BREAD AN

Tony Anderson was born i......read English at Oxford, and has taught both in Britain and abroad. He has worked as an editor and writer for television, books and theatre, and has recently edited works on Russian/Caucasian subjects. He lives in Somerset.

Tony Anderson

BREAD AND ASHES

A Walk Through the
Mountains of Georgia

WITH PHOTOGRAPHS BY
Chris Willoughby

VINTAGE

Published by Vintage 2004

4 6 8 10 9 7 5

Copyright © Tony Anderson 2003
Photographs copyright © Chris Willoughby
Maps by Reginald Piggott

Tony Anderson has asserted his right under the Copyright,
Designs and Patents Act, 1988 to be identified as the author
of this work

First published in Great Britain in 2003 by
Jonathan Cape

Vintage
Random House, 20 Vauxhall Bridge Road,
London SW1V 2SA

www.rbooks.co.uk

Addresses for companies within
The Random House Group Limited can be found at:
www.randomhouse.co.uk/offices.htm

The Random House Group Limited Reg. No. 954009

A CIP catalogue record for this book
is available from the British Library

ISBN 9780099437871

The Random House Group Limited supports The Forest Stewardship
Council (FSC), the leading international forest certification organisation.
All our titles that are printed on Greenpeace approved FSC certified paper
carry the FSC logo. Our paper procurement policy can be found at:
www.rbooks.co.uk/environment

Printed and bound in Great Britain by
CPI Antony Rowe, Chippenham, Wiltshire

*This book is dedicated to Lucy, Charlie and Sarah
with love and thanks*

and to the memory of Chris Willoughby 1947–2000

CONTENTS

CONTENTS

THE CAUCASUS
and surrounding regions

A I O N D A G H E S T A N

CASPIAN

SEA

r. Terek

Grozny
CHECHNYA

Mahachkala

INGUSHETI

Itum-Kale
Kazbegi Shatili
Kobi
Omalo
Gunib
Derbent
Akhmeta Pshaveli
I A Telavi
Mtskheta Lagodekhi
Tbilisi Zakataly
Rustavi Ilisu
r. Alazan Gach
Sheki

Lake
Sevan
Mingechevir

A Z E R B A I J A N
Baku

E N I A
Yerevan

Barda

NAGORNO-KARABAKH
Agdam

r. Kura

r. Araks

Lachin

NAKHICHEVAN
Nakhichevan

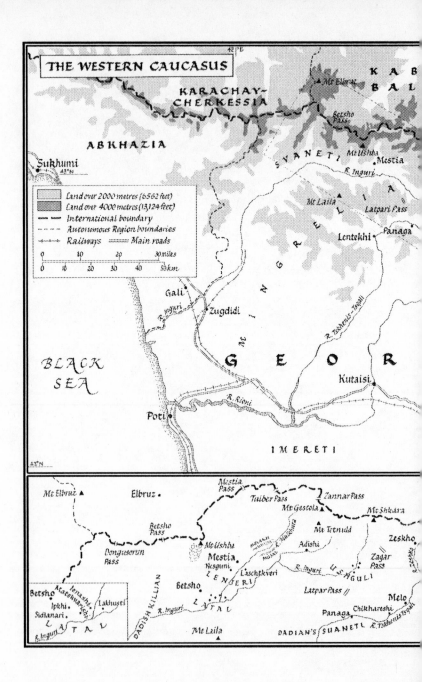

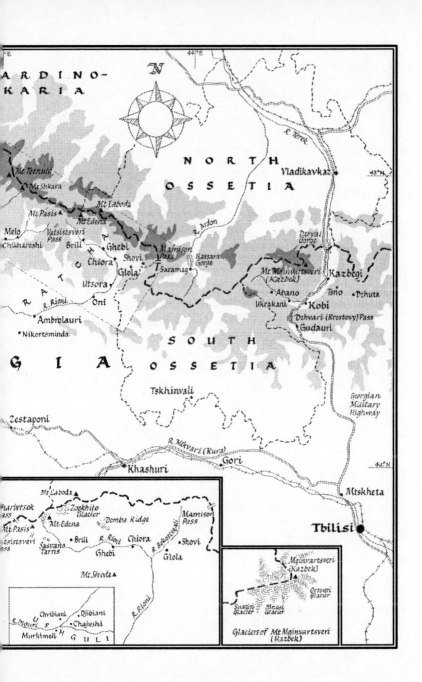

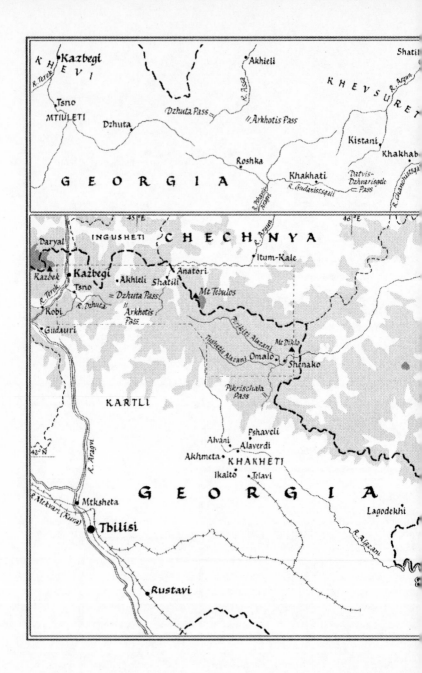

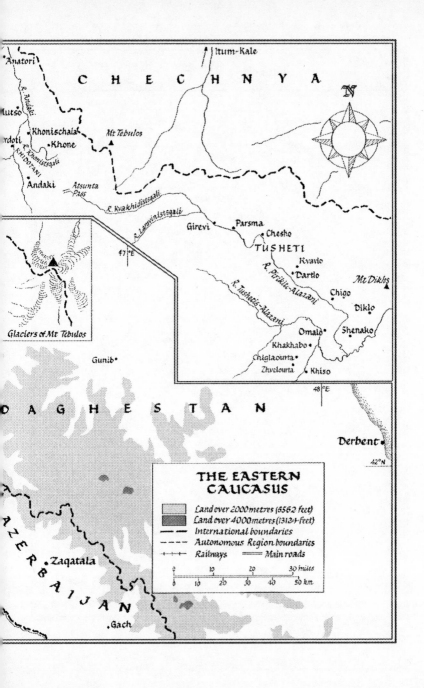

Anatori

CHECHNYA

Itum-Kale

Mutso
Khonischala
Khone
rdoti

Mt Tebulos

Andaki

Atsunta
Pass

R. Kvakhidistsgali

R. Larovinistsgali

Girevi

Parsma

Chesho

TUSHETI

Kvavlo

Dartlo

Mt Dikhos

Chigo

Diklo

R. Pirikiti-Alazani

R. Tushetis-Alazani

Shenako

Omalo

Khakhabo

Chiglaourta

Zhvelourta

Khiso

47°E

48°E

Glaciers of Mt Tebulos

Gunib

DAGHESTAN

Derbent

42°N

THE EASTERN CAUCASUS

Land over 2000 metres (6562 feet)

Land over 4000 metres (13124 feet)

International boundaries

Autonomous Region boundaries

Railways   Main roads

0   10   20   30 miles

0 10 20 30 40 50 km

AZERBAIJAN

Zaqatala

Gach

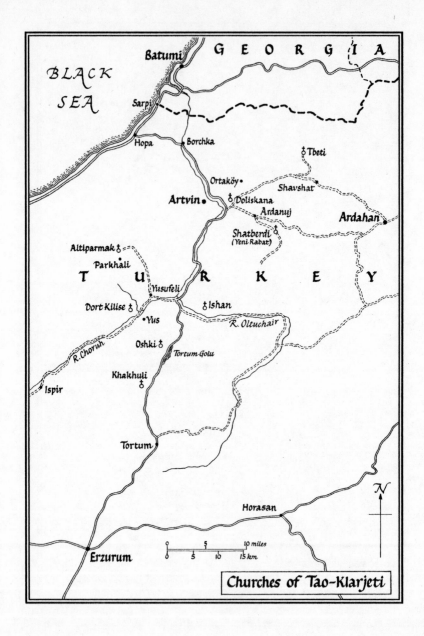

Churches of Tao-Klarjeti

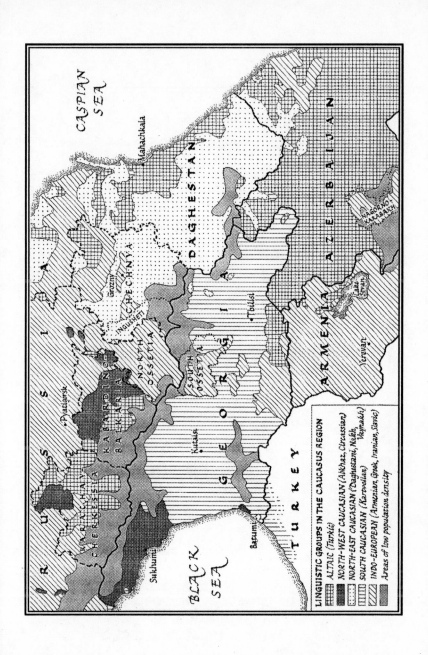

LINGUISTIC GROUPS IN THE CAUCASUS REGION

⬚ ALTAIC (Turkic)
■ NORTH-WEST CAUCASIAN (Abkhaz, Circassian)
⬚ NORTH-EAST CAUCASIAN (Daghestani, Nakh)
▨ SOUTH CAUCASIAN (Kartvelian)
▥ INDO-EUROPEAN (Armenian, Greek, Iranian, Slavic)
▨ Areas of low population density

CASPIAN SEA

Makhachkala

DAGHESTAN

NAGORNO-KARABAKH

AZERBAIJAN

Grozny

CHECHNYA

INGUSHETI

Lake Sevan

NORTH OSSETIA

SOUTH OSSETIA

Tbilisi

ARMENIA

Yerevan

R U S S I A

Pyatigorsk

KABARDINO-BALKARIA

KARACHAY-CHERKESSIA

G E O R G I A

Kutaisi

Sukhumi

BLACK SEA

Batumi

TURKEY

ACKNOWLEDGEMENTS

Many people have helped me during my travels through Georgia and the Caucasus. To all those whose kindness and hospitality I can never hope to repay sufficiently, to chance-met Azeris, Khevsurs, Tush, Ratchuelians, Mingrelians and Svans, I owe a great debt of gratitude and thanks. I would like to thank, particularly, in Azerbaijan, Carol Morgan and the staff of Children's Aid Direct and Dr Raghib Mamehdov; in Georgia, Beka Gotsadze and Mindia Chincharaouli for all their help and guidance, Dr Sasha and Dr Irina Aleksidze for their hospitality, Tsira Gugushvili for her years of friendship and support, Marika Didebulidze and Mako Maisuradze, for all of the above, for their tireless help with all my enquiries, and for their enthusiastic involvement with so much of this story.

Yiannis Sarzetakis on Syros and Robert Temple in Somerset added greatly to my understanding of the Promethean legends. Professor Richard Villems of Tartu University answered all my queries on the genetic background of Georgians and Caucasians with great clarity and patience. From Cameroon, David Zeitlyn and Anna Rayne provided a recipe for snake. From Tbilisi, Levan Butkhuzi told me all about hyenas in Georgia. Zura Revazishvili has helped and entertained me for many years in all matters Anglo-Georgian. Frances Howard-Gordon and Tom and Caryne Clark were instrumental, and there at the beginning. Alan Bell of the London Library gave much advice and dug deep amongst the archives. I am grateful to Hutchinson for permission to quote from Tim Severin's *The Jason Voyage*. Lady Cicely Nepean kindly allowed me access to all the Baddeley material in her possession, and to her memories of her intrepid great-uncle, John Baddeley. Dr Tamara Dragadze and Professor George Hewitt have both liberally given of their learning and time, and both have applied their academic rigour to certain sections of this book. Professor David Braund must deserve my special thanks and some kind of award for reading through my entire manuscript and making many valuable suggestions. All mistakes, inconsistencies and diversions from the straight and narrow are of my own making.

My own family I thank for their patience and indulgence over a rather surprisingly protracted period.

Finally, I must thank Judy Willoughby for permission to publish some of Chris Willoughby's splendid photographs of Georgia. To him I owe a very special debt. The book is dedicated, in part, to his memory. He died not long after the last journey we made together.

AUTHOR'S NOTE

Although the walk which provides the central narrative for this book took place over the summer of 1998, I refer frequently to other journeys and visits to Georgia, from the period just before the break-up of the Soviet Union to the present. Although the mountains of Georgia, and the people of the mountains, are the primary focus of my journey, the history, politics and culture of the area provide ample scope for unabashed digression. I have drawn upon the work of scholars but this book is not an academic treatise on the Caucasus. My spellings and transliterations will not please everyone. Many words, especially place names and proper names, arrive in English from their original Caucasian tongue via another language, particularly Russian. There are often, therefore, many variants, all equally valid. A person from Ossetia may be an Ossete, an Ossetine or an Ossetian; the greatest of Georgian monarchs may equally be represented as Queen Tamara or Queen Tamar; the river that runs through Tbilisi is both the Kura and the Mtkvari, or more properly the *mtkvari*, for Georgian uses no capital letters. The Georgian alphabet includes various letters which represent glottalised sounds that do not occur, normally, in English; I have settled for the nearest English equivalent. I have tried, with the valiant help of my editors, to be consistent where necessary. I only hope that by the time the reader has finished this book, he or she is a little less confused than I was when I first went to Georgia.

I, who am maddened to frenzy by love,
have composed these lines.
She, whom vast armies call mistress,
has deprived me of reason.

From *The Knight in the Panther's Skin*
by Shota Rustaveli

CHAPTER 1

ILISU

'The Understanding of an Ass'

How we came from Tbilisi to Baku
and started back again

'Do you have a gun?' asks Akhmed.

'A gun?'

'Yes, a gun, do you have one?'

'No,' I say, 'no gun.'

'Would you like one? A rifle? A Kalashnikov?'

'No, no thank you.'

'Here, take mine.' He passes over his old hunting rifle, made of a Soviet army barrel from the last war, a Turkish breech dated 1919 and a stock he had carved himself.

'No, thank you. I thought you said this was a peaceful place.'

'Yes, of course, it is a completely safe and peaceful place, *ochen spakoynoye mesto*, but there are bears and even wolves.'

'But the bears are no problem,' I say, 'are they?'

'No, no, absolutely not,' Akhmed assures me, 'but there are people.'

'People?'

'Yes.'

'Ah, so you would not say it was entirely safe.'

'No. It is completely safe.'

We sat on a grassy slope above the village, watching the great mountains darken, the fireflies and the stars coming out. Below, on the low wall of the little border post, a young guard coughed and lit a cigarette. It glowed comfortingly, way off in the night. His friends inside played cards and drank endless cups of tea, like soldiers everywhere. Akhmed, leaving reluctantly, had told them to watch over us. So we settled down and drifted into sleep, listening.

Later, suddenly, there were noises and then cries: 'hooo, hooo, ahooo'. The tent flap was pushed aside and there they were, Akhmed and Assa and the brother. Of course, they had brought vodka and bits of dried and salted bear and their weapons. They would stay with us and we would drink. So we drank and we drank, and I tried to chew the bear, but it was clear that there was more to their visit than eating bear. It would be far, far better if we came with them, back down to the village. Their families wanted to welcome us, mother, sister, father, brother were all waiting. Though it was one o'clock in the morning, they were ready. 'No, thank you,' we said. 'We are fine here, we are tired. Thank you so much.' Well, if that was the way it was, they would just have to stay with us all night. It was cold; it would get colder, but they would not leave us. We were their guests; our beds were made. Their beds were made. In the village was every comfort. But . . .

So we got up. They clapped us on the back and led us off down the mountain through the dark and silent village. And as we walked down, along the muddy lanes, I began to get an inkling, an intimation of something I recognised. I had been here before. Not in this place, of course, but the situation was somehow familiar. All this was leading to some old conclusion I had not yet quite grasped: a meeting far from home; a sudden and uneasy friendship; a journey through the night. We turned into a pitch-dark, narrow alley and stumbled up some steps. Double doors were flung open and we were bundled inside. This was what I had sensed in the gravid night: in the dim and smoke-stained light men were wailing and clapping and dancing. They had been hard at it for hours and the long tables were littered with bottles, ash-strewn plates, bits of old meat and roasted chickpeas. We were at the bad boys' disco in Ilisu.

I heard Chris groan. His stomach was delicate. From Tbilisi to

Baku he had managed to maintain a moderate lifestyle, and back through the old khanates of Azerbaijan he had sipped at hospitality politely. But now he was for it. The company roared as we walked in. Hurriedly an exhausted boy cleared a space and brought vodka and sweet champagne. Glasses were filled and we were toasted and glasses were filled again. And we toasted and filled glasses and called for more bottles and were toasted. In every man the fire was stoked, lit and roaring. Alcohol and cigarettes and crunchy things were passed around and around. In the gaps between, Assa sang loud impromptu verses of greeting, of love, of loss. The men jumped up and clapped and danced again.

Then, some unseen signal passed through the company and by common accord everything stopped. We were once more in the little lane walking God-knows-where through the night. The air was wonderfully cool, the tin roofs of the houses gleamed under bright stars, only the crunch of our boots and some distant, fading laughter disturbed the quiet. The village slept. Down Main Street Akhmed and Assa unslung their rifles and fired into the night sky for pure joy; their bullets, glowing red like firework rockets, threaded their way through the stars. The roar of the guns nearly knocked me flat and echoed up the lanes and battered against the houses. No one stirred, no dogs barked, no sirens wailed, the soldiers in their barracks beyond did nothing. Then we fired too, and the rifles roared again and Akhmed, Assa and the brother laughed their approval. We stepped through a little wooden gate, across a cobbled yard with a patch of vegetables to one side and into a low wooden hut with a porch and a corrugated roof, comfortingly like a cricket pavilion. The lamp was lit, we were given more guns to inspect, admired the head of a tûr* which Akhmed had shot high in the mountains last year, and were ushered courteously to our beds, all lined up neatly against the far wall. As I lay between fresh, white sheets just on the very edge of sleep, the Three Bears appeared and looked down at me.

The next morning at eight as promised, Fasil arrived from his fly-blown rooms in Gach to find us drinking tea on the stoop of

---

* *Capra caucasia* or *Capra cylindricornis*.

the old pavilion. He seemed more substantial here, excited, and was greeted with loud cries of 'Saoo! Saoo!' and much hand-slapping from all Akhmed's friends and relations who had gathered to inspect us. It was already hot and clear, a perfect day for the mountains.

We set off through the village, Akhmed leading the way, past the little border post and the soldiers waving in the bright morning sunshine. The houses, built of stone, were large, their gardens full and bright with flowers and fruit; all seemed peaceful, the road through the village broad and easy. A little boy of three or four ran down towards us laughing, carrying in his arms a bewildered turkey twice as big as himself. The village looked cheerful and prosperous but as I admired the scene Akhmed said that life here was hopeless. There was nothing to do, nobody had any work, nobody had any money. (Out of the corner of his eye the brother shot me a vulpine glance.) They had long ago sold off their cattle and their sheep and could not afford to buy more. To bring in something, at least, Akhmed went into the mountains to hunt: wild goats mostly and bear sometimes and, if he was very persevering, tûr, the horns of which might fetch twenty-five dollars if he was lucky, though it was both dangerous and illegal. He seemed for a moment genuinely worried that I might tell the police. Nowadays they did not even own a horse, and what was life without a horse? Fasil nodded his agreement. He, of course, a refugee from Karabakh, had absolutely nothing, not a home nor even a patch of ground to grow a few potatoes.

Akhmed was small, wiry and hard like a Sherpa, like mountain men everywhere. His brother was taller, more powerfully built but not so light on his feet; Fasil seemed almost ponderous beside them. They all set off at a tremendous pace as we headed north towards the mountains. Up there, somewhere, was the hammam of which I had heard rumours, a natural spring of hot, healing waters with miraculous properties, they all agreed, just this side of Daghestan. As we walked over the rubble of the river-bed, Fasil picked flowers and showed us, delighted, plants that grew also in Karabakh. Here, one for all stomach complaints, there, wild plums, and over there a berberis, for all problems of the heart, emotional

4

and physiological. This for the liver: it looked to me like angelica, though far larger than any I had seen before, and Fasil stooped to cut it down, whittling the plant to its inner stem which he cut into slices and passed around. It was horribly bitter but they chewed it with apparent relish and laughed at us. The water from the river, ice-cold, clear and sweet, washed it down.

As we climbed, all the humid torpor of the plains was blown away. The great snow-covered ridge of the Caucasus gleamed ahead, poplars, birch, chestnut and oak grew about us. We passed occasional cultivated plots, full with potatoes and beans. A few little calves pottered about, charming till one saw their back ends. Fasil was moved to frequent cries of 'Nature! Nature!' as he threw his arms wide in exultation. He praised everything, particularly the water which was so pure here and so plentiful, he assured us, that quite spectacular cucumbers might be grown. As if to emphasise his point a great waterfall, with its attendant rainbow, appeared in front of us. I stood in its spray to cool down.

Ilisu – or Illisu or Elisu as it appears on various maps – sitting along the ancient and important trade route from east to west across the Caucasian isthmus, was once prosperous and fought-over. It has had its moments in history. Formerly part of the eastern Georgian kingdom of Kakheti, and the borderland between Georgia and the fierce Lesghian tribes to the north in Daghestan, it was a country rich in orchards and game, where silk, rice and cotton were once grown. Towards the end of the sixteenth century, the Georgian King Alexander of Kakheti granted Ilisu in fiefdom to the exiled ruler of Ghimri, from over the mountains in Daghestan, in the hope that he might restrain his rapacious countrymen. This splendidly titled Shevkal of Ghimri, sometimes known as Ilisu Sultan, was on the run from the far more powerful Shevkal of Tarku, over by the Caspian Sea around what is now Mahachkala. The Shevkals of Tarku proved over the years to be the most deadly nuisance to the Georgians, mounting expeditionary raids almost yearly into eastern Georgia, for plunder and for slaves. It has been said that hardly an *aoul* (mountain village) in Daghestan was without Georgian blood, and Georgian slaves were sold and given in tribute to the Persians, who preferred boys, and to the

Turks, who preferred girls. Because of the depredations of the Shevkals of Tarku, King Alexander of Kakheti tried to establish an alliance with the Russians, seeking their aid against the formidable tribes of Daghestan. He did not know, of course, what he had started.

When the Russians finally annexed Georgia and moved down in force against the peoples of the Caucasus at the beginning of the nineteenth century, the Sultan of Ilisu made a brief gesture of resistance. The Russian commander-in-chief, Tsitsianoff, himself a Georgian, a man of great courage and energy, was determined to subdue all the petty princedoms of the mountains and bring the khans to heel, to put an end to centuries of squabble, feud and strife. He was outraged by the resistance and prevarication of the Sultan of Ilisu and wrote him a letter, a masterpiece of vituperation, saying: 'Shameless Sultan with the soul of a Persian – so you still dare to write to me! Yours is the soul of a dog and the understanding of an ass, yet you think to deceive me with your specious phrases. Know that until you become a loyal vassal of my Emperor I shall only long to wash my boots in your blood.' The Sultan of Ilisu and his allies submitted, swore allegiance to Russia and were forced to pay tribute.

Forty years later, in 1844, Ilisu was in turmoil again. Sultan Daniel, who had till then been loyal in his allegiance to Russia, a major-general in Russian service, had become alienated, like many others, by the offensive and unjust terms of Russian rule and ran off into the mountains to join in the war against the Russians then raging fiercely under the command of the great Avar leader, Shamyl. Sultan Daniel tried, unsuccessfully, to regain control of Ilisu and for fifteen years he and his countrymen fought bravely by Shamyl's side battling against the Russians as they closed in around the jagged heights and dark defiles of Daghestan. However, by 1859, he knew the end was close and once again negotiated with the Russians. He tried to broker a peace between them and Shamyl but Shamyl rejected him and so he rode out of the war and into the Russian camp to beg, and receive, pardon.

Akhmed and I talked of Imam Shamyl, still a great hero throughout the Caucasus, of his many daring exploits and his last stand at

Gounib where, with his last five hund'
surrounded by a force of 40,000 Russian sol(
he finally surrendered. As we sat on a boul
fist, full of onion tops, slashed in an arc
became Shamyl, cutting a path through m.
us fastidiously with bread, cheese and herbs and .
packet of sausages from Byelorus. I was beginning a no.
attempt to explain that the finest account in English of Shamy.
exploits had been written by Chris's great-great-uncle, John
Baddeley, when I looked across to Chris for confirmation. He was
sitting on a stone, puzzled, eating one of the sausages from Byelorus
from which he had failed to remove the plastic covering. 'You
know,' he said, 'this sausage has the most remarkable texture.'

This may have undermined some faith in our capabilities.
Akhmed's brother, at least, tried to persuade us that the hammam
was too far, another three hours or so, the way too difficult. I
thought of Tsitsianoff's words to the Sultan of Ilisu but managed
a more diplomatic response. After some discussion it was decided
that he should return to the village on his own. As he stood to go
he reached across into my shirt pocket and pulled out the few
notes I had there. It was nothing, a few pence. Even so I looked
after him uneasily as he strode off, helpfully, with our packs.

The walk to the hammam was as fine an introduction to the
mountains as we could have wanted. The great pleasure in such
journeys is in seeing and feeling what no map can tell, no matter
for how long pored over in the quiet of a room at home or in the
basement of the Royal Geographical Society. Of course, the
romance of maps lies in their mystery, in the names of far-off places
in strange tongues, such a powerful seduction: Ilisu, Shatili,
Ushguli, Batumi, Tbilisi, Baku. I have sometimes imagined a
turbanned man of my age sitting cross-legged on the floor of his
dwelling in Samarkand with a map of Britain open in front of him,
mouthing gently to himself, while a small shiver of pleasure
descends his spine, 'Saffron Walden, Gateshead, Chipping Sodbury,
Clacton-on-Sea.'

We set off up the Ilisu River – the valley narrowing all the way –
stopping briefly here and there to examine the prints of bears or

wild strawberries of a flavour so intense it made us laugh.
uted to each other over the noise of the river which charged
ugh a debris of broken bits of mountain, boulders and smashed
es. Birches grew sideways out of crags and often, far too often,
as the mountains closed in or landslides blocked our path, we had
to cross the river and its crazy tributaries. Our guides skipped across,
Akhmed smoking a cigarette, the turn-ups of his trousers not even
damp. Chris and I slithered and splashed our way onwards, scrambling for footholds and slipping into deeper waters. But far worse
were the bridges. At various points trunks of trees and sometimes
poles, no bigger than those I use for growing runner beans, were
thrown across. At one or two of these even Fasil, a little out of
practice perhaps, looked, for a moment, doubtful. But then he too
would skip across like a tightrope walker and turn, concerned, to
watch our progress. I could not help looking where I was going
and, as everyone knows, staring at the water produces a peculiar,
dizzying effect. There, just below the plunge of white water where
the river goes, for a moment, clear, my gaze was held with a
disturbing power. I knew that I should look away but, despite plenty
of practice in the weeks to come, I never quite managed to free
myself. As we attempted to walk along one particularly absurd stick
– hesitating between paralysis and panic, having tried wading and
even crawling across – I was just explaining to Chris that it was far
better not to concentrate too hard but to walk lightly, confidently,
when I fell in. Akhmed turned slightly aside so as not to give too
much offence by his laughter but Fasil was quite overcome and
had to lie down on a small hillock. I just managed to catch hold
of the pole as I entered the water and to prevent myself from being
swept rapidly down the mountain. Akhmed reassured me later by
saying that he himself had fallen in from time to time, when coming
back down this way, at night.

The mountainside steepened, the gorge grew deeper and
narrower, the river madder, till there, at last, but on the other side
was the hammam. Somehow, unbelievably, the villagers had
managed to come up here and reinforce the entrance into the
mountain with a portal of cement. We saw a narrow dark hole and
all around was streaked a brown, green, yellow, mineral ooze. I

could not imagine, at first, how we were to cross but a few broken poles and some useful rocks pointed the way. Chris and I jumped, waded and fell to the other side.

Unsure of the etiquette, I waited till Fasil and Akhmed had stripped down to their underpants and then we crawled through a low tunnel into the dark. A Gollum cave; dark, hot and magical. The water was waist-high, warm as a baby's bath and smelling not unpleasantly of sulphur. Light filtered through from the entrance and we drifted about for some time in a torpid daze, speechless, gazing up at the roof of the cave which curved into a gentle dome above us. Water poured in from a high lip of rock and we stood under it in turn, massaged by the fall. Here, inside the mountain, away from all the natural drama of the outside world, it was comfortable, peaceful, wet and warm and I thought how pleasant it would be to stay. Akhmed, though, had other ideas and said that if we didn't mind a little climb there was more to see. The others were too happy to move so I followed him outside, feeling a little vulnerable after the closeness of the cave and in my underpants, though they were quite new. We climbed the precipice above. Higher up and further into the gorge hung a small, battered wooden platform and from this we stepped into a basin of rock into which flowed very hot mineral water. A hole had been drilled through the basin; Akhmed rammed in a wooden plug and our bath filled up. One end of the bath jutted right out into the narrow defile, the river and the rocks far below. We lay on our backs, staring up at the bare sides of the gorge and the narrow strip of sky above. An eagle drifted lazily across. How far away the land of Billy Bunter! Here was my perfect fantasy of the Caucasus, high in the mountains, floating with this kind Azeri in his underpants. Even he could not stop himself from smiling. In all my trips through Georgia this image, then nebulous, nugatory, had been forming in my mind. I thought of Baddeley and of Freshfield and all the other travellers' tales I had read and reread and particularly of Negley Farson's story of bathing in the Narzan Springs miles west of here. He found himself sharing his small pool with two locals who, like the villagers of Ilisu, insisted on the magical and curative properties of the waters. When Farson asked them which particular complaints they hoped to be cured of they replied, laughing, that they were both suffering from venereal disease.

Akhmed had hesitantly, courteously and with a small furrow of concern across his brow, broached the subject of my psoriatic skin. After I had dispelled his fears of contagion, he assured me that were I to stay here for a week, bathing regularly, I should be healed without a doubt. I could not quite follow the list of known illnesses dispelled in this way but it seemed to include leprosy, angina, diseases of the lung and kidney, migraine, stomach ache and gout. I have, over the years, attempted many strange and wonderful cures, including a month in the hills of eastern Turkey, in early winter, lying in pools all day long, a woolly hat upon my head, icicles hanging from the trees, an insane Russian by my side, with a small collection of Turks in all kinds of conditions, being eaten alive by voracious fish that stripped the skin till the blood flowed. There, I think, I came near to death and developed a certain sensitivity towards prolonged bathing in pools. However, always tempted by the miraculous, I considered, for a moment, spending a week alone up here with the eagles and the bears. Whatever happened to my skin I should certainly be mad on my return.

It was time to leave. The water was powerful but debilitating if lain in for too long. We scrambled down and joined Chris and Fasil who were sitting in a patch of sunlight on the far side of the river. We ate a leisurely sausage and started back for Ilisu. Chris and I staggered with tiredness and I gave up all attempts to walk on top of the pole bridges but waded into the river and clung to them and hauled my way across. It was much faster and less terrifying, and the water in my boots and up my back refreshing. Fasil continued to pick huge bunches of herbs and flowers for his family in Gach, till he looked like a lost florist's assistant or a man off to feed a favourite donkey. His pleasure in our walk was as great as mine, underscored by a deep nostalgia for his home village of Lachin and the mountains of Karabakh.

Back in Ilisu we sank around the table in Akhmed's yard. It felt like days since we had left and we were greeted and fussed over like long-lost cousins. Tea, welcome and beneficent, was quickly placed in front of us, such is the understanding between the tea-drinking peoples of the world. More young men came over, greeted each other affectionately with many cries of 'Saoo!' and sat to talk. Asser, Akhmed's brother-in-law, putting his little daughter gently from his lap, stood to try on my pack and walked happily up and down with it, exclaiming. It was so comfortable! So light! Why, in the army they had to carry 34 kilos all day long, what was this? 17 kilos! Nothing! And they all had a go. Only the brother asked for something, a shirt, or some of our clothing. I explained that we were far from home, that we had weeks of travel ahead of us, that we had brought the bare minimum and that everything was needed. They all understood, of course, of course, but the brother looked away angrily. We promised to send what we could through friends in Baku.

Naturally and undeniably, however modest we might be, to them we looked like two big sacks of swag with dollar signs all over. Faced with such difficulty in life, such comparative poverty, such frustration of hope and opportunity, it was impossible not to be conscious of this, not to feel a deep unease. This was not a fear of robbery or assault but a diffidence about appearing in certain places at all. Our very presence – so free, so easy – was a kind of affront. Walking through the mountains with our strange garb and stranger faces, I felt, at first, a tremor of timidity as we approached each new village and ran the gauntlet of appraisal. But my discomfort was soon dispelled: the natural courtesy of nearly everyone we met soon made us forget our deep, dividing, differences.

I looked at the faces about me: some looked almost Armenian, others Turkish or Georgian, even French or English for that matter, a great mix as one might expect from this ancient province, poised above the route from the Caspian to the Black Sea and backing on to the mountains with all the tribal confusion of Daghestan behind. One man in particular engaged me in conversation, a Bruce Lee lookalike, quite obviously the descendant of one of the Mongol Hordes, a wandering Nogay or a Tatar-Mongol Khan. He was the toughest-looking man I have ever seen, with a face as hard as a bulldozer's shovel. He would bang the table with his fist or poke me in the chest with his finger, quite nicely, whenever he wanted to make a point, roaring with laughter all the while:

'I was in Moscow for ten years.' Poke, poke, crash. 'Then they kicked me out because they said I was Mafia! Dog shit! Everyone's the Mafia. The whole place is the shitting Mafia! Who the fuck wants to live in Moscow anyway? They had nothing on me!' Crash, poke. 'This problem that you have with your skin, I have seen it before. I knew a man in Moscow, brilliant man and he would make up this stuff. You must do this, you must. You take some tar from a stovepipe and mix it with sump oil and eggs and rub it all over you. The whole thing will clear up immediately. No shit!' Crash, poke, crash! Everyone roared with laughter and he jumped up and down getting more and more excited, telling them that they were all idiots and knew nothing. But he was not so mad. Tar has been used for years and oil helps. Maybe it's the answer.

A car arrived, mysteriously, to take us to Gach. We said our good-byes and as I climbed in I noticed Fasil handing over money to the brother who ran round, opened the door and gave me a warm kiss. Ah, love! love! cupid, cupidity and the whole mess. As we drove I asked Fasil to explain: he had handed over most of the money I had given him and Akhmed because it was necessary, an obligation. Apparently our invitation to the disco had been made without the funds to support it and there were previous bills to be taken into account. I refunded Fasil and we all dozed happily on the tree-lined, buffalo-spattered road to Gach. In the desolate *auberge* of this decrepit town a charming elderly lady served us with tea and hot water for shaving and talked to us in perfect English, unused for thirty years. It was pitch-dark and utterly still as we slipped into our sagging beds. I felt my brain fizz briefly then go out, like a turned-off television.

*

It was the summer of 1998. We had started our journey from the Caspian to the Black Sea in the middle, in Tbilisi, seeing friends and trying to organise our route. My original plan had been to walk all the way across the isthmus over the mountains of Azerbaijan and Georgia but it soon became clear that there would not be enough time. So we decided to travel through Azerbaijan as best we could, then to start walking in earnest in the mountains of eastern Georgia and try to reach Svaneti in the west, where Chris and I had been some years before. Particularly, I wanted to visit the people of the high valleys of Georgia, the Pshavs, the Tush, the Khevsurs, the Ratchuelians and Svans, so often described as living in isolation in their upland glens; to try and cross the passes that separated them, to see just how isolated they really were and whether their distinctive mountain cultures still survived. Since I had first visited Georgia in 1989, as the Soviet Union was disintegrating, and in the half-dozen trips I had made since then, this idea of a mountain walk had been forming in my mind. My friendship with Chris Willoughby had by chance produced a further impetus: a professional photographer, he had reasons beyond photography for wanting to travel to the Caucasus. He had grown up with stories of 'Uncle Jack', John Baddeley, who had spent years travelling through and writing about the mountains. Chris's father had inherited Baddeley's old home and had passed on to Chris many of Baddeley's books and photographs. Indeed, Chris's aunt, Lady Cicely Nepean, still remembers her great-uncle Jack well, and possesses many of his books, diaries and notes. Though Chris and I had been friends for years it was only when I first travelled to Georgia that I discovered all this, by which time Baddeley had already become a major source for my interest in the area. It was the happiest of coincidences.

Baddeley had bequeathed a large collection of books and papers about the Caucasus to the London Library. It's a terrible place the London Library, the largest independent lending library in the world, its body opening out impossibly, Tardis-like, across London, its discreet façade offering no clue as to the confusion within: the Byzantine cataloguing systems, the labyrinthine arrangement of the shelves. There are distractions at every turn, so that it soon becomes almost impossible to remember what original purpose might have led one down a particular stack. Often I have fled in mounting panic from Topography to History and back again, unable to find the exit. There are many tales of libraries where professors have been found dead, after weeks struggling exhausted towards the light. Here bodies lie motionless, wedged between the stacks, surrounded by piles of books, uncleared for days. It is the ideal setting for a murder: blood drips slowly from floor to floor through the patterned holes in the iron walkways; in Amharic, a famous scholar slumps, his fingers clutch the slowly turning pages of *The Secret History of the Mongols*, the last page torn out, an ornate dagger of ancient, Sasanian design stuck deeply into his cranium.

Addled by all this, emerging from days spent trying to flee Albania (a phase), I strode off purposefully to find the Caucasus, determined to resolve a great muddle. Despite finding myself back in Albania a number of times on the way, I eventually settled in the half-light and began my search. Why was there an Albania in the Caucasus? And what was Iberia doing there as well? And why did Armenia appear in western Turkey, five hundred miles from where it should have been? Such innocent questions led me on. Caucasian Albania had nothing to do with Albania as we know it but was, roughly, the country we now call Azerbaijan, Albania its ancient Greek and Roman name, for a time the easternmost outpost of the Roman empire. And the Rupenid Armenian Kingdom in Cilicia, in western Turkey, was an Armenian state founded after the Seljuk Turks had overrun Armenia proper. And Iberia was Georgia, though the Georgians have never called their country by either name but rather, after its unification in the eleventh century, Sakartvelo, the Country of the Kartvelians. Even in Roman times there was confusion and speculation that the peoples of both Iberias, Spanish and Georgian, were related, that Spanish colonists had moved from sunset to sunrise, from the western to the eastern edge of the Roman empire; or else that the common term Iberia was a mere coincidence of names derived and distorted from founding tribes. Of course, everything immediately becomes more complicated: Graeco-Roman Iberia, for example, was eastern Georgia at first, the western part was Colchis (Egrisi to its own inhabitants), where Jason stole the Golden Fleece.

There is much complex discussion, too, over the origins of the name 'Georgia'. No one quite knows how it arrived. It was once thought to have derived from the worship of Saint George, so prevalent in Georgia, though now most scholars believe it to have come through an Arabic or Persian distortion of a Georgian toponym, either Egrisi itself or one of the provinces of ancient Georgia, Gugareti, giving Gurdjan or Djurdjan, thus Gruzya in Russian and so to Georgia. I prefer a Greek derivation. A Greek friend, Yiannis Sarzetakis, phoned me once to say, in some excitement, that he had found two wonderful old books on Georgia in a bookshop in Athens. Would I like them? Of course I would! I then got another call to say that these books were, in fact, about farming, an easy mistake as the Greek words for agriculture and Georgia are the same. When the ancient Greeks arrived in Colchis they were deeply impressed by the abundance of fruits, vines and other produce and there seems to have been something of a farming cult within the Colchian religion: their kings were buried with agricultural implements, extremely unusual in ancient cultures. So the Greeks returned with this idea of a land of farmers or a land where farming was especially venerated and started their present confusion of names, though it has to be said that Georgia was never a name used by the Greeks in antiquity.

There is another puzzle here: why are Europeans called Caucasians? Quite clearly they did not all come from the Caucasus and among the native peoples of the Caucasus there is a great variation of physical types, though not many blonds – about 10 per cent, according to the anthropologist Alexander Javakhishvili. So how did this name come to describe native Europeans and north African Berbers, dark Sicilians and blond Norwegians and then all the white-skinned people of the world? This is a tale of love between an eighteenth-century anthropologist and a skull. In 1795 Johann Blumenbach was trying to categorise the races of the world and using skull types as one of the bases for his work. He came across a particularly beautiful skull, one that he felt represented the loveliest characteristics of the majority of European types. It had belonged to a Georgian woman. In truth his reasoning was slightly more convoluted: he thought that his *Varietas caucasia* not only represented the most beautiful stock of human beings but that mankind had originated in the Caucasus and that all the divergences of human types – from 'Mongol' to 'Aethiopian' – developed subsequently. From this stemmed the idea that there was a Caucasian, or Caucasoid, race, a notion that dominated anthropological science for years after and became particularly widespread during the time of mass immigration into America at the beginning of the twentieth century, when the officials who welcomed the migrants off the boats had to note down their racial origins and described anyone white as Caucasian. Other anthropologists have commented that it would be hard to find a less suitable name for the 'European race'. The population of the Caucasus is extremely diverse and few are typical of any large section of Europids.

Among all these diversions and the books on Georgia and the Caucasus that I found piling up around me on the floor of the London Library, was Baddeley's collection which included his own publications. He wrote four great books: *Russia in the Eighties; Russia, Mongolia and China; The Russian Conquest of the Caucasus* and *The Rugged Flanks of the Caucasus.* The two last are particularly fine. He was a remarkable man: adventurer, journalist, writer, linguist and businessman (though not so remarkable in this). He had arrived in Russia in 1879, aged twenty-five, after a couple of years travelling in South America. He had been taken up by Count Shuvaloff, the Russian ambassador to London and a friend of his family. Quite how much of a friend will never be known but Baddeley's mother was a lively and attractive woman, left a widow after his father's early death, and Shuvaloff (Shovel-off to the English) was a notable seducer, a man of great brilliance, one of the major architects of the Treaty of Berlin, along with Beaconsfield and Bismarck. For whatever reason, Shuvaloff took Baddeley under his wing and they became very close. Years later he died in Baddeley's arms. Invited to Moscow by the count, the young man set to work learning Russian with tremendous energy, studying fourteen hours a day and, for light relief, improving his Spanish by reading *Don Quixote* before bed. Dissatisfied with the progress he was making, he took himself off to a small village where he lived and worked among the peasants and so came under suspicion of having revolutionary sympathies. The following year he became Russian correspondent for the *Standard* and wrote for that paper for many years at a fascinating time in Russian history and a tense and dangerous time in the relationship between Russia and Great Britain.

Travelling widely through the Russian empire, Baddeley was drawn more and more to the 'wild freedom' of the Caucasus and he conceived the idea of a journey from the Black Sea to the Caspian through the mountains from west to east. He never quite managed this, though his many journeys on horseback with his Ossetian guide, Ourousbi, in the early years of the twentieth century became the basis for his *Rugged Flanks of the Caucasus*. He spent the last years of his life in Oxford writing up his journals from these travels, though, sadly, the book was not published until after his death in 1940.

Most of his work has been long out of print, though *The Russian Conquest of the Caucasus* has recently been republished due to the interest aroused by the disgraceful Russian wars in Chechnya in 1996 and 1999. This new edition has a preface by Professor Moshe Gammer from Tel Aviv University, an eminent Caucasologist who unfortunately knew nothing of Baddeley, nor bothered to find out any more, thus missing the opportunity of writing some brief biography of this fascinating man. However, the professor did recognise Baddeley's extraordinary clear-sightedness, an objectivity remarkable for a man of his times. On the one hand, himself a child of empire, Baddeley felt that under Russian hegemony there was real hope for peaceful progress in such disrupted, disruptive lands; on the other, while admiring the extraordinary bravery and hardihood of combatants from both sides, he utterly condemned the ruthless brutality with which the Russians took control of the Caucasus. He writes brilliantly of Yermoloff, commander-in-chief in Georgia with jurisdiction over the whole Caucasus for ten years, from 1817 until 1827, the soldier who more than anyone exemplified, indeed formed, Russia's strategy here. Yermoloff was a giant of a man with a vast head and a voice like thunder who claimed a specious descent from Genghis Khan to add glamour to his name and impress the natives. Incredibly brave, winning the cross of St George at the age of sixteen, he had fought the French, the Poles and the Persians and, at the taking of Paris in 1815, commanded both the Russian and Prussian Guard. His soldiers loved him. He was said to have been at least as cruel as the natives themselves and wrote that he desired that 'the terror of my name should guard our frontiers more potently than chains of fortresses, that my word should be for the natives a law more inevitable than death.' Another

Russian soldier, General Potto, who wrote a book on the Caucasian wars, remarked that 'in his hands the former system of bribery and subsidies gave place to one of severe punishments, of harsh, even cruel measures, but always combined with justice and magnanimity.' Baddeley commented that 'Politically it is difficult to see where justice came in, but in this respect Russia was only doing what England and all other civilised states have done, and still do, whenever they come in contact with savage or semi-savage races. By force or by fraud a portion of the country is taken, and, sooner or later, on one excuse or another the rest is bound to follow.' He questioned the justice, particularly, of a policy of subjugation which included the wholesale destruction of entire villages with their populations, men, women and children alike, if they showed any inclination to resist. This has horrific echoes in the present day. He wrote: '. . . if once we allow Russia's claim to exact submission from the tribes; if, further, we allow the right of man to play the part of Providence in punishing the innocent with the guilty and both alike with the utmost severity, then Yermoloff's justification is complete. Yet a tolerance so wide would vindicate not his misdeeds alone but the crimes of a Tamerlane . . .'

Baddeley also believed that the means undermined the ends and that such brutality could only lead, eventually, in one direction. The Chechens, Ingush, Lesghians and the Avars, all the mountain tribes, trained from early youth in war, were (and still are) a ferocious enemy and it took the Russians more than forty years of fighting to subdue them, roused by their imams, particularly Imam Shamyl, in Ghazavat (holy war) against the invader. Now, of course, the weapons used are far worse: vacuum bombs that destroy whole villages and suck lungs inside out, helicopter gunships and rockets. The purpose is the same, to kill, destroy, subdue, control, and in the end the result no different: death, hatred and an eternity of trouble. In the light of the present problems one reads Baddeley with an appalling sense of history; it has all happened before. When Yeltsin stood up in the Duma to justify his actions in Chechnya he said, 'Chechnya is Russia.' Of course it is not. It has merely been ruled by Russia. Even the words of hatred quoted by Baddeley in his book, describing the Russians as animals, worse than animals,

are exactly the same as those used by Chechens toda
them weeping in front of the television cameras. Bad
on Russia and the Caucasus are still a great source
trying to understand the complex history of the native p
their relationship with the great empire to the north. A ı discovered, every moment of this history – Tsarist, then Soviet, now
post-Soviet – has been fiercely branded on to the collective
consciousness of all who live in these fractured, fractious lands.

*

On arriving in Tbilisi to start our journey, Chris and I had two
appointments. The first was with Beka Gotsadze, a young architect
who had created a building company in the capital, one of a new
breed trying to rise out of the chaos of post-Soviet Georgia. He
was importing equipment from Europe through Istanbul, setting
up a brick factory, trying to secure supplies of cement, battling
against a chaotic economic situation, Mafia gangs, political unrest
and the sheer novelty of such an enterprise in a country with little
infrastructure to support it and an utterly bewildered population.
Even his father had difficulty in really grasping the fact that Beka
was his own boss, did not have to answer to someone in Moscow,
was responsible for his own decisions. In his office on Chavchavadze
Prospekt, Beka, with his partners Levan and Vasca, all graduates
from the School of Architecture in Tbilisi, cleared off a table and
rolled out some maps. As I explained my plan to walk through the
mountains they became more and more excited: when not working,
this was their great pleasure, to head up to Khevsureti and over the
border into Chechnya to hunt bear or tûr among the high peaks.
Beka had promised to find us a guide, a lad from Shatili, the Khevsur
capital, who knew the mountains well and would take us on our
journey from east to west, but now they all wanted to come too.

'We will take you where we went last year with our Chechen
friends. We killed some bears and the mountains are so beautiful.
But maybe you need a rifle?' Beka asked.

'Well, thank you, but we are fine,' I replied. Chris looked instantly
relieved.

'It is not so easy,' Vasca said. 'The mountains can be hard. You will have to cross a lot of snow. Maybe you will need ropes. You must not spend too much time in Azerbaijan. Anyway it is not interesting.'

They all agreed, Azerbaijan was a waste of time and the mountains there nothing to compare with their own mountains and the people dangerous and not to be trusted. (Everyone in the Caucasus says this about everyone else.) It would be much better to spend more time in Georgia.

'We will come with you. Definitely!' Beka said. 'We cannot possibly let you go on your own.'

'But you are getting us a guide and we shall be gone for weeks. Can you take so much time away from this?' I asked

It would not be possible, they had work to do, they had just got the franchise to build the first McDonald's in Tbilisi. I accused them of being responsible for the death of Georgian culture but they laughed. If Georgian culture could survive the Persians, the Turks, the Arabs, the Mongols and the Russians it could survive McDonald's. Perhaps. Also, if they came they would miss the World Cup on television. Still it was tempting. They might be able to join us for a few days. So we left it at that and, having arranged to meet our guide in Telavi in eastern Georgia in a week's time, set off for our second appointment, just as Beka was answering the phone to the Chief of Police in Chechnya who had rung their office rather than any government ministry (utterly useless, they all agreed) to arrange for a car to bring him to Tbilisi.

I had become peripherally involved with a small aid agency that had been helping Georgian refugees from Abkhazia and Azeri refugees from Nagorno-Karabakh. We were going to see if we could raise a little money for them and Chris was to take photographs in the camps. I knew next to nothing of the world of international aid, apart from a trip to Zugdidi in Mingrelia, western Georgia, a few years previously where I had interviewed some of the Georgian refugees who had been cleared out of Abkhazia during the Georgian–Abkhaz conflict of 1992 and were living in dreadful misery in a decrepit hospital. Unfortunately, CAD, Children's Aid Direct, who had had an office there, was forced to close it due to lack of funds but they were still operating in Azerbaijan. We went to meet their local representative, Ghia, and sat in the little park off Rustaveli Prospekt where the Kazbegi beer company had set up a jolly stall with a very pretty barmaid. Ghia drank only lemonade, the only teetotaller I ever met in Georgia. He talked of the difficulty of life in Tbilisi, how it had changed. There was 70 per cent unemployment and the city swarmed with strangers, all the IDPs (that anodyne acronym), the Internally Displaced Persons, from the west; he used to know everybody here, now he recognised no one. But I saw the new shops and the beer and the cafés and thought how much more open and cheerful the city looked, despite its awful problems.

We went together to the United Nations building. Outside, the aid world mingled, delegates gathered for some conference, the roads jammed with convoys of white Toyotas. Among them we found our CAD driver, who would take us to Mingechevir, our first stop in Azerbaijan. We climbed aboard, waved to Ghia and set off along the dusty road, through Rustavi, heading east. Our Azeri driver, a charming man, himself a refugee from Karabakh and delighted to have found such a job, asked us frequently if we thought he was going in the right direction. He was absolutely terrified of taking a wrong turning and finding himself in Armenia by accident. The Armenians would slit his throat immediately, he said, drawing his finger across his prominent Adam's apple in the universal gesture. To his great relief, after a number of alarms, we arrived safely at the correct frontier.

There is always some *frisson* of excitement at crossing strange borders. Were our papers in order? Did our arranged expressions of innocence betray our guilty hearts? Here the Georgian soldiers waved us through nonchalantly, but the Azeris stopped us half a dozen times at hundred-yard intervals to check our passports. We crossed over the lovely old bridge, the *Krasnaya Most*, now falling down, past a stream of lorries going nowhere, backed up for miles. Little stalls and kiosks selling cigarettes, juice and biscuits lined the road. We choked in clouds of diesel fumes as buses and trucks jostled with us for position. This was supposed to be part of the Traceca corridor, the great highway that would carry trade and bring prosperity, linking Central Asia and the Caucasus with Europe, the new Silk Route. It was chaos. From the optimistic chatter I had heard in London I had expected something a little broader. Throughout the 1990s I had attended an annual conference (more of a small get-together) at the School of Oriental and African Studies in London University, organised by Dr Tamara Dragadze who has helped me over the years with various knotty Georgian matters. A small number of academics and amateurs gathered for this Georgian Studies Day to listen to lectures on Georgian culture, the problems of translating Shakespeare into Georgian, Persian influence on the poetry of Shota Rustaveli, that sort of thing. Suddenly, at the end of the decade, we were all moved to the Lloyd's building, our numbers multiplied hugely by businessmen discussing oil, the new pipeline from the Caspian, harbour facilities at Poti, insurance problems, security and the development of the Traceca route. All exciting and compelling subjects but I now began to wonder if the Traceca enthusiasts had actually ever tried driving over the border.

The road to Mingechevir – at first lined with trees and fields full of men scything and hoeing, herding sheep, goats, buffalo and cattle – descends after a while into a great and desolate plain. The temperature soared and heat basted us through the open window of the car. Our driver laughed. 'India,' he said, 'we call this India here.' At nine that night we dripped into the town, a modern creation, all cement factories and a huge power station, now closed down, empty and falling into ruin. Mosquitoes buzzed and droned: into these torrid and malarial lowlands, inhabited by serpents, the refugees from mountain Karabakh had been dumped. At first they huddled in the open and in tents; a few still stand. Now most were housed in breeze-block huts that broiled them in the summer heat. All dreamt of the cool mountain air of home, though many of the children that we met, playing up and down the camps or learning lessons in the schoolroom CAD had built for them, remembered nothing of that life; home had been here for the last five years, since the Armenians had driven them from Karabakh.

We spent the next day in the camps, then visited the new computer centre in town and the family-planning clinic, scenes replicated across the globe, I imagine, where aid agencies struggle to meet the needs of all the dispossessed. Here, in Azerbaijan, a country of seven million people, there were over a million, scattered here and there, reliant almost totally upon the help of foreign money for all their basic needs, but full of a remarkable energy and spirit. The promised wealth from the new oil fields in the Caspian, from the great oil deals struck by the President, Haydar Aliev, and all the concomitant business, had made no difference to these refugees. They had seen none of it. Nesdan, a lovely, bright Azeri girl, a Russian teacher, fluent in English, and Kerim, middle-aged, repectable with a mouth full of gold, a university professor, both now working for CAD, took us to the Unfinished Hotel. This was started under Gorbachev but left roofless. Intended as a winter base for the Soviet Olympic rowing team when Russian rivers froze, built on the edge of the Kura which ran bright blue and clear (unrecognisable as the muddy brown river that raced through Tbilisi), the hotel now provided shelter of a sort for some few dozen families. All were refugees from Agdam, just under the lee of the eastern tip of Karabakh and, in the summer of 1993, the scene of one of the most awful Azeri disasters. Abandoned by their own government, the citizens of Agdam had fought off waves of Armenian attacks till, encircled, with a narrow corridor into Azerbaijan deliberately left open, 200,000 fled the city and the surrounding villages. In the Unfinished Hotel families lived with their geese and ducks among the rubble, desperate for clothes, for shoes, for bedding and for a roof. All their troubles they blamed unhesitatingly on President Gorbachev. He had started the rot and brought down chaos. All came out to meet us and to talk and, as Chris took photographs, led us with pride around the kitchen gardens they had created. There were, I think, only two men among them, most of the others had died in the fighting, a few had found work elsewhere. The women ran the group. Their elected representative, a sturdy and impressive lady, burnt by the sun, led us proudly around her garden plot, presented us with cucumbers of an enormous size and eyed us shrewdly. Others had come, talked, taken photographs but nothing had changed. We could promise little. However, as the seeds they sowed all came from Europe, we were able to have a most satisfying discussion on their cultivation. The seeds and garden tools, the little greenhouses CAD had provided, were perhaps the most helpful of all the aid they had been given and rows of beans, sweetcorn, tomatoes and lettuce marched across the ground. The endive puzzled them. Why were they so bitter? I showed them how to tie the outer leaves to blanch the plants, my most glorious moment.

Kerim took us for tea by the reservoir outside Mingechevir, the water level low in case the Armenians should blow the dams, he said, and flood the country. He started on the usual Turkish nonsense about the Armenians: how they all originally came from Russia and did not really belong in their country, how the Russians had deliberately placed them to disrupt the Turkish commonwealth which would otherwise have stretched uninterrupted from Istanbul to Siberia. The same old stuff! I gently pointed out that the Turks themselves did not originally come from here or from Turkey and Kerim agreed that this was true but went strangely quiet for a while. However, he insisted that the Azeris and the Armenians could live in peace together, that this present trouble was a post-Soviet problem, that he liked Russians and thought of Azerbaijan as inextricably linked to Russia, the source of books, education and industry. He just despised the Russian government. In his home in Karabakh he had grown up with Armenians and had had many Armenian friends. Not now, though. But he liked Georgians. Georgians were OK. And it is curious that relations between Georgia and Azerbaijan have often been rather good, whereas Armenia has, of course, terrible problems with Azerbaijan and a sometimes rather uneasy time with Georgia, despite the fact that they are obvious allies and partners, two mostly Christian countries that have shared a great deal of history and many of the same difficulties. There are disputes between them which occasionally flare up, particularly in the Georgian towns with a mainly Armenian population near the border – though this can also be true of towns with a large Azeri population. Tbilisi has had for centuries a large and active Armenian community, controlling much of the trade and business of the city, indeed of all the Caucasus, and this has, over the years, caused some resentment. Georgians always joke that

Armenians much prefer to live in beautiful Georgia than in their own country, a harsh, high, barren, granite plateau. Towards the end of the First World War, in November 1917, when Armenia, Georgia and Azerbaijan were all seeking recognition from the great powers, faced with the Bolshevik threat from the north and the Turkish threat from the south, the three countries actually managed to unite into a committee of government, a Seim, of Transcaucasian States, which led to the declaration of Transcaucasia as an independent Democratic Federative Republic in April 1918, recognised by the Ottoman empire. The peoples of the north Caucasus, Daghestan and Abkhazia had also joined to set up a Union of United Mountain Peoples of the Caucasus. Both were short-lived. The Seim fell apart primarily due to differences in the face of Turkish actions in and claims to Transcaucasia. The Azeris welcomed the Turks, the Armenians retreated in blood before them and the Georgians declared their independence. It seems extraordinary now that such a Seim could ever have been contemplated. Shortly after, in 1920, a war broke out between Armenia and Azerbaijan and at the Versailles Conference Armenia and Georgia, who had fought each other briefly in 1918, fell out over Armenian territorial claims which included the port of Batumi. The Georgians and Azeris seemed much more in accord though, again, the relationship was far from simple: Azerbaijan had given tacit support to a federation of the Muslim areas of the south-west Caucasus which briefly declared a republic and most of which was rapidly incorporated into Georgia and Armenia. As happens so often in the Caucasus, history repeats itself tiresomely and the disputes and conflicts between Georgia, Armenia and Azerbaijan from 1917 to 1921 echo weirdly through the 1990s.

Early the next day we left Mingechevir and drove off towards Baku. After Agdash the road winds up for a while through the foothills of the Caucasus and becomes lovely. Here we stopped to drink tea under the trees and change cars. Another CAD worker had come to collect us and drove us down through barren hills of baked mud and then the great empty plain before Baku. During our few days there, when not discussing plans in the CAD office or chatting with the local Oxfam representatives, we wandered the streets. It was livelier, more open, seemed more prosperous than Tbilisi: in the evening air couples strolled up and down the squares or sat to drink and eat while children buzzed about on bikes. All the men had mobile phones strapped to their belts, the new status symbol, and stopped ostentatiously every few minutes to converse. Gleaming and enormous jeeps, covered in chrome, raced about. But most of them were armoured and in them, and all around, standing outside buildings, sitting in offices, were bodyguards, carrying arms, wearing the regulation shades, smoking Marlboro cigarettes. No one could accuse Tbilisi of a regenerate orderliness but I had never seen there these wandering scrimmages of squat, broad-shouldered men in sharp suits. The reason for them was, of course, oil and the unfortunate habit business competitors had, still have, throughout the old Soviet Union, of killing each other. Everywhere old buildings were being restored, new office blocks built, as the oil men of the world and all their trailing business partners established themselves in town. Into one of these shimmering new blocks – all glass and metal outside, Italian marble within – Chris and I walked, out of the hammering heat of the mid-morning sun. At the reception desk smart, polyglot girls with American accents welcomed us. The air-conditioning hummed gently. 'My God!' I said to one. 'This is by far the coolest place in town.' 'Well, thank you!' she replied, delighted, her command of the vernacular too good by half. Stephanie, my contact here, was waiting for us. The Minaret Group, an investment company, had just opened offices in Baku and had expressed an interest in helping some of the Azeri refugees. I had spent the morning in the CAD office preparing a proposal with the help of a computer and Elnara, the CAD local representative, a fabulous Azeri girl. I wanted to persuade Minaret to help the people of the Unfinished Hotel.

Stephanie ordered us coffees and took us into the conference room. At the far end of a vast polished table, three very wide men sat in their shirtsleeves, shoulder-holsters tight across their smart white shirts. As they left, I spread maps, proposal and photographs across the table and, getting into my stride, waved my arms about and knocked Chris's coffee across the lot. Not a good start.

Stephanie, unperturbed, listened to the spiel, became more and more excited, said this was just what was wanted, so we left after an hour feeling buoyant and pleased with ourselves. Much later, back in England, I telephoned CAD and, indeed, Stephanie had rallied her staff, visited the refugees and started to help rebuild the hotel. Unfortunately, in my innocence, I had not reckoned with the usual Caucasian complexities. I had managed to involve CAD in one of the great corruption scandals of the time. Minaret, it turned out, were not all they should have been, investors from the US and Europe had lost fortunes and CAD had had to steer rapidly away from such a tainted association. Viktor Kozeny, the Czech businessman who had set up Minaret, known to his enemies as the 'Pirate of Prague', had persuaded investors to part with $450 million by dangling the prospect of privatisation vouchers in front of them. These vouchers, offered but never quite released by the Azeri government, could be bought cheaply and later used, in theory, to grab pieces of the newly privatised state industries, especially the oil industry and the huge state-owned oil company, Socar. Investors included major real-estate companies in America and even George Mitchell, the leader of the US Senate, who had flown into Baku to attend Minaret's gala opening, just before Chris and I arrived. Later it became clear that Kozeny had got away with exactly the same sort of scam in the Czech Republic. He was quite fantastically wealthy.

Our business done, we went to see the sights. We wanted to see the Maiden Tower, *Kyz Kalasy*, Baku's famous landmark, a surviving fire-temple (later converted) of the Zoroastrian religion which dominated this land for so many centuries when it lay under Persian rule, before the coming of Christianity and then Islam. The present border of Azerbaijan with Persia, dating from the Russo–Persian wars at the beginning of the nineteenth century, divides the ancient province in two, the Persian half also called Azerbaijan, the Garden of Fire. The flickering fires that flamed above the oil which seeped continuously to the surface of the ground made it the natural home of fire-worship and, after the Zoroastrian religion gave way to Islam in Azerbaijan, parties of Parsees from Bombay, Indian Zoroastrians, would come to Baku to tend the 'eternal flame' and conduct religious ceremonies.

John Baddeley came to Baku a number of times at the end of the nineteenth century, to try and profit from the great oil boom, without a great deal of success, but he also gathered material for his journalism and probably did a certain amount of work as a spy. Certainly his great friend from St Petersburg, Sir Edward FitzGerald Law, whom he met up with in Baku in 1893, worked for the British government as well as writing for the *Daily Telegraph*. He was the Commercial Attaché of the British Embassy in St Petersburg. Together they visited the Zoroastrian Temple at Surakhani, set among the oil wells just outside Baku. The population of Baku had recently soared, workers from around the Russian empire attracted to the boom-town, and the place was a focus of political ferment. The Tsar was about to visit and the police were out in force. Baddeley and FitzGerald Law fell into conversation with a group of Parsees who had gathered to conduct ceremonies at the Fire Temple, after journeying through Kabul, Herat and Bokhara. Law had lived for years in India and spoke fluent Hindi. The authorities and a group of bystanders gathered round them and tried to arrest Baddeley and Law as spies – the British and the Indians were obviously plotting some dastardly deed against Russia and the Tsar. Both men had important friends in the Russian government and managed to repel their assailants by threatening them with dire retribution and employing a stream of well-chosen Russian abuse. However, it was not an unreasonable assumption and it is odd, given the difficulties that existed between Britain and Russia at the time, that both Baddeley and Law seemed free to travel wherever they liked throughout the Russian empire, gathering information. Both men's views were well known, particularly Law's. He regarded the Caucasus as essential to British interests in Persia and India and the potential site of possible military operations against Russia if the threat presented to India became a reality. These, of course, were the years of the Great Game, the *Bolshaya Igra*, and Russian actions against the British in India were not confined to their *agents provocateurs* in Central Asia and Afghanistan; there were real plans to attack India by sending a force along the route taken by the Parsees and down through the Khyber Pass, rousing the Afghans and Punjabis on the way. Fears that Herat and Kandahar might fall to the Russians had led the so-called 'forward' thinkers in British Military Intelligence to insist that 'there can never be a real settlement of the Anglo-Russian question till Russia is driven out of the Caucasus and Turkistan'.* Law himself had written forcefully about the need to ensure that Russia was kept out of Istanbul as the Ottoman empire collapsed, and he considered the Caucasus as the key, Russia's soft underbelly: 'The vulnerable point of Russia is not the Black Sea littoral, not the Baltic, but the Trans-Caucasus and her southern frontier. A campaign based on a successful occupation of the Trans-Caucasus attacks her vitals.'† Law felt that the native populations here would not need a great deal of encouragement to rise against their Russian masters. It was, after all, not long since Shamyl had been finally captured in 1859. In fact, Shamyl, fully understanding the British position, had personally written to Queen Victoria to ask for help; the British were fighting the Russians in the Crimea and any diversion of Russian forces would certainly have been most useful. In 1855 Sir Richard Burton had been called in by Lord Stratford who proposed that the great explorer should travel to the Caucasus to assess the situation and to make contact with Shamyl; when Burton discovered that he could neither promise arms nor money he declined to go. To the frustration of many of the 'forward' party, the British government had baulked at Shamyl's request and left 'the greatest guerrilla leader in the history of war' to pursue his struggle on his own. In the west of the Caucasus similar brave and determined resistance by the Circassians had aroused much British sympathy and their most famous supporter, David Urquhart, First Secretary to the British Embassy in Constantinople, passionately advocated their cause, even succeeded in smuggling arms to them. Although Baddeley accused Urquhart and his friends of deluding the Circassians with the hope of British support, he wrote in *The Russian Conquest of the Caucasus* that the Allies had 'totally failed to take advantage of the situation created by Muridism [the religious movement that inspired the struggle for liberty] in the Caucasus'.

* MacGregor, *The Defence of India*, 1884.
† T. Morrison and G. Hutchinson, *The Life of Sir Edward FitzGerald Law.*

Our visit to the Maiden Tower was far less interesting than Baddeley's and Law's to Surakhani, though the building itself is grand, a sort of fat chimney pot with a piece of great buttressing wall attached, a remnant of the fortress walls of the old inner city. There has been some debate about its origins – it has been used for defensive purposes and may have been a lighthouse at one time. However, though the legend which gives it its name is much later (all about a maiden escaping her incestuous father and jumping off it) the latest archaeological work suggests that it dates from around 800BC and that it was indeed a fire-temple, each of its seven floors devoted to a separate god in the holy pantheon of Ahura-Mazda. Now, somewhat less dramatically, it has become a trinket shop.

Walking up through the narrow streets of the old city we went off to find Baku's museum. Housed in one of the grand old buildings of the oil barons, it seemed utterly deserted. We groped our way through the silent, imperial penumbra until, at the far end of a long, dark corridor, we came across a family crouched on the floor cooking lunch over a primus stove beneath a dusty exhibit of the Stone Age. They waved us on and we pottered about, peering at odds and ends through the gloom, the place obviously untouched for years. Azeri historians and archaeologists are sensitive about dates: they try to push back as far as possible the time of the arrival of Turks in the Caucasus, to give their historical claims to the land a greater weight and antique dignity. Here there was little to celebrate the Caucasian Albanians whom the Turks had conquered and mixed with. There is, of course, not a great deal that is certain about these Albanians or their origins – described as 'an indefinable Paleocaucasian population', speaking many languages, of which one, Udi, spoken by some 3,000 people in three villages (two in Azerbaijan and one in eastern Georgia) is thought by some to be the sole descendant. Although the Romans under Pompey almost reached Baku and conquered the country, the Albanians fell more within the Armeno-Persian world than their Georgian neighbours – albeit that Pompey claimed a special link between them and the Romans by virtue of a mythical common descent from the population of Italian Alba, on which basis we could join them to Balkan Albanians and the Britons of Albion. They were converted to

Christianity during the fifth century AD, though the earliest Christian missionary activity began much earlier. Their alphabet, still incompletely understood and surviving only in fragments, was given to them, according to Armenian historians, by the Armenian monk Mesrop Mashots in the fifth century at the same time as he invented alphabets for the Armenians and the Georgians, an assertion hotly denied by Georgian historians. The first Turks to appear were probably the Huns around the middle of the fourth century, though they were almost certainly not wholly Turkish and remained for the most part to the north of the mountains, as did the Khazars nearly three centuries later. Azeri historians have argued that there were Turkish or Turkic tribes settled in the area during the first millennium BC, though most other scholars suggest that only from the fourth century AD can any real interaction between Turkic peoples and Caucasians be certain, and that Turkic settlement is much later. Only from the eleventh century with the arrival of the Seljuks can the land be properly described as Turkish.

The Seljuks were a branch of the Oghuz Turks and something of the culture of these extraordinary warriors can still be felt in the great *dastan* of the Oghuz, claimed by the Azeris as one of their national treasures and displayed in the museum: *The Book of Dede Korkut*. These ornate oral histories, gathered by Father Korkut, high priest and bard of the Oghuz, and probably first written down sometime during the fourteenth century, refer to a much earlier world: ancient tribal beliefs and customs break through the later Islamic veneer the stories were given. They are wonderful, verbose, bombastic tales, often surprisingly funny, full of abuse, tricks and ruses; women are bright, leaping flames or waving cypresses, everyone cries tears of blood and war is the only noble occupation. The Oghuz fight the Georgians, they fight the Abkhaz, they fight each other. Captured by the Georgians, the Prince Salur Kazan takes his lute and declaims modestly:

> When I saw ten thousand enemies I attended
> to them,
> When I saw twenty thousand enemies I dented
> them,

When I saw thirty thousand enemies I thwarted them,
When I saw forty thousand enemies I bore it with forti-
tude,
When I saw fifty thousand enemies I sifted them,
When I saw sixty thousand enemies I was never sickly at
the sight of them,
When I saw seventy thousand enemies I circumvented
them,
When I saw eighty thousand enemies I castigated them,
When I saw ninety thousand enemies I was not nice to
them,
When I saw a hundred thousand enemies I thundered
at them.
I took up my unswerving sword,
I wielded it for the love of the faith of Muhammed,
In the white arena I cut off round heads like balls,
Even then I did not boast 'I am a warrior, I am a prince',
Never have I looked kindly on warriors who boasted,
Now that you have caught me, infidel, kill me,
Drive your black sword at my neck, cut off my head,
I shall not flinch from your sword,
I do not defame my own stock, my own root.

*

A large section of the museum is still devoted to the early Soviet
years and there, in a glass case, is a framed certificate signed by a
delegation of British Trade Unionists in November 1924,
proclaiming the 'fraternal goodwill and comradely feelings, close
understanding and unity of purpose' between the workers of Great
Britain and Russia, all of which seems now wonderfully archaic:
'Long live the World Federation of the Proletariat! Long live the
Unity of the British and Russian Workers!'

The British delegation had been taken on a tour of the oil fields,
then in their heyday. Much has been written recently of the dere-
liction of the old oil workings of the Caspian, of the bright new
platforms built in the middle of the sea, of the enormous wealth

that has flown and will, possibly, flow out of Baku, the old and new pipelines, their profound effect on the politics, economics and stability of the whole area and on international relations, the hope and the anarchy that pours out with the crude. Just how important Baku was globally in the past is sometimes forgotten, though nicely illustrated by the story of Hitler's Birthday Cake: when presented with a cake on which was drawn a map of Europe and Russia, Hitler cut himself a great slice around Baku. In 1901 more oil was produced in Baku than in all the US fields added together. In the ten years previously the population of oil workers in the town had risen from just over a thousand to nearly 28,000. The wealth, the corruption, the lawlessness and the misery, the political turmoil that this engendered can hardly be exaggerated. As the Nobel brothers, the Rothschilds and the other oil barons made their great fortunes, the workers, Russian, Azeri, Daghestani and the rest, lived in appalling conditions, ripe grounds for Joseph Stalin – Dzhugashvili as he was then – and his fellow Bolshevik conspirators: 'The thousands and thousands of workers lived in damp, unlighted, dark, dirty barracks, where three slept together on a small, uncovered wooden cot . . . The work at the oil-wells under the burning sun was hardly easier than toiling in coal-mines. The working day lasted for sixteen hours without interruption; even that seemed too short to some of the owners.'

When we left the museum Chris and I went to look, without success, for the house of Essad Bey, author of this description. I had stumbled across his *Blood and Oil in the Orient*, a book which gives a wonderful portrait of Baku and its inhabitants at the turn of the nineteenth century, and he had become something of a favourite of mine. He wrote more than a dozen books during the 1920s and 30s, among them *The Twelve Secrets of the Caucasus*, a highly romanticised and fantastical account of the mountains and the mountain people. He described himself as the son of a wealthy Muslim oil magnate, living in great luxury in Baku, with an intimate knowledge of the tribes of Azerbaijan and Daghestan. But there was a mystery here: in my further rummagings through second-hand bookshops I picked up another book set in Baku at the same period by one Kurban Said, *Ali and Nino*, a fabulous,

romantic tale of the love and the clash of cultures between Muslim
Ali and Georgian Nino among the flames of war and massacre,
Muslim against Armenian, Bolshevik against nationalist, as Soviets,
Turks, White Russians and British closed in around Baku. It is
immediately obvious that *Ali and Nino* was written by the author
of *Blood and Oil*, the style and content are so similar, so who was
Kurban Said or Essad Bey and why did he write under two names?
I wish I could say that I found the answer myself but in 1999 there
appeared a long article in the *New Yorker* by an American journalist,
Tom Reiss, who had read *Ali and Nino* while working in Baku and
had set out to discover more about its author. It is a fantastic piece
of detective work. Indeed, Said and Bey were one and the same,
but far from being a Muslim Azeri he was, in fact, Jewish, a certain
Lev Nussimbaum. Reiss's research uncovered an extraordinary story
of false identity, Nazi persecution, Italian Fascist police, publishing
greed and a mad baroness in an Austrian castle. Nussimbaum had
indeed been born in Baku, had grown up in a wealthy, cosmo-
politan household, but had fled the city with his father in 1919
when he was fifteen years old and gone to live in Berlin where his
books, all written in German, were published. There he had
become, in Reiss's words, 'a professional man of the Caucasus' and
a 'Weimar media star'. Even at school he dressed as an Azeri Muslim
which intensely irritated the local Muslim community. Representatives of the Azeri, Persian, Georgian and Turkestani communities
in Berlin published a denunciation in various newspapers, writing
that 'He is no Oriental and his name is not Essad Bey'. This explains
the Kurban Said persona. His cover had been blown. As the Nazis
grew in strength and refused to allow Jewish authors to publish he
had to find another identity. He fled Berlin, went to Vienna in
1935 and finally to Italy where, somewhat foolishly, he proposed
himself as Mussolini's biographer in 1937. Denounced as a Jew,
again, he was pursued south by the Fascist police. He died in 1939,
hungry and penniless, of an infected foot brought on by Raynaud's
disease.

It was time to head back towards Georgia and to start walking. At
nine the next morning Chris and I caused a minor riot at the Baku

taxi rank when we loudly announced that we wanted to go to Sheki. We were saved from having to pay a price equivalent to the cost of a round-the-world cruise by the fierce altercations and knock-down auction that ensued. Diving into a cab just as the scuffle threatened to turn ugly, we found ourselves in the company of two good-humoured brothers who roared off with a great blaring of horn and screeching of tyres. Immediately the bargaining process started again, their efforts redoubled with pleas of costly tyres and irreplaceable gearbox when I told them I wanted to take the slow mountain road. After the town of Ismayilli the road winds through the foothills of the Caucasus, green, tree-lined and cool. At first, on either side, walnut and chestnut trees mingle, then, particularly between Sheki and Lagodekhi, walnuts march all the way – the longest avenue of walnut trees in the world. I once corresponded with an Englishman who had walked it in autumn and had survived on nothing but fresh walnuts for days. In Sheki we found our CAD contact, Dr Raghib Mamehdov, who worked with a group of colleagues among the refugees from Karabakh. Small, dark, energetic but exhausted, he whisked us off on a grim tour of the local camps. Again, I could not help wondering which perverse authority had decided to house all these destitute people down on the sweltering plain. Certainly it was a way of lessening the impact on existing communities but this seemed too high a price to pay. One group of refugees from Lachin occupied a mouldering building, an old power-plant, which they had worked hard to make habitable and homelike with mats and rugs and pots of flowers. But still the walls were full of holes, there were no windows, the roof and floors were dangerously weak and there was no sanitation or electricity and little water. Flies and mosquitoes buzzed all around. Everyone looked tired and ill. Raghib, patient and kind, spoke to all in turn, gently reassuring them.

When we returned to his house, his two colleagues from the Mobile Health Unit had just arrived back from another camp with their driver, Serefim, and all immediately declared – with typical Azeri kindness and relieved, perhaps, by the distraction of our visit – that we must have a picnic. So we gathered up supplies and left for the pleasure gardens of Sheki. Here, amid trees and little streams, tables had been set up about the hillside, a Turkish dream of paradise, and as Serefim cooked kebabs, we settled to talk and drink. The youngest of the doctors was a tall fair Russian, Volodya, born in Baku where he had lived all his thirty-five years. The other, Aydan, a bright, sharp woman, had worked with the refugees since their arrival and was frustrated and bitter. Some of her anger she directed at her own government but most she kept for the Armenians.

'We must fight them and we must kill them,' she said, flatly. 'We must and shall take back Karabakh. It is the land of our people.'

'But when you see all the present misery, do you think more fighting will help? Isn't there already too much to do just to survive?' I asked.

'Do you leave a thief to steal? Do you leave a murderer to murder? We can never have peace with these people, we can never forget what they have done.'

Unusually, she did not blame everything on the Russians and felt a terrible sense of loss, of bewilderment at the fracturing of what she called 'my world'.

'I used to travel often to Moscow or St Petersburg, I have many friends there. I have not been for seven years. I cannot afford to travel, to go abroad, to do anything any more.'

Valodya was chain-smoking, his fingers trembling as he puffed his cigarettes. He wanted desperately to know what we had heard, what we thought and specifically what we knew of the terrible massacre of Armenians in Baku in January 1990. I told him what I knew: hundreds of Armenians had been dragged from their homes, chased about the streets and killed, causing most of Baku's 300,000 Armenians to flee the city and the country their families had lived in for generations. Then a week later the Soviet tanks had rolled in, just as they had done in Tbilisi, in Dushanbe, in the Baltic states, and two hundred more people had been killed, many crushed under the tanks, though this time they were Azeris. In Azerbaijan, as in Georgia, many thought that the riots or demonstrations and the subsequent repression were all part of a Soviet or Russian or KGB plot to destabilise and then control the fledgling independence movements of the countries, that Russia would never allow her influence in Azerbaijan, with all its oil, to be threatened. Everyone now, of course, points to Chechnya and its vital oil pipeline as the great example of how far Russia is prepared to go to protect its interests. As a Russian, Valodya was, naturally, extremely sensitive to this but his loyalties were to Azerbaijan: he had been born here, his child had been born here, and he would stay. He was convinced that in the pogrom against the Armenians dark and mysterious forces had been at work:

'I do not know who was really responsible. That night I was in my flat when I heard shooting outside. I rushed down to the street and saw a car that had swerved on to the pavement. My blood froze. I knew the car, it was my best friend's. He was inside, dead, shot in the head. He had probably been coming to see me. Soldiers were running about the streets shooting. But they looked strange, I am sure they were not Azeris. I thought they looked Syrian, perhaps. They had no badges or flashings on their uniforms. I think they were mercenaries, *agents provocateurs*.'

I began to understand why his hands trembled so. I have heard various different versions of these events: that the massacre started when an Armenian shopkeeper went for some Azeri thugs with a knife, that refugees from Karabakh deliberately set out for revenge or simply with bloodlust against the Armenian community, as Azeris had in Sumgait in 1988. Whatever the reason given for the initial acts, there is always a conspiracy theory to explain the violence.

They all wanted to know why Chris and I were going to Georgia and when I explained our grand plan, our walk, Serefim, another refugee, once a teacher, now a driver, decided that he would take us on to Ilisu, but that first we should come on a little expedition with him.

So next morning, with Raghib and Serefim and his friend Elderim, we drove to a small village, Bash Lagski, a mainly Lesghian affair up by the border with Daghestan. Stopping briefly for another friend, a Lesghian, Shakir, and bumping tediously over rocks and river beds (they absolutely would not let us get out and walk) we eventually came to a halt by a stream and clambered out. A few bored soldiers came over from their border post, were hugely entertained by the two odd Englishmen, cadged some cigarettes and wandered off. We all sat under a tree in the rain while Serefim and Elderim tried desperately to light a fire. A little elf appeared. He had a broad, sad face and deep bloodshot eyes and on his head he wore a brown bonnet with a red ribbon around its brim, Harvey Nichols *circa* 1940. He was riding a tiny brown horse. The Karabakhis let out cries of delight, grabbed the horse, persuaded the elf to sit upon a rock, and raced about happily doing cowboy tricks. They stood on the saddle then jumped down to the ground, then swung back into the saddle again and galloped about. At length they returned the horse to its bemused owner and laid out our picnic, aghast that they had forgotten to bring along a table-cloth: tomatoes and cheese, cucumbers and herbs, tins of a peculiar meat they tried to warm on the sputtering fire and lots of vodka. The Lesghian quickly became rather drunk and surly then fell asleep but the men from Karabakh continued to race about, picking herbs, talking of their mountain home, explaining that there in Lachin (where hundreds of Kurds and Azeris had been slaughtered by Armenians) this or that was different from, or the same as, that or this, excited to be half way up a mountain once again.

As night fell, we drove off to Gach and there Serefim, handing us on in this game of pass-the-parcel, introduced us to Akhmed and Fasil in the dark and filthy hostel where Fasil now lived with his family in one small room. Fasil and Akhmed agreed to take us to the hammam the following morning and so we drove on to Ilisu, left Raghib, Serefim and Elderim with much ceremony and many promises of future contact, and found ourselves walking through the village with Akhmed, meeting his brother and Assa, being taken to a ridge above Ilisu to pitch our tent, and then being suddenly left alone in the still, dark Caucasian night. But just before he left us Akhmed asked:

'Do you have a gun?'

CHAPTER 2

TUSHETI

'ra lamazia tusheti'

How we met the Mindis, their uncles,
their cousins and tried to keep up

The old Intourist Hotel in Telavi, where I had arranged to meet our Georgian guide, was a wreck. I had stayed there ten years before for a few days and it was grim then, but now it looked as though it had just been trashed by a Mongol Horde. The hotel was falling apart; piles of rubbish and broken glass lay about, doors perilously half-hinged hung open. We wandered in through a knot of little boys playing football in the empty ornamental pond and made hopeful noises. We peered into grimy, deserted rooms. I backed hastily out of a lavatory: a camel, a herd of camels, just down from fresh pasture, had been in. Then a young man appeared. His hair was neat and his black trousers immaculate and creased; his shirt, in this heat, cool, white, perfect. I stared at him in amazement. He greeted us courteously, smiling. He was terribly, terribly sorry. There were no rooms. There was no electricity, no water, no one to run the hotel, nothing. Not even a simple bed. All gone, all broken. 'Ah!' I said. 'Closed for repairs.' 'No, just closed.' He smiled and spread his hands wide. Best to try the old Hotel Telavi down the road.

The old hotel was dark and dusty. A tiny, shambling, ancient man shuffled out of the gloom and peered at us over the front desk. Yes, there was a room. No, there was no water. Electricity, maybe, sometimes. We must pay now. Could we see the room first?

What is to see? The room is a room. He was four feet tall with a shrunken head, straight out of the Pitt-Rivers Museum. He glared at me. I glared back. A Mexican stand-off. He shrugged and moved away. I paid.

He softened slightly and told us there was a fountain across the way, we could wash there. The room was a room. We dumped our packs and went down to the water. It flowed, abundant and clear from wide spigots set in an ornate wall, and fell into three stone basins below. There was all Telavi: drinking, gargling, shaving, filling buckets and water bottles, washing clothes and, discreetly, bodies; everyone relaxed, laughing, waiting their turn. Smiling boys smoked cigarettes and splashed giggling girls who pretended to be annoyed. Here, at the village pump, all was well with the world.

Cleaner, refreshed, we wandered through the town in the torrid heat, peering into empty shops, buying obscure tins of food at little kiosks where private enterprise struggled to bloom among dried fish, bottles of vodka, cigarettes, bars of chocolate, green and blue liqueurs, all ancient produce from the old empire. In a tiny cobbler's shop we sat and drank tea in the cool darkness while Chris had the stitching on his boots repaired. The young cobbler was infinitely amused by us. What on earth were we doing here? Everyone in Telavi was trying to leave. How much did we earn? How much were shoes in England? How much was a Mercedes? There was nothing to see here, and in the mountains even less. The boots were perfect.

That evening we sat on the landing of the old hotel in the thick, hot dust in the no, maybe, never light and dined experimentally off tins of horrid little fish in what Chris, with his naval background, suggested was whale oil, all washed away with good Kazbegi beer. In the middle of the night an old lady in her nightgown shuffled into our room, looked around by the beam of her torch and left, sweetly murmuring to herself.

The next morning our guides found us. I had only expected one but Mindia had brought along his older cousin, also called Mindia. They were both Mindi for short, they explained at length. I tried to think of something witty about having two minders called

Mindi but gave up. Dark, good-looking lads drenched in sweat and carrying huge old canvas rucksacks, smiling and excited, both Khevsurs from mountain villages through which we would pass. The older Mindi had walked a little of our route before and knew some of the mountain passes. He was tall, strong and broad; the younger was smaller, lighter with dark intelligent eyes.

The Mindis led us sweating to the usual chaos of the bus: a long wait in the heat while crowds of people clambered on and off with impossible baggages, unsure of when or where the bus would go. Old, wasted men hawked cigarettes and snacks, tired women waddled through the crowd with huge boxes, shouting, 'Ice-cream! Ice-cream!' Young girls offered bubble-gum and sticky drinks. Snot-nosed boys raced here and there on their own wild trajectories. At last the bus rattled off. Crushed tightly in the back, Chris was soon fast asleep, a rare talent. I have seen him sleeping in a luggage rack on a train in Armenia, surrounded by an admiring crowd; I have seen him sleeping while standing up wedged tight in another bus in Georgia between two enormous Svan women who shared a complicated meal across his chest and shouted at each other as we zigzagged and bumped down a mountain road.

The Mindis and I discussed the plan: we would leave the bus at Alvani, stay the night and early the next morning catch a lift in a lorry, they hoped, up into the mountains to Omalo. From there we would strike off north, then west through Diklo, Dartlo and along the Pirikiti-Alazani River. Though the Mindis now lived in Gamarjweba, a suburb of Tbilisi, they spent much time in the mountains. Both the younger's parents came from Mutso, in Khevsureti, the older Mindi's father, too, though his mother was a Tush from Diklo. The Khevsurs and the Tush are peoples with long and turbulent histories, like that of Georgia itself. High in the mountains, for centuries they pastured their cattle and fought their neighbours and invaders from the north and east. They were famous as poets and as warriors. When the great Imam Shamyl led his men in holy war against the Russians and tried to subdue the mountain tribes to his will, the Khevsurs, Christians (though like all the mountain tribes also strongly pagan), defeated him at Shatili and beat his men back over the passes into Chechnya and

Daghestan. When, in the seventeenth century, the Georgian King Alexander of Kakheti fought off the assaults of the Persians and their Lesghian allies, he called upon an army of Tush, Pshavs and Khevsurs many thousands strong. Though, of course, the old life has gone, underlying values remain alive. The Mindis would say, only half-joking, that what Khevsur men loved best were guns, horses and women.

Baddeley was fascinated by the Khevsurs and though he never managed to reach Shatili, or further south into Khevsureti than the Arkhotis Pass, he wrote at some length about their folklore, their towers, their birthing chambers and their strange customs and taboos. Like every other writer who has touched on their history, he tells the legend of their origin as a lost band of Crusaders who struggled into the mountains after some catastrophe on the way to, or back from, the Holy Land. Though the dates are all wrong and their history goes back much further (they are certainly, for the most part, Kartvelians, Georgians), there is a mystery here. Even now a good number of the Khevsurs, though not the Mindis, are fair-skinned with fair hair and blue eyes. Their traditional dress, of which there are many accounts, was of chain-mail, with a Christian cross on their shields and smocks. I have seen some of these Khevsur crosses, on old rings, on necklaces and embroidered into shirts and jackets, and they look exactly like the Maltese cross or cross patée; again, associations with the Crusades are difficult to ignore. Though other writers have dismissed as myth these tales of Khevsurs dressed as Crusading knights, Baddeley writes of one of the great sights of late tsarist times:

In old times the Imperial Convoy consisted of representatives of all the tribes wearing each his national costume, and one of the privileged sights of St Petersburg in the time of Alexander II was the Sunday *razvod*, or parade, in the great Michael riding school (*manège*), in winter, when all these wild horsemen – the Toushi and Khevsours in chain armour – were put through their paces and then with a wild yell charged up to the very feet of the Emperor, who sat impassive on his horse surrounded by the Grand Dukes and a brilliant staff.

When Baddeley reached Khevsureti, he had for a guide over the mountains a Khevsur 'clad in hauberk of chain-mail, with iron shield, sword, dagger and rifle, and a bridle decorated alternately with cowrie-shells and beads of turquoise blue.' That much, at least, is clear but strange tales and legends accumulate around the Khevsurs: Essad Bey wrote that the Khevsurs lived in a deep, impenetrable valley surrounded by mountains and cliffs so precipitous that no stranger could ever find the way in. Only those who knew the route could descend into the secret valley, and then they had to lower themselves down by rope. As might be imagined, I was full of eager anticipation.

We rode in the old, battered bus across the plains, through herds of buffalo and cattle, past shepherds and their flocks of sheep until, finally, we ground to a halt at Alvani. We shouldered our packs and walked through the village, neatly laid out with gardens full of peppers and aubergines, onions and fruit trees. The air was thick, the sky had darkened, huge black clouds raced towards us, hurled from the mountains ahead. Thunder cracked and boomed. We quickened our pace and arrived, just as the storm broke, at the house of the Mindis' cousins.

It was typical of village houses across the Caucasus: square, built of stone with a broad wooden veranda running all along the front on the first floor. We sat here, drank tea and watched the storm flatten the onions and send the chickens running off in panic. The cousins, two quiet men in their thirties, strangely lacking in animation for Georgians, borrowed a neighbour's car and took us, moving warily through the flood, along the road for a few miles to the great eleventh-century cathedral of Alaverdi. Georgian churches are largely unmentioned in most western European accounts of our culture – not even one word in Kenneth Clark's *Civilisation*, for example. These churches represent more than a thousand years of continuous evolution, and range from the tiny seventh-century churches of Svaneti to the splendours of Svetitskhoveli and Gelati and the vast and magnificent cathedrals of Tao, in what is now north-eastern Turkey.

Alaverdi, built at the beginning of the eleventh century, is the tallest of Georgia's cathedrals and, silhouetted against the great mountains behind, its outline dominates the valley of the Alazani. I had been some years before when the entire floor was bare earth and rubble. Now, all had been restored. The church has an elegance and a monumental solemnity which is particular to Georgian architecture and we walked quietly around, lighting candles which sent their smoke curling against the walls, adding to the blackened streaks left by all the thousands of prayers before. The church was almost empty but on my previous visit it was so densely packed that, had it not been for the enthusiasm of Mr Shota, I would not have had the courage to burrow my way in. Mr Shota, tiny, brown, elegant, taught English literature at Telavi University and had attached himself to the theatre company I was travelling with. The actors had just performed at the theatre in Telavi and Mr Shota so loved the show that he had returned the following morning to present the actresses with copies of *The Knight in the Panther's Skin*, by Shota Rustaveli, Georgia's national poem. He somehow appeared on the bus with us as we drove to Alaverdi. I saw him lean over to Bronwen, our lady musician, and say:

'My dear, as Dickens wrote, "A woman is a mirror to the twin."' A shiver of bewilderment passed over Bron's face.

'I am sorry,' she said, 'what was that?'

'A woman's twin is in the mirror,' replied Mr Shota, nodding vigorously.

'Oh. Er, could you repeat that, I didn't quite catch it?'

'Yes, of course. As Dickens wrote, "A woman's mirror is the twin to a woman."'

'Ah!'

Mr Shota freshened us up with sudden plunges into the canon of English literature while the bus ploughed slowly forward through great crowds of milling celebrants. It was Alaverdi's feast day and all along the road to the cathedral people were picnicking in the mud. Many had tied black canopies to the trees and sat under them eating and drinking like so many extras in a biblical epic. Sheep and chickens were butchered furiously, fires stoked, shashliks prepared. The roadside fence was hung with the bodies of the slaughtered. As we got ready to leave the bus, Mr Shota looked up at me and said:

'In Georgian we say that a man who chooses will never grow a moustache.'

'Indeed, indeed. Could you say that again?'

'Certainly young fellow. A man will not grow a moustache if he chooses.'

'I see. What does that mean, in fact?'

'I mean what I say! That is it!'

A fair had sprung up outside the entrance to the church. Ladies sold hats and shawls and bric-à-brac. Men gambled loudly over the three-thimble trick. Mr Shota led us round the church, moving calmly through the throng. 'Come on, young fellows, follow me.' He pointed lovingly to the new iconostasis and bemoaned the few and faded frescos, so much lost, so much destroyed. But Alaverdi had survived more than Communist neglect and suppression; damaged by earthquake and almost razed by the troops of the Persian Shah Abbas in his attempt to level all Kakheti and massacre its population in 1615, the cathedral had stood its ground for almost a thousand years.

*

Now, as the rain stopped and the sky cleared, we left the empty church and drove back to Alvani. The air was wonderfully fresh and we climbed on to the roof of a neighbour's house to look at *diklos mta*, Mount Diklos, towering in the distance, tomorrow's destination, snow-covered, glowing in the sun.

After a night clouded by home-brewed *chacha*, a fierce spirit with nothing to recommend it besides its alcoholic content, and pierced by the screams of a psychotic cockerel, insane with the thought of dawn, madder even than my own, we were up at five and standing by the road. Much to my amazement, the lorry soon appeared: an old, green, Soviet army truck. We climbed up into the back and stood among sacks of rock salt, separated by a hurdle from a huddle of calves, destined for the mountain pastures. A young Tush boy stood smiling by the cab, an electric-blue baseball cap on his head with the mysterious legend 'Holiday Saving Punch' printed across it. Off and up, desperately clinging to the sides of the truck, through the village of Pshavelli and into Pshaveti, the country of the Pshavs.

Pshaveti shares much of the culture and history of its more northerly neighbours, Khevsureti and Tusheti. Bound for the high mountains, I could not stop this time. My main interest in Pshaveti was, in any case, poetic. Perhaps the most interesting of all Georgian poets, Vazha Pshavela, was the son of a great mountain clan, the Razikashvilis, his *nom de plume* meaning, simply, a lad from Pshaveti. Not quite the wild, uneducated free spirit made out by some, he had been educated in Telavi and Tbilisi, and even, for a year, in Moscow till forced out by poverty. In the late 1880s he returned to Pshaveti to live as a peasant, riding occasionally into Tbilisi with his saddle-bags stuffed with poems. At first ridiculed as a sort of mad bumpkin, he was later championed by an older poet, the great, saintly Ilia Chavchavadze, and became a huge figure in the spiritual and artistic life of the nation. When he died in Tbilisi in 1915, crowds wept in the streets. I soon discovered that young Mindi, not uncommonly, could recite by heart large sections of Pshavela's poetry. Written largely in the idioms of Khevsureti and Pshaveti, his poems contain and celebrate mountain life and culture and yet – and this is what makes him so distinctive – they also subvert and challenge much that such a life entails. The best account of him that I have read is in Donald Rayfield's overview, *The Literature of Georgia*, and I quote and paraphrase from Rayfield's book here. Pshavela, steeped in folklore and song, romantic, heroic, pantheistic, evolved a philosophy in his poetry which is strangely incisive and demanding. One of his greatest poems, 'Host and Guest' (*stumar-maspindzeli*), is almost a critique of mountain custom: the dire laws of the blood-feud and the equally irrefragable laws of hospitality come into conflict and end in death. It is deeply pessimistic. In the poem a Khevsur, Zviadauri, out hunting, comes across his blood enemy, Joqola, a Chechen. Joqola does not recognise him in the mist and offers him hospitality but his fellow-villagers drag Zviadauri off and kill him. Joqola is outraged and he and his wife stand guard over the body of Zviadauri. They, in their turn, are condemned to die by their fellow Chechens.

Pshavela's masterpiece and, says Rayfield (though many

Georgians would disagree), 'Georgian poetry's supreme achievement' is 'The Snake-Eater' (*gvelis mchameli*). The hero, Mindia, of course, is the archetypal 'poet-shaman unable to coexist with family or community'. He is taken by wizards, *khajis*, and forced to eat snake flesh, strongly taboo. This gives him magical powers but he finds himself no longer able to cut down trees or take the life of animals and he becomes a kind of complex Pshav visionary, a holy, romantic, pantheist who finds himself trapped between his reverence for nature and its cruelty and indifference:

> This is the wrong that nature does us,
> the cause of our eternal grief:
> evil and good, it kills them all,
> no one has it ever spared.

He begs his fellows, hopelessly, to spare all living things and eventually, in despair, commits suicide. There is no easy resolution. Vazha Pshavela's pacifism and his sensitivity to and awareness of nature in all its forms is especially remarkable given the prevailing mountain culture of the warrior and hunter. He drew largely upon a great corpus of oral folk poetry and legend that links the Georgian mountain tribes with the other mountain peoples of the Caucasus: the Chechens, the Ingush, the Circassians and the tribes of Daghestan. Theirs is a pagan world of local deities and minor spirits and their poems and songs allow the living to commune with these spirits and with the dead in their dark land, *suleti*, the land of souls.

After Pshavelli, the lorry stopped, the differential was changed and the road soon became a boulder-strewn track. Great lumps of rock hung over us, water poured across our path or crashed over us, the mountain sheer above and below. The driver powered his way up zigzag bends, throwing us all in a heap towards the back. Young Mindi picked himself off the floor and remarked that the driver was terribly good. I was not so sure. As the track curved up, he started a series of three-point turns to get us round the bends, backing the lorry over the precipice till the back wheels spun, half in the void. Chris and I got ready to jump. The Mindis grinned.

Stone and rock fell away from under our wheels until there really seemed no possible way forward. The regions of hazel and mountain ash, chestnut and oak, dropped away behind us, the mountains now blanketed with wild azalea and fir. Above the lorry's roar we yelled; only the poor calves moaned. At every violent lurch upwards, at each sharp turn, they were hurled against the back and sides of the truck into a pile of twisted legs and huge, frightened eyes. They lay there, tangled and broken, staring up at us. I could not look and turned away towards a vertical world of rock and snow. Nature and human nature, each in conflict with itself and with the other, pure Pshavela.

Here, above the tree line, into Tusheti, along a steep slope covered with mountain rubble, we crossed over the Pikrischala Pass into a great wide bowl of peaks, the heart of the Caucasus. The track was blocked. A landslide of boulders covered it entirely. Everyone leapt out. An ancient shepherd wearing three jumpers, two jackets and what looked like a whole sheep on his head, came out of nowhere and started to direct operations. With sledge-hammers and crowbars, hammering, pushing and levering, we rolled the rocks to the edge and watched them bounce and spin, thousands of feet below. In the cold air, at this great height, I was beginning to feel a little peculiar. A headache, slight dizziness. Was it, perhaps, altitude sickness? Or the *chacha* from the night before? I could not work it out and tried, oxymoronically, to stay alert for signs of clouded consciousness – a sure way to know, apparently, that you need to descend. But how, I wondered, in all this fog of consciousness, could one possibly tell?

The driver thought he might now just get through and we all walked forward as he came slowly towards us, the truck tilting over impossibly, the better part of the outside wheels over the edge, rubble and earth slipping out from under them and pouring away. He was through and we were off again, down and down towards the river, rushing along a narrow gorge, clogged with broken trees. Old power cables dangled from pylons, nearly decapitating us as we raced past; high above in the remaining lines, huge trunks of trees hung suspended like trapped prey in a web. Here, perched on the slopes ahead, were the first settlements, Khiso and

Chiglaourta and there, at the head of the valley as the gorge narrowed, a ruined tower guarding the way to Omalo. As the road turned up again and left the river, more towers lined the gorge high on our left and then more again by the hamlet of Khakhabo. In 1984 Eduard Shevardnadze, then President of Soviet Georgia, came here by helicopter to celebrate the Tushetoba and had a spring named after him. These 'obas', festivals, occur in summer throughout mountain Georgia, each village celebrating its particular saint in an entirely pagan riot of drinking and eating. Beer, particularly, is specially brewed for the occasion and consumed in huge quantities with great fortitude; the stuff that I have drunk resembling nothing so much as the yeasty sludge left over from unsuccessful home-brewing fiascos of my youth.

We stopped to pick up a couple of boys carrying Kalashnikovs: off hunting, they said; then up and over a near-vertical piece of mountain and into a wide grassland, very lovely, a half-dozen more towers on a crag above, pine trees covering the high slopes around, birch lower down and flowers everywhere. Omalo, the capital village of high Tusheti, at the eastern edge of the valley of the Pirikiti-Alazani, the 'far' or northern branch of the Alazani River. Like many of the settlements of Tusheti and Khevsureti, the old village of fortified tower houses sits high on the upper slopes, for the most part deserted, while the new village clusters along the river valley and the track. New Omalo is a strange place of half-built houses: hostels for young people or holiday makers from the cities, ideas conceived but never finished in the late days of Communism, oddly disconcerting in this pristine setting of mountains and alpine meadows, rushing water, clear air and quiet, contented cattle.

We were keen to move after our hours of battering in the lorry and the Mindis warned of afternoon storms, so we walked out of Omalo to the north-east, past an old graveyard with broken headstones, small houses with decorative verandas, a couple hoeing a patch of potatoes, and past the little church of Queen Tamar and her son Giorgi Lasha, 'Light of the World'. All over Georgia there are churches and castles dedicated to Queen Tamar, or said to have been built by her or even visited by her, a queen so great that she is always called *tamar mepe*, King Tamar. During her reign

(1184–1212) she held the country under her firm and careful hand (bringing Tusheti also to heel) and ruled from the Black Sea to the Caspian. The kingdom knew unparalleled prosperity, her court was full of poets and philosophers and the 'peasants were like nobles, the nobles like princes, the princes like kings'.* Unfortunately her son, a brave but dissolute man, found himself in the path of the Mongols and, going out with 90,000 knights to see who on earth these strange people were who had just devastated Armenia, was utterly routed, and finally died of his wounds in 1223.

It was a gentle four- or five-hour walk through the meadows to Diklo, at the eastern edge Tusheti. To the north, Daghestan lay in the shade. Mount Diklos towered above. The lower slopes, felt-like, had just been scythed, the hay stacked in stooks around. We walked into the village, over a football pitch at forty-five degrees, with trees as goal posts, where the Mindis had played as children. Just ahead was big Mindi's tower, his ancestral home, half-ruined to be sure but still his own, a tangible link with history, last inhabited, he thought, in his great grandfather's time.

The towers of the Caucasus seem to grow out of the mountains and, as much as the high mountains themselves, define the character and the culture of the place. Some have seen them as unique; this is not the case. Similar villages of tower-houses exist in the Mani in Greece, in Albania, in Persia and, of course, in Italy at San Gimignano. Baddeley compared them closely to the towers of Ireland. Perhaps nowhere, though, are there so many. The plan is always much the same, though there are discernible local variations: massive stone walls, a door often on the first floor only reached by ladder (which would be pulled up in times of trouble), angled slots from which to fire upon intruders, covering all the ground around. Even now one can see how well, how beautifully they were built: huge courses of stone laid immaculately, tapering upwards, the corners still sharp and strong where they remain. Until the Russians arrived, lugging their artillery over the mountains, these towers must have been all but impregnable, susceptible only to trickery and starvation.

* C. Toumanoff, *Armenia and Georgia*, pp. 624–5.

Often in this part of the Caucasus there is also, with each village or group of tower-houses, sometimes standing alone, sometimes within the village cluster, a more elegant, taller, more tapering tower with a pitched, pyramidal roof of thick slates. These have survived rather better than the broader, squatter, flat-roofed tower-houses around them, perhaps deliberately maintained for longer, perhaps inherently more sound. Most agree that these were lookout towers; Baddeley calls them defensive towers, though the tower-houses themselves were also capable of being defended. The explanation often given, that they had fires lit at the top to warn of danger, does not ring true. Certainly, here in Tusheti this would have formed a wonderful line of beacons all along the valley, but it is difficult to see why fires could not have been built more simply on high ground, of which there is a plentiful supply. Anyway, I made careful examinations and there are no blackened stones, no marks of fire or smoke. The roofs, too, though with openings underneath, would have got in the way of any fire and must frequently have burnt down, something of a disadvantage. It is far more likely that other methods were used – perhaps, simply, calling or the ringing of bells or flashing mirrors. I like to think of mirrors flashing warnings up and down the mountain passes; I'm sure Red Indians, or perhaps the cavalry, used to do this to good effect in many stirring cowboy films of my youth. Unfortunately, there is no evidence for this at all and there might have been a problem at night. However, looking along the valley of the Pirikiti-Alazani, towers receding into the distance and curling round into each side valley, along every ridge to the north guarding the passes and high peaks beyond, it is clear that a rapid and effective system of warning and of calling to arms would have evolved. One must never speculate too wildly, of course. My own house in the lowlands has a bell on the roof which I always thought must have been rung in times of flood until I was told that it was used to call in the farmer to his lunch.

John Baddeley, travelling mainly in the northern Caucasus, found these tall 'defensive' towers particularly among the Galgais or Ingush where he describes them clustered in groups. This is something I never saw in Georgia. Such towers here are almost always solitary, two together at the most, and that rarely. Baddeley has some fine illustrations of them in *The Rugged Flanks* and so I have always called them Galgais towers, though who first built them, or the tower-houses, is not at all clear. The Galgais told Baddeley that they had been built by those who had lived there before, some said by the Greeks and the *pirgi*, the towers of the Mani come to mind again. To the west, the towers of Tchegem were said to have been built by Svan masons who came over the passes, but no one knows when. Dates from the seventh century (contemporary with many of the early Svan churches) to the seventeenth are suggested. One rather eccentric and excited local historian in Mestia suggested to me that the towers were Sumerian in origin, that they were as old as history itself. Whatever the case, masons moved considerable distances over the years. The towers of Ushguli in Svaneti are, for example, identical to those in the mountain villages of the Kupat Dagh in north-west Persia, far to the east. They have the same dimensions, above all the same distinctive machicolations and design of roof that I have seen nowhere else.

Just as the predicted afternoon storm broke, we came to a low wooden hut in the middle of Diklo. The Mindis called out and opened the door. Two grizzled old men, uncles, leapt up, embraced the lads and shook our hands warmly, greeting us, over and over again, with '*gamarjobat*', the normal Georgian 'hello', but literally translated as 'victory to you', a greeting replete with Georgia's troubled history. The little hut was warm: a tin stove glowed in the corner, against the walls two old plank beds, in the middle of the earth floor a rickety table and a couple of chairs. Cheeses wrapped in cloth hung from a beam, the whey collecting in buckets underneath. The uncles had been having a jolly afternoon drinking with friends and nothing could possibly have been more delightful than to continue. One dashed outside and instantly returned clutching a vast demijohn of wine. Bread and cheese were spread over the table, more cheese heated over the stove to make, well, hot cheese, *khachuerebo*, a sort of Georgian *fondue*. We all set to, though not without considerable ceremony, the mandatory rounds of toasting and response. This ritual is rarely omitted and, however formulaic, contains subtle variations appropriate to the occasion, the company and the place. As I grew to appreciate, the younger Mindi was a master of these ceremonies: always polite, reverential as host or guest, his discourse listened to with grave attention, his responses serious and full.

As we drank our wine, ate our hot and cold cheese, nibbled bunches of a basil-like herb, *khakhouna*, the uncles told us that they arrived every spring as soon as the spring melt allowed and stayed through till the end of September. Only a few old couples now stayed through the bitter winter, taking their cattle on to the high south-facing slopes where the sun warmed them and kept the snow from settling. Everyone lived simply, growing a few onions and potatoes, herbs. Sometimes a trader arrived and they could buy cigarettes and soap, a few essentials, or, if they needed to, they could go shopping in Mahachkala. Shopping in Mahachkala? In Daghestan? Really? Yes, of course; it took only six hours or so to walk from Diklo over the pass to the first village where they had Lesghian friends who gave them a lift the forty-odd miles to the town.

The storm battered the hut, the wine flowed freely, a particular theory whirred in my head. Historians and travellers hand down and repeat clichés about the Caucasus from book to book, one of the most persistent being that the mountains stretch like a wall from sea to sea, impermeable, impregnable. The way through was either by sea along the coast of Abkhazia to the west; or through the Iron Gates (or the Gate of Gates) at Derbent by the Caspian to the east; or, with more difficulty, along the River Terek and through the Daryal Pass in the centre where the Georgian Military Highway now cuts over the mountains. But the mountains were, at the appropriate season, always more permeable than this, from north to south and east to west. My own planned route beneath the southern crest of the Caucasus was, in part, an attempt to see just how impenetrable this landscape really was, to see how much truth lay behind all the stories of tribes living in isolation from the world, cut off and enclosed by dark ravines and towering heights. The Russian military map of the Caucasus, till the break-up of the Soviet Union a secret document but now becoming more available, shows a multitude of passes, and W. E. D. Allen, in his edition of *Russian Embassies to the Georgian Kings*, numbers seventy tracks and paths across the main chain. Professor David Braund in his *Georgia in Antiquity* indicates many of these passes in use two thousand years ago. There are five passes leading north from the valley of the Pirikiti-Alazani alone. Of course, a distinction must be made between peaceful passage to and fro and any attempt to lead an army through the mountains, though even this could be done: Tamerlane sent his hordes ravaging into Pshaveti, Tusheti, Khevsureti and Svaneti, and the Huns rampaged through Svaneti a thousand years before him. However, it was difficult and being half insane with the lust for slaughter, like Tamerlane, certainly helped. The Russians took almost fifty years to subdue the mountains. When, in 1832, they set off to punish the Galgais for refusing to deliver up some of their fellows guilty of murdering a few missionaries, a column of 3,000 regular troops and 500 Ossetine militia was held up for three days by one tower guarding a pass. When the Russians finally managed to dig their way through solid rock to the base of the tower and lay a mine, the defending force gave up. It consisted of two ragged Galgais.

As the thousands of towers suggest, warfare and raiding across the mountains was a permanent reality here. With local knowledge, a degree of hardihood and determination, success was possible. Certainly the two uncles with their shopping trips show that peaceful passage was quite usual. There is much evidence for this: the Khevsurs, for example, have for centuries gone into Chechnya and Ingusheti to buy horses, and shepherds yearly drove their sheep up through the passes and down on to their summer pastures beyond. The common customs, traditions, folklore, legends, buildings and costumes of the mountain people show not just a local adaptation to a shared environment but a continuous contact, a common culture that transcended all divisions into Christian or Muslim or particular alliances to any state or ruler. One of the earliest writers on the Caucasus, Strabo, the Greek geographer, writing at around the beginning of the Christian era, insists that not only were the mountain Georgians close neighbours to the tribes of the north, they were actually kinsmen and they would call upon their northern kin in times of war. This is an ancient community, relatively isolated, certainly, but by no means utterly cut off. Time and again in the mountains I was struck by the fact that, contrary to all the stereotypes, the Khevsurs and the Tush expressed nothing but friendly regard for their neighbours to the north, often outright admiration, especially for the Chechens in their struggle against Russia. Throughout history all these peoples and tribes raided, traded and fought with and against each other and successive waves of invaders. The Caucasus were far from the 'impenetrable barrier' that is often described.

The storm and the wine were finished. I had a headache and Chris looked definitely odd. He was staring intently at a large lump of cheese, trying to decide whether it would do him more good than harm. He rejected it and took out his camera. On their plank beds the uncles slept wrapped in their burkas, *nabadi* in Georgian, those huge woollen cloaks with impossible winged shoulders more like a tent than a garment, an all-in-one sleeping bag and raincoat. Mindi dropped one on to my shoulders and I nearly fell to the floor. It was staggeringly heavy. The uncles wore them with pride as Chris took their photographs.

We decided to walk in the remaining hours of daylight towards the border with Daghestan. Here, still in Tusheti, there are two small villages of Lesghians, *lekhi* to the Georgians. The name is often used of all Daghestanis though, more properly, it applies to a particular people, about 400,000 of them, in southern Daghestan. In the scholarly chaos of translation and transliteration they also appear as Lazghi, Lakz, Lezgi, Lezgin, and every variation between; *lak* or *lag* in the local languages meaning, simply, a man. Indeed, there is a tribe called Lak to the north, along the border with Chechnya – the tribe of Man. There were Lesghians here in Tusheti but also many others nearby: within a few miles east of this north-eastern corner of Georgia was one of the most confused and linguistically diverse areas of Daghestan. Butting up against us was a patchwork of tribes: Dido, Ginukh, Hunzib, Bezhita, Khwarshi, Tindi, Karata, to name a few, and within the borders of Tusheti itself there were Batsbi, Udi and Chechens or Kists. Most speak their own north-east Caucasian languages. Many of these communities are only a few thousand, even a few hundred, strong.

As we walked, a young Lesghian boy overtook us. He was carrying a transistor radio and wearing an England Euro '96 football shirt. The Mindis treated him with amused disdain and he mumbled his replies in Russian and stared at his feet. He went off to warn his friends of our approach. Despite the centuries when raiders from Daghestan seasonally tormented and pillaged eastern Georgia, bringing it at times to the point of desolation, there was no present problem between the two countries. We passed a small shrine, a pagan holy place where sheep are still killed in sacrifice, and walked out along a finger of rock, a promontory where the mountain drops sheer away on all sides, and into the ruins of a fortress perched here, guarding the way into Daghestan. We climbed down through the middle of the fort over rocks and the sliding remnants of the walls and clung to the edge, peering nervously out into the ravine. At least no enemy could take us from behind.

On our way out we were ambushed. Four huge white dogs came at us, snarling. The Mindis stood with Chris and I sandwiched in between, determined to sell their lives dearly. As the dogs closed in we wielded our sticks to some effect but they kept coming, low to the ground and fast from all sides. One had just got hold of a Mindi's trouser leg and we were all bashing away when a tiny child of perhaps four or five came rushing upon us, shouting and waving its arms. Utterly cowed, the dogs slunk away. Sheepdogs are the terror of such places. They would have caused us considerable damage had not the baby intervened. In eastern Turkey, around the town of Kangal, a particularly huge and fierce race of these dogs is bred and buyers come from far away, all over Asia Minor, the Caucasus and the Middle East, to purchase them at great price. They roam the hills around in packs. They are terrifying and I once asked a local shepherd what to do if attacked. He said, with absolute conviction, that one must immediately sit down in front of them. I imagined myself sat for days on the ground while these creatures slavered and growled around me. I never tried it: in the heat of battle it does not seem a worthwhile experiment.

We came upon the little girl's father, camped under a canvas awning stretched between two pine trees, stripping a couple of carcasses, sheep taken by wolves the previous night. So much for the dogs! A Tush, he spoke Lesghian and called out cheerfully to a small group, hard-looking men, who came strolling past his camp. 'Good people,' he said. He sold them cheese and mutton. It was getting dark now and we hurried back to Diklo. The dogs were waiting. They came at us in fury but the child had followed and called them imperiously away.

The next morning I awoke, walked out of the hut, tried to jump the fence, fell over and brought half of it down. An uncle, laughing, helped me up, politely pointed out that the fence was a gate and opened it for me. In gumboots, a clean apron tied across his front, he was tending a fire, heating a great cauldron of milk and stirring it from time to time. He was going to make *shebolili sulguni*, a smoked cheese that lasts for years, the best cheese in Georgia. I had admired great stacks of it, small, round, brown truckles, piled up in the old market, the *bazari*, in Tbilisi. We breakfasted (bread and cheese), said our farewells and set off for Dartlo about twenty-five kilometres away. The storm which had brought us rain the day before had brought fresh snow to the mountains and the peak of Mount Diklos stood dusted in brilliant white like some giant fairy cake. We walked past Shenako and then, heading into the west, along a little track winding up way above new Omalo, through the old village perched on its crag. Some of its towers were still roofed, a little house had recently been repaired with an ornate balcony of carved wood which looked out along the Pirikiti-Alazani: a hidden world here in the mountains, an immense valley, beautiful, its slopes an astonishing and intense green, towers scattered along the northern edge all the way as far as the eye could see, and flowers so thick upon the ground one scarcely dared to tread. It was a botanist's dream: gentians, auriculas, fritillaries and a thousand flowers I could not name. As we walked young Mindi taught me a song of Tusheti:

> *ra lamazia tusheti*
> *da lasharoba tushuri*
> *rkeb dagrekhili tchedula*
> *santlit shubl-gadatusuli.*

How beautiful Tusheti is
And the Tush Lasharoba,
The crooked-horned ram,
Its forehead scorched with candles.

I sang this incessantly for days, irritating everyone because I could only really remember the first, and most apposite, line. The verse is not as obscure as it at first appears: the Lasharoba is a great Tush Christian–pagan festival at which a ram is sacrificed, and the ram's head is scorched because the sign of the cross is made on it with candle smoke.

It became increasingly hard to keep up with the Mindis. Along the flat, Chris and I did quite well, but they walked at a run and never seemed to alter their pace; uphill and downhill they went with the same light tread, wearing only plimsolls on their feet, never stumbling on the loose stones and the rocks that lay hidden under the smooth covering of grass and flowers. It was an education to watch them, whenever I was close enough to see. The concept of guiding was something quite new to them, though, and they had a tendency to disappear over the edge of the landscape, leaving us utterly alone in the middle of the Caucasus. However, Chris and I had been in training: we had gone for weekend walks over the Quantocks, carrying packs filled with books. There, in the Somerset hills, with compass, Ordnance Survey map and a good knowledge of the local languages, we had frequently got lost. Nor did we ever manage to resolve the central dilemma, a clash between two opposing schools of thought: should we train hard or should we save ourselves? Whatever we had done, it was not quite enough.

We had been walking for nearly eight hours as we came down through the woods towards Dartlo. Storm clouds gathered once more and a fierce wind ripped about us. Two woodcutters carrying huge bundles of birch led us along a short cut to the village. They spoke to each other in Tush, the local dialect which the boys understood much of, though it has marked differences with standard Georgian. A little further on there is a community of Tsova-Tush, originally a completely different people and language, also called Bats or Batsbi, closely related to the Chechens and professing a strange mixture of Islam, Christianity and paganism. They are said to have moved into Tusheti from the north at the end of the sixteenth century, originally to pasture their flocks during summer, with the special permission of the kings of Kakheti. Nearby there is also a community of Kists, a Chechen tribe, who have also lived here for centuries. It's ethnological mayhem. The Mindis seemed to use the words *kistebi* and *chechenebi*, Kists and Chechens, inter-changeably. Clarity is not at all helped by the fact that very often names of peoples come to us through other languages, Russian particularly, and each group will refer to itself, and to its neigh-bours, differently. Georgians, of course, are, to themselves, *kartvelebi*, and Georgia, *sakartvelo*; Chechens call themselves *nokhchi*, the ethnonym 'Chechen' given them by the Russians after the name of the first village the Russians encountered when invading the country. The Ingush refer to themselves as *ghalgay* or *galgais* – like all these ethnonyms the word in English has many variant spellings. Even great scholars like W. E. D. Allen seem muddled, telling us that Galgais is the name the Ingush give themselves and then sepa-rating them on his maps.

As we scrambled down towards the river, huge black clouds gath-ered ahead, thunder cracked and rolled over the peaks. I could make out, high on a crest, the great, dark towers of Dartlo pointing to the sky, and all around more towers. We passed by a graveyard of simple slate headstones pushed into the earth and more massive sepulchres roofed with overlapping slabs of stone, all scattered up the slope, separated from the village in sacred ground. We crossed over the river on a terrifying bridge and struggled up towards Dartlo, resting for a while by the ruin of an old church. Within its broken walls stands a memorial for the men of the village who perished in the Second World War, thirteen of them. This must represent a high proportion of the men of fighting age. The Georgians always claim, as do the Azeris (and, probably, every other ex-Soviet country), that they lost a greater proportion of their men during the war than other republics, and they use this to counter-act suggestions that they were particularly favoured under Stalin, who was, of course, a Georgian. In truth the Georgians did contribute enormously to the Soviet war effort. From a population of three and a half million in 1939 over half a million Georgians joined the armed forces of the USSR, that is about 15 per cent of the population which, by the end of the war, had fallen by over three hundred thousand.* The death-rate among the mountain men was especially high, truly terrible, owing to the fierce fighting encountered by the particular regiment in which most were enrolled; indeed, it helped to depopulate the mountains.†

I wandered off and sat by the river, dangling my feet and washing my socks, watching the chickens that scuttled about and greeting a grand old lady who came to clean her herbs. Smoke poured out of the front door of her little house, the lower part of which was rendered with mud and dung, bits of old tin tacked on to the walls and covering the roof. All around the mountains crowded in and great waterfalls poured down, silent in the distance. As night came on we pitched our tents on a strip of flattish land by the river and ate tins of Korean spam, of which the Mindis, we discovered, had a tediously inexhaustible supply. As they chucked the empty tins into the grass and flowers about, I burst into *ra lamazia tusheti*. It was subtle and it did not work. I dropped into a fitful sleep, the river roaring in my head, reading, in between fits, *Nicholas Nickleby* by the light of my torch. Dickens is such a comfort.

At five thirty the following morning I crawled out of the tent. Chris was still fast asleep, sitting curiously upright, his head poking out of the top of his green ribbed sleeping bag, looking for all the world just like the caterpillar in *Alice in Wonderland*. I peered into his face; no, he really was asleep, though I would not have been at all surprised if he had suddenly said, 'You! who are you?' The sun had just touched the far end of the valley. It was quiet, cold and damp and, despite the hot midday sun of mid-June, snow still clung to the banks of the river. Cattle were already spreading up into their high pastures, donkeys wandered after them. As the mist rose and the valley brightened I saw, again, wrinkling the slopes almost to the very top, the marks of what I took to be ancient terracing. None of the locals were very definite about this but,

---

* R. G. Suny, *The Making of the Georgian Nation*, p. 284.
† Donald Rayfield, *The Literature of Georgia*, p. 220.

clearly, here was more than some effect of rain and snow or the traces of cattle. It all looked man-made. Indeed there is archaeo-logical and environmental evidence to suggest that throughout mountain Georgia there was an ancient, traditional system of land management, of terracing and of forest maintenance which prevented soil erosion and allowed widespread cultivation.* If so, it would help to explain the self-sufficiency of this ancient province and the large population it seems once to have supported. Though pastoralists rather than agriculturalists, the people would have grown grain for bread, at least, and there was very little flat land around. Above Dartlo I saw patches of potatoes no more than three feet wide, clinging to the mountainside, terraced with stone. Terracing of some sort would have helped to prevent the rain and the spring-melt from scouring all the earth from the slopes into the river. Indeed, Strabo describes these mountains as more popu-lous than the plains below and specifically writes that while the mountaineers shared the pastoral habits of their neighbours to the north, driving their beasts each summer across the main range into southern Daghestan and into the steppe lands at the foot of the mountains, they also practised agriculture extensively, just like their cousins in the plains.

I could not count all the towers in Tusheti but if there were, say, thirty tower-houses in Dartlo alone and in each tower an extended family of ten or fifteen, then a village such as this would have had a population of 300 to 450 souls. There were towers everywhere in this western part of upper Tusheti. What can the population here have been in centuries gone by? Perhaps five thousand people, just in this valley? And many more in lower Tusheti to the south. I began to understand how armies of Tush and Khevsurs were raised from these mountains, and also what rich plunder, in cattle and in slaves, Tusheti must have represented to the covetous eyes of the tribes over the mountains. Now this world is almost empty but the Mongol Census of 1251 gives the population for the whole of Georgia as 5,000,000. That is rather more than its population today and is a figure taken after the devastation of the Mongols

* Tamila Tsagareishvili, *traditsiuli kultura da ecosystemebi*.

themselves, though before, admittedly, Tamerlane, the plague, the Turks, Shah Abbas and the rest. Even if we allow that the Georgia they measured was geographically larger than today, this is an extraordinary figure. It is as though Britain, not long after the Norman invasion, had had a population of 60,000,000 which then declined to such an extent in the succeeding centuries that only in the twentieth century did we near that total once more. The Mongols, too, were accurate people; they liked to know exactly how many troops they could levy, calculated at the rate of one armed man for every nine peasant families, which does not seem too terrible, unless it was your son or husband taken. This meant that in Georgia they could expect to raise an army of 90,000; exactly the number said to have been raised by Giorgi Lasha against them. Just to illustrate something of what happened to Georgia over the centuries, the painful process of its history, to explain a little of this extraordinary crash in population, I shall attempt a very brief and condensed version of the campaigns of Tamerlane:

At the beginning of the fourteenth century Georgia was in a dreadful state after a hundred years of Mongol rule. King Giorgi the Magnificent managed to reunite the country and he, and then Bagrat the Great, were just beginning to restore some measure of prosperity and calm when, in 1366, the Black Death struck with the most horrible ferocity. Then, as the country began to breathe again, in 1386 Tamerlane made his first attacks against Georgia. He waged a blitzkrieg of terror, killing purposefully, ravaged the country and took Tbilisi with much slaughter. Then he went off to devastate Azerbaijan leaving Georgia a little time to recover, six years. He came back in 1392, took Tbilisi again, killed any who opposed him and laid waste the land. Off he went again but came back a year later and repeated the process. Tamerlane then rode away to India, and the Georgians, thinking he had gone for good, tried to retake some of the territories they had lost and pushed into Azerbaijan themselves. Not a good idea. On Tamerlane's fourth invasion he ordered his troops to destroy everything – crops, orchards, churches, houses – but a particularly fierce winter and a lack of fodder for his horses forced him to retreat to Karabakh. On Tamerlane's fifth invasion, in 1400 (and if this is beginning to sound ridiculous one must imagine how the Georgians felt) he again ordered a mass destruction and pursued the Georgians into their mountains where they hid. Despite going after them in caves (into which he shot arrows wrapped in naphtha) and down ravines (where he had his bowmen lowered in baskets) he was unable to capture King Giorgi and met fierce resistance. The Georgians now decided to pay him tribute, to furnish him with troops and to be especially kind to Muslims. However Tamerlane still came after them and massacred any who held out against him. In 1403 he started all over again, devastated Kartli once more, drove into western Georgia, cut down forests (just like the Russians in Chechnya four hundred years later), destroyed towns and villages and monasteries, left ruin and desolation everywhere. Finally in December 1403, his own army by this time completely exhausted by the whole process, he stopped, had a great banquet and moved off into Karabakh again, though he left most of the army in Georgia. God only knows what he would have done next but, thankfully, he died in 1405. Many parts of Georgia remained a wasteland for two hundred years – there were just not enough people left to culti- vate the fields and tend the crops and animals. The country was utterly ruined, almost all but the most basic activity ceased: there was no building, writing, painting. Names of once-prosperous communities litter old maps: *nakalakari*, site of an old town; *nasophlari*, site of an old village; *nasakhlari*, site of an old house; *pardakhti*, wasteland. In the years of chaos and desolation that followed, Georgia's corpse was picked over by her warring nobles, and, at each stuttering sign of recovery, hacked at by Turkman tribes, by Osmanli Turks, by Savafid Persians.

*

It was half past nine and I was desperately trying to galvanise the Mindis. Perhaps if we started earlier we should not have to walk quite so fast. However, I encountered a definite counter-movement. Not for the first or last time I wondered who, exactly, was supposed to be in charge here. It was an extension of family life: starting out with some illusions of control, slowly but surely one gives up entirely. Eventually the Mindis decided that we could not leave until we had managed to buy enough bread for the next three days – there would be no possibility of finding any food ahead.

'Fine,' I said. 'Good idea, let's buy bread.'

'Well, the bread is not made yet. They'll have to make the bread.'

'OK. Let's get the bread made.'

'Right, but we've asked the old lady there and she says we shall have to wait. The wind's in the wrong direction.'

'The wind's in the wrong direction! We could be here for weeks!'

'No, no, it'll turn later this morning.'

And sure enough, there was the fine old lady of the herbs from the night before, sticking twigs and wood into her outdoor bread oven, smiling at us and going off to make the dough. The Mindis started to pack their tent. It was an ancient, high canvas affair that I would have hesitated to put on a camel. At night, if we were near a village, a Mindi would borrow a hoe and dig a small moat around it, to carry off any sudden flood water. It was barely waterproof. My little almost-two-man tent, the sort of thing you put in your top pocket, take out with a flick and it's up, was tremendously admired and at the end of my journey I gave it to young Mindi. Chris, expert after many years of camping in the rain along desolate beaches in the south-west of England, with all the chaos of a wife, children, dog, a boat and various friends and relations, could pack our tent in no time flat. The Mindis, meanwhile, struggled with their monster, each finding some excuse to wander off and do something really important.

'Hey, bitcho, I'm going to fill the water bottles.'

'No, bitcho, I've got to have a shave anyway, I'll fill the bottles.'

'Hey, bitcho, I'm really hungry, I'll open some spam.'

'Oh, you old bitcho.'

Well, it went something like that. Georgian boys and young men use 'bitcho', 'boy', in the same way that Americans use 'man', but it has a strange and unsettling ring in English ears which made me feel, till I got used to it, that perfectly loving conversations were about to degenerate into quarrels. I noticed an odd thing, though: walking through the Caucasus I saw remarkably few birds. There were eagles, certainly, and years before I had seen great numbers of lammergeiers around Mount Kazbek. Of course, there were birds about but in those lush upland valleys, walking by rivers and through meadows full with flowers and pollen and insect life, I had expected flocks and herds of bee-eaters and fly-eaters and ant-eaters, hoopoes, bulbuls, all manner of exotic creature. No such thing. Numbers of larks and insignificant little brown jobs I never got a clear sight of. However, these would call to each other incessantly and their call was 'bitcho, bitcho, bitcho!' Perhaps this was some race of mynah bird.

Waiting for the wind to change, young Mindi, Chris and I set off up the mountain for Kvavlo, just above Dartlo. We made our way up through the flowers, an exhaustingly steep climb, into a mass of rubble and fallen stone. Standing among the ruins, giddy and out of breath, we peered down at the settlement below and looked out over another valley, with more massive towers, heading north into Chechnya. Because of the way the Caucasus was formed, not with a single vertical upward thrust, but in ridges, overlapping and bursting up criss-cross, the valleys run both north to south and east to west. I always thought of the shape of the mountains as something like the hand game, played as a child: 'Here's the church, there's the steeple'. Hence the constant surprise, as you walk or climb along, of further valleys, suddenly opening out to right and left. W. E. D. Allen describes the Caucasus, less fancifully, as 'a series of parallel ridges. These ridges are linked by necks or saddles which give access from north to south of the main chain. The connecting ridges form wide upland glens, often at a great elevation. Typical examples are upper Svaneti and the Tush and Khevsur glens in northern Kakheti. Here communities have lived in almost complete isolation during all the known period of history.' Well, the isolation is overdone: the Tush would hardly have needed to defend themselves with so many towers if no one was liable to come through the passes. In fact, the threat from the north is a major theme of the *Georgian Chronicles, kartlis tskhovreba,* a great compilation of Georgian history, originally put together in the twelfth century but added to until the seventeenth and the basis for most historical studies since. This threat was, of course, not just from next-door neighbours over the mountain ridge but from the peoples beyond: Scythians, Sarmatians, Alans, Khazars, Huns and all the rest of history's great vagabonds.

Here, in the old village of Kvavlo, was the most beautiful Galgais tower, tapering to the sky, built right to the very edge of the mountain, only a crack up one side, its roof still perfect and intact. Presumably its builders worked from the inside as they went up; even so they eventually would have had to climb out on to some sort of scaffolding to lay the distinctive, overlapping roof slabs. The thought gave the imagination vertigo. As Chris, in the true tradition, stepped perilously backwards to take his photographs, Mindi and I climbed up among the ruins. I mangled in my mind something out of John Ford:

> Alas, poor towers,
> You look not like the ruins of your youth
> But like the ruins of those ruins.

As we got ready to pour nasty things on to the heads of our enemies and sighted our ancient rifles through the gunslots, calling out for more ammunition, a tiny old lady appeared round the corner of a tower and smiled at us, inviting us into her house for a drink. Tiny and neat as its owner, built among the rubble from the plentiful supply of stone, the house clung to the very edge of the old village. A narrow veranda looked out to the east. On the sill of massive slate she was kneading her dough and, in a frying pan over a glowing stove, flat loaves were cooking. Cheeses hung everywhere. A pet lamb eyed us nervously. The pots and pans, the flagstone floor, everything was scoured bright and clean. She dipped mugs into a bucket of clear spring water and set plates of fried potatoes and cheese before us. It was terribly good but we ate only enough to be polite, not wishing to ravage her supplies. How did she bring provisions up here? Well, of course, her husband bought things up on his horse, but she would walk down to the village and back again almost every day. Like all the people here she had not an ounce of spare flesh on her. She was hale, full of vigour and merriment. Just to sit by her was bracing. She and her husband lived here year round, right through the fierce, snow-bound winter.

At one o'clock our bread was ready, five or six flat, round loaves. The boys poked them, critically, unsure, the wind never having properly turned about, but we packed them away and set off, along the roaring Pirikiti-Alazani, past a hawser bridge with a pulley and metal basket that hung below, the first such I had seen in Tusheti. The valley narrows, opens out, narrows and opens again, past the hamlets of Chesho, Parsma, Baso and on towards Girevi. All along and above are towers – some, around Parsma, built conjoined to form a larger fort – and then even grander fortifications, still higher, just visible in ruins on the valley's rim. Even with my fondness for towers I was running out of exclamations and having continuously to revise upwards my calculations of past populations. The track, muddy and loose at first, became more difficult and narrow and we had to scramble over the rocks at the river's edge. Comfortingly dotted along the way, shrines commemorate those drowned in the river: a memorial slate and a spout of mountain water, with a tin mug or a glass for passers-by. By Parsma an intelligent-looking shepherd, an old man with a grizzled and intense face, stopped to chat and warned us that the Atsunta Pass, the way through into Khevsureti which we hoped to reach the day after next, was very difficult and dangerous at present. I wondered what he meant.

Around six that evening, in the face of a stinging, bitter wind we hauled ourselves into Girevi, just as the rain started to pour from an ink-dark sky. The Mindis began a complex discussion on where we should pitch our tents, for the sake of propriety and in proper consideration of the inhabitants, and also in an attempt to avoid the cow shit and the waves of water flowing down the slopes. I suggested we knock on the door of the large wooden hut ahead and gather some local knowledge. A young man poked out his head, laughed to see us standing there, incongruous, beached upon his porch and promptly beckoned us all inside. Naturally, we would stay the night and, naturally, though not quite cousins, the Mindis knew his family and he theirs. In the hut were beds, a wooden table, cheese-making equipment and a radio which played, surreally, Judy Garland singing something even more dreadful than usual. As Chris and I struggled into all our clothes (it was bitterly cold in the hut) the music changed to Bob Marley's 'No woman, no cry'. It was very odd.

Our host disappeared to milk his cows which were gently munching hay in a small open-sided barn behind the hut. We made some packet soup in celebration and put our medicinal supply of *chacha* on the table with more Korean spam, bread and cheese. Our host, 'a very good man', Mindi insisted, and he was, produced a great jar of cherry jam and butter and more cheese. Nothing could have been finer. In the dozy glow of food and drink we sank on to our truckle beds. Well, Chris and I had beds; the Mindis, quite rightly, slept on the floor.

Sheep like maggots wriggled way below us as we cut across the steep slope early the next morning, trying to find a way over the river. The route ahead was blocked by landslides and we needed to leave the Pirikiti-Alazani as it curled round to the south and follow the course of the Kvakhidistsqali, its northerly tributary, pointing west. North of Girevi three major side valleys head towards Chechnya, only two or three kilometres away, dozens of towers and forts guarding them and the pass beyond. We followed, at first, a narrow cow trail, then dropped perilously down and forded an ice-cold torrent, flowing from the great glaciers that lie high on the ridge of mountains between Tusheti and Chechnya. Then we climbed up through grass and flowers to drop down again, made another crossing and worked our way up on to a rise where we passed a hodgepodge tent of felt stretched across two poles. Two wild and hairy shepherds rushed out at us, clutching a bottle. They desperately wanted a party. Their cheeses hung about the tent and bits of sheep decorated a low wall. We managed gently to decline the invitation, to the shepherds' amazement and despair, but as we walked away one came running after us and tried to press his bottle upon us as a parting gift. 'Good men, good men,' said Mindi.

We walked on into an empty land. No more ruined towers, no people, no cows, no sheep, just birds crying 'bitcho! bitcho!' and the river roaring under a bridge of ice and snow. We crossed over tentatively, poking ahead with our sticks, climbed up a sheer slope of broken scree, dropped down again, scrambled over river rubble and through blankets of wild azalea and thickets of raspberries, sadly not yet ripe. The snow lay thick about us and the way was often blocked by fallen rock so that we were forced to cross and re-cross the river and its tributary streams, walking sometimes high above it, sometimes along its broken bank. Often the valley narrowed and hung perpendicular on both sides, seeming impassable. We stormed along at a run, forcing a path across mud and shale as the ground slipped from beneath our feet into the river below, like motorcyclists on a Wall of Death, held to the sides by our own velocity. We slid across more snow bridges, the river rushing underneath until, after six exhausting hours, just past a little shrine, the mountains opened out around us, great peaks ahead, rivulets of water flowing down through the flowers. It was utterly quiet. Four huge eagles circled above, eyeing us quizzically. The great peak of Mount Tebulos, *tebulos mta*, loomed over us to the north, at 4,500 metres (14,775 feet) one of the highest in the Caucasus, permanently swaddled in snow and girdled with its glaciers and ice fields. Ahead, somewhere, lay the Atsunta Pass through which we must climb tomorrow.

Now, fierce black clouds raced up behind us from the east and the storm broke fast, before the Mindis could put up their tent. We all huddled in mine, knees tight against our ears, laughing as the thunder crashed against the mountains and shook the ground about us. The sky emptied itself and immense prongs of lightning stabbed down till we shone inside the tent in a lurid, yellow light, crouching, odd little humans exposed like woodlice in a bonfire. It was a dark and stormy night, so the Mindis entertained us by reciting verses from the *vepkhistqaosani*, *The Knight in the Panther's Skin*, by Shota Rustaveli. This is Georgia's national epic and, to an astonishing degree, almost universally throughout Georgia in my experience, large portions of the poem's sixteen hundred verses are known by heart. The poem is still given to every new bride and it is her responsibility to teach it to her children, especially to her sons. This to an Englishman, from a country where hardly anyone recites poetry by heart any more, induces a sense of shame. I have frequently sat listening to Georgians sing songs and recite poems inexhaustibly – but when English guests are invited to contribute from their national repertoire most go blank, or sing a few snatches from Beatles songs. Young Mindi, not unusually, could not only give a fine tour of Georgian poetry but also knew many Russian poems and could do bits of Shakespeare in both Russian and Georgian.

Shota Rustaveli wrote the *vepkhistqaosani* towards the end of the twelfth century at the court of Queen Tamar. He describes it as a 'Persian tale', though no source, no original version, has ever been found. Most likely this is a poetic conceit, and the story and verse entirely of his own making, though with the 'sun-like heroes', the hyperbolic allusions to physical beauty, the longing of the lovers, the heroic deeds, the amazing lamentations, the influence of Persia is clear. Rustaveli sets his poem in Arabia and India and refers to Athenian sages, Persian princes, the empire of Cathay, Negro slaves, merchants from Baghdad, caravans from Egypt, the Khwarazmian Sha, 'the teachings of Plato'. Rustaveli was educated for some time at a Neoplatonist academy and was deeply influenced by the Platonists, who taught that love was the expression of the yearning of the soul after perfection, an idea that informs his whole poem. Strangely, as has often been remarked, there are no direct references to Christianity or to Islam, though there are echoes from the Bible and perorations to 'One God, who has created the form of every man's body'. The story is above all one of love – spiritual, erotic and platonic: 'I speak of love's highest form', sings the poet, 'elevated, pure and heavenly'. Love and friendship, established through loyalty and selfless heroism, lead to harmony and stability, symbolised by marriage, and so the poem is as much about the Georgian state and its glorious incarnation in the person of Queen Tamar (and her husband David Soslan), as it is, on the surface, about the adventures and tribulations of its fictional lovers. Indeed, the prologue explicitly states the poet's own love for his queen, thought not to have been a mere conceit. The poem starts thus:

> He who created the firmament by the omnipotent might of
>   his power,
> Gave breath to all living creatures and to man spirits celestial,
> Gave us the world to possess with all its unlimited varieties,

And Kings ordained by Him, each in his own image.

One God, who has created the form of every man's body,
Assist us, give us strength, to conquer the wiles of Satan;
Fill us with longing for love, endless, enduring to death!
Lighten the load of sins we must bear to the world to come!

I sing of the lion whom the use of the lance, shield and sword
  adorns,
Of Tamar, the Queen of Queens, the ruby-cheeked and jet-
  haired,
How shall I dare pay tribute to her in praiseworthy verses,
Whom to look upon is to feast upon the choicest of honey?

Tears of blood flow profusely as I exult our Queen Tamar
Whose praises I have uttered forth in well-chosen words.
For ink I have used a lake of jet and for pen a pliant reed.
My words, like jagged spears, will pierce the heart of the hearer.

I was told to compose in her honour stately and sweet-
  sounding verses,
To laud her eyebrows and lashes, her hair, her lips and her
  teeth –
Badakhshan ruby and cut crystal arrayed in two even ranks.
An anvil of lead can break even the hardest stone.

Fire my mind and tongue with skill and power for utterance
Which I need, O Lord, for the making of majestic and praiseworthy verses;
Thus will the deeds of Tariel be remembered in eloquent
  language,
And of the three star-like heroes who faithfully served one
  another.

Come, let us sit together and weep with undrying tears for
  Tariel.
There never breathed a man born under the same star as his.

I, Rustaveli, whose heart is pierced through by his sorrows
   have threaded
Like a necklace of pearls a tale told until now as a tale.

I, who am maddened to frenzy by love, have composed these
   lines.
She, whom vast armies call mistress has deprived me of life
   and reason.
Thus sickened am I by love for which there exists no cure.
She alone can cure me or leave me to death and the grave.

I have found this Persian tale and have set it in Georgian
   verse.
Until now like a peerless pearl it was rolled on the palm of
   the hand.
I have done this praiseworthy and disputable deed for her;
Therefore let her who has robbed me of heart and of reason
   judge it.

(translated by Venera Urushadze)

Of course, one advantage Georgians have is that the language of Rustaveli is still perfectly intelligible to them. It would be quite impossible to imagine the English happily reciting some late twelfth-century poem in the original, like Layamon's tedious *Brut*, for example, not that it's worth remembering. We have to wait till Chaucer to find a poet both writing in a language that is comprehensible and producing work of such stature, something that helped to define and characterise the people and its literature. In no other way is Chaucer comparable, of course, and it is difficult to cast around for an English equivalent of Rustaveli. There is none, though there are elements that are familiar enough, especially the ideals of courtly love, prefigured in the poem, and the romance of the quest or hero's journey, even if their expression is perhaps a little ornate and oriental for the English sensibility. Spenser's *Faerie Queen* probably gets as close as anything we have. Of course, this was written four hundred years later and in a deliberately archaic style, but Spenser's glorification of Queen Elizabeth as

Gloriana, his political and moral intentions, his use of the theme of courtly love as a kind of template for human and moral inter-action, are all somewhat comparable to Rustaveli's work. If one takes the pair of lovers from *Orlando Furioso* and the central friend-ship between Gilgamesh and Enkadil from the *Epic of Gilgamesh* and mixes this up with bits of Spenser's *Faerie Queen*, one might get some sort of ghastly international cocktail that gave some flavour of *The Knight in the Panther's Skin*. Much better just to read the poem itself. Even in translation it has a marvellous, forceful certainty of purpose and direction and – despite all the mayhem of sorcerers and monsters, dreadful battles, the three couples with their interwoven tales – a singular clarity. Rustaveli has no doubts about his task and its purpose, for his understanding tells us that poetry is, first of all, a branch of wisdom. The poem ends, like a Shakespearean Comedy, with a vision of love and harmony estab-lished between the couples and within the state:

> So the three sovereigns parted, yet they fulfilled their prom-
> ises,
> And often left their own homes and visited one another.
> Those who disputed their rule were at once put to the sword
> and humbled.
> Thus they enlarged their kingdoms and increased the might
> of their power.
>
> They poured upon all alike their mercy like snowflakes from
> heaven,
> The orphans and widows, the helpless and poor were en-
> riched, made happy.
> Evil-doers dared not appear but recoiled and vanished.
> Harmony reigned; like sheep, goat and wolf fed together.

*

Chris and I started to drift towards sleep and, during a lull in the storm, the Mindis left us to put up their tent. We crawled into our sleeping bags and found ourselves sliding headfirst down a steep incline, so struggled outside once more to turn the tent around. Afterwards I wondered why we did not just turn round in the tent. We seemed, moreover, to have camped on the edge of a cliff, though Chris said that there was no need to worry as he had seen a ledge which might break our fall, some dozen yards below. As I drifted into sleep I thought I heard him mumble, 'Why? What? Where?' In the night I dreamt that we awoke to find that the Mindis had gone and left us, quite alone in the Caucasus, standing in this great and empty space.

They were still with us and by nine the following morning, stopping for breakfast, we had already walked for more than an hour, a fine tramp, stung to pieces by towering nettles. We noticed numbers of adders slithering away from us through the grass which struck me as odd at this height, around 2,500 metres, over 8,000 feet. The Mindis could not be discouraged from killing them, though they reacted with horror at my suggestion that we should cook them for breakfast in honour of Vazha Pshavela, the *khajis* and Mindia. This was a great disappointment as I had recently been sent a recipe for viper by a friend, an anthropologist working in Cameroon, and I was eager to try it:

'La vipère, une fois tuée, sa tête et sa queue sont coupée et enterrés. La vipère dont la ventre a été ouvert afin d'en enlever les viscères est ensuite découpée en morceaux . . .'

Instead, we finished the Korean spam; the Mindis chucked away the tins, I sang *ra lamazia tusheti* and we set off for the foot of the Atsunta Pass.

The way looked easy at first but walking was often difficult, traversing steep slopes of shale or following deep ruts, boulders and sharp stones concealed beneath the grass, ascending and descending all the while. We forded the torrents that flowed down from Tebulos to the north and curled round beneath the great snow-capped peak above us. The land was hard to read, rising and falling in folds, and though we climbed steadily, the ground would suddenly drop away and there ahead was yet another rise climbing away towards the west. Where was the pass? It seemed to come no nearer. Straight ahead a great wall of mountains stretched out, jet-

black and shining in the sun with their varnish of ice, streaked
with snow. We struggled up an endless green precipice only to find
that this, too, fell away, back down to the river again. As we slithered across fields of snow, an icy wind blew off the mountains,
freezing the breath in our throats. Hardly daring to waste the
energy, I turned to look back the way we had come: great fingers
of mountain closed like a zip towards us. Massive and dark, the
peaks towered ahead.

The final part of our ascent seemed interminable: a great, bald
shoulder covered in fine scree and rubble which rose at sixty
degrees up to the pass. I felt as though I was standing on the edge
of the world, like a matchstick stuck on the surface of an orange.
We kicked our boots in and zigzagged slowly up. Chris was concen-
trating on his feet and, indeed, as he stepped forward his face was
only a few inches from them. 'Chris, take a photograph,' I
suggested. 'I'm fucking not doing anything but look at my boot-
laces till we get off this thing,' he answered, reasonably. A mild-
mannered man, he only swore under extreme provocation. Every
few minutes we paused for breath.

We crawled on up and then, at last, through the thick and
freezing cloud that now swirled about us, the Mindis were cheering
and waving. We had reached the top of the Atsunta Pass. I threw
off my pack and fell flat. But could this really be the pass? We lay,
it seemed, on the edge of a knife. I peered through the mist: the
mountain dropped sharply into nothingness beyond. At that
moment I was too tired to register anything beyond a shiver of
doubt but I had expected something, well, broader, perhaps tree-
lined with the odd café. Nevertheless, in celebration, we carved
our names on a projecting rock then, putting on all the clothes
we had, huddled down behind it to eat our bread and cheese.
Chris started to play with his GPS machine, something he had
bought for his sailing trips, usually around the waters of the Fal
but with vast and complex projects in mind, mostly involving cata-
marans and Polynesia. He would announce, every so often, exactly
how far we were from his back garden in Somerset. Despite a relationship with machinery nearly as troubled as my own, Chris was
enraptured. I never did quite understand the point of this gadget.

Not only did we have to wait for contact with three satellites (and every time I could not help looking up and scanning the skies) but it seemed utterly incapable of telling us where we were without the use of an accurate map, which we did not have. And if we had an accurate map . . . Well, I got no further. However, now it was telling us how high we were: 11,500 feet; 11,650; 11,800. And on it went, never quite deciding. Far too high, anyway, for a respectable person. Later I looked on the Russian military map: the Atsunta Pass is marked at 3,431 metres (11,265 feet) making it the highest pass in Georgia, and in all the Caucasus topped only by a few passes around Mount Elbruz and Mount Ushba, though our machine insisted that we were hundreds of feet higher than this. Here the summits of the mountain chain were at eye level, spreading like a row of teeth both east and west. Only a few peaks far to the west and glinting briefly through the mist seemed higher than us. I thought I could see Mount Kazbek, some sixty kilometres away, or perhaps it was Elbruz beyond, the greatest of all the peaks in the Caucasus.

It was time to leave Tusheti and enter the land of the Khevsurs. But how? The Mindis were nervous. We knelt on the edge of this so-called pass and looked about. To our left an impassable barrier of rock; to our right, the way we wanted to go, a huge collar of thick snow; and then there was straight down. I looked in vain for Essad Bey's rope. Big Mindi took my stick and approached the snow. Prodding, he felt his way forward, looking grim. A few yards into the snow he fell through and felt the mountain, sheer beneath him, start to move. Carefully, gently, he returned. Much too dangerous, impossible. The Mindis, deep in conference, shook their heads.

Young Mindi came and patted me on the shoulder. 'I am sorry,' he said, 'really sorry but we shall have to turn back.' Back? All the way back, down that interminable slope, back all along through Tusheti and back down into the plains? I could not bear it. Besides, I was far too tired to go back. I went to look again straight down the mountain. My thinking was not, just then, at its clearest but the way down did not seem utterly impossible. The drop was not quite sheer but sloped at about seventy degrees. It was covered in loose rock and ice and under this, the Mindis assured us, lay the trapped and frozen waters from the snow. The mountainside was poised to slide. Besides this, what lay beyond? A chasm? A precipice perhaps? We might get some way down but could we climb back up if we had to? At the very least we needed ropes. Young Mindi shrugged. On his own he might have a go, but with us?

Would it be safe and reasonable, I asked, for him to go a little way down and have a look? Perhaps the descent became easier further on? Chris looked troubled but the Mindis brightened and declared that it could be done. So young Mindi, lighter and less likely to start an avalanche, reached into his pack, took out his stout shoes and started to cut notches in their soles with his hunting knife. Then he slid gently over the edge. One long whistle and we were to follow, two short and he was in trouble, nothing and he was heading back – or dead.

We saw him pick his way carefully down, slipping now and then and studying his retreat. Then he disappeared from view. We waited nervously on the lip of the pass, straining to hear. After an age came a long, low whistle. This was it. Chris and I shouldered our packs and Big Mindi, who carried his cousin's as well as his own, urged us to take the slope as fast as possible. With the three of us the scree would start to slide, so we should slalom our way down in steep zigzags and outrun it. He pointed out a route. I would go first, then Chris and Mindi in the rear. Without stopping to think, I stepped over the edge, felt the wind rush at me and, crazy with fear and excitement, ran, slipped, fell, jumped up and roared downwards, bouncing off the mountain, dimly aware of Chris and Mindi behind and the rocks and shale rushing down in my wake. As I hit terminal velocity I thought my legs would surely give way but somehow the automatic body took over and then there below was Mindi, leaning on an outcrop and far, far below him a valley, criss-crossed with streams, peaceful in the sun. I hit the outcrop at speed, flat on my back, then Chris arrived safe in a shower of rubble and then Big Mindi, dragging the extra pack, with his personal avalanche around him.

CHAPTER 3

KHEVSURETI

Khevsurs, Chechens, the Russian Shaitan and the Fate of Georgia

How we came through to Shatili and what was said there

We lay stunned and laughing. I could have lain there for ever, shut my eyes and slept but the lads were keen to move off the mountain before bad weather or night did for us. There was still a long and difficult way down. We shook the stones out of our boots, picked ourselves up and lapped at some ice-cold melt-water. Chris swore he would never again go anywhere that could not be reached in a Toyota land-cruiser and declared that if that was a pass he was a Dutchman. As we turned to look back, it did seem, even to the Mindis, absurd. The pass rose like a sheer black wall with nothing to distinguish it from the mountains around. I vowed that I would never cross it again, a silly thing to do, inviting Fate's reply. Young Mindi said I should compose a victory ode; I could find nothing to rhyme with Atsunta but junta.

Edging our way down into Khevsureti, Chris and I were in trouble. Lame, hobbling, shattered, we muttered encouragements to each other as we passed through the zone of rock into the zone of flowers. Huge blue gentians nodded kindly at us. Down we went through swathes of white azaleas and into the silence of the valley. Even the streams were silent. Not a breath of wind, no bird's cry, no clicks and whirrs in the long grasses. We had found the still centre of the turning world. A mute strangeness enveloped us; I had forgotten to breathe for some long time and forced myself to do so, hardly feeling the air pass into my lungs. We had entered a vacuum. Chris and I needed to stop, just to stay here and lie down but the Mindis, with the scent of their Khevsur homes strong in their nostrils, had disappeared into the distance ahead. So we followed along as best we could.

Three hours later, in the throat of the valley, we saw a black felt tent and outside it an old man with a few cattle and a young boy of six or seven who, mysteriously, jumped on to a large horse as we approached and galloped furiously off. It came as a shock to see another human, something almost unnatural. The old man waved cheerily and pointed us towards the Mindis. We found them settled on a tiny ledge, tent up, old cheese and stale crumbs spread nicely for us on a rock and Mindi cleaning his pistol. I had felt strongly disinclined to carry a gun, though frequently offered one; I was keen, in general, to avoid mishaps. But weapons for Khevsurs have an almost talismanic significance and Mindi smiled happily at me and cried, 'Target practice, only for target practice.' The day had obviously passed too quietly for him. He set up some stones on a rock and blasted away blissfully, then reloaded and we all joined in.

Chris, delving into the rank depths of his pack, had produced with a flourish, like some amateur prestidigitator on stage in a village hall, a few packets of minestrone soup. In such strange forms comfort lies. As we warmed ourselves by the glow of our fire and the hot soup spread out along our limbs the Mindis, entranced by the packets, stood under the stars sonorously declaiming the cooking instructions to the mountains, in English, French and Italian. As I drifted off to sleep I could hear them in their tent laughing hysterically, correcting each other, repeating over and over again in the most exaggerated and melodramatic tones: Empty the Contents into a Saucepan, Add one pint of Water, Bring to the Boil Stirring all the Time.

Had we been able to supply them with a sufficient number of packets of soup they would have been fluent in a week. I had heard young Mindi's minimal English grow day by day. We would swap words and phrases as we went along – he always remembered them far better than I. Given their geographical position and their history it is not surprising that many Georgians are able linguists. Other languages are both natural and necessary: bilingual in Georgian and Russian or, if Svans or Mingrelians, trilingual, the comparatively simple grammar of English, for example, presents few problems.

It is said that only Papua New Guinea shows a more densely variegated linguistic map than the Caucasus, called 'The Mountain of Languages' by the Arabs and approached by the Romans, according to Pliny, with the help of 130 interpreters. There are actually about forty native languages in the Caucasus, an area roughly half the size of France, though this rather pales in comparison with many modern cities and their recent immigrant populations: London, now, is home to speakers of over 300 different languages. Gurdjieff, in his fabulous book of quasi-Sufic tales, *Meetings with Remarkable Men*, describes living in Tbilisi in a cheerfully polyglot environment, where speaking five or six languages was nothing uncommon. He claimed, later, to speak eighteen himself, though his friend, Abram Yelov, spoke thirty. Gurdjieff was drawn to Tbilisi during his youth because he could find there the most fantastic selection of rare and wonderful books in many tongues. When I first went in 1989, I rambled around the city in search of the old book market where Yelov traded near the Alexander Gardens, eagerly bending my ears to any passing chatter, straining towards the exotic and hearing, quite mistakenly I am sure, the natter of a dozen peculiar nations at every street corner.

Many of the languages of the Caucasus share a terrible complexity: Tabasaran in south-eastern Daghestan, spoken by about 90,000 people, has, I was once assured by a tipsy linguist, eight genders. Scholars, he assured me, enjoyed introducing new, unfamiliar objects to the Tabasars to see to which gender they might be assigned. Apparently a samovar was unanimously assigned to the seventh gender, though no one could say why. This story may be apocryphal but Bats, spoken only in one village in Tusheti, really does have eight genders. Goodness knows what for. Essad Bey insisted that Tabasaran was so difficult that the Tabasars themselves (the name is said to mean 'Hatchet Heads') preferred to borrow an easier, neighbouring tongue. Many languages here also have a prolix proliferation of cases: one analysis of Tsez detected forty-two different locative case markers which can describe precisely which kind of space someone or something is in, at, under, by, near, away from: a hollow space, a flat space, a space that might be a trifle uncomfortable or sadly lacking in alcohol. Even the maddening case endings of Russian must come as light relief. Words are often formed by accreting suffixes and prefixes and fixes in the middle and so grow alarmingly. Clusters of consonants hang together like mussels on a rock, though far more difficult to swallow. Indeed, it is hardly surprising that a number of Caucasian languages now have few native speakers: Archi perhaps 1,000, Hunzib only 600, the last speaker of Ubykh sadly died just a few years ago. Many must have choked to death on their own consonants: Ubykh had eighty! (A bad joke and I apologise for it: the disappearance and decline of these languages is a great tragedy.) Others have fifty or sixty. Abkhaz, a notoriously difficult language, has fifty-eight; one of its dialects, Bzyp, has sixty-seven. Despite having an Abkhazian mother, Evliya Chelebi, the great Turkish traveller, described the language as 'extraordinary and surprising'. Scholars trying to recreate Proto-North-Caucasian have postulated a scarcely believable total of 180 consonants or consonantal phonemes. Georgian, by comparison, is in this respect quite modest, though Georgians like listening to visitors choking over words that contain groups of consonants which seem to be sounded half way down the throat, unsoftened by any intrusion of vowel. Grammar, particularly verbal forms, presents further problems: lurking beneath the surface are Georgian polypersonal verbs which are best left entirely alone, though Avar verbs, with their special forms indicating whether the speaker was a witness of what he relates or merely heard it from others; their thirty-six forms in the indicative; twenty-six forms in the conditional; twenty-seven gerundives and the rest, totalling 117 distinct verbal forms, must represent the most terrifying piece of grammatical information I have yet unearthed.

Of all the Caucasian languages only Georgian had, until the late nineteenth or early twentieth century, a surviving written form. (Armenian is not classified as a Caucasian language.) Now most are written in Cyrillic script but the difficulties this presents, jamming the jagged mountain sounds into the soft porridge of a Slavonic alphabet, are well illustrated by the poor Abkhaz: given a Cyrillic orthography with fifty-five characters in 1909, toying with a Roman-based system in the twenties and thirties, then moving, in 1939, to a Georgian one. (This 'gift' of an orthography by a dominant people to a minority is, of course, always a highly political act.) In 1953, on the death of Stalin, they reverted to a newly devised though still unsatisfactory Cyrillic script again. This is still in use and though the Georgian alphabet is the best basis for the representation of any Caucasian language, according to the Georgian and Caucasian scholar George Hewitt, present animosities and grievances make it extremely unlikely that the Abkhaz will adopt such a system. Instead Professor Hewitt proposes a new Roman alphabet. For the time being they will have to make do with their bastardised Russian script which looks most peculiar and horribly complex. By contrast the Georgian alphabet is a rare thing, a work of beauty. Some of the letters seem almost recognisable, others are strange and exotic. The Georgian equivalent of our 'j' looks rather like the sign we use on maps for a battle-field; one of the 't' letters is a lovely, flowing figure eight with a long, curved cat's tail; one of the 'ch' letters looks like a key with a ribbon tied around. However, there are also some letters that are more recognisable: there is a definite upside-down omega for 'o', and 'a', 'b' and 'g' are not far off their Greek or Latin equivalents. The alphabet, *anbani*, has thirty-three letters and words read from left to right and follow, to a large extent, the Greek order. Armenian scholars insist that the Georgian alphabet was created by the Armenian monk Mesrop Mashots early in the fifth century, along with the Caucasian Albanian and Armenian alphabets. One form of Georgian writing, *kutkhovani*, the capital-letter script, does resemble the ancient Armenian, with lots of verticals and sharp angles, suitable for carving on stone. However, Georgian scholars vigorously disagree with this Armenian provenance, insisting that their alphabet was created during the reign of their first king, Parnavazi, in the third century BC. Most western scholars believe that the alphabet coalesced during the fourth century AD from a variety of sources, including Greek,

Persian and Aramaic, under the influence and guidance of Byzantine missionaries. It does seem that some of the letters of the Georgian alphabet were influenced by Christian symbolism, thus giving the later date for its invention a certain weight: Donald Rayfield in *The Literature of Georgia* shows how the old Georgian aspirated 'k' was based on the form of the cross, and the penultimate letter was a combination of the cross and Jesus' initial. However, the alphabetic order reflects an older pattern: pre-Christian Hellenistic, rather than Byzantine, Greek.

ა ბ გ დ ე ვ ზ თ ი კ ლ
მ ნ ო პ ჟ რ ს ტ უ ფ ქ
ღ ყ შ ჩ ც ძ წ ჭ ხ ჯ ჰ

Linguists traditionally divide the great Babel of Caucasian languages into various groups, though there is continuous debate over how far they relate to each other. There are two non-Caucasian language families in the area: Turkic, of which Azeri has by far the largest number of speakers, and the Indo-European languages like Russian and Armenian with a sub-group of Iranian languages such as Ossetian and Tat, a mixture of Hebrew and old Persian spoken by 20,000 Jewish Daghestanis near Derbent (though there are also Muslim and Christian Tats). Then there are three divisions of Caucasian languages: North-West Caucasian like Abkhaz and Adyghe; North-East Caucasian, which includes most of the languages of Daghestan and also Chechen, Ingush, Bats (the Veinakh or Nakh language-family; the words mean, simply, 'our people' in all three languages); and, finally, South Caucasian, the Georgian (more properly Kartvelian) group of languages, consisting of Georgian, Mingrelian, Laz and Svan. Though various attempts have been made to relate the Kartvelian group to both North-East and North-West Caucasian, they have been largely unconvincing and so Kartvelian seems to be that fascinating phenomenon, a language family isolate with no obvious relationship to any other language on God's earth.

If the current understanding of evolution is correct it is difficult not to believe that all languages, like all people, are, however distantly, related. Eminent professors have spent their lives involved in the fearful process of lexicostatistical glottochronology, deriving family trees and branches of descent back, so that a Proto-Caucasian language would have split into the North-Caucasian and Kartvelian groups roughly ten thousand years ago, Georgian and Mingrelian diverging perhaps two thousand years ago. Ultimately, all these calculations lead back to a hypothetical first language, an Ur-language. One of these, Proto-Nostratic, constructed or reconstructed by the great Russian linguist Vladislav Illich Svytich, inspires an annual dinner in certain American universities, during which only it may be spoken. Isolates like Kartvelian excite considerable debate and many energetic attempts to fit them into the great scheme; they are intriguing and irritating anomalies.

One of the most captivating hypotheses relates Georgian to that other baffling language isolate, Basque, a subscript or echo of the purported relationship between the two classical Iberias. This theory enjoyed considerable popularity (among the two or three people who were interested) until recently when such investigators as the distinguished scholar of Basque, R. L. Trask, dismissed it with some finality. It is still popular in Georgia and, of course, like so many questions of language, has evolved to support a fiercely political thesis. Zviad Gamsakhurdia, the first, luckless, freely elected President of Georgia, who died in mysterious circumstances after only nine months in office during the bloody civil and separatist wars which followed the collapse of the Soviet Union, wrote an extraordinary book, *The Spiritual Mission of Georgia*. In this, linguistic arguments are brought in to serve the most disturbing nationalist cant. Briefly, Gamsakhurdia declares that Georgian and Basque represent the extreme eastern and western remnants of the original European, pre-Indo-European, language. This is then elaborated and developed through the medium of certain esoteric Christian Georgian texts, theosophical mumbo-jumbo (not in itself evidence of madness but worrying in a president with pronounced tendencies towards ethnomania), alchemical mysteries buried in the Caucasus, the identification of the Golden Fleece with the Holy Grail ('The bringing of the Grail to Georgia is a fact') and much, much more, into a Messianic nationalism with an ostensibly spiritual and cultural focus: the Georgians are the original, autochthonous inhabitants of their lands, and have a God-given destiny to reunite East and West under their spiritual guidance. He derives this whole mess from erroneous theories about the Georgian language and a proto-Iberian world which represented, and will bring forth again, a pre-Hellenistic, more spiritual, more rapturous communion between mankind. He quotes portentously from the medieval Georgian *Praise and Glorification of the Georgian Language*.

> . . . the Georgian nation and its language, adorned and blessed in the name of the Lord, is a Lazarus among the nations and languages, and will rise in the future and gain its universal position as mankind's spiritual teacher and at the second coming of Christ will become exposer of sinful humanity.

Clearly Gamsakhurdia identified himself with David the Builder, *davit aghmashenebeli*, perhaps the greatest of all Georgian kings, when he wrote that King David 'combined the struggle with Georgia's foes and the building of the Georgian state with an extensive religious, philosophical and scholarly activity that is truly astonishing.' The book is a piece of self-indulgent, nationalistic cathexis.

The followers of Zviad Gamsakhurdia and his clan, known as Zviadists, *zviadistebi*, still have much support in Georgia, particularly in his Mingrelian homeland. Gamsakhurdia is often seen as a determined anti-Communist and dissident, imprisoned for his heresies, a nationalist hero. He was also a poet. It's a strange phenomenon, this business of poetry, extreme nationalism and deranged leadership. Radovan Karadzic of the Bosnian Serbs and Eugene Terre Blanche, leader of the white supremacist party in South Africa (and author of the immortal line 'The little bird goes tweet, tweet, tweet') share this distinction in our times. Stalin too, of course, wrote poetry in his youth, though he's rather better known for executing poets and driving them to suicide. Gamsakhurdia was, besides, a linguist of some genius, translator of Shakespeare, Baudelaire, Gogol, and author of works on Shota Rustaveli and Georgian culture. He inspired tremendous devotion, not to say fanaticism, in his followers. I remember groups of them, mostly women, that would camp outside the Parliament buildings on Rustaveli Prospekt holding up his photograph and chanting his praise during the early, disputatious days of independence. Hence the 87 per cent vote which brought him to office. However, if anyone doubts that the man was, fundamentally, dangerous let him read *The Spiritual Mission*. 'Ultimately,' he wrote, 'we shall lose Tbilisi too, for anti-Georgian tendencies and an influx of non-Georgians are increasing in the city.' It was not far from this to the decidedly eccentric proofs of Georgian ethnicity that he began to demand of his people: two hundred years of ancestral residence in the country. Censorship, discrimination and militant nationalism soon followed and, though this does not entirely justify the bloody coup that ousted him and all the subsequent mess, it does help to explain it.

Gamsakhurdia's world-view was obviously not based entirely upon his enthusiasm for the theory that linked together Georgian with Basque but it was a building block in the ethnocentric, nationalist edifice that he constructed. He drew extensively upon the works of linguists and scholars, particularly on the writings of Nikolai Marr, an eccentric Georgian-Scot who linked Caucasian languages not only with Basque but also Etruscan. Marr's theories had considerable influence and underpin much of the linguistic speculation in W. E. D. Allen's *History of the Georgian People*, a wonderful, poetical book that may be greatly blamed for my own enthusiasms. Much of this kind of linguistic deduction can be simply if harshly summarised as the comparison of words from different languages with a vaguely similar sound and meaning, these words being taken as cognates and so being held to prove an earlier relationship. R. L. Trask exposed this for what it is worth by a forceful demonstration using a Hungarian dictionary and a knowledge of Basque – he had no understanding of Hungarian: any two languages are susceptible to this kind of 'proof'. However, the possibility of some relationship, though not verifiable by any linguistic method so far devised, is still intriguing. I wondered whether a real genetic test, an analysis of DNA, could settle the question.

My son Charlie was studying biology at University College London and working in the Department of Genetic Anthropology. The studies taking place there and in other such departments cast light upon the genetic relationship between the peoples of the world and the mix within races and nations. Myths of racial purity have been thoroughly dismantled. Both Georgian and Basque DNA have been sampled but, despite my best efforts, I have so far failed to persuade any of the overworked researchers to take up the task of a direct genetic comparison between the two. However, Gamsakhurdia's idea that the Basques and Georgians are together descended from the ancient, original stock of Europe and that other Europeans were later immigrants has been shown to be untrue. Most geneticists now agree that almost all Europeans, more than 80 per cent, have been in Europe since Upper Paleolithic times and that their gene lineages cannot be ascribed to later Neolithic diffusion. The old idea that farmers from the fertile crescent moved into Europe about ten thousand years ago and scattered its inhabitants to the winds is quite wrong; the Europeans have been in Europe for far longer than was once believed. In fact, far from being close, the Georgians and Basques are at either end of the European genetic pool. Richard Villems, Professor of Genetics at the University of Tartu, introduced to me by the team at UCL, kindly tried to explain all this to me:

'Kartvelian and Basque mt [mitochondrial – so inherited from the mother] DNA are quite dissimilar within the European context. The Basques have the highest frequency in Europe of haplogroup H – the main European variant of human maternal lineages – above 60 per cent. Usually in Europe it is about 40–45 per cent, though lower in the south, about 35 per cent around the Mediterranean. In this sense Kartvelians seem to be at the opposite end – their H is below 20 per cent – and that is a very significant difference indeed. Hence any typical genetic difference calculus would put them automatically rather distant from each other though, of course, the differences are within a pool of pan-European maternal lineage variation.'

So in fact the absolute opposite of Gamsakhurdia's thesis is true: Basques and Georgians are about as far apart as it is possible to be within Europe, something that should come as no surprise when one considers their geographical positions. They are both more closely related to just about any other Europeans than to each other. All this underlines the dangers of trying to hijack some sort of linguistic 'proof' into the service of a particular political, cultural or ethnic theory. In the wrong climate, misuse is almost inevitable.

*

Under a fierce morning sun we started to climb again, leaving Tebulos behind and fighting our way against the wind up on to a high ridge. Way below a tiny settlement of scattered huts came into view and then two valleys branched out in front to left and right. The right hand valley pointed north to Mutso, the Mindis' ancestral home which they both claimed they could see in the distance. I looked hard but saw nothing. Then Chris brought out his telephoto lens and there, at the utmost end of our vision, we could just make out one or two dim towers blending with the rocks behind. But the Mindis had decided to take a small diversion through Khevsureti for personal and touristic reasons, I think, and so we crossed the ridge and went down, down, down, away from the bare and sculpted heights, across a grassy knoll and through the scrub towards the winter settlement of upper Ardotti. It was steep. Our legs, shattered by the Atsunta, worked improperly. My knees had failed and Chris had developed a strange gait, his left leg completely stiff. We hobbled down for hours until we reached the hamlet: conical haystacks, a neat field of potatoes with a woven fence around, a garden of onions, great stacks of birch piled high against the walls of the few small houses, ready for winter. Wheat was growing on the slopes around, almost ripe for the scythe. The people of Ardotti move up here in winter towards the sun, away from the valley bottom where the snow lies deep and avalanches tumble.

The Mindis, of course, had disappeared ahead but after five hours of descent we struck a little track along the mountain edge, running just above the Andaki river. I thought of my home on the moors of Somerset: how wonderful it was to be walking, for a moment, along the level. The way to the lower village was lovely; crossing and re-crossing the river on little pole bridges, we walked through a narrowing gorge till we saw its ancient towers, a few houses perched on a hill and a church above. We climbed up through the ruins and the rubble and Chris and I sat in the shade of an old wall and looked about while the Mindis strode off to forage for bread and cheese. We saw them away in the distance, specks against the mountain, making their way to an isolated homestead surrounded by grazing cattle. Around us a few little houses stood among the ruins, some with newly galvanised roofs; narrow tracks wove in between. Red-breasted birds chirruped in the clear air. We lay in a stupor in the heat, baked like the stones, immobile.

Eventually we were gently moved aside by a young girl leading a file of cattle through the village. She paused to greet us. She was, naturally, a cousin of the Mindis. With blonde hair and bright blue eyes she was my first fair-haired, blue-eyed Khevsur. I was all set to enquire delicately into her parentage and ancestry when she was gone with a smile and a wave, trotting off after her line of cows.

The boys returned with no bread but with some fresh cheese that was so salty we filled our mouths with water to eat it; then we passed down through the village shrines, some with the horns of tûr leant outside them on a ledge. Here the old pagan beliefs of the mountains still mingle freely with Christianity, and the mountain tûr which leads the hunter sometimes to destruction, sometimes to a kind of revelation, has a magical and symbolic significance. I have seen many dozens of these horns piled high in churches in Svaneti, and they are laid upon shrines and tombs throughout the mountains. The prowess of the hunter is mixed with and transmuted into the Christian valour of the more martial of the saints, especially St George, slayer of dragons, the favourite saint of Georgia, as of England. The fact that he was a Cappadocian, like St Nino the great Illuminatrix of Georgia, added to his lustre. He remains particularly beloved of the Khevsurs and of the Svans and, though not worshipped above Christ, as some commentators suggest (old Khevsur songs say 'Let us praise first the Lord and then St George'), he is probably preferred, appealed to and worshipped more frequently.

The way soon became more difficult and we had to leave our track: great slides of mud and stone had blocked it entirely. We forced our way up through loose shale and slid down to the river, crossing by a rocky outcrop in mid-stream with another shrine on it, peculiarly built with a mysterious chimney on top. The Mindis, practising their George-like qualities, amused themselves by killing more snakes in an effort to exterminate the entire species. We scrambled along the right bank of the river, throwing ourselves about in a most enjoyable way, over rock and the debris of spring storms. As we leapt and slipped above the torrent, Chris immersed himself almost entirely and was about to sail off for Chechnya when young Mindi hauled him ashore. I looked at him pityingly. Then, swinging along the water's edge by the supple birch trees that thrust their way through the boulders, I found my pack suddenly stuck fast in an overhanging branch. As I dangled like a mad haddock from a rod, bending ever nearer to the surface of the racing water, the Mindis managed to reach out and undo the straps on my pack. Recovering my dignity with difficulty, I thanked them warmly, forgetting for the moment that I had recently been cursing them for their terrible speed. I had reason to be grateful: we tried to ford the river a number of times but it flowed too fierce and all along were shrines to the drowned. Eventually we came to a pole bridge of the kind I particularly dislike: two sticks with a little mud plastered between, the water raging below. Bullied by Mindi, I managed somehow to walk across. Chris, owing to his nautical past spent mainly walking along yardarms and such, did rather better.

Here was a mean and nondescript hamlet, Andaki: three battered houses stuck about with tin and black plastic, and an old ruin, fast by the river. It was not a good place to camp, the ground uneven and rocky and entirely covered in cow shit. While big Mindi was let, rather furtively, into one of the houses, young Mindi discovered that he had dropped his camera, an ancient Zenith in a leather case of which he was terribly fond. So he disappeared back the way we had come. Would he manage to retrieve it, possibly half way up the Atsunta Pass, and still be home in time for tea? Of course.

We found a marginally less vile place for our tent and Chris did useful things and made some tea. I encouraged him by describing the negotiations big Mindi was without doubt now entering into and his certain and imminent arrival with a large roast capon and four bottles of claret. I drifted to the water's edge and amused myself by staring at the rushing river and then shifting my gaze to the ground in front of me, enjoying the weird sensation that this produced. My innards seemed to flow into the water, drawn out and away as it raced downstream. An hour later I was feeling very odd when I became aware of Chris muttering, 'He's probably in there drinking beer, lying on a divan and eating fish fingers.' A small party of cows ambled past us, one with its back-end hanging off, savaged by a wolf. Then the Mindis reappeared together, suddenly from the wings, like conspirators meeting on a stage: the camera was found and a great dish of fried potatoes and onions produced. We ate slowly; nothing could have been more delectable. We finished our meal in utter darkness.

That night in our tent, by the light of my torch, I came to the end of *Nicholas Nickleby*. My addiction to text meant extra weight to carry but Penguin £1 paperbacks in the Classics series were, I felt, disposable and my load would lighten as I went along. In fact, I had a double purpose for these books but could not finally bring myself to use their pages as I had intended. Instead, I carefully cut through the spines and, section by section as I finished them, left them on our trail, under a rock or in a cleft in the mountainside, so that anyone who followed from Tusheti to Svaneti would be able to find comfort, too, in *Nicholas Nickleby*, *Bleak House*, *David Copperfield*, *Nostromo* and *Victory*.

The local inhabitants felt none of my qualms with regard to text. In the open, of course, one manages discreetly, as best one can, but many villages have dunnies a little way off: four poles driven into the ground, covered in felt or blocked in with planks, and a boarded floor with a hole set above a seething pit. I had dreadful imaginings, not to be gone into, about dropping my valuables down such a hole and would clutch my pockets tightly. Often on a sharp hook on one wall, paper was thoughtfully spiked. In the mountains newspapers, traditional in such circumstances, hardly ever come and I began to take an interest in the various works I found. I realised after some weeks that most of the pages were torn from Communist texts. I thought I had discovered a delightful Georgian joke but could never quite bring myself to broach the subject with any of my various hosts. This was a country, after all, where blowing one's nose in public was thought indelicate, as I once found out to my shame in a theatre in Tbilisi.

The next morning we washed in the river as the mist began to break away and the sun crept through. We set off back northwards towards Ardotti, at first encountering the same difficulties as on the previous day: the track washed away in sections, mad dashes across precipices of mud and rock, Chris and I holding desperately to the hillside as we went, the Mindis stepping surely across the slopes. Past Ardotti the way became easier and we rested a while at a corner under a tree where the little River Chanchakhistsqali flows into the Andaki from the south. Beyond this lay a wrecked Russian helicopter, its fuselage adapted as a dwelling of sorts. Numbers of these wrecks, brought down during the Chechen War, littered the mountains, modernist shrines to the dead. The ancient dead lay here, too, in their sepulchres of massive stone, though some of these structures were taboo houses, used as isolation wards in times of plague or cholera and for women in childbirth or during menstruation.

John Baddeley was fascinated by the Khevsurs, though in all his journeys over the mountains he only reached one Khevsur village, Akhieli, about thirty kilometres to the west and north of Ardotti, one of the Khevsur settlements most isolated from the south. He got stuck with his horses in deep snow while trying to cross over the Arkhotis Pass from the north and had to retreat into Ingusheti. It was October and already far too late. At the time of his journey, 1901, the local Khevsurs and Ingush were involved in a fierce blood-feud: there had been twenty-seven murders in the previous two years just along the valley of the Assa where Akhieli stands and no Khevsur would go alone into Ingush territory. They travelled heavily armed in groups of at least twenty. Despite such tensions, at the time of Baddeley's visit the Khevsurs were well-disposed and hospitable and showed him around the village, posed for photographs and talked freely of their customs and way of life. He saw the 'hovel' where the girls and women were obliged to go during their periods and photographed a group of them outside it and also went to the separate birthing house where 'every woman about to have a child had to retire, there to remain, along with her babe, until forty days had elapsed and she could be considered "clean" again. Women relatives might take her food and water and deposit them outside the hovel, but nothing more – no contact was allowed on any consideration, no propinquity even. The husband's part was to prowl around at night with friends, and if the unfortunate woman cried or groaned, fire off his gun to scare the Evil One.' In Baddeley's time the Russian authorities had made such practices illegal and exacted, if they could, heavy fines.

Such customs had long since ceased, the Mindis assured me, though the forty days after the birth of a child were still considered a time of great vulnerability. This echoed my own experience of small communities in rural Greece where during this time the new mother is not permitted outside the home and all manner of prophylaxes against the Evil Eye are still used. Frazer makes much of the universality of such beliefs and practices in *The Golden Bough* and writes of the seclusion of menstruous women, the fear of menstrual blood, the isolation of women during childbirth in special huts set apart or in sacred ground and their separation from all human contact. Through the dangerous mists of cultural relativism it does not take much empathy to imagine the misery, pain and fear of a young girl come for the first time to childbed in such circumstances!

Beyond Ardotti, through a gorge with stark, bare cliffs, craggy and dramatic, the path widened; great wedges of rock and boulders had fallen all about giving the way an air of cataclysmic beauty. Big Mindi left us for a while and nipped off along the Khonistsqali, flowing into the Andaki here from the foot of Mount Tebulos, to the village of Khonischala where he had a cousin who had, young Mindi said, fine blue eyes and fair hair, quite long and almost wavy. Just beyond the point where the two rivers meet we had our first clear view of Mutso, to my mind the finest, though most ruined, of all the tower-villages of Khevsureti. Its sad, dark towers filled the imagination with cries of war, the fury of raid and vendetta. High in the gorge the towers cling, overlooking the angry river. Great blades of rock slice and jag up into the sky. Half way down the mountain and right across the river, despite the summer's heat, the snow and ice lay gleaming, packed and solid, scattered over with timber and mountain rubble. We passed another shrine to the drowned, a little girl whose name and portrait were etched into a slate, a shelf underneath with a bottle. Mindi poured a libation on to the earth and we drank to her and to the dead.

As we toiled up towards the towers we wound our way through the tombs and sepulchres of Mutso. Perhaps five feet high by six feet wide and twelve feet long, with pitched roofs of thick slate, they were beautifully, solidly built of massive stone. Most had been broken into, by Russians, young Mindi said, looking for gold. Peering inside we could see quite clearly: all along the length of the tomb shelves of slate projected from the walls and on them, and on the floor, disturbed and scattered all about, lay bones and skulls and teeth, all the skeletal remains of long-dead Khevsurs. In one tomb a female and a baby lay quiet, side by side upon a shelf, their skin still clinging to their ribs. At the far end the wall was strangely shaped into the suggestion of a hearth, small shelves above it. Bones lay everywhere. Clinging to the very edge of the precipice, these sepulchres are so sturdily built that they have remained far better preserved than the towers and tower-houses. Perhaps they are still, and ever have been, carefully tended. Instead of a door they have a square of thin slate, like a window, built into one wall. Presumably this was broken and replaced at each new interment; now all are open. On either side of this 'window' is a small alcove or post-hole, perhaps suggesting a bar across, in which I found, in two or three instances, freshly laid green herbs or the dried remains of others.

It would be an exaggeration to talk of an extant cult of the dead in Georgia but, certainly, the dead are profoundly venerated. At any gathering, though the toast to peace is properly first, the toasts to the dead often follow, even before the sacred toast to the mother-land. In the mountains, as far as I have seen, before the toast a libation is always made, wine or spirit poured on the ground, though beer may never be used for such purposes. The toasts are listened to with great solemnity and answered with an equal gravity and in the proper manner. If the recent dead are referred to, espe-cially if they were dear and close family or friends, such rites, though formalised, are charged with deep emotion and spiritual force. Though grief is never wild or abandoned, the tears of grief may flow unashamedly. Particularly in the mountains, at night, in the open, the power of such rites seems intensified to an overwhelming degree, the spell cast only broken when the round of toasts moves on, to Georgia, to mothers, to fathers, to children, to friendship. This ongoing relationship with the dead is something we have lost except in the most private way. Ahdef Soueif, a contemporary Arab writer, remarked that in the twenty years she had lived in England, she 'never found out how the English mourn. There seems to be a funeral and then – nothing'.

In Georgia in ancient times and in many parts of the Caucasus the obsequies were prolonged and various. There are references to funeral games such as wrestling and fighting but, most particu-larly, to horse racing, and Khevsur races in honour of the dead are well-attested. They may have had their origin in the custom of sacri-ficing horses and burying them along with the dead, a habit prob-ably shared with the Scythians in the steppes to the north of the mountains. Many horse burials have been unearthed, especially in western Georgia. These races might last for days and cover immense distances over the mountains, with many contestants. They still occur in rather less extended forms. Another possible remnant of the ancient obsequies persists, though no longer linked to funerals. It is a sort of mad polo, *tskhenburti* (literally, horseball), where any number of players charge through the mountains from village to village, chasing a ball, brandishing fearsome hockey sticks. There seem to be no other rules and I was desperate to see the game in action. Sadly, so far, I have had no luck, though there are some wonderful illustrations of it drawn by an Italian artist, Castelli, who spent many years in Georgia during the seventeenth century.

We scrambled up over rock and ruin, past one great tower still standing, and sat for a moment drawing breath in another little graveyard. There were gravestones sticking up everywhere and more tombs, one perfect, with graffiti in Georgian and Russian scratched about, some very ancient, some dated, the earliest I could find from 1560. Chris, busy with his camera, backed, as usual, perilously towards the edge. Young Mindi and I went on up. Towards the top no track was discernible and our scramble turned into a rock climb as we came to the base of the towers. About us the broken walls closed in, pierced with gunslots, arched doorways high above the ground. It was the most extraordinary place. There were many towers here, most massive. Using the ancient fingertip-to-nose method I measured eight yards along each side as they tapered in along the level of the first floor. Great slates and blocks of mountain, finely placed, the facing true and exact, carried here and built with what effort on such a high and impossible crag? Such skill, such prowess was well rewarded: Mutso is said never to have fallen to an enemy. Not to the Chechens, nor Shamyl, nor even to the Russians. Only time and neglect have finally reduced Mutso to rubble.

It is difficult to realise fully the necessity which drove these Khevsurs to build in so high, so difficult, so inaccessible a spot and to have lived here through so many centuries. The place itself illustrates, far better than any words of history, the desperate and dangerous times that passed through generation after generation of Khevsur life. Existence was hard and fierce, death never far distant. They lived close to their graves. In these ruins we could read their struggle for survival, their ferocious independence, the bitterness of raid and vendetta. I thought of the strange and blood-curdling nursery rhyme that all Georgians know and sing. It has a light, charming, lilting tune:

> *zhuzhuna tsvima movida*
> *didi mindori danama*

vints chvenze tsudi rame tkvas
guli gaupos danama.

A light rain has fallen
moistening the great field
If anybody says anything bad about us
Let our daggers rip his heart out.

Big Mindi's family tower, the Diaouli tower, still leant in ruins
but young Mindi's, the Chincharaouli tower, had fallen and quite
disappeared. Right at the top was a patch of sacred ground across
which Mindi refused to walk. He could step around it, he said, but
only to the left, not the right. While a child, an uncle had told
him that to walk this ground unbidden was certain peril: he would
instantly turn into a great goat with horns like the Devil. The sense
of taboo was palpable and mostly from respect but partly from
unease (a momentary, atavistic shudder), I too avoided this fearful
place. Only certain priests and elders and a few spiritually gifted
men (never women) might walk there at all times, and even they
in strict observance of the laws. This was the *khati*, the sacred space
where religious rituals are performed, where people gather to make
offerings, to eat and drink and sacrifice and also to dance and sing
ritual, improvised songs, the *kaphiaoba*. The word *khati* has other
significant religious and spiritual meanings: it is the name given
to the Sons of God, pre-Christian deities like *gudani* and *lashari*, to
whom the mountain people gave special devotion, and it also means
'icon' or just 'image'.

I was unable to penetrate much beyond this with Mindi but
others later muttered vague warnings and there seemed to be a
general feeling that old Mutso was not to be trifled with, not to be
lightly ventured into, especially not at night. I was intrigued by this
and by Mindi's talk of the spiritually gifted men who might penetrate its mysteries. Years before I had been told about certain
people, called in Georgian *mkadre*: quite ordinary men, sometimes
thought of as deeply unfortunate men, who were suddenly transformed in the midst of life, often reluctantly, by some epiphany,
touched by God. They lived alone in the mountains in communion

with the Spirits and with God, touched by his will, and were said to possess extraordinary powers, though quite what these were I never could discover.

At the bottom of old Mutso we found big Mindi playfully kicking two little boys, more cousins, of course. We walked a little way along the river and set up camp by a settlement so mean as to have no name on the Russian military map, but called by Mindi Khoniskhevi or something rather like it: an abandoned armoured car and two green-painted wooden huts, their roofs covered in black plastic, so depressingly ubiquitous. Two families lived here with their children and cattle.

Dark clouds marched down the mountains and a huge storm began to break as a desperate and melancholy bunch of Kists walked by, on their way from Chechnya to Telavi. Thunder crashed and lightning flickered and struck the ground about us so that the earth trembled and shook. We huddled in our tents and I tried to remember whether I should or should not hold on to the tent pole. The cows mooed pitiably in their fright. Pity, too, the poor Kists! At around nine o'clock that night a strange brightness filled the sky so that for a moment I thought I had missed something and it was morning. Chris said that after our days in the wilderness among such extravagant displays of nature, living on a diet of barely leavened bread and cheese, with such physical torments and constant reminders of the frailty of the body, the mind purified of tax returns and news, he felt an almost biblical derangement. He was waiting, now, for the visions to begin.

It had poured, flashed and thundered all through the sleepless night. We crawled half-dazed into a world still there and a morning full of cloud and moisture and set off past new Mutso, new but ruined too, past young Mindi's father's house lying in decay. He had left when still a child in the early 1950s and had been brought down to Gamarjweba in the plains around Tbilisi by his parents. It was a final abandonment and they never returned. However, they did keep some tangible remembrance of their past: embroidered Khevsur jackets, their Khevsur crosses and rings, some daggers. These Mindi treasured. His father remembered living in Mutso when many still wore traditional

Khevsur dress. Later, in Shatili, Mindi produced some of these wonderful embroidered jackets, covered in Khevsur crosses, carefully kept by his aunt. I had seen, too, Khevsur jewellery at the home of my friend Mako Maisuradze, collected by her father years before. It is, I suppose, absurd to regret the disappearance of traditional dress, the visitor's requirement for the picturesque a pointless and irrelevant nostalgia when set against the times and the convenience of the universal norm. But how drab the new is in comparison! I remember the first time I visited the Topkapi Palace and in one of the chambers saw the display, in glass cabinets arranged around the walls, of the clothes of the Sultan and his family from earliest times until the end of the Sultanate in the twentieth century. The costumes are wonderful, full of colour and grace; but how sad and drear the final cabinet! The little Sultan has thrown off the garments of his ancestors in favour of top hat and tails, and grey and black appear for the first time instead of shimmering emerald and gold.

All along the banks of the Andaki River were shrines with spouts from which poured clear mountain water. As we passed we drank and added white stones and crystals to those already piled on top. We paused a while at the shrine of Mindi Daraouli's grandfather, his name and dates engraved on slate, and spent a reflective moment there. Walking on, Chris rather destroyed my developing rhapsody on the wayside shrines of Khevsureti.

'They are exactly like our park benches,' he insisted. 'In England, when you die you get a park bench with a plaque and passers-by sit there and rest. Here it's the same, only with water and spouts and a cup.'

Where was the romance in that? The mystery? It seemed far too banal a comparison. He was right, of course. Perhaps Khevsurs wandering through the villages of central Somerset would find an equal rapture in the dedicated park bench. It is a strange custom, after all. Out of what dim antiquity did it develop?

The river, swollen by the night's storm, roared and raced beside us with a fantastic power and ferocity; boulders and trees rolled and crashed in its course as it fell steeply. We crossed, thank God, upon a substantial bridge of girders, poles and planks laid on top, and looked across the valley to Anatori, where the Andaki flows into the Tchanti-Argoun. Anatori is a Khevsur necropolis and John Baddeley had sat on a rock, a hundred years ago, not ten miles north of here, near Djarego, and 'cast many a longing glance up the Argoun' towards Anatori and its tombs. Hampered by deep snow, again, he was unable to cross the pass and had to be 'content for the present with dreaming of a journey southward through the valleys of the Kists and Khevsurs'.

The tombs were larger than those of Mutso though built in the same fashion. The 'windows', similarly smashed open, were barred. Through the bars we could see skulls and bones lying thick within. In one massive charnel house a shrivelled hand pointed out, ribcages, legs and arms strewn around. In another a body lay intact, parchment skin stretched tight, hands folded across chest, someone's child. Here were the ancient dead, still visible and present, half way between this world and the next, clinging to a precipice. Curiously, the tombs here and in Mutso were unadorned and bore no mark or symbol of Christianity, nor of any other faith. The Georgians were converted to Christianity by St Nino in or around AD 337 and can claim to be the oldest Christian nation after the Armenians (by a few years); so, though over the centuries paganism, Christianity, Mazdaism and Islam all left their mark in Georgia, gaining and giving ground, it is strange that these Khevsur tombs suggest so little. In fact, burial grounds all over the mountains are similarly stark and though tombs I have seen in Ossetia have a slightly different shape, and those in Ingusheti or Chechnya are a little different again, their material, size, situation and aspect all argue for some degree of homogeneity, for a common mountain heritage and culture.

Anatori lies just beneath the Chechen border and as we turned south towards Shatili, the Khevsur 'capital', we passed an army checkpoint: four young soldiers sitting about a little hut, keeping an eye on Chechens coming through the pass. They expressed only the mildest interest in us, chatted amiably to the Mindis and waved away our passports. Their uniform was a strange mixture of clothing, all of it either too large or too small: fake Adidas track-suit bottoms, a medley of boots and shoes, assorted camouflage jackets, though these last with smart new shoulder flashings on which 'Border Patrol' was embroidered in Georgian and in English, not, noticeably, in Russian.

Shatili is the only one of the tower-villages that still stands; well-preserved into modern times, it was partly restored in the 1970s under the Soviets. As we approached we could see its massive tower-houses squat against the base of the mountainside, over-looking the Argoun River on its passage north through the moun-tains to Chechnya and the Caspian Sea beyond. Shatili's tower-houses are not perched upon some impossible height but cluster just above the Argoun, signalling a degree of strength and a security unmatched elsewhere. Certainly the heights around were heavily guarded and just across the river on a hill not far off we could make out the ruins of a fort. Wooden balconies projected from the huddled towers, and narrow paths wound up through them scarcely wide enough for two abreast. Life was close, confined, guarded, stony and difficult. Inside all was dark and damp. A hearth was built into one wall on the ground floor, but no chimney or other outlet for smoke. There was no separate byre for cattle as in the towers of Svaneti and on a winter's night, locked in, smoke filling the room, humans and animals crouched together, the atmosphere must have been rich. In one tower-house we found lovely carved wooden chests and, inside these, old Khevsur clothes all damp and falling into decay. The towers were uninhabited. No one wanted to live such a life again: too dark, too hard. But in the vast space all about there must have been some comfort, as well as safety, in living so densely packed together. Indeed it is easy to jump from flat roof to flat roof, and it is not difficult to imagine a community sitting here, mending their rifles, spreading crops to dry, calling to each other, watching the river and the sun set along the valley, enjoying some contentment.

Around the river and beyond were scattered huts and a ragbag of dwellings made from this and that. In front of the towers two small but fine old homes with carved balconies were falling gently back into the mountainside. We left our packs by a long low wooden hut that later I would know well as Dato's home, and strolled along to see the Mindis' uncle and aunt. Up a steep flight of wooden steps we found them, ancient and benign, sitting on a small veranda, sewing socks and pocking maize. Cousins appeared from all sides, smart girls from Tbilisi up for the holidays in improbable shoes, a mass of skirmishing little ones of indeterminate sizes and shapes, Eldar in his late twenties, blue-eyed and blond, who was to come with us on the next leg of our journey, and dark Dato of the hut. All were delighted to see the Mindis and embraced them warmly. With us they were kindly and polite but not at all amazed. Shatili had frequent visitors, though they arrived from the south, up the mountain road from Tbilisi. Why, only a month before an elderly Dutchman had arrived on a bicycle, giving rise to the expression 'I'll be a Dutchman on a bicycle' which has since passed into the local vernacular. Inside the house, in a dark, low room with smoke-blackened timbers and a tiny window, we sat at a little table on a sloping earth floor and were served with bread, butter and cheese and blessed cups of tea, followed by hot cheese.

After our meal we thanked our hosts, still smiling and pocking, and walked up the narrow track through the towers to new Shatili, which had been invisible from the direction of our approach. At the top of the old village, across a meadow that was at once football pitch, grazing ground and helicopter landing place, we entered a short lane of Soviet semis. Incongruous and something of a shock, they were by no means as ugly as might have been expected; care had been taken to build them on the edge of the hillside with wide balconies looking out over the Argoun River. We were let in to number 6, I think. Inside were fitted cabinets and a couple of ornamental televisions and a bathroom, of all things. It felt very peculiar after our days in the open: strange underfoot and the space–air–light ratio was all wrong. The Mindis threw their packs down and left us. Chris and I stood in the middle of the sitting room and looked at each other. What were we supposed to do here? Sit, obviously. So we sat on the sofa and looked at the televisions. No, there was something not quite right. We moved out on to the balcony. On it were the skins of four large black bears and half a dozen mountain goats, all quite fresh and drying in the breeze. Water flowed around us in torrents but in the bathroom, in observance of the ancient Soviet tradition, it trickled wanly from the taps. After some difficult but determined washing we hung our socks up with the bears and then lay down. Our bodies, settling slowly in disbelief on to the beds, gave up willingly. We fell asleep.

I had sent Mindi off with some money to try to buy food. A chicken, I thought, might be rather nice. We pictured a plump roasted bird or casseroled, perhaps, with a few onions and potatoes. Past travellers in the Caucasus often wrote of the difficulty of finding food in the mountains and would describe hard bargaining with fierce tribesmen over the mangy carcass of some sheep. In his *Caucasian Journey*, Negley Farson lamented the fact that even after paying handsomely for his dinner those who had sold it to him would always invite themselves to the subsequent meal and polish it off with vigour. I was not so ambitious. A chicken would be fine.

Chris and I were already sitting at the table when the Mindis and Eldar arrived carrying a plastic bag.

'Here it is,' said Mindi, proudly. A pale, scrawny, boiled chicken plopped, naked, on to the table. It was grotesque. We were overcome. I tried to pierce it with a variety of knives, two forks and a small hatchet but it was so unaccountably bouncy that it resisted all our increasingly violent efforts. I suggested a game of basket ball and Chris wondered if there were any power tools nearby, a band-saw, perhaps. Eldar, a quiet man, a man of few words who would sometimes open his mouth to speak then, considering, close it again, was noiselessly crying in a corner. He began to look so unwell that I thought we had better send the chicken away and asked Mindi to try and have it turned into soup. Our combined mental powers had by this time degenerated to such an extent that this most reasonable request proved far too much and no more sense was to be had from anyone.

Later that evening a group of men followed by a troop of small boys came into the house with a large jug of *chacha*. Prominent among them was Bakar, by far the biggest man I had seen in the mountains. There was a good six and a half feet of him, topped with black hair, a black beard and searching, dark eyes. It was he, always deferred to, who led most of the conversation, with occasional comments coming from his Chechen friend, Ismael. They made a fine pair: Ismael was a foot shorter, twice as broad, with a stomach that bulged through his open (fake Adidas) tracksuit top, the only even vaguely podgy person I had seen for days. Bakar was in his mid-thirties, Ismael probably my age, late forties. Bakar and all the Khevsur men were dignified drunk but Ismael refused the *chacha* and all tobacco. As for many Chechens, the war with the Russians had caused him to reaffirm his allegiance to Islam and its laws. He had the face and figure, however, of a Chechen Brezhnev, tough, square, jowelled and lined, and had certainly been familiar with the bottle and its joys in the not-too-distant past.

The men were all armed. They had leant their Kalashnikovs against a wall, an odd sight in this strangely suburban room. As the evening wore on they amused themselves by stripping down their weapons, cleaning and oiling them, comparing their actions and their attributes. Guns and knives were passed around for general approbation. Bakar, however, did not give up his Kalashnikov. He never did. I was to learn later, when I slept by him, that he always kept it by his side. I found such proximity to so many guns rather unsettling.

Smiling, Bakar looked at me and asked, 'How do we know that you are not KGB?'

It was, I think, almost entirely a joke but I felt a small tug of apprehension. I said something quite fatuous. 'Do I look like KGB? Besides, I speak such bad Russian.'

'Ho, ho, ho,' he laughed, 'but if you were really KGB such truly execrable Russian would be the best of disguises. In fact, it is difficult to believe that anyone who speaks such bad Russian is not doing it deliberately. But perhaps you are CIA or FBI or MI5?'

'Yes, or WXYZ or LMNOP.'

'Ha! ha! or BMW or IBM or BBC,' and he dismissed the subject with an airy wave. But having got up speed I could not stop.

'Or perhaps I am an agent of SPECTRE,' I said.

'SPECTRE? What do you know of SPECTRE?' His eyes narrowed.

'Counter-espionage. I think it's the evil organisation that James Bond fights against, or perhaps that's SMERSH.'

'Bah! James Bond is for children.' His lip curled derisively, then his eyes brightened. 'But Robin Hood! There was a great English-man. Or Richard the Lionheart! A great king, a marvellous man. I am particularly fond of the novels of Sir Walter Scott. And Jack London, an American, of course. Is Jack London much read in England?'

'Well, a bit, I think, yes.'

'*The Call of the Wild! White Fang!* Wonderful books! The moun-tains! The snow! Hunting! Is there much hunting in England?'

'Well, you cannot just go and shoot whatever you want,' I replied, 'besides there is not much to shoot: rabbits, pigeons, a few deer in Scotland. Although they hunt deer on horseback with dogs near where I live.'

Bakar, who had been looking more and more depressed, became suddenly alert. 'Ah! Like wild boar. That is excellent hunting.'

'No, I am afraid we have no wild boar.'

'No wild boar! But I am sure there were wild boar in Robin Hood.'

'Well, he must have had the last of them. No boars, no bears, no wolves.' There was a stir in the room. The Khevsurs rustled in disbelief.

'But in the mountains?' Bakar continued. 'There must be wolves in the mountains.'

'I am afraid that our highest mountain is in Scotland and, even there, there are no wolves. And it is only one and a half thousand metres.'

The Khevsurs laughed and shook their heads. What a sorry place, they seemed to say, with no bears, no boars, no mountains.

Bakar and Ismael were involved in a major cattle deal, trying to buy up some two hundred head, more if they could get them, to drive over the mountains to Chechnya where they would fetch a good price. The road through from Itoum-Kale had now been built to within five miles of the Georgian border and was planned, even-tually, to push all the way to Shatili. Just a little more road, a bridge, and it would be complete. President Dudaev and the Chechen government, and a shadowy group of Chechen businessmen, were proposing to pay for the continuation of the road in Georgia itself, but it was difficult work and the hard winters destroyed the road as it was being built. It needed continuous repair. This route through Georgia had become increasingly important to the Chechens since the first Russo-Chechen war of the 1990s and they wanted to be able to avoid passing through the lands under Russian control which surrounded them to the east, west and north. Georgia was vital to them. Of course, the Russians did not like this at all and since the second Chechen War the passes are heavily guarded by Russian troops and the Georgians keep a wary eye on them. During the hostilities of 1999 bombs from Russian planes fell on Georgian soil – around Omalo, in fact, from where we started in Tusheti, injuring three villagers, and again by Mutso where three Mi-8 helicopters not only dropped anti-personnel mines but opened fire, though, thankfully, there were no casualities. The Russians claim that they made an unfortunate mistake but the Georgians are not so sure – more of a threat and a warning, they say. Most feel that the Russians are poised, ready, waiting for some excuse to interfere blatantly in Georgian affairs, as they have elsewhere throughout the old Soviet Union. The Russians have made a particular point of accusing the Georgian government of harbouring terrorists, though the Georgian government insists that only women and children, the old and the sick, have been let through. In fact, we know that some bands of Chechen guerrillas were, and still are, able to make use of the passes over the mountains, not just for escaping from Chechnya but also in order to get back in and continue their struggle. Local people know, of course, though they might not say, but there is also evidence from a very remarkable and courageous Russian journalist, Andrei Babitsky, who reported from Chechnya throughout the war till caught in a vicious Russian trap and ruthlessly murdered. He accompanied a group of Chechens from Georgia across the mountains to Grozny, and stayed with them in the battles that followed, broadcasting regularly back to Moscow. The situation here is still incredibly tense. Shortly after I thought I had finished this book, in August 2002, the Russians bombed the mountain villages of Georgia again, killing numbers of innocent people, going after Chechens hiding in the Pankisi Gorge, not very far from Omalo. The ancient Kist communities in the Pankisi have provided refuge for many Chechens, seven thousand at one estimate, though how they all fit there is a mystery. There are also numbers of guerrillas, maybe 500, maybe 2,000, including some Arabs. The gorge has lately become notorious as a centre for drug smuggling, kidnapping and criminality with the woefully useless and sporadically corrupt Georgian army powerless to intervene there. Outbreaks of violence between the Kists or Chechens and local Georgians give ominous warnings for the future. And now the Americans have become involved.

Ismael and a close friend had bought a bulldozer and were working on the construction of the Shatili road. Unfortunately, his friend had been shot and killed the previous year. Each village along the way through Chechnya demanded some profit from the deal and someone, aggrieved and dissatisfied, had made plain his anger. The vendetta and its laws still obtain, just like the Kanon in Albania, and sooner or later this man, or his family, will pay for his deed. However, all agreed that revenge killings were no longer as common as they had once been. The Khevsurs said the last they could remember here was fifteen years ago. It was almost always possible to pay in goods rather than in blood: forty cows for the life of a man, perhaps fifteen cows and thirty kilos of cheese for a woman. They made their own laws here, the police never came, they were too frightened and nowhere nearly so well armed. A century ago Baddeley, sitting in Akhieli, had a similar conversation with his Khevsur host, though the value of human life seems to have plummeted in the intervening years.

'The figures given to me', he wrote, 'were these: 60 cows for a life: 15 cows for each ear cut off: 30 cows for an eye: 5 cows for a thumb, and 4,3,2,1 for the fingers successively.'

In fact there was an elaborate system of blood-price, called *siskhli* (simply, blood) codified and set down in charters during the early Middle Ages, which obtained throughout Georgia, though this was especially directed at the aristocracy. W. E. D. Allen quotes the example of a certain family, the Avshandadze, who, in the eleventh century, were able to exact a price, for the loss of one of their men, of five thousand pounds sterling plus 12 peasants, 12 white mules, 12 falcons, 12 running dogs, 12 stone falcons and some satin legs of boots. In other words the blood-price, among the aristocracy at least, was deliberately set to be prohibitive, to ruin the aggressor.

Bakar poured out more *chacha*. He began to speak of the many hunting trips he had made in Chechnya. I asked if that was how he had met Ismael, but Ismael was not a hunter, not of animals. They had met while fighting Russians. Bakar had lived in Grozny for three years, was there all through the first war and had fought alongside his Chechen friends.

'I have seen,' he said, looking at me intently, impressing his words upon me with his gaze, 'the Russians bombing villages, I have been in villages when they were bombed, I have seen Russian troops setting fire to women and children and killing them like cattle. I wish only death to Russians, all of them!' Everyone nodded.

'Shaitan!' said Ismael. 'Shaitan!'

Bakar's hatred was not unmixed with a kind of contemptuous compassion for the young Russian conscripts drafted into Chechnya. Most had no idea what they were doing and little more idea of where they were. They just wanted to get drunk and go home. Bakar talked of trading beer for ammunition – a crate would buy three thousand rounds for his Kalashnikov. Some time later I was told that Bakar never separated from his Kalashnikov because he had been so badly traumatised during the fighting. He could face neither crowds nor cities and had not been to Tbilisi since the war. Later still I heard another version: that he had been accused of rustling cattle and Tbilisi was too hot for him.

Many Georgians are very ambivalent about the Chechens: some look upon them as murderous bastards, others – particularly young men and mountain people like the Khevsurs – admire them greatly. Though there were and still are Chechens who curse their patriots for bringing such catastrophe crashing about their heads, many Georgians feel that the Chechens are fighting a just and necessary war. Their own independence they see as incomplete and precarious. There are still five large Russian military bases in Georgia, part of the price paid by Shevardnadze for the release of weaponry and equipment to help him end the civil war. Under the terms of the Tashkent agreement after the break-up of the Soviet Union, Georgia (and the other independent states) was supposed to get a share of Soviet military hardware. Of course, it did not until Shevardnadze was installed as president and came to some accommodation with

Russia. There are many who think of him as little more than a Russian stooge. They look across the border to Azerbaijan which managed, despite its own bloody conflict with Armenia in Karabakh, to expel all Russian troops and they see the Chechens resisting, vowing never to submit, and they feel unmanned. They suspect Shevardnadze of collusion and mutter about dogs and tricks and leopards and spots, remembering his years as President of Georgia when it was a Soviet Republic. They remember, too, his treatment of dissidents and his links with the KGB. On the other hand, there are others who admire him enormously: he plays the Russians at their own game, he gives with one hand and takes with the other, not for nothing is he called *tetri melia*, the Old White Fox. He has an international profile which has put Georgia on the map and he has given the people some hope, at least, of being able to build a civil society out of all the anarchy, though, sadly, many of my Georgian friends say that such hope, along with any faith in their president, is fast fading.

These Khevsurs' attitude towards their Chechen neighbours intrigued me, partly because it supported the idea of a common bond throughout the mountains, partly because ancient enmities seemed to play no part here, but also because more recent events seemed strangely unremarked. During the Abkhaz separatist conflict of '92, when the Abkhaz fought fiercely against Georgian hegemony in Abkhazia, Chechen volunteers had travelled across the mountains in their support. Many accounts of appalling acts of savagery, torture and mutilation perpetrated on the Georgian population particularly blamed the Chechen fighters. I asked Bakar what he felt about this. There was just a moment of uncomfortable silence.

'There are,' he explained, 'bad men everywhere. Besides, those men were mercenaries, suborned with Russian money. Again, it is the Russians who constantly interfere in our affairs, they are doing the same now in Daghestan, there will soon be war there as well. They will try again in Chechnya, I promise you that. Dudaev has apologised for the part the Chechens played in Abkhazia, it was a mistake.'

Though prophetic, this seemed rather less than complete. The Chechens and Abkhaz have historic links and the Chechens who fought were screaming for holy war. After the First World War there was a great scheme by which the Chechens and the Abkhaz, along with other North Caucasian peoples, were to be united in a Federation of Mountain Peoples, with its capital in Sukhumi. It was granted a moment of favourable consideration at Versailles in 1918, saw a glimpse of day in 1920 and was then promptly trampled underfoot by the Bolsheviks, along with the rest. Here Ismael chimed in. 'Yes, we are a peaceful people, we only want to live in peace with our neighbours.' How often had I heard that from all kinds of unlikely quarters? And then, 'It is the Russians backed by the Jews who cause these problems.'

I thought, oh God, not again, and most of my sympathy flew out the window to join the bears. There were mutterings of disagreement, possibly a polite reaction to my own reaction, possibly not. I turned to Ismael.

'What', I asked, 'about the British hostages? If you are such pleasant people why abduct a young couple working for charity in Grozny, people who only wished to help you.'

These two aid workers came from the West Country and were, by chance, relatives of good friends of mine. They had been held captive for eighteen months and were finally released in September 1998 after a deal involving a large ransom, paid, it is said, by the Russian millionaire businessman and politician Berezovsky. They had both been badly beaten and abused, Camilla Carr repeatedly raped though I did not know that at the time, of course. However, despite her trials, she still manages to have considerable sympathy for the plight of the Chechen people. Perhaps this was, as Ismael replied, just a case of 'bad men' again.

Grozny became known as the kidnap capital of the world and in the West the newspapers related the gory details: a Russian diplomat was abducted, then dumped, strangled, on the border between Chechnya and Ingusheti. Worst of all, and later still, in October 1998, four telecommunications engineers, three British, one New Zealander, there to help rebuild the shattered telephone system, were taken by a Chechen gang from their 'safe house' in Grozny. They never came home. They were all beheaded. It is now thought that this particular gang, unusual in refusing a large ransom (about 10 million dollars), were closely connected to the Taliban in Afghanistan, where numbers of Chechens seem to have fought, and to Osama bin Laden and the Al-Qaeda network. There was at least one Arab in the gang, though it was headed by a Chechen, Barayev, who was eventually gunned down in 2001. This was a group of Islamic extremists with a reputation for viciousness. They kept the hostages in a tiny cell, starved them, forced one, Rudi Petchey, a Russian speaker, to make a confessional video in which he said that he and his colleagues had been spying for the West, collecting information against Islamic groups in Chechnya. The executions are grisly enough left to the imagination but the Chechens filmed them, celebrating their barbarism. Other hostages, Russians, men from other Caucasian nations, who were held at the same time, were ransomed successfully: the murders of the engineers were a terrible declaration of intent and seem to have been a response to the American missile attacks on Osama bin Laden's bases in Afghanistan and Sudan after the first bombing of the World Trade Centre in 1998. Of course, the horror of 11 September 2001 and the subsequent war against the Taliban and Al-Qaeda have eclipsed these earlier events but they gave another clear indication of what to expect. However, it is difficult to know with the Chechens how far the murders were driven by their Islamic jihad and how far by their vicious greed; probably both. One of the Russian hostages, now living in Moscow, reports a conversation he had with Barayev in which he was told that 'our Arab friends' had given thirty million dollars, three times the original ransom demand, for the deaths of the Telecom engineers.

What is this when set against the terrible torments of the Chechens themselves? Perhaps not so great a crime in the great and terrible scale of crimes, but it does little for the Chechens' protestations of innocence, for the righteousness of their moral outrage. Of course if, as Bakar and Ismael insisted, everything was the fault of the Russians and the Russians wished to discredit the Chechens in the eyes of the world, examples of savagery would be well worth paying for, though to associate the Russians with the murders of the engineers seems too far-fetched. With so much rumour, misinformation, disinformation, who knows where the real truth lies in such circumstances. Only the plain facts of death and destruction seem utterly unambiguous. In Tbilisi I was offered further evidence of Russian skulduggery, more plots to implicate Chechens in murder and terrorism: Shevardnadze had just survived another assassination attempt. A group of terrorists had fired upon the President from across the River Mtkvari (Kura in Russian) while he was driving along in convoy on the opposite bank. Extraordinarily enough, they had, again, filmed themselves while doing it, the film seized from them, or deliberately left, as they fled the scene. The film was shown on national television: a missile streaking across the river, an explosion, the quick action of the driver and bodyguards, gunfire, chaos. The terrorists got away but they left behind one dead. On him were found Chechen papers. Who on earth, many asked with some justification, would go into such an operation carrying papers? It was another crude Russian attempt to blame a black-arse (a common term of abuse for Chechens, Ingush and their neighbours) and to make trouble between Georgia and Chechnya. The later events leading up to the second Chechen War, the bomb explosions in blocks of flats in downtown Moscow where more than three hundred innocent Russians died, were blamed on Chechen terrorists and used by the Russian government as an excuse for another invasion. These, too, seem not as they first appeared. There are strong suggestions of Russian intelligence involvement here and, indeed, very many Russians now believe that their own government is implicated. In fact, Berezovsky, the millionaire politician, once one of Putin's strongest supporters, now in exile and a wanted man, believes that Putin himself was at least aware of, if not directly responsible for, the Moscow bombings. Such an accusation seems insane but in the present climate such mutterings are commonplace. Certainly, until the Russians take a very different approach to their problems with Chechnya such bombings, massacres, torments will continue.

Bakar and Ismael suggested that Chris and I should come with them into Chechnya. We could meet President Dudaev, we could meet Basayev (a military commander I had mentioned), no problem, they knew them well. When? Sometime soon, as soon as they had bought their cattle. We would all go together. I did, later, go into Chechnya with Bakar but only into the emptiness of the mountains and never met Basayev, though I should have liked to. He had appeared as a fearless guerrilla leader during the first Chechen War and in a rather roundabout way I had come to know something of his story. In 1996 I had edited a book about the extraordinary Russian faith-healer, Anatoly Kashpirovsky. At the height of his fame, at his television healing sessions, he attracted huge audiences of thirty million and he entranced his adoring, supplicating public at mass meetings held in football stadiums throughout the Soviet Union. He was chased out of Tbilisi, however, when set upon by angry Georgian priests and an assembled audience at a session in the Georgian State Television studio. He just managed to escape by a back door but the whole fracas was broadcast on Georgian television. He had made some less than tactful remarks in relation to the savagery meted out by Russian troops at a peaceful demonstration in central Tbilisi on 9 April 1989, just a few days before he had arrived, and a week or so before I first came to Georgia. Twenty people, mostly young women, had been killed and the entire nation was in mourning and very, very angry. Kashpirovsky said that he believed that the citizens of Tbilisi were suffering from mass hysteria, that there was a psychic epidemic.

Always outspoken and never an intelligent guardian of his own fame, Kashpirovsky had become involved with the right-wing madman Vladimir Zhirinovsky and his party; he split from him, returned, and left again, partly in an excess of temperament and partly, I believe, because of a growing revulsion at Zhirinovsky's ferocious and Fascist nationalism. However, he did enter the Duma on Zhirinovsky's party ticket and while he was there, on 15 June 1995, Chechen commandos under the leadership of Shamyl Basayev, in perhaps his most famous exploit, crossed into southern Russia and stormed the town of Budyonnovsk. They herded together more than two thousand hostages and locked them up in the local hospital, threatening to kill the lot unless Russia cleared out of Chechnya and ended the war. A team of crack troops was sent in to storm the building and at least 150 civilians were killed, most in the crossfire but some deliberately by the Chechens, before the Russians were forced to disengage. Basayev personally executed five Russian airforce officers, though no civilians. He had suffered horribly during the Chechen War, losing his wife, his six children and his two brothers to a Russian bomb.

Pavel Grachev, who had been in charge of the attack, was, amazingly enough, about to order a second assault when Viktor Chernomyrdin, acting president while Boris Yeltsin was away at a summit in Canada, managed to restrain him and during this respite Kashpirovsky jumped on a plane. He successfully arranged a meeting with Basayev who, it turned out, was a fan of his television seances. Other deputies from the Duma were also there, though unable to gain an audience with the Chechen commander. They had bravely arranged themselves as a human shield between the troops and the hospital, fearful that the soldiers would be given orders to attack once more. Desperate hostages waved white towels from the windows begging the Russian troops to hold their fire; tense Alpha Group commandos surrounded the hospital, arms at the ready; bullets whistled overhead sporadically. Kashpirovsky was allowed into the hospital and later described what he saw:

'Along the walls of the corridors, in two or three rows, a great crowd was standing or lying, perhaps three thousand people. In the service area were naked dead bodies swimming in pools of blood. There were many corpses in the wards as well; children without clothing were hiding under the beds, many were wounded. A terrible sight.'

Kashpirovsky was taken through to see Basayev and spent more than seven hours with him, successfully persuading the Chechen to release some hostages and also to scale down the extent of his demands. Eventually they received news that Chernomyrdin had agreed to negotiate on this basis and all the hostages were allowed to go. The extent to which Kashpirovsky was instrumental in this is controversial; he claims a pivotal role, many argue that he merely tried to grab the limelight. Rumours that Kashpirovsky had put Basayev under a hypnotic spell added a certain paranormal spice to the whole event. The Chechen commander managed to return home with his soldiers and lived on to fight again.

This was the man, then, that Chris and I had been invited to meet. Whether or not we would have returned from the meeting is open to question, though Bakar and Ismael insisted that the Chechens would give, in guarantee of our safety, two sons of prominent citizens to the Khevsurs in Shatili. Such was the usual practice. As we finished the *chacha* and said good night, anything seemed possible. Trying to sleep, I found that all the familiar, restful furniture of my mind had been removed and in its stead hordes of Georgians, Chechens and Russians charged around and would not settle down. My thoughts were fractured, incomplete. Many Chechens and some Georgians have a simple view: they hate the Russians and little more can be said. Both peoples have just cause, the Chechens particularly: none forget the Chechen Genocide of 23 February 1944 when Stalin deported almost the entire population to Central Asia on the spurious grounds that they were Nazi collaborators. Half of them died on the way. The estimated death toll from the Russian bombardment of Grozny in November 1994 is 50,000. Every family in the land has been shattered. But the Russians have always had a paradoxical relationship with their colonies in the Caucasus. Now, of course, Russian propaganda portrays the Chechens and others as terrorists or brutal mafiosi but historically the Russian view of the Caucasus has always been a strange mixture of *realpolitik* and romance. The story of Russian expansion southwards during the eighteenth and nineteenth centuries has been brilliantly told by John Baddeley in *The Russian Conquest of the Caucasus*: the steady and inexorable movement of Cossacks to the Terek River; the establishment of the Terek and the Lesghian lines; the building of Vladikavkaz (Ruler of the Caucasus) and of Grozny (The Terrible); the annexation of Georgia; the hard war in the mountains that lasted forty years; the final capture of Imam Shamyl at Gounib. For the Cossacks, so often such a vile bunch, the laws and customs of the mountains were agreeable and they often adopted the ways of the local people, intermarried and had a grudging respect for their foes as they cut them down. For the ordinary Russian soldier the reality of the Caucasus was often harsh: bad rations, disease, constant fear of ambush, incompetent leadership. But for the young officers from St Petersburg and Moscow, the Caucasus represented escape, opportunity, freedom and adventure. It was their 'Wild West', though this is more usually said of Siberia; perhaps 'Wild South' would be better. Indeed, the Caucasus was to the Russians what the Wild West was to the Americans and although there is not quite the Russian equivalent of the Hollywood Western (though the *Prisoner of the Caucasus*, directed by Sergei Bodrov is a contemporary masterpiece), there is no equivalent in American literature of Tolstoy's *Tales* or Lermontov's *Hero of Our Time*. The effect of such a geographically tiny area on the Russian imagination during the early years of the nineteenth century was profound and gave rise to a whole genre of literature, Russian 'Caucasica', both in poetry and prose, and almost to a special type of sensibility. It was Pushkin's *Caucasian Prisoner* that seems to have started Lermontov on his own poetic career and the younger poet, who had spent his summer holidays in the Caucasus as a child, wrote about the mountains and their people throughout his short, eventful life. As a young officer he was arrested and sent to the Caucasus for his passionate elegy on Pushkin's death – *Death of a Poet* – in which his references to the 'hungry crowd that swarms about the throne, Butchers of freedom, of genius and glory' made certain of his exile. In fact, nothing could have been more congenial to him but, though he bravely lead a troop of sharpshooters in fierce engagements against the Chechens, he was deeply critical of Russian aggression and expressed nothing but sympathy, even love, for the place and its people. Indeed, Lermontov has given rise to his own tourist industry and Russians now flock to Pyatigorsk to feel, by such proximity, the thrill of his death, so strangely echoing the death of his *Hero*'s unfortunate victim, Grushnitsky, fighting a duel in the Caucasus. Here was the Russian Byron, heir to Pushkin, writing odes to Mount Kazbek, gloriously talented, passionate and wild, dying young.

I had visited Pyatigorsk in the great and grim old days of Intourism and was marched about, with a small, charming and eccentric band of English, by an earnest Russian guide called Victor who found our endemic frivolity difficult to handle. He took us, almost by force, to see Lermontov's monument, a terribly fake Aeolian harp set in concrete, and failed to understand our merriment on finding that the distinctly unmelodious sounds that issued forth came from a hidden tape recorder.

'Now,' he said, 'you must get your cameras ready.' No one had a camera. 'The architects have placed in this pagoda, blablabla, Lermontov blablabla. You must be aware . . .' Lermontov poems, more Lermontov. '. . . and here you see the Upper Pushkin Baths and there the Lower, designed by Italian architects and especially popular with our women patients.'

'Why?'

'Er, er, here in this famous city we have more than 150,000 visitors each year.' Mud baths, hot springs, Lermontov, a Congress of Mountainous Women from the Caucasus to celebrate Lermontov. More Lermontov. The poor poet had simply become part of the Wild Caucasus package deal.

Tolstoy, brilliant, profound, and, like Lermontov, himself a soldier in the Caucasus as a young man, has much of interest to say on the subject of Russian colonialism here. He was entirely aware of the schizophrenic attitude of his countrymen towards the mountains and their people: love them and kill them, honour them and suppress them. He saw the fiction in the romance and in *The Cossacks* and *Hadji Murat* describes the strong attraction, the admiration, that the Caucasus and the mountain tribes inspired, even as they were being systematically destroyed. 'The mountains, the mountains, the mountains!' murmurs Olenin in *The Cossacks*, and Tolstoy writes that they 'permeated his every thought, his every feeling'. As Olenin approaches the mountains from Moscow he dreams of his future:

Everything was hazy and confused but the lure of fame and the threat of danger made that future interesting. Now, with unprecedented courage and a strength that astounded everybody, he was slaying and subduing an innumerable host of hillsmen; now he was himself a hillsman and was fighting on their side for independence from Russian dominion . . . he imagined fair Circassians and himself, crowned with glory, returning to Russia with an appointment as aide-de-camp to the Emperor, and a lovely wife.

Olenin eventually decides that he really is in love and will stay in the Caucasus with a young Cossack girl, far from the temptations of society, living his life in accordance with the laws of nature. But that, too, is a dream and finally he leaves for ever and returns to his proper home.

Tolstoy was not writing history, of course, but in *Hadji Murat* he does tell a true story. The facts can be found in Baddeley. Hadji Murat was Imam Shamyl's most trusted lieutenant and fought by his side against the Russians with great courage. However, they quarrelled and Hadji Murat went over to the Russians. Then, desperate about his wife and children who were held by Shamyl, he tried to escape and free them. He was hunted down by the Russians and their allies and, in an heroic last stand with his little band of faithful followers, was eventually killed. Tolstoy starts his story with a charming analogy. He is reminded of the tale of Hadji Murat one summer's day when out walking through the fields towards his home. He has been picking flowers. He sees a 'wonderful crimson thistle in full bloom', called 'the Tartar Thistle' and decides to pick it:

> However this was no easy matter: it was not just that the stalk pricked me at every turn, even through the handkerchief I had wrapped round my hand; it was so terribly tough that I was five minutes struggling with it, breaking through the fibres one by one. When at last I succeeded in plucking the flower the stalk was in shreds and the flower itself no longer seemed as fresh and beautiful as before. And apart from that it was too crude and clumsy to go with the delicate flowers I had in my bunch. I was sorry that I had needlessly destroyed a flower which had been fine where it was, and threw it away. But what strength and vigour, I thought, recalling the effort it had cost me to pluck it. How stoutly it defended itself, and how dearly it sold its life.

Looming behind all the excitement and action of the story is the figure of Tsar Nicholas, incompetent, immoral and utterly deranged by power (and certain contemporary parallels spring to mind), who, unforgettably, when agitated 'turned his mind to a subject which never failed to soothe him – his own greatness'. There are many other wonderful portraits of historical figures: Shamyl, as absolute an autocrat as the Tsar; Vorontsov, commander-in-chief of the Caucasus and Hadji Murat himself, brave, pious, thoughtful and sober, the immaculate warrior. The almost universal admiration for Hadji Murat among the Russian soldiers is best exemplified by the character of Butler (not, I think, an historical figure) who is 'captivated by the poetry of the peculiar, vigorous life led by the mountaineers. He got himself a jacket, cherkeska and leggings and he felt he was a mountaineer too, living the same life as these people.' Balanced against this romance is Tolstoy's clear and unflinching perception of the obverse reality it masked:

The emotion felt by every Chechen, old and young alike, was stronger than hatred, it was a refusal to recognise these Russian dogs as men at all, and a feeling of such disgust, revulsion and bewilderment at the senseless cruelty of these creatures that the urge to destroy them – like the urge to destroy rats, venomous spiders or wolves – was an instinct as natural as self preservation.

And Tolstoy goes on to analyse the dilemma facing the Chechens in 1840, exactly as it does today:

The villagers were faced with a choice: either to remain as before and by terrible exertions restore all that had been created with such labour and so easily and senselessly destroyed, while every minute expecting a repetition of the same thing, or they could act contrary to the law of their religion and, despite the revulsion and the scorn they felt for the Russians, submit to them.

Nothing finer nor more apposite has been written on the bombing of Grozny and the systematic destruction of Chechen towns and villages in the campaigns of the 1990s.

The Russian relationship with Georgia is, perhaps, more complex.

When John Steinbeck wrote his *Russian Journal,* just after the Second World War, he devoted a marvellous chapter to a brief visit he paid to Georgia, where, utterly exhausted and overwhelmed by Georgian hospitality, he produced one of the funniest and most exact accounts of what it is to be a foreign guest in that country. It could be said that in some respects he fell for the Georgian cliché, but still he reports what he saw and heard. He starts his chapter thus:

> Wherever we had been in Russia, in Moscow, in the Ukraine, in Stalingrad, the magical name of Georgia came up constantly. People who had never been there, and who possibly never could go there, spoke of Georgia with a kind of longing and a great admiration. They spoke of Georgians as supermen, as great drinkers, great dancers, great musicians, great workers and lovers. And they spoke of the country in the Caucasus and around the Black Sea as a kind of second heaven. Indeed, we began to believe that most Russians hope that if they live very good and virtuous lives, they will go not to heaven, but to Georgia, when they die.

There existed a peculiar inversion of the relationship between coloniser and colonised: a sense, certainly during the Soviet years, that however bad life might be in Georgia and for Georgians, it was probably far worse for most Russians in Russia. After the devastation of the Second World War many Ukrainian and Russian children were taken in and looked after by Georgian families. Many quite modest Georgian families had Russian maids, nurses and nannies; impossible to imagine such a thing, for example, in British India. Who, then, was colonising whom? All the peoples of the former Soviet Union were sustained by many jokes, especially the Russians themselves, most of them not terribly funny to a foreign sense of humour, but context is everything. One famous Russian comedian would move his audience to helpless hysteria by simply and slowly reading out a list of recipes. Of course, none of the ingredients was obtainable. In Georgia there were and are many jokes and one particular friend of mine is a great store of these. Most I forget but one I remember tells of two Georgian men making love to two Russian women in adjacent rooms. It is a few days before Georgia is to declare its independence. In the middle of his rapture one Georgian shouts out to the other, 'Must we really give up all this?' There was always a sense that the Russians were there to be had.

The Georgians, too, have a tremendous and visible culture: their Christianity, their architecture, their literature, their existence as a nation are all far more ancient than their large Russian neighbour's, with strong links that stretch back to ancient Greece and the empires of Persia. Tbilisi is eight hundred years older than Moscow and Tbilisi is the 'new' capital city! The old capital of Mtskheta, not far up the road, is more ancient still. There is a psychological strength that comes from such a history, such continuity, such coherence in the face of overwhelming odds. Not least among the singular facts about Georgia is that it survives at all. Fought over by the great empires of Romans, Persians, Byzantines, Arabs, Khazars, Turks and Mongols, harried by Avars, Lesghians and Chechens, torn by internecine strife, much of Georgia's history till the nineteenth century is a complicated pottage of endless war, alliance and fragmentation as the country broke into kingdoms and principalities, some joining with one power, some with another, most fighting each other in a desperate attempt to ride on whatever great geopolitical tide happened to be flowing at the time. If Georgia, or something vaguely like it, has existed for about 2,300 years – beginnings are always inchoate and everyone argues about them – then it has only been united for about four hundred of them. At the end of the eighteenth century, despite the heroic efforts of King Irakli Bagrationi (the 'Hercule' of Frederick the Great's famous remark: 'Moi en Europe, et en Asie l'invincible Hercule.'), the Turks and a briefly re-emergent Persia were carving their way through Georgia again. Poor Tbilisi was sacked and ravaged once more. In a desperate plight, Irakli, at the treaty of Georgievsk in 1783, placed the Georgian kingdoms of Kartli and Kakheti under the suzerainty of Catherine the Great of Russia, and in 1801 they were incorporated into the Russian empire. The Bagratid princes, who had reigned in Georgia for a thousand years and could claim the longest lineage of any ruling house in the world (as well as direct descent from the biblical King David!) were led off into exile in Russia – certainly not part of the treaty – though not before Princess Maria Bagrationi had first killed, with a dagger she had concealed among her skirts, the Russian general sent to escort her out of Tbilisi. Georgia had been saved and taken in one gesture and Russia became, at the same time, friend and enemy, saviour and oppressor.

Georgians bitterly complain that the loss of their independence and sovereignty was not supposed to have been part of the deal. The treaty promised to uphold the throne and to treat Georgia as a protectorate. However, in reality it is difficult to see what else they could have expected, especially in view of the fervent appeals sent to Tsar Paul by King Giorgi (Irakli's successor) begging him to take under his wing the Georgian crown. Tsitsianoff, the general in charge of the Caucasus, a Georgian whose family had lived in Russia for two generations, was convinced of the utter necessity of bringing Georgia into the Russian fold if it were to survive. A man of astonishing abilities, he did more in his few years of governor-ship to unite Georgia and bring the warring mountain tribes to heel than had been achieved by centuries of struggle.

Whatever its justification, the effects of Russian rule were, and still are, profound. For the first time in four hundred years, by 1810 – with the further incorporation of Imeretia, Gouria, Mingrelia and Abkhazia into Russia – Georgia, though split into two Russian Gubernias, was more or less united. At first there were outbreaks of rebellion and revolt, usually over issues of taxation and forced labour, some extremely violent and serious, though soon quashed, but in general the nineteenth century was perhaps one of the most peaceful periods in Georgian history. Of course, Georgian soldiers fought and distinguished themselves in the imperial armies and it is true that the Turks caused some problems in the south of the country, but in much of Georgia there was for the first time in centuries little war, not a lot of ravaging nor laying waste, not even much pillage. This was remarkable in a nation whose capital was said to have been devastated thirty-two times. Compare this with the history of Paris or London. I remember walking with a Georgian friend of mine up a little hill in Somerset by my house and pointing to the field where the last battle fought on English soil took place,

Refugees from Karabakh, Mingechevir.

The bad boy's disco, Ilisu.

The author and Fasil, walking to the hammam.

Akhmed, his brother and his mother, Ilisu.

Kvavlo, Tusheti.

Towers, Tusheti.

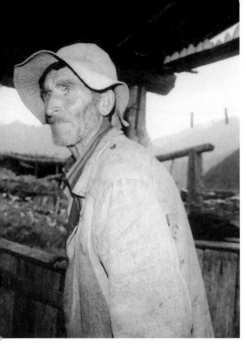

(*Above*) Making cheese, Diklo.
(*Below*) Drinking wine, Diklo.
(*Facing page, above and below*) Shatili.

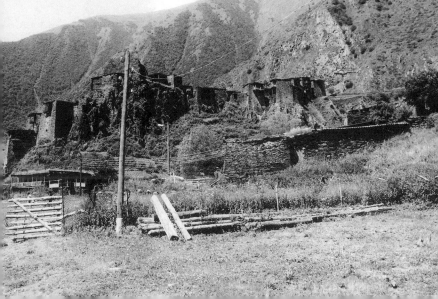

Mindi Chincharaouli.

Making bread, Dartlo.

Socks, Shatili.

Eldar, Akhieli.

Crossing the Dzhuta Pass.

even then a rebellion not an invasion and this in 1685. He was staggered by the thought that we might have fought abroad, suffered bombardment from the air, but that for many hundreds of years no foreign armies had rampaged across the land.

Under Russian 'protection' there was a great cultural renaissance in Georgia. Vorontsov, the viceroy, opened a Russian theatre in Tbilisi and a public library, invited Italian opera companies to perform Rossini and Donizetti. Young Georgians, travelling to university in Moscow and St Petersburg, looked out upon Europe, cut off from them since Constantinople had fallen to the Turks in 1453 and the Byzantine empire had crumbled away. They returned to reinvigorate Georgia, to bring a new sense, paradoxically, of Georgian nationhood, to reinforce the culture and the language. Almost all the great poets and writers of nineteenth-century Georgia made this journey. A new Georgian consciousness was born and a new intelligentsia rose from the experience of Russian rule. These writers and thinkers were self-consciously called the '*tergdaleulni*', 'those who have drunk of the Terek', those who had crossed over the River Terek in the north of Georgia and made their way into Russia. In Ilia Chavchavadze's *Notes of a Journey from Vladikavkaz to Tiflis*, the great poet describes his feelings on returning to Georgia after four years studying in St Petersburg. He, more than anyone, led this new awakening of the Georgian spirit and was called, by his English translator, Oliver Wardrop, 'the most remarkable man that Georgia possesses.' Resting in the posthouse at Lars, just a few miles north of Kazbegi, poised to return to his native land, he worries how his countrymen will receive him, a stranger now, and thinks back on the time he has spent away:

These four years are life's foundation, life's head waters, the hair-like bridge thrown between light and darkness. But not for all! Only for him who has gone to Russia to exercise his intelligence, to give his brain and his heart work, to move forward.

Then, a complete nincompoop of a Russian soldier comes in, cadges tea and cigarettes and, in a wonderfully funny series of dialogues, Chavchavadze sets forth the dreadful obtuseness of colonial condescension:

'Your country is not civilised, to use learned language, that is to say in the vulgar tongue it is uncivilised, do you understand?'

'Very clearly.'

'There, I told you I would simplify the learned language so that you would understand. Now I will begin from this: your country is not enlightened, that is, it is unenlightened. This tea is from Moscow?'

'No, I bought it in Stavropol.'

'It is all the same. Now let us begin as I said before with the fact that your country is not enlightened, which means that your country is dark. Do you understand?'

'Yes, quite well.'

'Now when we begin by saying that your country is not enlightened it is as if we said there is no light in it. I will explain this by an example: imagine a dark room . . .'

The conversation gets more and more marvellously absurd; it illustrates many of the contradictions and tensions inherent in the relationship between the two countries.

Without doubt, Georgia owes Russia a debt. Most would say that this has long since been cancelled, though Georgians remain as passionate about Russian culture, literature, music and art as the Russians themselves. They like the links, they just do not enjoy the bondage. As a famous line from Baratashvili's *The Fate of Georgia (bedi kartlisa)* has it: '*ra khelhqris pativs nazi bulbuli, galiashia datqvevebuli?*' – 'What pleasure does the tender nightingale receive from the honour of its cage?'

CHAPTER 4

KHEVSURETI CONTINUED

> Titan! To whose immortal eyes
> The sufferings of mortality,
> Seen in their sad reality,
> Were not as things that gods despise;
> What was thy pity's recompense?
> A silent suffering, and intense;
> The rock, the vulture, and the chain . . .

> *Prometheus*, Lord Byron

How we crossed the Dzhuta Pass
and came to Mount Kazbek

I awoke late the next morning to find Chris sitting on a bear on the balcony, talking to two donkeys below. He was trying to persuade them to pick up his socks which had blown away in the night. As neither he nor I knew the Georgian for sock the conversation was hopeless. We looked out across the river upon forested slopes. Bakar was heading up through the trees with his Kalashnikov towards a light sprinkling of tiny cows high on the hills above.

An elegant young woman from next door came to visit with her little daughter and invited us for a cup of tea. In her home were a bed, a table, a couple of chairs, a few clothes hanging from hooks on the wall, little else. She had fewer personal possessions than Chris and I carried in our packs. However, the Mindis had given her the fabulous fowl of the previous evening and she produced a great bowl of the most marvellous soup. The boys arrived (they

had been visiting cousins) and we all set to in a highly compli-
mentary fashion.

Later we walked down through the village and crossed the river,
past a small barracks with a few Georgian soldiers sitting about
decoratively, and inspected the old, ruined fort of Queen Tamar
(naturally). It was difficult to get up to and impossible to get in,
the doorway high above the ground. Even the Mindis could not
manage the assault without a ladder. Guarding the approach along
the river, its old stones cast grim shadows in the sunshine. Then a
sudden and tremendous clattering in the sky announced the arrival
of a huge yellow helicopter which landed on the football pitch and
disgorged an eminent Georgian gerontologist, his pretty handmaiden and a Japanese television crew. This was by far the strangest
sight I had seen in Khevsureti. The Japanese raced about in sharp
white shorts and set up cameras in front of a bemused but dignified old man who looked a hearty seventy but was, apparently, well
over one hundred. The Georgians have long been famous for their
centenarians and like other mountain people such as the Hunzas
they have a reputation for vigour in old age; the Japanese were
making a film about longevity and were hunting up ancient
Georgians across the territory. They had just come hotfoot from
Abkhazia which used to boast a substantial and famous choir
consisting entirely of men over one hundred. They had been on
the track of the Oldest Man in the World. Unfortunately, they told
me, he had died the very night they arrived.

Meanwhile the pretty handmaiden had been carried off, to her
great and evident delight, by a company of Khevsur knights and
placed upon a horse which promptly bolted along the river's edge
and threw her. This occasioned such outpourings of tenderness
from her escorts that her delight was greatly multiplied and she
was soon quite fetchingly restored. Big Mindi had said that he
would have to leave us and the opportunity presented by the helicopter and the handmaiden was too good to miss, so that evening
we said a warm farewell and watched him grinning wildly and
waving as he disappeared into the sky above Shatili, bound for
Tbilisi, home and other joys.

*

As the helicopter's clatter faded we turned and headed back down our lane. The house beyond ours was owned by an architect from Tbilisi, another Chincharaouli (almost everyone in Shatili is a Chincharaouli). He had many elaborate plans to turn his place into a guest-house for foreign visitors, walkers and climbers; I had, in fact, seen it advertised with staggering optimism in a small brochure. He had been trying to get to grips with things but they had eluded him, in that way things have. He had started drinking the week before and simply not managed to stop. His friends, a well-known artist and a lorry driver who had been trying to leave for days, were in a similar condition. The house had quite obviously just been ransacked and looted. As his friends poured the *chacha*, the nice architect swayed about picking things up, shaking his head mournfully and putting them down again. The artist was a great fisherman and had caught some fine trout but the whole prospect of preparation and cooking was far too much for them. The architect found a frying pan, struggled with it for a moment, then sat down in dismay, his kind face troubled. He spoke good English but most of it got caught at the back of his throat.

'I caghnnt, I carghghnnt, I can't sleep,' he said. 'That's the problem. Ghghghghohoho.'

'Goats?' I asked.

'No! No! It's the ghosts. Too many ghosts.'

'Oh dear,' I said and looked at Chris who was nodding his head in sympathy and understanding.

'That must be, er, difficult,' I said. 'Are there many ghosts here?'

'Oh many, many ghosts. Many ghosts.' And he took another drink to steady himself. I suggested that he might just be suffering from a bit of a hangover but he shook his head. No, it was not *nabacchusevi*, the wonderful Georgian word for hangover, it was ghosts.

I woke at six the next morning, not a ghost all night, to sounds of bloody revolution, gunfire and cries from the lane outside. I struggled into my trousers, ran to the door and was immediately surrounded. Beka, Levan and Vasca had arrived, driving through the night from Tbilisi. It was time for a party. Cheeses and salamis were cut and laid along the low wall outside our semi and we all stood in the lane, eating and talking and drinking from the jug of *chacha* that someone had inevitably produced. Beka looked shattered and was struggling manfully with the *chacha* pressed upon him; not only had he driven up through the night in his tough but battered four-wheel drive Niva (a tortuous journey of seven or eight hours, demanding even in daylight) but about ten miles outside Shatili the car had stuck fast in an avalanche of snow and they had abandoned it and walked. Thoughtfully they had carried up not only food, rifles and essential gear but also extra supplies for us: coffee, chocolate, batteries, tins of fish. I was amazed to see them, for though they had all wanted to join us at some stage on our journey, the World Cup was still being fought out and these three were crazy football fanatics who worshipped regularly at the shrines of Real Madrid and Manchester United. The tension between their generous instinct to help us along our path and their desire to stay in Tbilisi to watch the semi-finals on TV had been dreadful, painful to see when we were discussing our plans with them, but eventually they just could not bear the thought of Chris and I wandering lonely through the mountains and had come up to Shatili to make sure that we were all right. They disguised this as best they could by insisting that they were all going off to hunt bear which, of course, they never got around to, though they were splendidly attired in camouflage suits fit to fool any wandering bear and contrasting strangely with the traditional dress (T-shirts and jeans) of our Khevsur hosts. We all chattered at once, talking of the mountains, the stuff of our journey since we had left them in Tbilisi, and when Mindi recounted our descent of the Atsunta Pass, with many unintelligible embellishments, everyone clapped us on the back and fired their rifles in the air, shouting '*lomi! lomi!*', an endearing and encouraging epithet which young Georgian men use in praise of each other meaning, simply, 'lion'. Chris was so moved by this that he accidentally drank the *chacha* he had been trying to avoid and looked even more bemused than he had when he first stumbled forth into the morning, hesitating by the door of the semi like some ancient citizen unable to decide between one pint or two.

We finished off the cheese, the sausage, the *chacha* and wandered in a throng along the lane, across the helicopter-football-field and down through the narrow winding track between the towers, to a necessary breakfast on the veranda of Dato's hut by the Argoun. Girls appeared with food and *chacha*; omelettes arrived and bread and smetana and meats. Children were passed around. It soon became obvious that this was not the day to leave Shatili. We sat and drank and ate and talked and Beka made gentle enquiries after horses and the whereabouts of bears and then settled again, though I became more and more confused as he explained the plan to me, partly because, while speaking excellent English, he pronounced bears and beers in exactly the same way:

'No, no, thank you, I really don't need any beer.'

'Of course, but we will find beers, there are many here.'

'Really? Will they be cold?'

'Cold? No! They are used to it and they have very thick hairs.'

We spent much of the day arguing about my proposed route. I wanted to head due west to Akhieli, to see what had happened to the village that Baddeley had visited. Were the birthing rooms still there? How did life now compare to life in 1900? And then I wanted to go again due west to Kazbegi. You could draw an almost straight line between the three villages and this seemed to me rather tempting. It was about forty-five miles from Shatili via Akhieli to Kazbegi as the crow flies, though many more on the ground: mountains, rivers and glaciers got in the way and had to be crossed or circumvented and a succession of deep gorges and high ridges lay along the path. And this seemed to be the problem. Mindi, Beka, Dato and the rest all conspired against me and insisted that the best way lay along the road to the south and then across country to the west, missing out Akhieli altogether. Of course, I had no idea what lay ahead but I strongly suspected that neither did they, certainly Mindi had not done the journey before and had little idea where we were going, though, as he said, what was the point in having a guide if you don't go where he guides you? I explained about Baddeley and the birthing rooms but everyone agreed that this was terribly tedious, not worth the bother and that I could see birthing rooms in Shatili: here they had simply shut the women in the base of the towers and lowered food down to them on a rope. Yes, they were completely unattended and no, no one could go near them for forty days. Lurking in the back of the conversation I picked up fleeting references to lorries and caught a definite whiff of hijack in the air. After all, why walk if you could get a lift?

The men from Tbilisi extolled the purity of mountain life as the jug went round and round, and mourned the passing that they all foresaw, but they were by no means blind: boredom and drink lay in wait for many of the young men who seemed to make up the great proportion of Shatili's inhabitants, escaping from unemployment and the Mafia gangs in the cities to the ancestral homeland where they could, at least, subsist. But then boredom and drink affects young men everywhere and Shatili seemed no worse than many other places. At times I felt that the ritual drinking of the Georgians mitigated against excess, on other occasions it seemed to be little more than an excuse for it. Both could be enjoyable or irritating according to one's mood, the company, the situation. But the purity that Beka and Vasca referred to was more that despite the years of Russian and Communist rule and interference, the Khevsurs had managed to avoid the corruption of the plains and were not yet subject to the Coca-Cola culture that would surely, one day, come. A simple, good life was still to be had in Khevsureti, particularly if you were young and fit. Naturally, most people also wanted a decent road, better communications, some money, something to do, but they were also deeply conscious of their home as special and remote, and so were both worried by and eager for progress. And this is not a new self-consciousness: there is an extraordinary train line that stops some way below Shatili, part of a projected trans-Caucasian route that was planned to run from Tbilisi through the mountains to Pyatigorsk or Vladivkavaz. It was abandoned years ago after the Khevsurs and the Tush brought work on the line to a standstill, objecting to the cultural and environmental pollution that the railway would bring.

Late in the afternoon Dato decided to slaughter a beast. Our presence demanded celebration. In truth it was Beka's presence that was being honoured, for he was an important benefactor to the village. Two little boys were dispatched and returned after a short time dragging a small calf through the gathering dusk to the edge of our veranda. They were all roughly the same height, the calf no more than two or three weeks old. We tried to protest that such a magnanimous gesture was really unnecessary but Dato would have none of it and, pulling out his knife, walked over to the calf and cut its throat. The little creature sank to the ground and gently keeled over. A bowl was pushed under to catch the blood and then, the head severed and left lying on the grass, tongue protruding slightly from the mouth, its body was hung between a couple of fence posts and skinned, deftly and expertly. The men set to and within moments the carcass was butchered neatly, the organs taken off for soup, the best meat cut into cubes for shashlik. As night settled about us we gathered round the fire and watched and warmed ourselves while the meat was turned above the embers. This, I was warned, was absolutely the business, what Khevsurs liked best, 'strong meat', meat from calves that were still drinking their mothers' milk. And it was incredibly strong meat, with a deep, rich, powerful taste that I could barely stomach. The soup, however, was clear and good, though what I really needed was a light green salad. Throughout the feast villagers drifted into the orbit of the fire, ate and drank, toasted and talked. An ancient man came waving a huge bottle of spirit that burned and tasted like acid, *zhip-itaouri*, a kind of ur-*chacha*, if such a thing can be imagined. He bore down on Beka, forcing him to drink, holding his head back and pouring the stuff down him. 'Crazy people,' Beka muttered while the others, backing away from the ancient, answered, 'Tradition, tradition.'

The next morning I found Chris examining a pile of unknown men asleep on the bears on the balcony. We packed our gear and tried to wake Mindi. Eldar had long gone up into the high pastures with his cattle, promising to be back by mid-morning and ready to depart, but as usual there seemed to be a lack of impetus, a shortage of vim. I waved my arms about, much to Chris's amusement, then we both wandered off and sat on a grassy knoll overlooking the river. Later the boys found us, expressed some amazement at our lolling and lazing and marched us off down the hill to Dato's. As we were saying our goodbyes a large green lorry appeared along the track on the opposite bank of the Argoun, and drew to a halt by the bridge. It was the goods lorry from Tbilisi and soon the entire village had descended upon it and were dragging forth a great array of furniture and hardware: cupboards and beds, shelves and pots of paint, every man, woman and child carrying off what they could manage and filing slowly over the river and up the hill, like a great train of porters in some epic of exploration. Of course, Mindi and Eldar had to help and rushed off to seize a wardrobe or two.

Eventually all was done and we set off, heading along the Argoun in a suspiciously southerly direction and soon Mindi and Eldar were so far ahead that all we could do was follow on. We found them an hour later sitting nonchalantly by the track as the dim noise that I had at first taken for something internal grew into the roar of an approaching truck. It was the furniture lorry. It stopped by us, hands reached out from the back to haul us up over the tailgate and we found ourselves sitting on two wooden benches with a group of men, one clutching a *pandour*, a beautiful instrument rather like a three-stringed lute or bouzouki, and some youths sprawled sleepily on skins in the centre. I had been completely finessed. I think I started to protest but then the roar of the truck drowned out all possible conversation and the way was so rough that all my energy was consumed by the effort of hanging on. It was an old army lorry, the back covered by canvas stretched over metal frames to which Chris and I held tight as bits of us went off in different directions. We evolved a terrific technique, the orangutan position, in which we held on to the horizontal metal bar above our heads and kept our backsides off the bench, feet firmly planted on the floor. In this way, though exhausted, we could absorb the shocks and jolts without sustaining too much injury. Still the youths slept soundly on their skins, though thrown and tossed about on the bed of the truck. I tried to encourage Chris to take a photograph but he refused to let go.

Strange things were happening to our piece of sky behind the lorry. It went black and then white as great blows of thunder drove through my midriff, shaking my spine and overwhelming even the engine noise. Lightning cracked and shrieked all about us, huge sheets and forks bouncing off the mountains in a wild fandango, exhilarating and terrifying. And then the air went polar and suddenly quiet and the sky froze and fell on our heads. For a moment I had no idea what was going on and then the strange new sensation in my hands revealed itself as pain. Someone was beating my fingers with a ten-pound lump-hammer. Huge hail-stones were battering the lorry, striking the canvas roof so hard that it became impossible to hang on to the bars beneath. I clutched the seat and watched as stones an inch across bounced through the open back and struck indiscriminately. There was a sudden rush towards the front as we each tried to huddle behind the other in a unanimous fit of altruism. And in England we talk of weather! I believe that had I got my way, we should all have been walking merrily along some open ridge when the storm broke and would, undoubtedly, have been killed, battered to death by outrageous hail. No one could have survived without shelter. Perhaps I could have stuck my head in my rucksack but my bones would all have been smashed. There is almost certainly a moral here somewhere.

I was particularly delighted when the lorry slowed as the hail-storm lessened and one of the young boys who had been lying so coolly through the violent jolting and juddering of our progress ran to the back and was terribly sick. I felt slightly less pathetic myself, though deeply ashamed of such *schadenfreude*. We stopped for a second at the top of the Datvis-Jvaris Pass (Bear-Cross Pass) and from our 2,676 metres, or 8,748 feet, looked out on a white world covered in hailstones, like great drifts of polystyrene balls, that were already melting in a moment of fierce sunshine. To the west a chain of giant peaks stretched out, their snows glistening brilliantly. Below, a deep valley with great, green walls dropped steeply beneath us. We drove down through rivers of melting hail, lurching and bouncing through deep ruts and gullies in the track. Along the valley ridge ruins of ancient fortresses merged into the rocks around and we passed a truly lovely Galgais tower, tapering elegantly towards the sky, near which the now pale Khevsur with his unscathed and tightly clutched *pandour* alighted and with a wave turned and bounded up the hillside. Beyond the pass a tight series of bends dropped us down a thousand metres and the track turned westward through thickly wooded slopes as the valley opened out, past Khakhmati and Biso, alongside the little River Gudanistsqali flowing almost due west and into the Pshavis-Aragvi, running south towards Tbilisi. At this corner the track also heads off south with the river and here we crawled out of the lorry, stretched our bones and started to climb up the long, steep path heading on west to Roshka just as the rain began to pour down upon us. In the driving rain Chris and I were soon completely soaked, but Mindi and Eldar, each holding a square of plastic sheeting above their heads, remained quite dry. Eldar's technique was particularly fine: his arms were as tireless as his legs. He would hold his plastic up above his head for hours, trousers rolled up to the knee. When we stopped at night he would swap his wet daps (the light plimsolls that he and Mindi always walked in – imported from China and available, very cheap, in the outdoor market in Tbilisi) for the dry pair in his bag, roll down his trousers, pass his hands through his hair and look as though he'd just walked out of his front door and was off to see his grandmother for tea.

By Roshka, a hamlet of a few substantial houses, we pitched our tents as Mindi went off to make himself known and borrow a mattock. He came back with news of a boiling kettle and, after he had dug the customary ditch around his tent and we had changed out of our wet clothing, we settled down to hot coffee, Shatili bread and cheese. A spruce, neat old man in his late seventies appeared by our tents and invited us into his house to dry. We followed him willingly and soon decorated his living room with socks and trousers as we huddled round a brightly glowing stove, set in the centre of the room. The stovepipe took the smoke out across the room and through a far wall but, unfortunately, most of it came back in through the window, and soon we were all feeling queasy. The old man sat upright on a bench with his wife, who remained entirely silent throughout but smiled and beamed upon us. He welcomed us and apologised that he had little to offer except the warmth of his stove and his company and, indeed, I think his was the barest house I have ever seen. It gave an impression, in the growing darkness, of neatness and tidiness, everything was clean and dustless, the table, the bench, the one hard chair, polished spick and span, but they had nothing. In fact, the front room through which we had come was completely, shockingly, bare. They became, in my mind, Mr and Mrs Hubbard and I wondered what they ate. I noticed that in the morning Mindi had left our small jar of coffee and a smoked sausage discreetly behind. In the pitch dark Mr Hubbard slowly lit his one paraffin lamp, just for our pleasure and comfort I am sure, and invited us to sleep by the stove. Dry and warm now, we declined and made our way back to our tents with many thank-yous, *madlobt! madlobt!*, and goodnights, *ghame mshvidobisa!*

For some peculiar reason we had again pitched our tents right by the river and I was kept awake for much of the night by its roar and the thunder, rainstorms, pains in my head and body, swollen and cracked lips, and a terrible and frightening noise that came nearer and nearer. It was a grinding, crunching sound with a strange, intermittent whiffling behind. I lay rigid, trying to prod Chris awake, unsuccessfully, until it became clear that two or three very large bears were directly behind my head and about to gobble us up like sardines. I could feel the heavy pressure of their presence against the thin walls of the tent. I was just inflating myself for an enormous bellow and getting ready to leap forth when I thought, 'horse', and the sounds and images in my brain which had coalesced into bear dissolved slowly into harmlessness.

The next morning, Sunday 28 June, did not look good. We awoke to a continuous, heavy downpour and thick cloud enveloped us. Predictions that if it rained with the new moon we would have rain for a week seemed to be coming true. Mindi and Eldar, none too sure of the details of our route, looked glum and said they would have real trouble finding their way through the cloud. They disappeared and returned shortly with the promise of a guide, a guide for the guides; and I thought that at some stage he might need a guide, too, and so on until at last an enormous band of people, each following the other, with Chris and me at the very back, would spread slowly across the Caucasus. However, we would have to wait till the afternoon when some of the cloud should have cleared. So

Chris and I were just settling down to write our memoirs and Chris was telling me about the time when the first mate's whore got stuck in the porthole as his ship lay in for repairs off Caracas, when a young man appeared and said that we were leaving now, this minute, this second. We scrambled about madly packing up and followed him down through the houses where numbers of natives were tying sacks and bags on to a couple of horses, preparing carefully for the mountains ahead. My pack was taken from me and strapped on with the rest and the young man who had fetched us kindly insisted on taking Chris's, so, for the first time, we walked unburdened. It was wonderful to feel so light; the way proved hard and I am not at all sure that I could have kept up otherwise. The loads were given a final inspection and adjustment and then we were off with a lot of waving and cheerful parting.

Our group consisted of two horses, two lads in their twenties, a small boy of ten or eleven, a marvellous, striking woman in checked trousers and a black felt fedora whose name I never discovered and a tall man in his thirties, Paata, who was impossibly handsome, like some film idol of the early days of cinema, a Ronald Coleman, perhaps. Paata and the woman looked and dressed (he in a smart leather jacket) like gypsies and this was the first time I had seen a woman in the mountains so obviously in charge and in her element. She and Paata led the horses but she had the final say, it seemed to me, in loading them and in questions of direction along the way. She smiled broadly and set off at a tremendous pace, the little boy skipping about, the lad with Chris's pack hanging back a touch and keeping an eye on us. They all seemed possessed of an incredible strength and swiftness.

In his *Caucasian Journey*, Negley Farson vividly describes an attempt to cross the Klukhor Pass, south-west of Mount Elbruz, through thick snow and I often thought of that as a benchmark on my Richter scale of difficulties. However, Chris and I unanimously awarded ourselves five Negleys for our efforts that day. Heroes only to ourselves, we staggered along after our gang. The weather, the whole climate, changed from minute to minute. Barely able to see our way through freezing cloud one moment, the next instant beat upon by a fierce sun from a clear sky, we had just begun to peel off our sodden clothing when thunder crashed against the peaks and we were walking through such extravagant downpours that we breathed in the rain as it fell. Another second and hail bent us double like corn. The way towards the Arkhotis Pass was steep and the pace set made it difficult and soon I was so drenched in sweat that the rain made little difference. Lines of snot streamed constantly from my nose. Fording torrents and sliding across slopes of snow and ice, all care for bodily comfort was soon abandoned and, almost as soon, ceased to matter. As the lightning flashed over us and made the air fizz, I thought how beautiful was our line of horses and men, silhouetted against the snow, walking on through this wild confusion of rock and weather. There was something deep and durable about this little human band, struggling towards the mountain pass; at least the image seemed then preternaturally strong. I caught an echo from eternity and felt ancient, nomad ancestors calling somewhere in my blood. I looked across at Chris and he was smiling and suddenly I realised that I was extraordinarily happy.

Near the top we stopped for vodka and cheese and some serious toasting: here an old friend had died, struggling alone up the pass in bad winter weather, and our drinking was solemn and respectful with both Mindi and Eldar making grave speeches of commiseration, earnestly and appreciatively received. Our duty done we marched on over the pass (2,935 metres or 8,963 feet) where I very nearly seized up completely as the lightning forked around us once more and the thunder rolled through us and shook us like the insignificant specks and motes we really were. I was so exhausted that I ceased to exist as a sentient being and remember now little of the way down except for a blur of inelegant sliding across snow and ice, following the horses as they picked their careful way, and then an endless descent through ankle-breaking stones, mud and water until I could make out, through a gap in the cloud, away in the distance, down in the valley bottom, the single, tall tower of the hamlet of Arkhoti. We came down through the snow line, the tree line and then the cow line. Though reassuring, this lay around each settlement, a thick morass formed from the excrement of cattle which I greeted with a groan, my appetite for walking through mud and cow shit happily quite assuaged in the lane outside my own home in Somerset, old farmer Oram being always particularly obliging in this respect.

The hamlet, as far as I could see, consisted of a few houses, surprisingly large, with planked wooden walls and tin roofs, the tower, some haystacks, and a small, curious, arched shrine from which hung a large bell with a few attendant graves around. However, I noticed little as Paata stopped by the second house, fantasies of fire, food and rest occupying all the spare space in my brain. A woman appeared at the door, slim, fair, blue-eyed, and ushered us in. We barely had time to wave good-bye and our band was gone, scurrying through the rain to some other shelter. Inside, we laughed at our good fortune: in the corner of the room was a square, metal stove which gave off such heat that the air pulsed in waves around it. Soon the room was decorated with clothes, packs, sleeping bags, and books, money, drenched passports (mine still has not flattened out). Everything we possessed oozed and dripped on to the floor. The lady of the house was not only a friend of Paata's but, as it turned out, also known to Mindi and Eldar, in fact distantly related to both, of course. Again, I was immensely struck by the kindness and gentleness with which we were greeted, though so shy was our hostess that she would hardly look at Chris or me, let alone talk to us. This may, of course, have been because we were just too dreadful to contemplate. She immediately disappeared into the next room and soon we heard noises of preparation and cooking.

It is extraordinary how quickly exhaustion turns to contentment: dry, warm, with hot tea, *chadi* (maize-bread) and hot cheese inside us, I felt a pleasant, comfortable glow and looked more closely about. The house was immaculate, a grave disappointment as I had been hoping for some time to come across a properly filthy hovel, of the kind frequently referred to by earlier travellers, who noted with Victorian disdain each mark of dirt or squalor. J. Abercromby, in his *Trip through the Eastern Caucasus*, written in 1888, wrote of the Khevsurs that 'their perceptions regarding cleanliness are entirely rudimentary'. In Baddeley's copy of the book, now in the London Library, are his usual, forceful marginalia and he chides the author for his 'lamentable ignorance'. However, Abercromby, riding down through Anatori and Shatili from Chechnya at a cracking pace and covering all the route we had just done in our lorry, did look long enough to notice with some delight the costumes and adornments of the Khevsurs he encountered. In Kistani, a tiny hamlet a few miles north of the Datvis-Jvaris Pass, he noted of the natives that:

> Their general aspect was certainly wild, but not by any means ferocious. Like the men of Shatil they shave their beards, and some seem to have the whole head shorn. Their shirts were much embroidered about the neck and breast. On the latter a triangle or cross was worked in coloured thread. The edges of their trousers and beshmets and the backs of their sheep-skin coats were decorated with mother-of-pearl buttons and stitched patterns.

I quote this only because here, hanging on the walls and decorating the room, were wonderful Khevsur cloths and embroideries, belts and socks, with crosses and triangles, stitched patterns and coloured threads. All had been set out with artistry and care and for the first time in weeks I found myself in a house that appeared as a deliberate act rather than some more or less dreadful accident, and it made me quite nervous. It must be said that despite our continual drenchings and our recent wash, Chris and I were deeply filthy, our aspect certainly wild and we fell well below the standard set by our surroundings.

I believe that the only time I saw traditional Khevsur cloth still in use was as saddle-cloths for the horses: Paata had a particularly bright and colourful one, a reminder of past times when Khevsurs took the matter of adornment for their horses as seriously as for their own persons. Baddeley was particularly excited by the appearance of his Khevsur guide in Akhieli:

> . . . though not in chain armour, what with bashlyk and bourka, a banderol of brass-rimmed cartridges, silver-studded belt and pistol, two swords, short and long, a round, iron shield, slung

at the saddle-bow, and, last but not least, a bay horse stepping daintily, its bridle studded with beads of turquoise blue and cowrie shells set alternately . . .'

This brings me back to Akhieli and to a matter I had, at first, thought to fudge over; however, in the interest of truth and as a salutary warning to all those who think they know where they are, or where they are going, I must now confess that when I started to write this part of my book and looked closely at my notes and at the military map, I gradually came to realise that the journey I thought I had made seemed all wrong from beginning to end. I had imagined that on leaving Roshka we were heading west towards Dzhuta, and that the Arkhotis Pass lay roughly along a line between the two. In fact, quite clearly, the pass lies due north of Roshka. Why did we need to go north? This must have been due solely to the fact that Paata's group were heading that way first (Paata had agreed to take us all the way to Dzhuta) and we needed their guidance in the dreadful weather, for it is quite possible to leave Roshka and head directly westward. The assumptions I had made overrode all evidence to the contrary and in my exhaustion I never bothered to look at my compass (in fact, I do not think I ever looked at it) nor even to question Paata or the others. Well, we went a bit north, no matter. Unfortunately my confusion did not end there, for, again looking carefully at the map, there was no village called Arkhoti, in fact there was no village, hamlet or settlement at all going west between the Arkhotis Pass and Dzhuta. The mountains were empty. Only directly north of the pass was there a village, and looking at my notes and the description of the land below the pass, it was the only one that matched up, the only possibility. And the name of the village on the map was not Arkhoti but Akhieli. I had, in truth, been in Akhieli, the very village I had wanted to visit: Arkhoti and Akhieli were one and the same, a fact later confirmed by Mindi in a letter, though he never managed to explain why he did not tell me so at the time. Actually, the matter is slightly more complicated: Arkhoti is the name of the *temi*, the community, which consists of three related villages or hamlets around Akhieli, all bound together by common descent. These *temi* are frequently found in mountain Georgia: often of great antiquity they illustrate how society in ancient times was founded upon family and community, a way of life that still persists into the present.* So, I had been exactly where I had wanted to be without realising it. Such are the lessons that travel affords.

Had I known where we were I could have rushed about with Baddeley in mind and Chris could have stood proudly before Arkhoti's tower just as his forebear had done in 1901. As it was we remained in ignorance. Such confusion over names is not uncommon in the mountains and communities are often referred to by both the name of the *temi* and of the village, so that different names are used for the same place. Passes and mountains, too, can easily be confused, with local names differing widely from those found on any map. Often villages of the same name appear in different places. Even the Russian military map cannot wholly be relied upon: Mindi, Eldar and Paata all referred to the Dzhuta Pass and as such it appears on Baddeley's map though the name for it on the Russian military map is given as the Arkhotistavisgele (the top or higher Arkhotis Pass).

Untroubled by any of this at the time, Chris and I were just contemplating a gentle, exploratory stroll when two villagers and a tall, fair-haired, square-jawed man in his early thirties, appeared in the doorway.

'Hello! How extraordinary! How funny! I had heard that two Englishmen had arrived but I did not believe it. Where have you come from? What are you doing? My name is Hans.'

Hans sat down, introducing himself and his companions, Iago and Armazi. Iago – his mother liked the name, though, sadly, it is probably a Georgian form of Jacob rather than a reference to Shakespeare – equally tall, dark, nervous and quick, came from Dzhuta and taught German with Hans at the German School in Rustavi, near Tbilisi. They came into the mountains during the holidays to paint, walk and hunt, with Armazi, the smallest, oldest and most powerful of the three, as their guide. The other teachers in the school all flew back to Germany, tickets paid, but Hans

* W. E. D. Allen *A History of the Georgian People*, p. 221.

preferred to come here, though he had gone no further east into Khevsureti. He was a great enthusiast for the mountains, organising now the buying of a horse, for three hundred dollars, which Armazi was to fetch from Ingusheti.

He was not the first German to have come: for years during the 40s and 50s Alfred Kurella, author of *Der schöne Kaukasus*, and 'a paragon of socialist literature' in the former GDR, spent his summers here. His wife was killed in a riding accident just outside the village and her grave is there still, we had walked by it on the way. In fact, Germans have a long and interesting history in the Caucasus. The Ossetians have unsubstantiated tales of ancient Germans among their ancestors but in Kabarda, in the North Caucasus, there were villages of Germans who had set out from Württemberg led by a prophetess, to walk to Jerusalem, to wait for the Second Coming. Of the fifteen hundred families that left, most stopped in the Caucasus and never got to the holy city. Ten miles or so east of Tbilisi, not far from Rustavi, were the villages of Marienfeld and Freudenthal where German colonists had been invited by the first Viceroy of the Caucasus, Potemkin, in the 1780s, to help improve the existing industries of wine-making and silk culture. These names have long since disappeared, though quite plainly marked by Abercromby in his map from the 1880s. He wrote of the villages that 'nothing could have been more charming from a distance', surrounded as they were by a thick belt of poplars and fruit trees, though close up signs of dilapidation were then already apparent. Perhaps because of this long association and also a deep respect for German culture and German social democracy felt by Georgian leaders and intellectuals, there existed a strong Germanophile tendency in Tbilisi at the end of the First World War. This led to a treaty with Germany after 1917 and even the establishment of a German Protectorate over the newly and, alas, vainly formed independent Georgian Republic. German troops arrived in Tbilisi, German money circulated, Germany was given a monopoly over all raw materials. So when the Armistice was signed a few months later and the British arrived as the new power in Caucasia, they were decidedly cool towards the Georgians, not to say hostile, and the feeling was mutual. There is a wonderful

Georgian film, perhaps my favourite, *My English Grandfather*, set in this period, which captures some of this antagonism: the eponymous grandfather has the stuffing knocked out of him by a local Georgian Bolshevik in a boxing match he has foolishly agreed to. Of course, he wins and marries his Georgian girl in the end.

Hans, also, was off to Dzhuta, a journey of ten hours, he insisted with great precision, and was leaving at seven the following morning. I looked wistfully across the table at Mindi but knew there was no question of getting him up in time. Hans had tried coming over the pass with Armazi in mid-September but, their horses falling into deep snow, they had turned back, exhausted and frightened. Indeed, Arkhoti lies in one of the most isolated Khevsur glens, the passes to the south and west are two of the highest in Georgia and blocked for much of the year. It was easiest to go north, through into Ingusheti, Armazi told us, and relations with the Ingush had been good, now, for many years. It was a journey that he had done often, trading cattle and horses, the best of which were still to be had to the north and west, in Kabarda, or through into Chechnya.

I must admit to the shiver of excitement that Armazi produced in me, a sort of ethno-historical spasm: I felt like a deranged twitcher with a rare crested grebe in full view. First of all his name was the name of a god, not just a god but *the* god, god of gods, proclaimed as such by the first Kartlian king, Parnavazi, in the third century BC. The sound of old Persia is obvious here and Armazi is probably to be identified with Ahura-Mazda, the creator of the heavens and the earth. The worship of Persian (or, as some scholars insist, Hittite) Armazi coalesced with the older Georgian worship of astral, solar and lunar gods, and, according to W. E. D. Allen, was subsumed into the Christian–pagan worship of St George. At Armaziskhevi and Armazistsikhe, near Mtskheta, rich burial grounds have been discovered along with inscriptions in Armazian, a form of Aramaic script, once widely used in Georgia though still incompletely deciphered.*

Not only did our Khevsur Armazi possess such suggestive associations but he was also the *khevisberi*, elder of the valley or gorge,

* D. Braund, *Georgia in Antiquity*, pp. 206, 213

the headman and spiritual leader of the community of Arkhoti. In the long centuries of Khevsur history it was the *khevisberi*, far more than any distant priest or power, who directed the spiritual, ritual and moral affairs of the mountains. He was and is elected by his peers, not on the basis of age or wealth, but for his deeper qualities. Sometimes his office is given to him in dreams. He decides on all questions of law, presides over festivals and sacred ceremonies; he, alone, approaches the shrine and undertakes the sacrifice and in so doing brings peace to the dead and placates the deities. At the great Khevsur feasts Armazi would sacrifice sheep at the village shrine and distribute the meat to the celebrants. To some this is no more than handing out hot dogs at a village fête, to others it still has meaning.

Armazi blamed the years of Soviet rule for much that had been lost in village life, especially for the death of the traditional skills and expertise that had once made the mountain communities self-sufficient: it was impossible now to find the weavers of cloth, the saddle-makers and blacksmiths that had once served the community and handed on their craft down the generations; no one knew anything any more. He would have to travel far to find a decent saddle for Hans's horse and he would have to do it soon; in a couple of months, when the snows began again, the valley would be sealed off, and though it was possible with craft and strength to cross the snows in good weather, the mountains around were particularly prone to avalanche and had claimed many lives. A helicopter from Tbilisi was supposed to drop in once a month but even this was frequently put off by fierce storms.

The evening had darkened into night and as we lit our candles we moved towards the next room, constructed, it seemed, for no other purpose than to welcome us, with four beds neatly lined against the wall, miraculously ready with fresh white sheets and plumped pillows. Our three visitors departed with promises to meet again in Dzhuta, Armazi rushing off to see his baby tûr, an orphan he had found wandering in the mountains and was bottle-feeding with ewe's milk.

*

I awoke late after a deep and contented sleep to the sounds of Eldar chopping wood and the slap-slap of *khevsuruli khachapuri* – the Khevsur version of the Georgian pizza – being formed for breakfast. Mindi slept on soundly in his corner as I wandered out to the well with my toothbrush. Chris had found the nearest high point, a splendidly constructed pile of dung, ten feet tall, and was standing on top of it photographing the village tower, much to the displeasure of the village cockerel which was strutting disconsolately around, pecking and squawking in a fury of wounded pride. The morning was misty and dull, low cloud muffling the mountain peaks. The oldest inhabitant, wrapped up in a smart, thick overcoat and a battered wide-brimmed hat, came strolling down the lane and sat by me on a low wall. After examining us with ill-concealed amusement, a huge smile cracking his grizzled face, he posed intensely for Chris, framed in the arms of the valley. Under the eaves of the house, skins hung in a row to dry. Large stones held down the boundary walls, the roofs of the houses and the body of the well. Staves were bent tight over the conical haystacks, each topped with a small square of tarpaulin. A tidy garden of herbs and potatoes flourished in the soft morning air. The dunnies were particularly substantial. Everything seemed ordered and neat, in strong contrast to Baddeley's description of the village in October 1901:

> I noticed that men, women, some with babies in their arms, and children of both sexes sat contentedly out of doors, heedless of snow or rain, and no wonder when one saw the alternative! We went into one house – all were alike – and at first could see nothing at all. Presently a fire was lighted, stirred into life rather, on the floor, and I saw the whole interior made one large room, divided in the middle by a wattle fence 3 feet high, on one side of which were cattle – oxen, goats, and two or three sheep – on the other the whole family. Over the fire hung a chain and kettle, as in Ossetia. There were rudely carved cupboards, benches, and stools, but everything black with soot, the air cold and damp, the smell abominable. The streets outside were filthy, a sort of stony farm-yard all the way,

in which the men and women and children walked or stood about bare-footed in the slush and snow.

After a grand breakfast we brought buckets of water in from the well and tried to help but were soon shooed out of the way. Eldar finished chopping all the wood in the district, laid in kindling for the fire and repaired a couple of cassette recorders, while Mindi and I engaged in our ritual morning conversation:

'I really think we should get going, it's ten o'clock.'

'We must wait for Paata and the horse.'

'Well, it doesn't look as if he is coming: we'll be climbing down the Dzhuta Pass in the dark.'

'He'll come soon and we can walk fast.'

'But I'd like to walk slowly.'

'No, now you must walk fast!'

By half past ten Paata had still not appeared and I took a firm grip. Gradually, after many thanks and farewells, our hostess waving to us, half-hidden in her doorway, we set out, back along the way we had come, past the little arched shrine, across the terrible bridge and up the straight, sloping track that ran along the edge of the valley. A beautiful girl, in crisp fatigues with an AK47 slung round her shoulders, ambled nonchalantly by, the first and only time I saw a woman carrying arms in Georgia. As we walked, the sun broke through the cloud, birds twittered with pleasure and the valley glowed golden and green in the morning light. Every few minutes Mindi would slow down to make sure that we properly appreciated each mountain shape, accentuating with peculiar cooing noises or an owl-like whoop every dramatic sweep of land or jagged peak, and exhorting Chris to photograph. At midday, resting briefly on a rock, we looked back to see Paata and his horse climbing steadily towards us. While we waited, Eldar, insufficiently exercised, did press-ups on his knuckles across the narrow track.

We cheered and clapped as Paata drew up grinning, loaded our packs on the broad back of the stallion and, blissfully unburdened, bent into the steep slope. The little river ran now far below us on our left-hand side and as we climbed, the land around became more fractured and wild. Striations cut the rock-face like the claw marks of some great cat. Deep pockets of hard-packed snow and ice filled each hollow and declivity, waterfalls rushed down from the permanent snows above, the rich grasses and flowers grew small and tight and turned to moss. An hour or two beneath the pass we met Armazi, leading his horse, and we stopped to eat and take our one hundred grams, an amount of vodka specifically recommended and laid down by tradition to meet all the requirements of refreshment. Armazi had helped Hans and Iago to the top and left them to tackle the downward journey on their own.

We parted after a few minutes rest and found ourselves on a strange, boggy plateau that I thought at first must be the pass, until the ground curled sharply upwards once again and broke up entirely. Boulders and rocks, massive, mineral-coloured and lichen-covered, piled high above us, tumbled into impossible heaps by some giant in a seismic, geological fit. Paata led the horse along the rivers of snow and ice that wound their way upwards at a slightly less acute angle, while Chris and I foolishly followed Mindi and Eldar into the madness of the rocks. Laid along the seashore these would have been fine for leaping and scrambling, but here, ascending quite vertically, they almost did for me. I could not have made it with my pack. Heaving my bulk upwards through a crevice, spluttering, my efforts forced a great, ringing laugh from Eldar which echoed off the mountains; Chris looked nervously around for signs of avalanche. The lads skipped happily about, putting in a few extra miles searching for crystals, filling their pockets. Here I learnt one of the great lessons of life, one of the few that I can pass with certainty to my children: always follow the horse. Never follow after mountain men taking a short cut.

Suddenly we were out and on to the snow. We zigzagged slowly up and then, above the snow field, the ground beneath our feet a mess of shattered and split rock, we were on the Dzhuta Pass, marked by a cairn, at 3,287 metres (10,792 feet) the second highest pass in Georgia, after the Atsunta. To the north-east a great ridge of mountain peaks, almost 4,000 metres high, stretched out; due north more high peaks and glaciers crossed into Ingusheti; to the south the mountains closed about us. But to the west we looked down over the shoulder of the pass into a long and lovely valley, with little rushing streams tumbling towards the river below. Exposed to a fierce and freezing wind we quickly started our descent, lingering only to carve our names triumphantly upon the cairn.

The way was long but easy. We walked contentedly in silence, breathing in the emptiness, the absolute quiet, no sign or mark of human life around, even the wind falling away to stillness. We followed a tiny crease in the valley's side as it widened out, dropping gradually down towards the River Dzhuta, shining in the sun, fed from the great Nibishi glacier which spread across the heights above us. Trees grew thick along the southern slopes and, after some hours, a few cattle appeared in the distance. We dropped down beneath the cow line. Over a gentle rise three little boys stood watching us, astonished, and tagged along behind. Then a fence, two haystacks and a roof: Dzhuta. The journey from Arkhoti had taken us ten hours exactly.

Hans and Iago had invited us to stay with them but Paata would hear none of it and led us directly along a lane deep in cow shit and mud to his sister's house. Tiny children hurled themselves at his knees and his sister, emerging from the house, laughed and cried and clasped him. We were settled on a low bench by the front door, backs against the wall, looking out at the village, while crowds of relations, in comical plenitude, appeared to inspect us. The girls all disappeared inside once more, reappeared with glasses of water and with slippers and then rushed back: from within came the clunk and clatter of preparation. Houses of substance, each with a broad veranda, spread across the slopes, half-hidden behind great nettles and docks that sprang from the well-mucked ground. I could see no towers here and the village had a prosperous and solid presence, quite unlike any other I had seen in the mountains through Khevsureti and Tusheti. There were perhaps twenty or twenty-five families in Dzhuta, and each, if Paata's house and Iago's house were typical, had at least a dozen members living together, with roving populations of cousins and uncles that came and went as work dictated. Here Paata's sister, Nino, was married to the oldest son; there were two other sons, a daughter, a teenage girl, two little boys, two toddlers and a baby (one of the little boys carried the baby everywhere) and, of course, grandfather and grandmother. Families are difficult to know and understand even if you speak the same language – impossible in just a few hours – but both Chris and I sensed a subtle accord flowing through this family and a kind sagacity characterised all their interactions. The middle son, a fine-looking lad in his early twenties, was gently touched; when we were at last ushered into the front room and sat around the table, he brought in a home-made cassette player (a great tangle of wires and plastic) for our greater pleasure and proceeded to play *Disco Dance 3* at full volume, grinning with delight and dancing round the room. His brothers and sisters softly petted him, calmed him, stroked his face and turned the music down. Then he, laughing, turned it right up again, and the whole scene was re-enacted, time and time again with great goodwill.

Paata entered bearing a great chipped jug, full to the brim with *chacha*; the teenage daughter laid the table, setting down loaves, plates of cheese and butter, bunches of spring onions and herbs, a huge omelette. I looked at her fondly and suppressed a sudden desire to jump up and give her a hug; she reminded me so much of my own daughter with her long dark hair and smiling face, although there was certainly a difference in her approach to domesticity. The toasting began. We drank. Grandma appeared carrying a stack of steaming *khachapuri*, smeared them with butter till they dripped and encouraged us to eat, standing behind one of her sons and nodding with approval as we did so. Then grandfather arrived, a magnificent man, looking more like an old Cretan than a Khevsur, trousers tucked into tall leather boots, jacket draped across his broad shoulders, a woolly hat on his head and a great white moustache under a prominent nose. Everyone rose to their feet to welcome him and we remained standing while Paata greeted him with further toasts: toasts to the motherland, to our motherland (a peculiar concept for the English) and Mindi replied with toasts to the *mamasakhlisi* and to the *diasakhlisi*, the father of the house and the mother of the house. We emptied our glasses and then we all sat down again, grandfather pulling one of the toddlers on to his lap and feeding her with buttered *khachapuri* till her face gleamed golden under the light from the bare bulb overhead. Here in the mountains, conservative, traditional, I saw again how serious was this business of toasting, though I became a little confused:

sometimes we drank with the *tamada*, the toastmaster, and emptied our glasses as he did, sometimes only he drank and we waited for the reply. My hand moved nervously back and forth towards my glass as I tried to observe propriety. We were all called upon to make our responses: as Mindi did so with his usual courtesy, nods and murmurs of approval broke forth and grandfathers' eyes shone with pleasure. Eldar, so shy that he was scarcely audible, staring at his feet the while, was similarly received, while I, keeping to the safe and simple, toasted friends, *megobrebi*, and children, *bavshvebi*. Finally, Chris drew a great shout of approval when he lifted his glass and said, in English, 'Here's mud in your eye!' Friends from the city, from Tbilisi, often say that the whole tradition of the *tamada* and the rituals of toasting have become degenerate and fallen into decay, a mere drinking by rote. Indeed, it can be incredibly tedious with the *tamada* rambling on for hours and making all conversation impossible. Even worse is the propensity displayed by foreign guests to jump up and try to emulate their hosts. The result is so excruciating that I have often come close to killing good friends who could not be restrained from such tendencies. But this was not my experience in highland Georgia. At its best the tradition established a kind of intimacy among friends and strangers, re-affirmed custom and family ties, ties of friendship, and drew all together in a common bond. The table, with its heaps of food, became a sacred space, a pool of light and warmth set against the darkness outside. The alcohol consecrated the communion. My friend Marika would often talk of her grandfather, a doctor in Tbilisi, who was always in great demand as a *tamada* at weddings and feasts. A charming and witty man, a great raconteur, he would bind the company together with his words, though he drank only lemonade. I found this almost inconceivable: the drinking of wine or of spirits seemed so central to the whole ritual. My own favourite *tamada*, Sandro of Chegem, the hero of Fasil Iskander's wonderful stories of Abkhazia, was valued for his extraordinary ability to outdrink all other men and nations and thus uphold the honour of his hosts. He had developed a finely muscled roll of flesh at the back of his neck from the exercise of so much head-tipping.

Mindi's toasts to the *mamasakhlisi* and *diasakhlisi* have a resonance in Georgian that goes far beyond their rather dull English translation. Georgian has the odd distinction of being one of the few languages (Vlach is another) that reverses the almost universal sounds for mother and father, so that *mama* is father and *deda* is mother (*dia* is an ancient form of *deda*), a fact adduced by some scholars to underpin the theory that the Kart tribes were originally matriarchal, worshipping the sun, not the moon, as the supreme female deity and passing on the lines of descent through the mothers' side. Even today, though the Georgian language has no genders, the sun, *mze*, is thought of as feminine. There is an intriguing convergence, too, with the stories of the Amazons who were located by classical authors around Caucasia and the Black Sea. The Amazonian queen who was, according to legend, impregnated by Alexander the Great, at her own request, ruled a country that extended south to the River Phasis, the modern Rioni. Though Georgian society has been, through all the centuries of recorded history, strongly patriarchal, it is true that mothers are accorded a very special respect in Georgia. I never saw the desperate, twisting embarrassment they seem to inspire further west, particularly among teenage boys, rather the opposite: an open show of honour and of love.

The *mamasakhlisi*, the father of the house, was, in the distant past, in ancient pre-Christian Georgia, not merely the head of the household but of all households in the village and its related settlements, the *temi*.* Out of this the whole concept of kingship in Georgia grew. Though this broader, titular meaning fell away as Georgia organised itself into a complexity of ranks and classes under the influence of Persia, of Rome and of Byzantium, the title did linger on into the eighteenth century in parts of the mountains, while in the towns it came to mean, simply, the mayor. The *mamasakhlisi* held the family, the community together and directed its affairs. The point to be made out of all this is that something of the history of the Georgian family, of its great strength even today despite, or maybe because of, the fractures of invasion, repression, Sovietisation, this tremendous web of relations, of friends, of

* W. E. D. Allen, *A History of the Georgian People*, p. 31.

obligation and of duty which bind Georgians so tightly together, can be found in these words: *sakhli, diasakhlisi, mamasakhlisi.*

I was growing terribly tired and Chris, I saw, had reverted to the old trick of propping his eyes open, all innocent, with his hands. He was usually able to sip unobtrusively at his glass, or to pour it sneakily into mine, but the scrutiny of our hosts had made such deceptions impossible. We were battered and boozed. I gave up all efforts at concentration and my gaze wandered around the room, over the bed in the corner where the baby now lay asleep, over the slatted cupboard and the hook-nailed door, over the ancient curled calendar tacked on to the far wall, and came to rest on a familiar smiling face which stared down at me with intent. It was Uncle Joe, the Big Moustache himself, yellowed with age, it is true, but still there in his frame, keeping an eye on things. Grandfather knew where I was looking and eagerly took his cue. And there followed the Stalin Conversation, something that became so familiar, occurred so often and with such little variation that I think I shall save it for later and another old man in the mountains, further along in my journey. Besides, the memory of my tiredness is overwhelming and I must get us all to bed.

Chris and I got a son each. Linking their arms through ours they led us out into the dark, treading gingerly through the cow shit, round to the side of the house, till we found ourselves once more standing in the miracle of the spare room. Never have crisp sheets and a plump pillow been so welcome. I began to have guilty thoughts that each time we descended upon a village, entire families were forced to leave their beds and sleep huddled behind some rock outside. But no, Mindi assured me as we settled down, there was always room for guests in Khevsureti.

One of the minor problems for guests in Khevsureti is that, having enjoyed the hospitality of the previous evening, the whole process is likely to start again at breakfast. And so it proved. It has to be said frankly, and I hope not ungenerously, that *chacha* is not the pleasantest drink in the world and that morning, as I gulped it down, it seemed to me like the stale urine of a Bactrian camel.

Chris just shook his head in disbelief. Infinitely receptive, suffused with a gentle pleasure at every new encounter and experience, he simply could not understand *chacha* for breakfast. He had frequently observed that not even the Georgians seemed to like it and he nudged me to watch as each glass was thrown back, followed by a tremendous grimace of pain and a quick grab at the nearest food. The rain poured down outside and scotched any thought of departure; we were exhorted to stay the day, the night, the week, till suddenly I remembered Hans and said that we really, out of politeness, should go and see him. So we dashed down the hill to a house pointed out by Paata and there, round a table on a broad veranda, we found Hans and Iago and two ancient uncles, rehearsing the scene we had just left. Ah, well. Here there were some interesting pickled shoots, looking uncommonly like mares' tail, so I tried them with my *chacha*; goodness knows why anyone should want to eat such things.

Hans was packing his new four-wheel drive Mercedes, ready to leave for Tbilisi. It stood incongruous in the yard. He offered us a lift but I wanted to walk to Kazbegi and see again the lovely mountain first climbed by Douglas Freshfield.

'No,' said Hans, 'I think you are mistaken. Mount Kazbek was first climbed by a German.'

'No,' I replied, 'it was Freshfield in 1868. He was also the first to climb Tetnuld and Shoda, unless some unrecorded Georgian managed to get up there before him.'

And we grinned at each other, weighed down by history.

'Who was this German, anyway?'

'I think, Klaproth.'

'Oh dear. I am sure Klaproth never claimed to have climbed to the top of Mount Kazbek, though he did claim to have "discovered" the source of the Terek, which he also did not do.'

And I broke the sad news about Klaproth to Hans. Klaproth's *Travels in the Caucasus and Georgia*, written in 1808 at a time when very few other Western Europeans had ever undertaken such a journey, is a fascinating account, marred, unfortunately, by the fact that the author seems to have lifted whole passages from other sources without being entirely frank. He plagiarised the great work of Prince Vakhushti (or Wakhushti) Bagrationi, the *Geographical Description of Georgia*, completed some sixty years before and, according to Baddeley who spends some time tearing him apart and calls him the 'Prince of Plagiarists', described sights he could not possibly have seen and journeys he never made. Baddeley's own copy of Klaproth is heavily annotated with exclamations of disbelief and disgust. Poor old Klaproth, caught in the act. But Hans just looked at me sorrowfully, sad to see me led astray by my own prejudice.

The rain had stopped and it was time to leave, so, saying goodbye with many expressions of thanks and goodwill, Eldar, Mindi, Chris and I strode off down through Dzhuta, waving, and walked on to the track heading west to Tsno. The road declined gently to the broadening river, the valley wide and open with tall cliffs of rock topped by a green fuzz. We were leaving Khevsureti and entering Mtiuleti. It had been days since we had walked so simply, the ground so uncomplicated underfoot. And then, not far from Tsno, the road now almost level with the river, I stopped dead, and nearly fell down with shock. A hyena! A huge striped hyena had lolloped up from the water's edge and stood in the road, not twenty yards ahead, looking at us. The boys stood open-mouthed, Chris moved towards his unloaded camera and then frantically scrabbled for film. The hyena, unconcerned, padded slowly across the road and up the slope, turning once or twice as it stopped to watch us. Then it was up and over the ridge, gone. A hyena in Georgia? Mindi said it could not possibly have been a hyena, it must have been a funny kind of wolf. But it was a hyena, unmistakable with its sloping back and blunt dog's face. This one was really big with great dark stripes running down its shoulders and flanks. I got terribly excited and jumped up and down and everyone laughed and we carried on. Later, in Tbilisi, my friends patted my arm and said, 'There, there,' and made enormously amusing remarks about the effects of wandering about in the mountains for so long. Later still, in England, I spent some time trying to contact Georgian naturalists and, eventually, with the help of the World Wildlife Organisation, tracked down the Georgian hyena man and sent him an email. And, indeed, there were hyenas in Georgia, though very few now, and sightings were extremely rare. None had been made for many years so far west, only in the eastern mountains near Azerbaijan, in very remote areas. It was absurd: this was the most populous place I had been in since Telavi, the road almost a public highway. There were hamlets and even greenhouses a little further on and the land was imminent with man.

Levan Butkhuzi, the hyena expert, was excited and amazed:

Thank you very much for your very important information. First let me introduce myself and after I will explain why your information is so important and actually invaluable for my personal research and the NACRES conservation project.

I co-ordinate programs and projects within the Noah's Ark Centre for the Recovery of Endangered Species (NACRES). At the same time I am the member of the IUCN Species Survival Commission, Hyena Specialist Group. I have been researching the biology of the striped hyena in the Caucasus since 1994 when NACRES received a small grant from Flora and Fauna International (UK) to make an assessment of the critically endangered population at the border of Georgia and Azerbaijan.

As you might be aware, the striped hyena is one of the least-researched species from the Hyaenidae family. The Caucasus is the extreme northern border of the striped hyena's present range. In the last century the hyena was widely distributed in Georgia where it was found in the Iori Plateau and in the Mtkvari and Alazani river valleys.

My first project was elaborated as a result of NACRES' findings in the south-eastern part of Georgia (Iori Plateau) which showed that the species could disappear soon, given its extremely low population numbers.

Unfortunately, before the project there had been no research carried out on population assessment or other aspects of the species' ecology in Georgia. The Georgian Red Data Book qualifies striped hyenas as extinct in the wild or inhabiting 'inaccessible regions in the south-eastern parts of the country'. However, reports from hunters and shepherds showed that this was not correct and habitat inaccessibility did not inhibit our research. But frankly, we had no clear picture of the population's conditions before we began.

Research was carried out mostly in the south-eastern regions of Georgia. Unfortunately we could sight only three adult individuals in two different seasons. Tracking and scat analysis have revealed that the investigated territory in Georgia is probably shelter for five individuals only.

The study showed that human disturbance is probably the most serious factor significantly affecting population numbers. This happens in two main ways: habitat destruction and the loss of prey diversity in the ecosystem. Human hostility towards the animal causes killing on every convenient occasion by hunters or villagers. We should also take into account tremendously increased poaching in the country. Human activity has significantly affected other species in the region. This territory falls under great pressure from non-sustainable farming, since the area is intensively used as winter grazing grounds for livestock. Thus a significant part of the area suffers serious erosion causing a decrease in hyena food bases. Some ungulates have critically declined or disappeared (such as Jeiran's Gazelle – *Gazella subgutturosa*).

We made a detailed literature survey in order to get a clear picture of where the animals could be. It is interesting that only one author (Dinnik) mentioned in his book (about the wildlife of the Caucasus, published in 1914) that historically the population range included Tbilisi and even further north to the Greater Caucasus Range. When we came across this information we assumed it was a mistake since the habitat in the mountains was considered absolutely unsuitable for the species and, moreover, NOBODY else (neither scientist nor local population) has ever recorded any sign of a hyena's presence in that area. Later on, during the implementation of the project, a shepherd from the Iori Plateau offered some interesting information about the animal. He said that the hyena inhabited some of the eastern gorges of Tousheti where he had seen it himself. However, we became alert, though still remain sceptical as local populations often confuse hyena and lynx – the Georgian words for the animals are extremely similar. On the other hand the information on the existence of the hyena in Tousheti seemed to be very interesting not only from the zoological point of view (the species presence in an unusual habitat) but also from an ecological viewpoint, and I thought it needed separate investigation.

Last year I went to Tousheti (to Omalo) and met a hunter who said he had killed a hyena and gave the pelt to the head of the Akhmeta Reserve, Mr Ashir Abashidze. I immediately went to Akhmeta and asked Abashidze about it. He confirmed the fact and with a very proud face showed me a pelt of a lynx. Can you imagine my disappointment?

I became really tired of all these contradictions and came to the conclusion that these stories of the hyena's presence in the mountains was all a big mistake. Now your information shocked me again! Could you give me a more precise description of the place where you saw the animal? I guess you did not take a photograph, did you?

I am currently looking for funds to carry out more detailed research on the biology of the striped hyena and will definitely include the Greater Caucasus in my proposal.

Thank you again,
Levan Butkhuzi.

After the hyena I needed a beer, two beers. The road had turned to cobble and then, in Tsno, to tarmac and a bus roared by, more astonishing and more terrifying than any hyena. People wandered here and there and little pigs rooted about, willow trees lined the river's banks. In the centre of the village a crumbling tower stood proud from the ruins of surrounding walls, said to be a church, but looking most unlike one, built on a massive twist of rock which jutted from the plain. On the heights beyond, a ruined fort guarded the way back into Khevsureti.

Suddenly we were out on the main road, the Georgian Military Highway. Cars and trucks zipped crazily by, such terrible speed, such dangerous monsters! In fact, the road was almost empty and the traffic that did move upon it was slowed by huge potholes and cracks. It had, a few years ago, been full of lorries going back and forth into Russia but times had changed and this great artery throbbed gently, with a slow pulse. One of the very first projects the Russians had instigated after Potemkin (first cousin of Catherine the Great's famous lover of the same name) became Viceroy of the Caucasus, was the construction of this road, or at any rate its ancestor, an extraordinary undertaking carried out in 1783 by 800 Russian soldiers under his direction.* In October of the same year the Viceroy was able to drive in his horse-drawn carriage all the way from Vladikavkaz to Tbilisi. Then the road had to be kept open, of course, a constant battle against snow and ice and truculent Ossetians. Now, neglected in Georgia's parlous poverty, the tunnels leak ominously, the road buckles and slides.

Potemkin's road, with all its subsequent improvements, was essential to the passage of armies, goods and men, to Russia's access to Georgia and the south, and to control over the mountains and all Caucasia. However, since history began, this passage through the mountains had always been one of the great gateways of the world. Just beyond Kazbek lies the Daryal Gorge; here the River Terek flows north and out into the lands of Gog and Magog, the terrible lands of the steppes where hordes massed and moved: Scythians, Cimmerians, Sarmatians, Huns, Khazars and all their frightful friends and relations. The gorge lay in the territory of the Alans, the ancestors of the Ossetians who still live across the Central Caucasus, north of the main chain in North Ossetia, part of Russia, and south in South Ossetia, part of Georgia. The gorge itself takes its name from them: the Dar-i-alan, the Gate of the Alans. It should also be said that in the usual mad confusion of Caucasian ethnography, some historians of Karachay and Balkaria, just to the west of North Ossetia, claim that they are the true descendants of the Alans, mixed over the centuries with Bulgars and Khazars, and report that Karachays and Balkarians still use the word 'Alan' to address each other, in the sense of 'kinsman' or 'tribesman'.

The Alans themselves were a once-mighty people, a Sarmatian

---

* Baddeley, *The Russian Conquest of the Caucasus*, p. 20.

tribe or confederation of tribes, nomads of Indo-Iranian origin, who appeared around the Black Sea in the first century BC and pushed the Scythians towards Europe and the west. They themselves were later similarly propelled by the masses behind, by other successive nomad eruptions from Central Asia, particularly by the Huns, and Alan bands were thrust westwards and up into the high mountains of the Caucasus, washed up by this great wave of moving populations. They swirled in complicated patterns across Asia and Europe, pressing, during the last years of the Roman empire, into Galicia and France where they left few obvious marks beyond, perhaps, a whisper of their name: Alençon, Hourgette d'Alans, Alène. It is also possible that the common British and French names Allen, Alan, Alain derive from them, and that the most British of creatures, the bulldog, as well as the French Dogue de Bordeaux, known originally as Alaunts, are descended from the fierce fighting dogs, the mastiffs, of the Alans. Some of the noble houses of Brittany and Normandy were probably, in origin, Alanic, and came with the Normans to fight at the Battle of Hastings and rule in England, most famously as the great family of the FitzAlans. In the Arthurian tales, so popular with these Norman knights, the story of the Sword in the Stone may well derive from Alanic rituals and there are echoes of Excalibur, too, in some Ossetian legends. The Alans were established in France by the middle of the fifth century AD, had fought alongside the Romans (and also, in some versions, against them) in the last great battle of imperial Rome helping to disperse the terrible Attila and his Huns at Chalons in 451, at the battle of the Catalaunian Fields. They created a kingdom in the Crimea, known well into the Middle Ages as Alania and the Sea of Azov is still their sea: for the Russians knew them as As or Os, hence Ossetia. The Caucasian Alans are thought to be of mixed descent, mingling with their neighbours, here in the south with mountain Georgians among others, as they came over the passes and through the Daryal.* They made frequent raids into Georgia and were settled in some numbers by the thirteenth century. In the fifteenth century they tried to take Gori (Stalin's birthplace) but

---

* W. E. D. Allen, A History of the Georgian People, p. 31.

were booted out by King Giorgi the Magnificent. The great Georgian Queen, Tamar (or Tamara), having rid herself of her first husband, the Russian Prince George Bogolyubski, a vicious sot (though an effective soldier in his campaigns against Muslim forces in Shirvan, Aran and Armenia), married the Ossetian Prince David Soslan with whom she lived happily and fruitfully. Though the Ossetians living around Daryal later gained a terrible reputation as bandits, pillaging travellers and extracting huge tolls at every step, running a great racket through the mountains which Lermontov describes wonderfully in *A Hero of Our Time*, in their strongholds they were sought after as allies by the great powers: by the Rus from as early as the fifth century, but more by the empires of Persia and Byzantium as these two giants wrestled for control. In fact, here, they were both more concerned to keep out the wild peoples of the north than to fight each other, and the Persians, particularly, tried again and again to organise a carve-up, proposing that both empires should share the cost of maintaining troops in the Daryal, of paying the Alans to police the border. The Byzantines rather liked the idea of Persia paying for this by itself, much to the fury and frustration of various Persians.*

The passage through the Daryal gorge was said to have been blocked by huge gates, or beams, sheathed in iron, according to Pliny, and there are many references to other smaller passes being similarly guarded, forming the great Caucasian Wall, the north-western frontier of the Sasanian empire. One thousand Alans were posted day and night to guard the Daryal.† Baddeley, among others, suggests sites for other 'gates' and mentions, particularly, the Crooked Gates, the Zilin-Douar, above Alaghir, though the idea of a gate – Dar, Douar, Der (as in Derbent), our own 'door' – may be metaphorical, a way through. However, although no gate could have spanned the entire shoreline beyond the mountains, there were certainly massive gates at Derbent, made of pure iron, set in a huge defensive wall.‡ Fed on travellers' tales and woolly bits of

* D. Braund, *Georgia in Antiquity*, p. 270.

† W. E. D. Allen, *Russian Embassies to the Georgian Kings*, p. 301.

‡ W. E. D. Allen, *Russian Embassies to the Georgian Kings*, and V. Minorsky, *A History of Sharvan and Darband*.

history, I had vaguely imagined that in the Daryal itself some vast gate was once hinged to one side of the gorge and closed upon the other. This was obviously nonsense, though there does seem to be plenty of evidence for real and substantial gates of some kind and there are frequent references to them from classical times under various different names: The Caucasian Gates, The Daryal Gates, even The Caspian Gates and Alexander's Gates, though the Caspian is miles away and Alexander went nowhere near them.

I had thought to find a narrow ravine, cutting and twisting through the mountains, with great beetling cliffs that overhung and blocked out the light. In fact, when I came through the Daryal a few years before, I had found, much to my disappointment, that it was rather broad. It is true that the cliffs shoot up nearly two thousand feet sheer on each side, and it is a little dark and damp, but there is a ruined fort in the middle near the lower end of the gorge, as well as what are said to be the remains of Queen Tamar's summer palace high on one side. Though dramatic, the Daryal is relatively spacious. Baddeley was convinced that the Daryal was far too difficult a prospect for it ever to have been a major route of invasion like the route by Derbent but I am not so sure: a bribed guard, a night-time assault and half of Mongolia could have poured through. There is evidence, indeed, that the Scythians pushed through the Daryal early in the eighth century BC on their way to devastate Urartu, the ancient Armenian empire – or else the ancient completely un-Armenian empire, depending on the scholarship one chooses.* Baddeley says that the first recorded passage by a military force was that of General Todleben, a German adventurer in Russian employ, a man with a reputation among the Georgians for duplicity and treachery. He forced his way through the Daryal and along the bed of the Terek in 1769 with four regiments and cannon, to meet up with the forces of King Irakli at Kobi, an 'astonishing feat' according to Baddeley. (This was the Irakli already mentioned who signed the treaty of 1783 with Catherine the Great and who won admiration throughout Europe for his campaigns against the Turks.) According to Georgian historians, Todleben's 'astonishing feat' was accomplished not in

* R. G. Suny, *The Making of the Georgian Nation*, p. 7.

order to help Irakli but rather to gain control of Tbilisi for himself, while the Turks dealt with the Georgian king. All his efforts were in vain, for 'l'invincible Hercule' was victorious again and Todleben was sent home. In his assessment of the Daryal route, Baddeley seems to have ignored the evidence of Arab historians who describe, probably with some exaggeration, vast armies of Arabs and Khazars, up to 300,000 men, attacking each other through the Daryal in their continuous, push-me-pull-you wars of the eighth century.*

We strode manfully by the road's edge after Todleben and Irakli, Arab and Khazar, and after an hour or so found ourselves wandering through the streets of Kazbegi. In Baddeley's time it had been a tiny village; when I first arrived in 1989 it had long been a town, Russified in a dreary kind of way but functioning. Now it seemed desolate: the buildings neglected, deep craters in the roads, hardly anyone about. The usual sad story. In the central square, more of an emptiness than a square, a few battered kiosks catered to the trickle of passing trade. We bought many bottles of good Kazbegi beer, some old sausage, more tins of Korean spam, much to my disgust, and – from an old lady sitting on a box, who seemed delighted to see us and obviously thought we might buy her entire stock – a huge bag of plums and a jar of *tqemali*, a most delicious plum sauce, a sort of chutney, sharp and slightly sour, that I liked to put on almost everything. With our picnic, we walked up the hill to the little hotel that I had stayed in ten years before. A fine sow nursed her litter on the grass outside but all was not well within. Along the corridors the floorboards were buckled, twisted and missing, the rooms broken and deserted. After much hallooing, a harrowed old man shuffled out of the dark, agreed that we could stay, found us some serviceable beds, charged us a few dollars and disappeared.

We took our beers and settled on a long bench by the front door. Here was the real delight of this hotel, for rising sharply in front of us, despite the line of poplars that some idiot had planted just beyond the pig, was the most wonderful sight: Mount Kazbek.

* D. M. Dunlop, *The History of the Jewish Khazars*, pp. 65–87.

The mountain seemed close enough to touch, the perfect image of everything a mountain should be, its great cone topped with a cupola of snow, brilliant white and tinged around the edges with pink in the evening sun. We sat silently before it and then Chris took photographs and Mindi took photographs and Mindi and Eldar went off foraging for bread while I delivered a short discourse to Chris and the piglets.

The mountain has always been considered sacred: when Russian engineers decided brightly, a few years ago, to build a cable car up its southern slopes, the local people, Georgians and Ossetians, rose up and destroyed the works. The wreckage can still be seen. Ilia Chavchavdze set his long poem *The Hermit* here, a strange story of an old hermit, living in an ancient, sacred cave called 'Bethlehem', tempted by the arrival of a beautiful young shepherdess during a terrible storm. Seduced by her beauty, he almost allows himself to kiss her, resists, but dies in the end:

> There, where Mount Kazbek rears his noble brow,
> Where eagle cannot soar nor vulture fly,
> Where, never melted by the sun's warm rays,
> The frozen rain and snow eternal lie;
> Far from the world's wild uproar set apart,
> There, in the awful solitude and calm,
> Where thunder's mighty roar rules o'er these realms,
> Where frost does dwell and winds sing forth their psalms;
> There stood, in former days, a house of God,
> Built by devout and holy men, the fame
> Of that old temple still the folk hold dear,
> And Bethlehem is still, to-day, its name.

When Douglas Freshfield, the great explorer and mountaineer, arrived to climb Kazbek in 1868, he was told that no man could possibly walk upon its summit, that he would never come down again and would simply disappear. On the top, it was said, was the tent of Abraham or even the cradle of Christ, and one of its old names, before the Russians called it Kazbek after a local family, was 'Christ's Mountain'. (The modern Georgian name is *mqinvartsveri*,

Peak of Ice or Ice Mountain.) Freshfield's guides all fled but they had reckoned without his ice axe, a wonderful innovation with which, not without some considerable difficulty, he cut steps into the ice up the steep curve to the top. For much of the time he and his three companions were reduced to crawling on hands and knees up the slippery slope, using their ice axes as anchors, at one point nearly pulled to their deaths as one of the party lost his footing and shot head-first over a chasm. This in no way discouraged the redoubtable Freshfield who returned to climb in the Caucasus three times in subsequent years, conquering many more summits. On their descent Freshfield was greeted with amazement and fêted, his conquest undoubted because his trail was quite visible from below and he had popped out and terrified a poor shepherd boy who was grazing sheep just beneath the snows.

The fear and awe which Mount Kazbek inspires come from a great tangle of myth and legend that hangs about it and the mountains around. A race of supernatural heroes, the Narts, inhabit the place, drinking copiously, fighting among themselves and any other beings convenient for the purpose – giants, ogres, genies, angels, archangels – misbehaving in a sadly degenerate and thoroughly Olympian fashion. Despite the many eccentricities and strange abilities of the great Nart heroes (they could rise from the dead, ascend to heaven, transform themselves into metal), they were essentially prototypic mountain men, concerned above all with their honour, their pride, their daring as warriors, as raiders, their love of feasting and fantastic bouts of drinking. The Nart legends are thought by many to have been brought along by the Ossetians, and thus to point back through the Alans to the Sarmatians and to the ancient beliefs of the Sarmato-Scythian nomads who roamed the steppes to the north of the Caucasian chain. George Dumézil, the great French collector and collator of the Nart legends wrote, memorably, that: '. . . *les contes sur les Narts, à défaut des documents anciens, permettent parfois d'évoquer, à travers les brouillards naturels du folklore, l'ombre d'un dieu Scythique.*' (The Nart tales, in the absence of ancient documents, allow us to glimpse from time to time, through the mists and fogs of folklore, the shadow of a Scythian God.)

However, local scholars insist that they are indigenous and, indeed, Nart epics occur from Abkhazia and Circassia right across the Central Caucasus.* Baddeley's guide Ourousbi, an Ossetian, claimed to have a huge ancestral Nart skeleton which he kept in his family sanctuary, a cave. Indeed, many Ossetine families claimed descent from various Narts and Baddeley suggested that the Narts may have been a tribe of tall Europeans who once inhabited the area, though this seems a trifle dull. Whoever the Narts may have been, wherever they came from, their stories give us a kaleidoscopic synthesis, strange, chaotic, surprising, even beautiful at times, of an Ur-Caucasia. Dumézil writes that their stories demonstrate the unity of spirit, the '*unité d'âme*' of the mountain peoples of the Caucasus:

Ces traditions héroïque donnaient à l'un des coins les plus morcelés du monde une véritable unité d'âme; chrétiens, musulmans, païens, tous y trouvaient l'illustration des vertus que requiert leur montagne: courage, ruse, résistance aux peines comme aux excès, colère sans frein, mémoire des injures, et – des quelques cas sévèrement comptés – miséricorde. Partout le plus bel éloge qui se pût faire d'un homme était de le comparer à un Nart.

(These heroic traditions give to one of the most fragmented corners of the world a true unity of spirit: Christians, Muslims, pagans, all find pictured in them the virtues which their mountains demand of them: courage, craft, resistance to hardship as to excess, unbridled anger, the memory of past injuries, and – in some cases severely calculated – mercy. Everywhere the greatest praise that could be given to a man was to compare him with a Nart.)

The Nart epics were kept alive by wandering bards who would turn up at any great occasion, especially funerals, and, as well as extemporising upon all matters of moment, would recite the old tales of the Nart heroes. Sadly the last of these bards died sometime in the 1850s and the tales have been recorded by professional folklorists who arrived upon the scene during the nineteenth century.

* D. Rayfield, *The Literature of Georgia*, p. 218n.

I first heard of Narts on my bus journey down the Military Highway in 1989, just after suffering deeply from an excess of Lermontov in Pyatigorsk. I could make neither head nor tail of them. As we careened along, the noise of the engine and the frequent crashing of gears drowned out the best efforts of our expert, Marika Didebulidze, who stood, desperately hanging on at the front of the bus, regaling us with their exploits. One moment convinced that she was talking about her close relatives, the next that we were listening to a sorry story of contemporary misdemeanours, I fell into a strange and confused reverie where screaming brakes, sun symbols, thunder gods and Narts, Narts, Narts, briefly occupied and suddenly fled the foggy mirror of my mind. Marika, not in fact a folklorist but an expert on early Georgian church frescos, now a close friend, later explained all. She had been coerced into joining our group by her boss at the university who was under the mistaken impression that a party of British folklorists was about to descend. Marika, knowing nothing whatever about Narts, had spent days in the library of Tbilisi university, desperately mugging up the subject. This was in itself heroic; more serious, though, was the fact that she had done this at a truly dreadful time. She joined us only a few days after the appalling events of 9 April 1989, Georgia's Bloody Sunday. As Russian troops battered and killed demonstrators with spades and rifle butts and thousands ran through the streets of Tbilisi through mists of CS gas, Marika was searching the city for her Russian nanny, senile and frail, who had wandered in her nightgown into the turmoil of the battle. She found and rescued her old nanny but with twenty dead (mostly young women) and many thousands ill and injured, there was not a person in Tbilisi who was unaffected by this pogrom. So when she met us, Narts were hardly her first concern. To do justice to her efforts and to give an example of the flavour of the Nart legends, I offer a translation of one of Dumézil's tales, *How Uryzmag Killed the Giant Shepherd*, chosen for its strange familiarity, a Nartian version of the Cyclops tale which mirrors the Greek myth with extraordinary exactness:

One day, Uryzmag, returning from an expedition, found the Narts all gathered together but very abashed. 'What on earth has happened to them?' he asked Satana. 'They are listening to their stomachs,' she replied. 'Ah! Ah! young Narts,' cried the old hero, 'to see you one would think that each of you had lost his dearest parent.' And so he took the best of them hunting.

From afar they saw a shepherd of gigantic size, with a flock of sheep. 'Hey, young Narts, which of you will go and get us a sheep for supper?' No one budged. 'Well, it's going to have to be the oldest who does it.' And Uryzmag rushed off. When he reached the sheep, he jumped from his horse and seized the most beautiful ram, as big as a huge ox. But it was the ram who carried him off and tossed him into the arms of the shepherd, a monstrous giant with only one eye. 'Thank you, my little sun,' said the giant to his beast, and he threw Uryzmag into his sack; Uryzmag tried to escape but the shepherd just mocked him.

When the sun went down the shepherd returned with his flock to a cave. He shut the entrance with a great rock. He called over his son, told him to fetch an iron spit, skewered the unfortunate Nart, set him above the fire and immediately went to sleep. Luckily the spit passed between Uryzmag's body and his clothes without harming him. Hardly had the giant dozed off when Uryzmag freed himself, seized the spit, stuck it in the giant's eye, then killed his son. All night, groping about, the giant tried to grab his assailant, but in vain. At dawn he half-opened the door, just enough to let out his sheep one by one. He felt each one as it went. But Uryzmag had marked out the best of the flock, the shepherd's favourite, and killed it. He skinned it and wearing the skin left at the head of the flock, while the giant caressed him and muttered advice: 'Go, my Gurchi, look after the flock till the evening and then bring all back to the house. I am blind but I shall chastise the miscreant, go, go . . .' Uryzmag did not need coaxing. When, behind him, the whole troop had filed out of the cave, he shouted to the giant: 'Hey! You blind ass! Here I am!' and ran off. Soon the whole flock had been seized by the Narts. All that remained after they had feasted was shared out in the Nart village. The hunters got equal portions but one Nart protested: 'No! No! We must give Uryzmag the portion which should rightly go to the oldest. Without him we would have died of hunger.' No one disagreed. Each took some beasts from their own share and gave them to Uryzmag.

One of the great heroes of Georgian mythology, Amirani, corresponds in many ways to the Ossetian Nart hero Batradz. He is celebrated in the medieval epic *Amirandarejaniani*, where, transformed into a courtly knight with supernatural powers, he pursues a fearful race of giants, the Devi, and fights and kills a particularly noisome one, Baqbaqi, who had three heads, from each of which (after Amirani had cut it off) issued a worm which grew into a dragon that in turn fought with and was slain by Amirani. His exploits, his appetites were those of warrior-hero and Nart: 'Astounding was the quantity of wine he drank and food he ate. For dinner he a bull devoured; for supper more than three he ate.'

Amirani was the son, or in some versions the husband, of the goddess of hunting, Dali; even so he needed help from God in his battle. God gave him the gift of fantastic strength but, having overcome the giant, Amirani decided to challenge God himself (or Jesus Christ) and for his pains was imprisoned in, or on, Mount Kazbek. If this begins to sound familiar, too, it is so. Amirani has long been known as the Georgian Prometheus, though, as David Braund points out in his *Georgia in Antiquity*, it is a rather confused parallel: both challenged God in their ways, both were punished by being stuck on or under a mountain in the Caucasus, but Amirani was not the great benefactor of mankind (in fact quite the opposite in some versions), did not bring the gift of fire and does not seem to have had any problems with eagles. However, the origins of the Amirani legends spring from deep antiquity, from the second millennium BC according to some scholars, and the Georgians have had plenty of time to confuse or conflate the two stories.

The two great Greek myths located in the Caucasus are the story of the Golden Fleece, with all its attendant business of the Argonauts and Medea, and that of Prometheus. Though the first Greek settlements along the coast of Georgia have been dated at about 600 BC, first contacts and these tales are far, far earlier and they represented, in the Greek imagination, the fabulous edge of the world where time and humanity began. Prometheus was one of the Titans, another fearsome race of giants, children of Uranus and Ge, defeated by Zeus and the Olympian gods in a terrible war. Then Prometheus, in some of the many variants of the story, created man by moulding him out of clay and breathing life into him. Zeus was deeply unimpressed and tried to destroy mankind but Prometheus stole the gift of fire from heaven (or the forge of Hephaestus) and gave it to man, enabling him to survive. For his trouble he was chained to a mountain in the Caucasus and an eagle was sent to torment him by pecking away at his liver. This is a terrible redaction of the myth but already it contains so much that it becomes difficult to disentangle.

To begin: which mountain in the Caucasus was supposed to have been the site of Prometheus' torment? Early Greek authors are not much help, merely referring to Mount Caucasus without a very certain grasp of where this might be. Aeschylus, for example, in *Prometheus Bound*, seems to place Mount Caucasus somewhere in Arabia, though he may have meant the Urals. However, later classical authors like Arrian do locate the Caucasus correctly and even visit them in order to see the site where Prometheus was said to have been chained. Within the Caucasus there are two obvious candidates for this: Mount Elbruz, the highest of all, and Mount Kazbek, the second highest and the most central. Elbruz is preferred by most, because it is nearer to the Black Sea and because of the purported Greek derivation of its name from '*strobilos*' meaning cone-shaped. However, Kazbek is a far more perfect and beautiful cone – Elbruz has twin summits – and because of its great significance in local legend and its majesty, I follow others, like Alexandre Dumas, and imagine Prometheus bound to Mount Kazbek. Elbruz is not in Georgia and Kazbek is, and though this had no relevance thousands of years ago, the currency of the legend in historical times in Georgia and its synthesis with the Georgian Amirani may add some weight to my preference for Kazbek. It is interesting that while in Greece there is no evidence of any cult centre or temple for Prometheus, in the Caucasus he was revered along with his eventual rescuer, Hercules, both worshipped before Zeus himself who was rather mistrusted for his antipathy to Prometheus and his creation, man. This might suggest that the Promethean myth was laid on top of, or even derived from, an earlier strand of the Amirani story.

Prometheus' name has a very precise meaning in ancient Greek: 'foresight'. (His brother, Epimetheus, possessed the gift, or curse, of hindsight and, beguiled by Pandora, let out all humanity's ills from her famous box.) Why, if he had foresight, did Prometheus allow himself to get into such a dreadful situation? The answer is that despite knowing the outcome he took this suffering upon himself for the sake of mankind. Here again one finds a specifically Georgian, though this time Christian, synthesis, for Amirani is often identified with Christ, something that makes no sense in this great muddle of myth without the Promethean intermediary and his willing acceptance of suffering for the sake of mankind. Freshfield, remember, was told that Christ's Cradle was located on top of Mount Kazbek; there seem to be no equivalent tales about Elbruz, though there are, of course, giants chained to it or imprisoned beneath.

Why did the eagle gnaw at Prometheus' liver and not his nose, or his eyes, or his testicles? First, there is a Georgian explanation for this, though it may not satisfy everyone. In the Georgian language the words for liver, *ghvidzli*, and the word for watchfulness or surveillance, *ghvidzili*, are nearly identical. The liver is said to be 'the organ of the psychic force that controls the moment of transition from the waking state to sleep.' And so, by extension, Prometheus' organ of awareness is constantly attacked, though the author of this explanation, Grigol Robakidze, suggests that in this way Prometheus is kept constantly awake, cursed never to rest, never to cease watching. Robert Temple, an old friend, has a much clearer explanation in his books *Conversations with Eternity* and *The Crystal Sun*. He was intrigued by the many references in ancient literature to divination by the use of animal entrails, extispicy or haruspication, and particularly by the use of the liver. In his investigation into the 'fanatical liver science of the Babylonians' he finds a clay model of a liver, dating from 2,000 BC, which shows the fifty-five zones of the liver where the diviner should look for significant signs. Many of the greatest oracular centres of ancient Greece practised extispicy, the liver focusing, it was thought, the divine rays from which priests could read the future. Robert, being of an enquiring, scientific and thoroughly eccentric disposition, went along to a slaughter-house and, lifting out the livers of freshly slaughtered lambs, noticed that he could see his own face in the organs' shiny surface in the few minutes before exposure to the air dulled them. Indeed, he finds many references to just that: the liver is the divine mirror in which fate and the future are foretold. So that, it would seem, is the real significance of Prometheus' liver: it is the organ of prophecy, of foresight. The eagle, for its part in Prometheus' torment, was often despised in the Caucasus and the bird persecuted by the inhabitants because of this ancient complicity.

One final observation on the Prometheus legend and its local significance: Prometheus stole fire from heaven and brought it to mankind. Fire has been taken variously to mean the animating spirit, the imagination, that which enabled mankind to rise above his animal origin, to conquer his own nature and the natural world around. The chains that bind Prometheus are said to be of bronze or iron, both of which metals have their own significance. Local versions of the Prometheus–Amirani tale feature blacksmiths who try to break or forge anew these chains. It's all rather muddled by strange additions such as dogs or horses that try to lick the chains away, perhaps some primitive embodiment of the powers of rust! The ancient Greeks were well aware of the Caucasus as a source of mineral wealth and many archaeologists suggest that in the Caucasus were the original, or certainly some of the earliest, sites for the discovery and practice of metallurgy. Certainly many of the Nart legends contain references to a heavenly forge and Batradz himself was said to have been tempered within it for two weeks. The gift of fire enabled mankind to work metal and took him out of his natural state and beyond the age of stone.

*

The stars shone bright around Mount Kazbek. Chris was fast asleep on the bench; Eldar and Mindi had slipped away to bed. I sat in solitary contemplation, enjoying the silence of the night and finishing my beer with a certain sadness. It was time for Chris to return to England, his one month quite used up, and we were heading back to Tbilisi the next day. I prodded him with my bottle.

'They were frightfully drunk,' he said, 'the captain, all the crew, dead drunk.'

'What did you do?' I asked.

'What could I do, in the middle of the ocean? I couldn't even steer the ship.'

'What could you do? What could anyone do?' And I pushed him, somnambulant, to his bed.

Next morning I discovered him lying on the floor, half under my bed, with his camera in one hand and a sausage in the other.

'Look,' I said, 'you can see Mount Kazbek through the window.'

'Shh! Don't make a sound! I've found one of your creatures.'

Maddened by missing the hyena, determined to enter for the World Wildlife Photographer of the Year competition, he was tempting something out of the darkness. A small, grey mouse appeared and started to nibble the sausage.

'That's a mouse, Chris.'

'Damn! Are you sure? It's rather nice.'

'It's very nice but what did you think it was?'

'One of those rat things.'

'I don't think mole-rats appear above ground. Anyway, they are blind, naked and quite repulsive. And they don't eat sausage.'

The tale of the blind mole-rat, or long-clawed mole-vole, *Prometheomys schaposchnikowi*, is a tragic one, despite the excellent choice of name. The mole-rat lives buried beneath the slopes of Mount Kazbek and around, in long, dark tunnels. A sadly unattractive animal, hairless and white like a great termite, it is nevertheless of interest to biologists studying circadian rhythms, those mysterious cycles of sleep and wakefulness that complicate diurnal time. When I first stayed in the blessed Hotel Kazbegi, in 1989, an old friend, Tom Clark (who reappears largely in my story later on), told me the tale of his uncle Bancroft who had come to Kazbek in the 1920s as part of an expedition searching for mole-rats, intending to take some back for London Zoo. They dug furiously about and eventually, with the help of bemused but enthusiastic locals, captured a number of these creatures, crated them up, and boarded the train for Moscow. Unfortunately, during the long train journey, the mole-rats fell desperately ill, tormented by parasites which they had rubbed off or not been prey to in their dark, cold burrows. Bancroft Clark had a brilliant idea. He would kill the parasites. From the restaurant car he bought bottles of vodka and poured the alcohol over the mole rats. The parasites succumbed at once but the vodka gave the mole-rats such a shock (presumably by suddenly lowering their body temperature) that they, too, all keeled over and died. It is almost unbearable. The post-mortem gave 'lung infection' as the cause of death. I went to the Natural History Museum in London and there they lie: a few skins and skulls, some of their labels bearing the name of Bancroft Clark.

Mindi and Eldar went off to find a car. I had no time to revisit the little church of Gergeti, up on a hill opposite Mount Kazbek, no time to rediscover the Ossetian shrines along the Terek with their great mounds of empty bottles and horns of tûr. There's hardly time even to mention them. However, I did want to stop at Kobi, a few miles south of Kazbek, and walk up along the River Terek a little way towards its source. Soon a car arrived with a very worried driver who was not at all sure that we would get far. We all piled in and chugged slowly down the Military Highway to Kobi.

Along the road, on the slopes and ridges about, for many miles, the crumbling ruins of fortifications and towers are plainly visible. This land is called *Khevi*, the Valley, and has its own special character and place in Georgian history. Its strategic importance is obvious, guarding the eastern and western mountain approaches into the heartlands of Georgia, and most particularly the Terek route through Daryal to the north. The Terek, with its southern confluent the Sounzha, formed the main highway from the Caspian to the south for all those who wanted to avoid Derbent, the hostile tribes of the eastern mountains or the terrible Shevkal of Tarku. The astonishing Genoese, who had established trading posts around the Black Sea and into the Caspian, were using the Terek route for their trans-isthmian traffic as early as the thirteenth century.* Fifteenth-century Italian maps show Kobi plainly marked. Genoese caravans went down the Terek to Kobi in order to reach the silk-producing districts of Kakheti in the south-east. Unhappily, most of these Italian traders were later wiped out by a fanatical bunch of dervishes from Derbent. But long before this, during the sixth century, the passage through the Daryal and down to Kobi had formed part of the Silk Route. At this time Byzantium and Persia were at war and the precious caravans of silk were unable to cross Persian territory. Emperor Justinian the Second had formed an alliance with the Western Turks of Central Asia under Khan Silzibul and the silk was brought from China, through Central Asia to the northern shores of the Caspian and then over the Daryal through Georgia to Trebizond from where it was shipped to Constantinople. However, the Turks became increasingly frustrated by Byzantine duplicity and the alliance broke up. The Daryal route seems to have been, in part, a ploy to convince the Turks of the difficulty of any approach towards Byzantine territory and Khan Tourxath, Silzibul's successor, wrote an angry reproach:

> Your emperor will answer to me for his behaviour, he who speaks to me of friendship and at the same time concludes an alliance with the Avars . . . Why, O Romans, do you always conduct my envoys across the Caucasus when they travel to Byzantium, and assure me there is no other route for them to take? You do this in the hope that I might forbear, because of the roughness of the ground, from invading Roman territory. But I know exactly where flow the Dnieper and the Danube and indeed the Maritsa. I am not ignorant of the extent of your forces: for the whole earth is subject to my dominion, from the first ray of the sun to the limits of the West.†

It took the Turks nearly another thousand years but eventually they made good the veiled threat implicit in Tourxath's letter.

* W.E.D. Allen, *Russian Embassies to the Georgian Kings*, p. 14.
† D. Obolensky, *The Byzantine Commonwealth*, chapter 6.

From the latter half of the sixteenth century, the Russians came down the same way to make contact with their co-religionists in Georgia, the Georgian kings urging them to tighten their grip on the route and so bring support and arms against the Persians, Turks and Avars that were tearing Georgia apart. By 1589 the Russians had taken Astrakhan at the mouth of the Volga and fortified it so that when, in that year, the first great Russian Embassy to Georgia was sent by the Tsar, it embarked there, sailed down the Caspian to the mouth of the Terek, went along the Terek to the Sounzha, followed the course of the latter till it almost meets the Terek again, came through the Daryal George and so on down to Kobi. Despite the fact that there were by now Free Cossack settlements along the lower Terek and the Sounzha, controlling the old summer pastures of the Golden Horde, the way was difficult and dangerous and the Embassy came under attack. The story of its journey is told in *Russian Embassies to the Georgian Kings*, brilliantly edited by W. E. D. Allen, whose commentaries and notes turn the letters sent by the ambassadors to the Tsar into an entire history of the region.

Kobi now consists of a few dilapidated shacks, mostly empty, and there is no sign of the old post-station where Baddeley and other travellers stayed and found fresh horses, something we never did, travelling being so much easier a hundred years ago, despite popular claims to the contrary. We turned there and drove as far as we could, with much pushing of the car, up along the Terek. Then we walked the broad track above the river which raced below us, a boiling turmoil of rock and debris, swollen by the melt-waters from the great glaciers beneath Mount Kazbek: the Ortsveri, the Mnasi and the Suatisi, just to the west. The Terek here squeezes through a narrow gorge which Baddeley gives as the Kasara, though Freshfield locates the Kasara further west where the River Ardon cuts through the Saramag valley. Whatever its name, the gorge is beautiful: a geological fantasy on the duel between water and rock. Slab-faced cliffs of strange formation rise from the river bed, stained and crusted by mineral springs that issue from cracks and crevices along the southern face of ravine. The river twists and scours under the northern bank, threatening the track and the Ossete settlements that perch beside it. By the first of these, a tiny hamlet and a tower, Ukrakani, we were met by two Ossetes on horseback who inclined politely from their saddles and asked us our business. They were armed with modern rifles, their horses magnificent and powerful. Mindi and Eldar were deeply impressed, though apprehensive, but the Ossetes waved us cheerily on our way and cantered off in a cloud of dust, heading towards Kobi.

With much regret, a little way before Abana where, I had heard, there are some interesting Ossetine towers, we had to turn back. I had originally intended to walk all through the upper part of Southern Ossetia, following the Terek towards its source, then on past Saramag, up over the Mamison Pass and so to Glola in Ratcha. Time and politics intervened and I had to come to Glola from Tbilisi. The problems were manifold: the route over the Mamison would have involved leaving and then re-entering Georgia, either illegally or with all the nonsense of days wasted queuing for visas which would probably not have been granted. Then there was a large Russian military presence spread all around the pass and I had been strongly advised to avoid any contact with the Russian military in the prevailing uncertain atmosphere. This border was extremely volatile, called by Thomas Goltz, an American journalist who spent six years in the Caucasus during the 1990s and wrote a tremendous account of his time there, *Azerbaijan Diary*, 'the most sensitive border in the former Soviet Union'. Mindi would certainly not have come with me and though I could, perhaps, have found an Ossetine guide, I had neither the opportunity nor time to do this. Finally there was the Ossetian Question. This was the source of Mindi's worries and all the discouragement I had received from my Georgian friends.

As the Soviet Union fell apart, riot and strife tore at the republics and the old geography imposed by Lenin and Stalin started to unravel: in the Caucasus, particularly, in Armenia, in Azerbaijan and in Georgia everyone seemed monstrously keen to grab for their guns. The problems this caused are still far from solution. Georgia suffered a terrible civil war, the war in Abkhazia, other difficulties around its borders in areas dominated by Azeris and Armenians and in Achara with its largely Muslim Georgian population, and here, in Ossetia, months of bloody turmoil. The

Southern Ossetians, like the Abkhaz, mistrusted the prospect of an independent Georgia, fearful for their future in the nascent, unfettered state. They wished to be united with their brethren to the north, to create a new, unified Ossetia, looking still towards Moscow rather than Tbilisi. The Georgians could not countenance such aspirations: the Ossetes were immigrants, they couldn't just run off with a great slab of Georgia under their arms. They must be stopped!

The Caucasus illustrate perfectly how political geography may be used as an instrument of power: Kabardines and Balkars thrust together, Chechens and Ingush, the whole confusing panoply of Autonomous Regions and Autonomous Republics brought to bear upon the contiguous and interpenetrating peoples of Caucasia. The Soviets divided closely related peoples from each other, pushed enemies together, made one people subordinate to another, created areas of discontent and resentment and so ruled. The idea promulgated by some academics and commentators that the problems in South Ossetia, or Abkhazia, were solely a response to Georgian chauvinism is simply wrong. Such endemic instability is symptomatic of post-colonial states and the inter-ethnic rivalries that spawn and flourish always present a terrible challenge to any new nation struggling to find its feet. As the Soviet Union broke up, and through the decade of the 1990s, there were problems everywhere; according to one analysis there were over thirty areas of inter-ethnic 'tension' within the Caucasus alone.

In 1989 the South Ossetian Autonomous Region decided it wanted to be an autonomous republic, still, apparently, within the Georgian Autonomous Republic, though goodness knows how this could have worked. The Georgian Supreme Soviet annulled the decision and, in November, a huge march was organised in South Ossetia by Georgians, many of whom lived within South Ossetia, some of whom had come from Georgia proper. For many South Ossetians the very fact that they were governed from Tbilisi had caused bitterness over the years; for Georgians who did not even use the name 'South Ossetia' to describe their province of Samachablo or Shida Kartli (Inner Kartli), any notions of secession were unthinkable. The 50,000 demonstrators were met by armed Ossetians and turned back. Clashes and hostilities followed swiftly and surely. The violence escalated and soon thousands of terrified refugees were pouring out of South Ossetia, Ossetians to the north, to Vladikavkaz, Georgians to the South, to Tbilisi. Whole villages, whole regions were emptied. 113,000 Ossetians, that is two-thirds of the Ossetian population in Georgia, many of whom lived outside the boundaries of South Ossetia, fled their homes. Many thousands of Georgians fled from South Ossetia. Tskhinvali, the regional capital with a large Georgian population, was devastated. Infrastructure broke down, houses, schools, hospitals were wrecked.

In 1990 Zviad Gamsakhurdia was elected as President of the Republic of Georgia. He refused any compromise with the leaders of South Ossetia and, as Soviet troops massed around Mineralnye Vody and the northern borders, accused Russia of stirring up trouble, provoking confrontation, desperate to hold on to its influence in Georgia. 'It is now perfectly clear', he said, 'that Mr Gorbachev is supporting terrorism in South Ossetia'* and he castigated its leaders, elected in polls held during December 1990 though not sanctioned by the Georgian government, as 'criminals, terrorists and usurpers of power'. In December 1990 the Georgian government abolished South Ossetia's status as an autonomous province. By the spring of 1991 the violence had spilled out beyond South Ossetia, and Georgian villagers reported atrocities from marauding gangs of Ossetes. Ossetes, subject to and fearful of similar treatment, turned to Soviet Interior Ministry troops for safety and these started to disarm Georgian police within the province.

At about this time Zviad Gamsakhurdia, instead of trying to step between the warring parties, to calm everybody down, started to rant about the 'very strict criteria' that would have to be met by non-Georgians who wished to be considered as citizens of Georgia. He decided that only those whose ancestors had settled in Georgia before the Russian annexation of 1801 would be eligible and announced that he intended to pass a law whereby all non-citizens

* *Independent,* 14 April 1991.

would be stripped of the right to inherit or own land. He could hardly have come up with anything more stupid or provocative and he played straight into the hands of all those who wished to desta-bilise the new state. The President's deepening paranoia only exac-erbated, here as elsewhere, an already desperate situation. By December of 1991 many Georgians had had enough and a bloody confrontation, the Tbilisi Revolution, forced Gamsakhurdia to flee the capital after fierce fighting and to take refuge first in Armenia, then in Grozny, in Chechnya, where President Dudaev granted him political asylum and, in February 1994, delivered the eulogy at his grave side.

Almost immediately after his flight, supporters of Gamsakhurdia and the forces of the new State Council of Georgia, headed by the uneasy triumvirate of Kitovani, Ioseliani and Sigua, came into conflict in Mingrelia, western Georgia. Georgia's civil war had started. Meanwhile a referendum was held in South Ossetia on seceding from Georgia and joining with Russia. The Georgian State Council responded by sending the National Guard into Tskhinvali. The armed conflict escalated.

Then in March 1992 Eduard Shevardnadze, having resigned as Soviet Foreign Minister, returned to his home in Georgia to head the State Council and by June an agreement was drawn up whereby a mixed group of Russians, Georgians and Ossetians formed a peacekeeping force and instituted a 15-kilometre-wide no-fire zone within South Ossetia. Despite some sporadic and fierce outbreaks, a measure of calm was restored, restoration work started in Tskhinvali and a few brave refugees headed back to their homes. Unfortunately the political status of South Ossetia remained, and remains still, unresolved. Outside the no-fire zone, gangs of bandits continued to wreak havoc, attacking the peace-keeping troops, murdering, rampaging through villages at night, taking hostages and preventing refugees from returning home. Tskhinvali re-mained closed to Georgians.

The peace-keepers did much important work and intervened to save both sides from attack and reprisal. However, they themselves had problems as time wore on. One in four of them was dismissed for drunkenness, hooliganism, theft, acts of violence and dealing in weapons and equipment. Georgians complained bitterly that Russian troops supported and armed the South Ossetians, but it seems probable that they were quite happy to sell or hire out weapons to either side – hire of an automatic rifle was set at about three hundred roubles. Rather than giving evidence of some Stalinesque plot it is more likely that the Russian forces, at least at ground level, were merely savagely corrupt. Now, after many meetings and talks between Georgians, Russians, Ossetians of the North and South, an edgy kind of peace is being maintained, though nothing has been resolved. The South Ossetians still say that Georgian refugees cannot return home until the Georgian government recognises their independence; the Georgian government, though hinting at some kind of special status for Ossetia, refuses to grant this.

And so Mindi and I decided not to walk through South Ossetia.

*

Our driver, Timur, was waiting for us by his car smoking a joint. Oh marvellous, I thought, the whole area is tense with enmity, the road's disintegrating, the car barely functions and our driver's stoned. But I was wrong on the last count; he was inhaling with great pleasure the acrid smoke from a *papiros*, and offered me one. These cigarettes are so redolent of Russia that smoking one is rather like inhaling a work of history. The filter is like the inner tube of a toilet roll, a sort of elemental roach, the cigarette itself a loose assembly of powders and dusts. I could not refuse it. We pushed the car along, jumped in as it fired and set off in a great cloud of smoke, exhaust fumes adding a certain piquancy to the tobacco. Chugging along the Military Road we soon started to climb towards the Cross (Dzhvari or Krestovy) Pass. 8,000 feet high, this had been a major barrier to travellers before the building of the road. Russian engineers constructed great chambers across the way to carry the winter snows that slid from the mountain heights and vast drifts, thirty or forty feet thick, rested on the tunnels' roofs. As we came to the top of the pass, Timur, a man of endless opinions, like taxi-drivers everywhere, turned to talk. Oh God, I muttered, help us now in our hour of need, let us descend gently from this great height. But the car seemed to know where it was going. I love the oriental splendour of Georgian names: Timur, Zurab, Merab, but I was amazed at the habit of calling so many male children after Georgia's greatest tormentor. It was rather as though the British had taken to calling all their boys 'Adolf'. However, this Timur, though garrulous, was not violent, and showed a scholarly turn of mind.

'Now,' he announced, 'we are in Asia.' Eldar looked about nervously. We all peered out of the windows. Chris said he did not care if it was the Arctic as long as the man looked where he was going. Mindi strongly disagreed with his geographical asseveration.

'Georgia is in Europe!'

'No, we are neither all Europe nor all Asia, we are both. Asia and Europe join here. We are the belt that holds the two continents together.'

And so we bounced along arguing affably and I remembered Baddeley worrying away at the matter while he was crossing the Mamisson Pass:

Now, it was on the Mamisson that I first began to be troubled by the question – where, in those meridians, did Europe end and Asia begin, and this for a purely practical reason. My insurance policy, an American one, contained a clause barring Asia absolutely from its field of operations. If I died in Europe my heirs would benefit to the amount of the policy. If I died in Asia they would get not one penny. Obviously, it would be well to know, if possible, in geographical terms, precisely what this meant. I thought there could be no difficulty about it but I was very much mistaken . . . it might depend, when crossing a razor-edged pass and losing my foothold, upon whether I slipped down one side or the other who would get or keep the sum insured!

Baddeley rehearses some of the geographical arguments and settles, with reservations, for the line of the Manitch, running from the sea of Azov to the Caspian, as the dividing line, thus excluding all of the Caucasus from Europe. Douglas Freshfield disagreed: 'It is hardly needful to repeat that the Caucasian Chain is the only suitable limit between the Continents. No natural boundary is perfect, but a wall is always preferable to a ditch, and the bisection of a river basin can be justified on no scientific ground. The Manytch has nothing in its favour, and the Don only classical tradition.' But there have been many other attempts to draw this boundary, attempts which shift not only around geographical arguments but around political and cultural ones as well. Looking at maps of Europe from the eighteenth century to the present most agree, with a few wobbles towards the Volga, that the line of the Urals, extended south towards the northern shores of the Caspian Sea, marks the eastern boundary of Europe. However, as soon as this line approaches the Caspian all kinds of wonderful meanderings and convolutions break forth. Sometimes the line misses the Caspian altogether, doubles back on itself, heads west then south then east then west in a desperate attempt to avoid all possible Asian elements (Hahn, Leipzig, 1881); sometimes it cuts off the top edge of the Caspian, veers off and runs down through the centre of the Caucasus, so dividing Georgia into Asian and European segments east and west of the line of the Daryal (Mackinder, London, 1919). This would have been understandable centuries ago when Persia dominated the eastern part of Georgia and Byzantium the western, but makes no sense, culturally or politically, today. Often the line is drawn down the middle of the Caspian Sea, running almost along its whole length north to south, then takes a sharp turn to the west, either just to the south (Cambridge Modern History Atlas, 1910) or just to the north (Philippson, Leipzig, 1928) of the Caucasus mountains. If to the south then not only is Georgia entirely in Europe but so is Azerbaijan; if to the north then the whole of Georgia is in Asia while Chechnya and Daghestan – about as European as the Rann of Kutch – are both in Europe. My own insurance policy decided that all of Georgia was in Europe and I can send a letter to a Georgian friend with the ordinary European stamp – not that it arrives.

All these complications show just how inadequate and even irrelevant rigid definitions of Europe and Asia can be. After all, the distinction arises from ancient Assyrian-Phoenician words meaning simply sunset (*ereb*) and sunrise (*acu*), so west and east, but both sets of words have taken on, if not geographically then certainly culturally, a huge weight and significance. The pervasive notion that Asia and Europe represent two vastly different, mutually exclusive and opposing forces is sometimes said to have derived from the time of the wars between Greece and Persia in 500BC; at this time, of course, both countries were already actively engaged in the lands that became Georgia. Here was the marchland, the frontier between the two powers for many centuries, indeed, all of Georgia's existence till the fall of Byzantium. So Georgia became or embodied, in a way, the very argument itself, was its synthesis.

Geography cannot ignore culture and politics; the boundaries between countries, after all, do not always follow convenient rivers and mountain ranges. But this makes things difficult. We have become used to thinking of Europe and Asia as separate entities. We might much more usefully think of one Eurasian continent and then annoying bits of geography like the Caucasus resolve themselves easily. It might be said that culturally Asia, or more specifically Persia, inhabits Georgia's past; most Georgians now would think of themselves as European, by religion, by culture and by inclination, even, by race. But the picture is more fractured. While paying ardent homage to the same nation and faith, middle-class intellectuals from Tbilisi would identify easily, of course, with a similar group in London, Paris or St Petersburg, while mountain Khevsurs or Tush would edge more closely towards their Ingush and Chechen neighbours. However Asian or European their tendencies, all remain unmistakably Georgian, a bit of both, a bit in between, something different. Essad Bey wrote at the end of *The Twelve Secrets of the Caucasus* that 'The Mountain-men are not Europeans, and they are not Asiatics; they are Caucasians – that is to say a special race of men that will endure.' In fact Baddeley comes, finally, to the same conclusion: 'Wherefore, for my part, while accepting, officially, the Manitch as the best possible conventional line, privately and personally I look upon the Caucasus as an independent portion of the globe's land surface, belonging to neither this continent nor to that.'

And so we left the matter, all agreeing that it was far too difficult to resolve and settling back to doze as the car chugged wearily down the mountains, ever nearer to Tbilisi.

CHAPTER 5

NIGHTBAR

'Close the Teashop of Argument, Open the Nightbar of Experience'

How I went to see Hamlet, got mixed up with
the theatre, and the Abkhazians

Tbilisi was hot. Horribly, clammily hot. In high summer, from the
tropics of Batumi to the deserts of Baku and through all the plains
between, the lands seethe and simmer. I felt as though I had been
smeared with honey and put to bake, like some fleshy baclava, and
longed for the freshness of the mountains. Chris and I dragged
our great filthiness through Sasha and Irina's flat. Hardworking
doctors, they had generously allowed us to use their home as our
base while in Tbilisi. Hospitably, they never referred to our condition. We washed, played with the children, Tazo and Nina, and
watched in admiration as they settled studiously to their hours of
chess lessons and piano practice. It seemed like home, but also
very strange. Normal things, like sitting in an armchair, were almost
disgracefully luxurious.

Next morning Beka took us to the airport. As I watched Chris
disappear through the barrier I felt, for a moment, bereft. We had
spent a month muttering inanely to each other in peculiar places
and grinning with the knowledge of each other's inadequacies as
we stumbled through our journey. I would miss my old friend. But
I was eager to continue. I returned to town. At Beka's office I met
up with Mindi and he decided, finally, to come through Ratcha
and Svaneti with me. He had been rather nervous of the Svans and

he did not know the route I wished to take but his curiosity and sense of adventure got the better of him. Still unconvinced of the need to slow down, though I had talked to him seriously about it, he now considered himself, quite rightly, my official guide to the mountains of Georgia and wanted to see the journey through to its end.

We all went up into the hills above Tbilisi to pass the day with Beka's parents in their little dacha in the woods. Here he had spent most of his holidays as a child. Ramshackle huts and cottages were sprinkled about among the trees and Beka's place was so like an ancient beach hut on the Devon coast that I felt instantly at ease, pottering about, fixing the water, fiddling with broken windows, sitting outside and discussing plans for imminent improvements that would never happen. Beka's stepfather, Gela, became at once enthusiastic about the walk through Ratcha. His own father had been a famous Georgian archaeologist, responsible for many of the digs at Brili, on the way to Svaneti, and he urged me to visit the old site, discoursing widely over Colchian gold, metallurgy, tree burials and the influence of Hellenic culture.

That evening, back in Tbilisi, I strolled to the top of Rustaveli Prospekt and looked at the washing hanging over the balconies of the Iveria Hotel. I had stayed there in 1989. Then, the lobby had been full of large men labelled 'Frank' and 'John Jnr' attending conferences of the 'Federated Nut and Bolt Union'. All sorts of odd beings loitered by the door. Everyone pointed to everyone else and hissed, 'KGB!' A large Armenian sat outside all day, holding court and eating sausages. Now, the building had been given over to refugees from Abkhazia.

I turned from the hotel and crossed the road. I was going to see a friend, Gocha Kapanadze, playing Hamlet. I found the theatre, a little underground cavern at the top of Rustaveli Prospekt which shared an entrance with a betting shop and snooker hall. It was so dark that I am sure half the audience were punters and had thought they were going to watch the dog-racing from White City, beamed direct to Tbilisi and displayed on an enormous screen. Occasionally we could hear cries and cheers from the next room, especially loud just as Gocha was starting on 'To be or not to be?

That is the question.' '*qopna ar-qopna? sakitkhavi ai es aris.*' His
performance was terribly moving, the production too, each moment choreographed precisely to convey intense emotion; a dark,
brooding, Caucasian Hamlet, fit for the place and the times. With
the tremendous energy of his swordplay and the overwhelming
heat of the cavern, by the time I went to congratulate him at the
end he had lost half his body weight. These conditions were a far
cry from those he had enjoyed in the days when we first met, in
1989, and he played in all the gilt and grandeur of the Rustaveli
Theatre. But everything had changed, money for the four
subsidised theatres of Tbilisi no longer flowed in, Rustaveli had
gone dark and actors had to shift as best they could. Though this
had led to personal hardship among the large acting and theatrical
community in the city it had also produced a new mentality: small
venues like the cavern were being created, actors, freed of the old
and rigid hierarchy, were able to take on new roles and branch
out in a way that would have been quite impossible before. Gocha
had just finished directing Lorca's *Blood Wedding*. Even style and
repertoire had changed. No longer could the companies afford to
rehearse each piece for six months, perfecting each movement,
each flicker of the eyebrow and then setting it in stone for twenty
years. I had seen *King Lear* and *The Caucasian Chalk Circle* and
Mother Courage at the Rustaveli, all quite wonderful, but with mostly
middle-aged actors who had, my friends told me, inhabited the
same roles, used the same gestures, since their youth.

My involvement with the theatre in Tbilisi stemmed from my
second trip to Georgia when I had attached myself to the Gog
Theatre Company, run by old friends, Tom and Caryne Clark. The
name was wonderfully redolent of the Caucasus: Gog and Magog
were the forces of darkness, the terrible tribes predicted, in the
Bible (Genesis 10:2 and Ezekiel 38:1–3), to break through from
the north and to destroy the civilised world. Of course, each nation
has a different idea of who Gog and Magog might actually be –
usually their neighbours, though the Russians, particularly, were
thought to fit the bill nicely. The Greeks thought Gog and Magog
were the Scythians, the Romans that they were the Huns or the
Goths. Tatars, Mongols, Khazars and many others all presented

themselves as likely candidates. Alexander's Gates at the Daryal were supposed to have been built to hold them back. In England, naturally, they have been transformed and confused into a pair of jolly giants at a mummer's play and stuck up outside the Guildhall in London. Two great oaks outside Glastonbury had been named after the giants and the theatre company after them. However, the name had got the actors into trouble and they had once been anathematised by an outraged priest in an African village.

I had done some work with Gog and my trip was my payment. The plan in Tbilisi was to join with the actors of the Young Rustaveli Theatre, to perform their own piece *Birdman*, and to put on some kind of collaborative show, the Young Rustavelis returning the following year to work in England. I had written a one-man performance for Tom (who had become known as The Great Marijuanavitch, for complicated reasons to do with a drunken actress, a mistaken identity and a strong proclivity) based on our experiences in Tbilisi the previous spring when the streets were full of mourning after the Russian pogrom and portraits of the dead hung around Sioni cathedral. It was set in the Nightbar of the Iveria Hotel (and subtitled 'Close the Teashop of Argument, Open the Nightbar of Experience'), full of anger and bewilderment, tormented Georgians, Armenian Mafiosi, wilting Natashas and the KGB. Caryne improvised a wonderfully manic piano accompaniment which gave the whole thing a disturbingly frayed edge. Thankfully, I have lost the text. Much of it had to do with Tom disappearing into the night in search of an English typewriter to type out his contract with the Rustaveli and reappearing instead with five bottles of brandy, three Bulgarians and a mad Armenian called Sam who had discovered the secret of cosmic energy. Anyway, the trip with Gog led to much toing and froing between Tbilisi and Somerset and a lot of what might loosely be called cultural exchange. Having very little to do with anything, I had spent a great deal of my time in the steamy café under the theatre, drinking ersatz coffee, watching famous actors selling contraband kippers and talking to Zura Revazishvili, Irina's brother, our interpreter, then teaching at the Language Institute in Tbilisi, now working for the BBC in London, his natural home. Zura, having announced

that he spoke 'just a smattering' of English, proffered the language
with the ready ease of a Gussie Fink-Nottle. He had spent his youth
ransacking the canon of English literature and watching Benny
Hill videos, that great actor enjoying the same peculiar cult status
in Georgia as Norman Wisdom did in Albania. This accounted for
Zura's odd sense of humour. We later wrote a tremendously
amusing and progressive Georgian–English phrase book together
which no one wanted to publish.

So the actors all embarked upon a steady stream of workshops,
rehearsals and performances, interspersed with frequent and
prolonged bouts of drinking and eating, and many expressions of
mutual adoration and goodwill. But in the streets outside other
movements were afoot. The large rehearsal room of the Rustaveli
Theatre opens on to a wide balcony overlooking Rustaveli Prospekt,
the great central avenue of Tbilisi. One afternoon during a typical
rehearsal ('Alex has lost his nose! Has anybody got a spare nose?
Where is everybody? Has anyone seen Annabelle? Does anyone
know where she is? Where's the blood? Has anyone checked the
blood? Tom, could you give Alex his blood? No? Alex, forget the
blood!'), we all became aware of a mighty tramping and rumbling
from the street and moved out on to the balcony. There, on the
Prospekt below, rivers of Georgians marched with their flags and
shouted for freedom, *tavisupleba!* and independence, *damoukide-
bloba!* and unity, *ertoba!* We had walked slap-bang into the middle
of an historical incident (as Fasil Iskander says of an earlier, equally
disturbed time), almost unavoidable, it is true, with dozens of political parties, over a hundred at one count, all clamouring on the
streets for their own version of independence. This was October
1990, just a few weeks before Gamsakhurdia was elected. There
had already been fighting in Ossetia and the Abkhazian crisis was
ripening horribly. Out on the balcony it was difficult to know quite
how to behave: waving to the crowds below turned one into Queen
Victoria, a more stationary gesture into Mussolini, just being there
seemed like an act of voyeurism. This was not my struggle and I
retreated from the balustrade and watched from a distance. It was
peculiarly fascinating.

A few days later, during the afternoon rehearsal for the final performance of *Birdman,* with the Georgian actors all taking part, chaos descended. A man with a black armband appeared in a terrible state of agitation saying that Merab Kostava had been killed. The play must be cancelled! Kostava was one of the leaders, with Gamsakhurdia, of the political opposition to the Communists. He had been imprisoned for ten years and was a great national hero. His car had, apparently, crashed into a cow. Immediately everyone began to shout. The story was false! The KGB had killed him! The cow was a KGB plant! It was a plot! No, it was an accident! Some railed, some cried, all were deeply upset. The show must go on, nothing would destroy them! The show must stop out of respect! Nobody knew what to do. Eventually rehearsals went ahead, some of the Georgian actors joining in, others hanging on to each other in clusters, shocked and bewildered.

That evening, after a minute's silence and a short address from Tom and from Ghizo, the manager of the Young Rustaveli, the play went ahead. The theatre was packed, audience and actors charged with emotion. There was much in the play that echoed the mood of the moment. It was a wild success and after the final song, the audience rose to its feet and clapped and cheered and demanded more. So the actors and musicians gave them all the songs again as great waves of applause broke over them. My neighbour, an elegant Georgian lady, turned to me and said:

'That was wonderful! I loved the songs, especially.'

'Yes, even I enjoyed them and I have heard them many times. Did you like the way they sang the Georgian songs they had learnt?'

'Quite fantastic. We were all amazed, they sung them so well! Mind you, I'm not sure they were quite as good as the Japanese choir which came here last year.'

'Really? How extraordinary! Do you get many such choirs coming to Tbilisi?'

'Quite a few. But tell me, who exactly was this Birdman?'

'Ah! Well, the Birdman is Bladud, King Lear's father, and he founded the city of Bath because he was driving his pigs over the Mendip hills and they fell into some hot springs and the pigs, which were all rather ill, were instantly cured. Just like stories of the hot springs of Tbilisi.'

'I see. But why did he have wings?'

'Well, he learnt to fly from Pythagoras. It's a sort of metaphor for freedom, I think.'

'I see. So King Lear's father knew Pythagoras?'

*

In all the ferment of Tbilisi it was impossible to remain impervious to the political turmoil in Georgia and even the most frivolous among us made some attempt to understand what was happening. Subsequent trips in 1991 and 1993, just before and after the civil war that ousted Gamsakhurdia, the Abkhaz separatist war and the coming to power of Eduard Shevardnadze, deepened my own involvement willy-nilly. I saw the distress of friends, the unrest, the violence, the crises of government and the economy. So in 1993, when I was asked to edit the English translation of a book on the Abkhaz-Georgian conflict, I agreed to do so. This was *Conflict in the Caucasus* by Svetlana Chervonnaya.

Frances Howard-Gordon, another old friend, had led the expedition to Georgia in April 1989 that I briefly described in Chapter 4, when we came down the Georgian Military Highway by bus, listened to Marika's lectures on the Narts and arrived just after the Russian pogrom against demonstrators in Tbilisi. Frances was publishing a series of books on the countries of the Soviet Union under her Gothic Image imprint and had been offered Professor Chervonnaya's work. It was published in 1994 and we had a little book-launch at Zwemmer's, the East European book shop in London. The ladies at Zwemmer's had laid on wine and sandwiches but as we were waiting for the party to begin, we got a phone-call from the police. They rang to warn us that they had received information that the bookshop was to be targeted by terrorists. It was probably a hoax but we should keep a careful watch on the proceedings. The Abkhaz were going to blow us up! Frances and I thought we might nip over the road to the pub. Nothing happened, of course, but why the fuss? What Chervonnaya had written was, very briefly, that this so-called 'ethnic conflict' between the Georgians and the Abkhaz who wished to secede from Georgia, or at least to separate into a confederacy of equals, was the result of a deliberate policy of destabilisation by reactionary forces within the old Soviet Union, the military and the KGB who wished to keep Abkhazia tied to Russia and its structures of power, to upset the independence movement in Georgia, and that the roots of the conflict could be traced through the activities of certain politicians and organisations both in Russia and Abkhazia itself. She was instantly branded, like others who took this line, as a Georgian propagandist or puppet who had at heart the basest of motives: to deny the right of the Abkhaz people to self-determination. Perhaps the most passionate advocate of the Abkhaz cause, George Hewitt, Professor of Georgian and Caucasian studies at London University's School of Oriental and African Studies and Honorary Consul of Abkhazia, came to our book-launch. I had read, and continue to read, George Hewitt's publications on Caucasian matters, always cogently argued and expressed in the most virile prose. He later very kindly wrote me an introductory letter to present to the Abkhaz in general should I ever manage to get into Abkhazia, which, so far, I have not. He had read Chervonnaya's book and hated it. So we were wary, though civil; no sandwiches were thrown. We agreed to lunch.

Professor Hewitt's position is, again very briefly, that there is no need to look to the wider political crisis within the old Soviet Union, that far from there being any conspiracy to wrest Abkhazia away from Georgia, precisely the opposite is true: there is and has been a Georgian conspiracy to subdue and overwhelm Abkhazia. Particularly during the Stalin years, after 1931, Abkhazians were subordinated to Tbilisi, denied language rights and political rights and their country was settled by Georgians (mostly Mingrelians) who further upset the demographic balance in their favour and became, if not the majority of the population (there are also large numbers of Armenians, Greeks, Russians and others), then the largest ethnic group within Abkhazia. Anti-Abkhazian policy, he says, was vigorously pursued by the mad nationalist Gamsakhurdia immediately after Georgia became independent (with Abkhazia within it) and continued by Eduard Shevardnadze whom he holds largely responsible for the war.

Both authors agree that the Abkhaz have suffered, though

Chervonnaya places this within the context of the oppression faced by many small nations within the Soviet empire; Stalin, after all, deported the Chechens, the Ingush, the Meskhetians, the Crimean Tatars and others in their entirety. Indeed, there were plans, never implemented, to do exactly that to the Abkhaz. Both authors agree that there was an outburst of appalling nationalist chauvinism under Gamsakhurdia. Both refer to independent Russian observers, though one describes the barbarity suffered by the Abkhaz at the hands of the Georgians and the other describes the barbarity suffered by the Georgians at the hands of the Abkhaz. They both agree that the conflict was absolutely unnecessary. On many of the details, however, they disagree and they certainly come to different conclusions about the reasons behind the trouble. To Professor Hewitt the whole conflict can be simply reduced to a struggle against oppression, to Professor Chervonnaya it expands into a chaos of conspiracy.

Whenever conflicts like this arise they are carried on by proxy in university departments across the globe. It is, I think, without any hint of irony that George Hewitt writes: 'Nor of course can the Georgian–Abkhaz conflict be resolved by these academic debates – what would certainly help would be for historians, linguists and ethnographers to refrain from besmirching their disciplines by placing them at the service of the nationalist politics of their nations in the first place.' To be fair, it is true that George Hewitt was specifically referring here to the absurd nonsense put about by some Georgian historians that the Abkhaz only arrived in Abkhazia in the seventeenth century. Again the mad I-was-here-first argument based on potty linguistic theories about the presence or absence of words for fish or pine tree or some such, proving that whoever did not have these words in their vocabularies must have come from elsewhere where there were no fish or pine trees. Even if this were the case, which it certainly is not, there would be no reason to abrogate any of their rights. But by the same token the Mingrelians and Georgians from Abkhazia – even if many settled there during the nineteenth century after the Russians had driven thousands of Abkhaz into exile in Turkey – should equally not be forced from their homes. Two hundred years seems a reasonable amount of time in which to become a resident. One of the tragic results of the Abkhaz conflict (and there were many, for both sides) was that between 160,000 and 250,000 Georgians (the figures are vigorously disputed), mostly Mingrelians, were forced to flee and ended up as refugees within Georgia proper. Many died on the high mountain passes as they tried to reach Svaneti. George Hewitt, at one of our affable lunches, thought that these people could be quite easily accommodated in the less-inhabited parts of south-eastern Georgia. Of course these parts are less inhabited for very good reasons – they are extremely inhospitable and overrun by large brown serpents. More seriously he has written that the refugees, those of peaceful intent at least, should be allowed back, but of course demographically this puts the Abkhaz in a tricky position: there are only about 80,000 Abkhaz, sharing the land with a quarter of a million Georgians.

It has to be said that the war in Abkhazia does not constitute one of the more glorious episodes in Georgian history. While many of the young Georgian men who went off to fight for their country did so out of the noblest of motives – to stop what they saw as their country's dismemberment – they were appallingly misled. Had a more rational being than Zviad Gamsakhurdia presided over the birth pangs of the new republic, and had Shevardnadze been more open to compromise and conciliation, more willing to countenance some new confederation of Georgia and Abkhazia (and Ossetia), then much suffering, death and hatred might have been avoided. This, however, is easy enough to say now, and at such a distance from the chaos of the times. Of course, the Abkhaz and their leaders were equally inflamed and inflammatory.

There had been warnings and alarms since 1988 and the beginning of the disintegration of the Soviet Union but the problems between Georgians and Abkhazians can be traced back further, at least to 1931 when Abkhazia became an autonomous republic within the Georgian SSR. Then, from 1937–1953, during the Stalin period and under the auspices of Lavrenti Beria, Abkhaz disaffection with Georgia increased: Georgian was imposed as the language of schooling, and publications in Abkhaz were repressed. Georgians and Mingrelians were encouraged to repopulate areas of Abkhazia left almost empty since the Abkhaz migrations of the 1860s (when many had fled to Ottoman Turkey after unsuccessfully rising against Russian rule). Many Russians also settled. The population was further affected by Stalin's removal of the Pontic Greeks to Kazakhstan during the Second World War. With remarkable regularity, every ten years or so, the Abkhaz petitioned the Soviet government in Moscow to be allowed to withdraw from the Georgian SSR and were constantly turned down. All this is seen as evidence of a Georgian conspiracy against Abkhazia. Indeed Beria – a Mingrelian born in Abkhazia, head of the Communist Party in Georgia and under the ultimate control of Stalin, a Georgian – savagely murdered and destroyed the Abkhaz intelligensia, tore apart the fabric of Abkhaz society. However, he had done very much the same in Mingrelia and throughout Georgia.

After Stalin's death, Abkhaz schools reopened and newspapers reappeared in Abkhazian, now written in an adapted Cyrillic script. The Abkhaz still felt that they were discriminated against by the government in Tbilisi and there were protests and petitions to Moscow – but the Abkhaz were always denied the right to secede from Georgia. Georgians were appointed to many of the most senior and most lucrative positions within the republic and certain language issues still remained unresolved. Tension in Georgian–Abkhaz relations was maintained, perhaps, as Professor Chervonnaya says, as part of a deliberate policy by the central powers who did much the same throughout the further reaches of the Soviet Union, from Lithuania to the Far East.

After Gorbachev started to loosen control from the centre with the promulgation of *perestroika* and *glasnost*, agitation within Georgia and Abkhazia gathered pace. In 1988 the Abkhazian Popular Forum, *Aidyglara*, was formed and, in March 1989, 30,000 Abkhaz met in Lykhny and called upon Moscow to recognise Abkhazia as a full Union republic. The Abkhaz Communist Party, particularly, demanded secession from Georgia and direct relations with Moscow. In April 1989, partly in response to this, though also to demand their own independence, thousands of demonstrators gathered in Tbilisi. They were brutally attacked by Soviet troops, almost certainly with Gorbachev's approval. Georgians point to the whole concatenation of events as evidence of collusion between Abkhaz officials, the Communist Party in Moscow and Abkhazia, the KGB and the Russian military, all acting to provoke the populations of Abkhazia and Georgia and thus to provide the opportunity and excuse for Russian military intervention. Abkhazians reply that if there was complicity between the separatists and the old Communist élite this should come as no surprise: they looked to Moscow for support as there was no other possible partner available to help counter Georgian oppression.

An attempt to open a branch of Tbilisi University in Sukhumi in July 1989 led to open confrontation between Georgians and Abkhazians in Abkhazia. In September, just as violence broke out in South Ossetia, the Abkhaz called a strike in protest against perceived Georgian violations. In August 1990 Georgia's Autonomous Soviet Socialist Republic of Abkhazia declared itself a full Soviet Socialist Republic independent of Georgia. By the spring of 1991 Georgia declared its own independence and elected Gamsakhurdia as President with an overwhelming 87 per cent of the vote. As I described in Chapter 4, events in South Ossetia unfolded grimly. There were problems in the Azeri and the Armenian areas of south and south-eastern Georgia. Gamsakhurdia's rantings only made matters worse and the Georgian people fell into a frenzy of despair and saw their country disintegrating before their eyes. At the beginning of 1992 when Gamsakhurdia was deposed in a *coup d'état* he fled into hiding, calling upon his supporters, mainly Mingrelians, to rise and defend their homeland against the traitors. The civil war began. Fighting in Ossetia also intensified. In April Shevardnadze returned to Georgia to head the Georgian State Council and the Abkhaz Supreme Soviet sent proposals to Georgia on a new federative treaty. This was ignored.

The precise nature and order of the events that led to all-out war in Abkhazia are still hotly disputed and it is almost impossible to make any comment on them without being accused of bias or ignorance. Even the spellings of place names betrays an inclination one way or the other: *Gal* and you are pro-Abkhaz, *Gali* and you must be pro-Georgian. Suffice it to say that in August the

Georgian National Guard (in reality a private army under the control of Tengiz Kitovani) went into Abkhazia, ostensibly to quell disturbances, secure railway lines, put an end to a spate of kidnappings (which were actually committed by Mingrelian supporters of Gamsakhurdia), and ended up occupying Sukhumi after storming the parliament building there. The Abkhaz government left for Gudauta. Fighting broke out across the country. As the months passed various ceasefires were brokered by the Russians and promptly broken. The Georgians, justifiably, accused the Russians of openly helping the Abkhaz and supplying them with arms. Chechens and other volunteers from the North Caucasus, as well as ethnic Abkhaz from the diaspora in Turkey and elsewhere, came to help the Abkhaz in their struggle. By the end of September 1993 Georgian forces were pushed from Abkhazia and many, if not most, of the Georgian population of Abkhazia fled across the border into Mingrelia and Svaneti. Thousands of Georgians and Abkhaz had been killed and the seeds of hatred sown will sprout for centuries.

Shevardnadze, who had himself very nearly been killed in the fighting in Sukhumi as Abkhaz forces retook the city, was forced to treat with the Russians who then helped him to quash the pro-Gamsakhurdia forces that were still causing mayhem in the west of the country. He had to allow Georgia to join the CIS (the Commonwealth of Independent States) and to allow Russia to keep its military bases in Georgia, to continue to man the Georgian border with Turkey. This was seen by many of his own countrymen as a terrible betrayal. The Russians had got their way and Abkhazia was lost.

One of the reasons that most Georgians find it so difficult to let go of Abkhazia, now *de facto* a separate state, is that they have all grown up with a history that describes the many centuries of co-evolution of the two peoples, of Abkhazians as part of the Georgian nation. This has been wilfully distorted at times – particularly recently in the post-Soviet cataclysm and the frenzied nationalism that it provoked – by the misrepresentations of certain Georgian historians who describe the Abkhaz either as relative newcomers to the area or, indeed, as ethnic Georgians. Unfortunately these fantasies exerted, and still exert, a grip on a part of the population who have received them as proof of the validity of Georgian claims over Abkhazia. But although the Abkhaz are not Georgians and Abkhaz is not a Kartvelian language (so not Georgian, Mingrelian, Svan or Laz) but one of the North-West Caucasian languages (with Circassian and Ubykh), proto-Kartvelian and proto-Abkhazian tribes have been linked since the beginning of the historical period. They together inhabited the eastern edge of the Black Sea and formed the Kingdom of Colchis (where Jason stole his Golden Fleece), the Laz Kingdom (which replaced Colchis) and the Kingdom of Abkhazia (with its capital in Kutaisi in western Georgia), which followed it and formed the basis of united Georgia. The first king of united Georgia, Bagrat, who came to the throne at the beginning of the eleventh century, had a Georgian father and an Abkhazian mother. Indeed, there has been much intermarriage over the centuries. These are strong family ties and George Hewitt himself writes that while the languages are different (referring here specifically to Mingrelian and Abkhazian), 'the linguistic evidence of language contact is testimony to a long period of symbiosis'. What is more, the argument that a separate language necessarily proves a separate ethnogenesis (Hewitt writes elsewhere that the Kartvelians and Abkhaz are 'totally unrelated'*) is not necessarily well-founded. It is quite possible for one group to speak a language completely unrelated to another and yet be genetically extremely close. Estonians and Latvians, for example, are as far apart linguistically as Europeans can be (Finno-Ugrics and Indo-Europeans) but they are genetically very close indeed in both their maternal and paternal gene lineages. And this seems to be the case with the Abkhaz and the Kartvelians (the Georgians, Mingrelians, Svans and Laz). After I discussed this with Richard Villems, the Professor of Genetics at Tartu University who had helped me with the Basque-Georgian relationship, he wrote:

But of course Georgians and Abkhaz are close genetically –

* G. Hewitt, *Central Asian Survey* (1995) 14 (2), pp. 285–310.

at least as far as their maternal lineages are concerned. The ethno-fundamentalists do not understand that our genetic legacy dates back tens of thousands of years, before any sensible person would put the split between North and South Caucasian languages. (On the other hand it also shows that genetics has little to do with the ethnic self-identification of people.)

Take a good archaeological (Paleolithic period) map of the Caucasus and you will see that the coastal part of the Black Sea has a high population density for at least 25,000 years – most importantly during the Last Glacial Maximum. People believe that the Abkhazian–North Georgian coastal area was one of the so-called 'refugiums' of the Last Glacial Maximum when huge areas of Europe became depopulated. I think that this is the key to the understanding and discussion of the genetic legacy and unity of the Caucasus populations, except where profoundly 'new' people are concerned like the Kalmyks and Nogays in the Terek and Kuban basins. Nothing to wonder at, knowing their history – they are, indeed, late newcomers.

So the Abkhaz separatists and some Georgian nationalists might like to think of themselves as completely unrelated to each other but they are not, they are genetically very close – not that this is any argument at all for the Georgian domination of an unwilling Abkhazia. It all goes back a bit, certainly, but nevertheless statements of absolute difference can be misused and help to drive another wedge between contending peoples. The history and culture of the Abkhaz and Georgians and their neighbours have so many points of commonality and similarity it seems almost perverse to exacerbate their differences rather than to stress what they have in common, an approach that I have not often come across.

One of the major difficulties for Western observers of the Abkhaz–Georgian conflict was that, having seen what had happened in Yugoslavia and what was happening at the break-up of the Soviet Union – the awful goblins of nationalism, violence and hatred that were released as soon as the lid was taken off the pot – they naturally started to see further fragmentation as productive only of appalling misery. All these moves towards separation just seemed to cause terrible violence – this was the phenomenon of dissolution. Suppressed 'ethnic hatred' explained everything, was deplored and the history behind such problems seemed so complex, tedious and refractory that it was oversimplified, misrepresented or ignored. All – commentators and antagonists alike – were caught in history's conundrum, between the need to remember and the need to forget. Past glories and past infamies were sifted and viewed in the refractive light of prejudice and partiality. Hundreds of years of history had to be deconstructed in a few months. Professor Villems's remarks about ethnic self-identification are most apposite: self-image is everything. People like to think of themselves in all sorts of peculiar ways, and selective history and scholarship of all kinds, as Professor Hewitt rightly insists, are used to reinforce or reinvent the national biography.

When *Conflict in the Caucasus* was published in 1994, Frances and I travelled to Georgia together to attend a conference in Tbilisi. We presented the book, gave a little talk (with Zura translating) and then I spent the rest of the day fending off angry Mingrelians who, somewhat illogically, wanted to have a go at us about George Hewitt's views, not just on Abkhazia but on the question of the Georgian suppression of Mingrelian culture and language. It was all part of his Georgian 'imperialist' thesis (one that subtly infiltrates the books written about the area which acknowledge George Hewitt's help – from Neal Ascherson's *Black Sea* to John Le Carré's *Our Game*). Did he not understand that they were all perfectly happy to be Mingrelian and Georgian, just as it was possible to be a Svan and Georgian, a Kakhetian and Georgian or, indeed, a Yorkshireman and English, that there was no contradiction or antipathy here? Why was he meddling in these matters? I tried to adumbrate the professor's concern for all the peoples and languages of the Caucasus, especially those threatened, both politically and demographically, with diminution or even extinction. My explanations were not well received. Soon I was exhausted and referred everyone to Frances who retreated in alarm.

We left to interview President Shevardnadze who had written a preface to the English edition of the book – at Frances's instigation: nothing to do with Professor Chervonnaya and not proof of 'blatant Georgian propaganda'. He was urbane, charming, affable and told us very little, really, no more than he wanted to, though the interview lasted over an hour. I asked him about the Georgian refugees, did he think they would return soon?

'It is very difficult to imagine a mass return soon. Two hundred and fifty thousand should go back but the Abkhaz will try now all they can to drag out the situation. The longer they manage to drag it out the easier it will be to make lawful the process of ethnic cleansing and the genocide in Abkhazia. In Sukhumi the main population were Georgians and now the separatists have brought in people from the mountains and from abroad and given them the Georgians' houses. And the authorities in Abkhazia are at the moment impeding the return of the refugees. I will be in Moscow soon and I want to clarify what Moscow's stance is. We have joined the CIS but we must take into consideration that we had no other options if we wanted to end the civil war here. When nothing came out of our appeals to the UN we had to turn to Russia. When I was in Sukhumi, just before it fell, I told the public that this would turn into a boomerang for Russia. If aggressive separatism is to prevail then this sets a very bad example within the Russian Federation and the CIS. I am sure that President Yeltsin wants to be helpful but how it will turn out in reality I cannot guess. The right decisions can sometimes take a long time to work through. It is still early days to assess the effectiveness of the Russian peace-keepers on the Abkhaz–Georgian border, but the fact that the representatives of only one country are there, the Russians, speaks of the weakness of the UN. The Security Council passed nine resolutions, good resolutions, but nothing came from them. We decided to take whatever help we could get. We have to consider one thing: during the course of the war Russian forces helped the separatists and today the peace-keepers are also Russians. If this action of peace-keeping turns out to be successful then obviously Russia will gain a lot of prestige from this. But so far they are not carrying out their mandate. Now is the most important moment, the time when the refugees should go back. We will see what happens next.'

So Frances and Zura and I went off to Zugdidi to see if we could see what had happened so far. The journey through Mingrelia was not entirely comfortable. Though Gamsakhurdia was dead, this was his home-base and his supporters still carried his torch. Gunfire, sometimes distant, sometimes very near, attenuated our nights. At almost every house we were shown bullet marks where Mkhedrioni thugs had, apparently, terrorised the inhabitants. (The Mkhedrioni, The Knights or Horsemen as they are known in English, were a Georgian paramilitary gang of ill-repute who had helped to topple Gamsakhurdia, done much to exacerbate the Abkhaz crisis and were held generally responsible for a great deal of lawless violence and criminal behaviour.) We were stopped, one night, by a group of armed men that I took to be soldiers. Negotiations to proceed seemed to take a while but it was not till we had driven some way along the road that our driver told us that they had been, in fact, bandits who had wanted to rob us. By chance, his cousin was one of the gang and had persuaded them to let us go. Family contacts are everything in Georgia.

In Zugdidi we spent a few days with the non-governmental organisations working among the refugees, particularly with the Oxfam office, and saw the miserable conditions in which thousands of bewildered and destitute people were living on the handouts of international aid. Each refugee had his or her own tragic story to tell. These were poor people, peasants who had lived off their land. Now they had nothing. All kinds of nasty diseases were endemic among the huddled masses and threatened to break out into the general population. There was, of course, not enough food, medicine, clothing, anything. The refugees were not being allowed to return to their homes. Some had tried and been driven away, some had not been allowed back by the Russian peace-keepers 'for their own safety'. We spent a day with the UN observers, mostly Norwegians, stationed by the bridge over the River Inguri which marks the boundary between Mingrelia and Abkhazia. We were not permitted to cross over ourselves. On the bridge gaggles of refugees waited for news of their homes. The Norwegian officers told us, off the record, that all attempts to return the refugees were being blocked by the Russians and by Abkhaz forces on the other side of the bridge. A Russian colonel, tall, tough and grim-faced, came to see us. He took out his notebook and demanded our names. So I took out my notebook and asked for his. He could not quite repress a grin. He gave his name, rank and number but he would not answer any of our questions.

Now, in 2001, some of the refugees do appear to have gone back home, particularly to the Gali border region. Precise figures are difficult to come by, but some say as many as 50,000. There is still trouble at the border, though. The Georgians and Abkhaz have come close to all-out war again. In 1998, particularly, a large number of returnees, perhaps as many as 30,000, were once more expelled from the Gali district by Abkhaz forces, their homes, rebuilt for them by international aid, burnt down and destroyed for a second time. The latest strange incursion involved a group of Georgians and Chechens causing mayhem across the Inguri. The Chechens had supported the Abkhaz in the war, now they, or some of them, have swapped sides. Georgia, of course, has become hugely important to them as the only neighbouring country that is not part of Russia. What they were hoping to achieve is difficult to discern. Conspiracy theories abound but mere banditry played a large part in the affair. The whole border area has become the playground of smuggling gangs from both sides. Peace would, of course, remove their livelihoods.

There is still no political solution and Shevardnadze is becoming more and more unpopular in Georgia, his government more futile, authoritarian, repressive, corrupt. The great hopes held for him – particularly by those in the West who saw him as the architect of the end of the Cold War – have all turned to ashes. The huge amount of money that America poured into Georgia (once the third largest recipient of American aid after Israel and Egypt) seems to have disappeared somewhere into the country's back pocket. There is little to show for it. Nobody, still, has much idea what might happen next. All must concur with Professor Hewitt's hope for the future: 'Every right-thinking person would advise that mutual co-operation between the patchwork of peoples living in the relatively small expanse of territory that constitutes the Caucasus was in all their interests. But this ideal will only be achieved when the integrity and rights of each of the peoples concerned are acknowledged and fully respected by their neighbours and international players alike.' The trouble is that all those concerned have such very different opinions as to what these rights of theirs, and of their neighbours, might actually be.

CHAPTER 6

RATCHA

The Jews of Oni, the Khazars and the Stalin Conversation

How we went from Oni, walked through
Ratcha to Svaneti and gazed upon the source
of the Phasis

In the awful heat and madness of Tbilisi bus station I met Mindi. This time he had brought along his friend Gia, known as Bomba for his explosive qualities, and also for his shape. Massive and gracefully elliptical, he towered above the crowds that parted about him as he forced a path to the bus, his great, expressive head split by a permanent grin and shining like a beacon on a torrid coast. Clever Mindi had, I am certain, selected him for his buffalo build; the pack he carried looked vast, topped with the great roll of Mindi's canvas tent. Mindi's own pack, by contrast, appeared delightfully small. Bomba's first concern – one which became a major theme of our journey – was for sustenance. As soon as we had wedged ourselves into the back of the bus he unfolded and dispatched a substantial meal. Feeling somewhat peckish soon after, he continued to snack on and off, while the bus trundled along towards Ratcha. There was something very reassuring about his bulk, his appetite and his constant good humour. Though only in his early twenties he was already married, had two tiny children, and was, to my great surprise, a student of banking. It seemed so incongruous, then, to be running off into the wilds with a baby banker; though in a striped shirt, braces and a suit he would have been utterly at home in some city wine bar, smoking a large cigar, and ordering more champagne.

Despite the official line coming from government in Tbilisi that all was calm and quiet now in South Ossetia, our driver refused to take the direct route to Oni, Ratcha's capital. So instead of going on the main road through Tskhinvali we skirted the bottom of the province (or autonomous region, or autonomous republic, or federated state or something quite new and undefined) and took the long road round. Our battered old bus puffed along slowly. Beyond Zestaponi, as we climbed into the hills of Ratcha and passed by Ambrolauri, the way grew green and lovely, great mixed forests covering the slopes. After eight hours we pulled into Oni.

Mindi had promised me that he had absolutely no relatives in Ratcha; as we climbed off the bus he fell into the arms of a cousin he'd quite forgotten about, recently married to a Ratchuelian man and now running a little general store in the centre of town. After a decent amount of amazement and delight, we left our packs among the blue plastic buckets and boxes of washing powder in her shop, and made for the museum. I had been urged to go and see its treasures by Beka's stepfather, Gela, and to contact the museum director, Gia Bereshvili. Unfortunately Oni had been hard-hit by an earthquake in 1991, many of its houses were cracked and twisted, and the museum was still shut for repairs – the familiar '*zakrit na remont*' sign jammed in the doorway – though there were few signs, in fact no signs at all, of any restoration. A neighbouring ancient pointed us to the director's house.

Mr Bereshvili lived with his old mother, neatly surrounded by fruit trees and ranks of onions. At first he seemed utterly bewildered by us but gradually he admitted that there was a museum, that it was shut, that he was in charge. I had been warned that one character-istic of the people of Ratcha was a certain slowness. They were kind, hospitable, immensely proud of their province and its traditions but not quick. Ratcha jokes are full of such slander: a stranger is trying to get to Oni. He gets a lift with a man from Ratcha. 'Is it far to Oni?' asks the stranger. 'Not far,' replies the Ratchuelian. Two hours pass in silence. Eventually the stranger asks again 'Is it far to Oni?' Unperturbed, the Ratchuelian replies, 'Now it is.'

Gia, warming gradually to us and to his subject, admitted sadly that after the earthquake all the contents of the museum had been removed to Kutaisi and it was now quite empty. However, we should not despair, he would show us something, something he had shown no one before. Leading us through to his study, impressing upon us the importance of Ratcha as a great centre of Kart civilisation, he opened the drawers of his desk and reverently placed upon its surface a variety of objects, such stuff that gladdens the hearts of archaeologists everywhere: fragments of ore mined in Ratcha 2,000 years before Christ, broken shards and bits of pot, bronze buckles and jewellery, smooth stones with magical purposes, strange symbols for stamping bread, a host of tiny artefacts of incredible age which he had excavated himself, many from the site at Brili which Gela had told me about. There could be no doubt, Gia said, with growing passion, that all this demonstrated the incredible sophistication of the Kartvelians and their great antiquity. His eyes shone as, well into his stride now, he raced with us through the Hittite confederacy, through Assyrian tablets and the Bible, through Herodotus and Xenophon, Pliny and Strabo and Arrian, and their references to ancient Kart tribes and their metallurgical skills: biblical Tubal and Meshech from Ezekiel, Xenophon's Taochi, Chalybes, Colchians, Phasians and Mossynoeci, the Heniochi and the Svanni and others of the Roman authors.

The Svans and Colchians have, from ancient times, been associated with mining or panning for gold. The Chalybes (possibly Homer's Halizones) of the Pontic coast were thought of by the Greeks as the discoverers of iron, and trade in iron between them dates probably from at least the seventh century BC, and is often given as the reason for the first Greek settlements along the eastern edge of the Black Sea. The black sand of the seashore there is still so rich in iron that it can be lifted with a magnet. Apollonius of Rhodes, writing in the third century BC, describes Jason and the Argonauts reaching the country of the Chalybes where the people 'do not use the ploughing ox. They not only grow no corn, plant no vines or trees for their delicious fruits, and graze no flocks in dewy pastures. Their task is to dig for iron in the stubborn ground, and they live by selling the metal they produce. To them no morning ever brings a holiday. In a black atmosphere of soot and smoke they live a life of unremitting toil.' Ratcha, too, was one of the great centres of iron production and there is evidence of ore extraction and smelting from before 1500 BC. Biblical references to the putative proto-Georgian tribes of Tubal and Meshech in Ezekiel associate them with metal and its trade. All this is evidence enough of a mining culture, a people familiar with metal and metalwork and indeed this is born out by the archaeological record. On Gia's wall, lovingly pinned, were photographic prints of some of the grave goods discovered in the barrow tombs of Trialeti, goblets of silver and gold decorated with precious stones and mysterious figures: A strange god with an animal mask sits on a throne; a procession of man-creatures with long tails and the masked heads of totem animals file up to him, offering vases or cups of some unearthly substance, possibly the 'Water of Life'; behind him grows the 'Tree of Life' and at his feet lie two animals, a ram and a goat, probably, though the latter looks rather like an armadillo; a huge bowl stands between them. Perhaps the man-creatures are pouring their liquid into it, or filling their cups from it. Underneath, in a separate frieze, deer race by. The goblet dates from early in the second millennium BC and its style, themes and motifs – immortality, fertility, arcane knowledge – link its creators unmistakably with other ancient peoples of Anatolia and the Near East: Assyrians, Babylonians, Hittites.

Xenophon's *Persian Expedition* (*Anabasis* in Greek, literally 'The Journey Up') is a great historical source for our knowledge of the people of Asia Minor and Transcaucasia and tells of his retreat with his ten thousand Greeks from Cunaxa after their failed attempt in 401 BC to help Cyrus overthrow his brother Artaxerxes the Second and seize the Persian throne. After fighting their way over the Armenian highlands and battling against wild Kurds, the Greeks eventually gain the heights overlooking the Black Sea near Trabzon and cry out in their joy, 'The sea! The sea!' as many of us over a certain age remember from our schooldays. Just before they arrive, however, they have to fight their way through the Georgian tribes that block their path to the coast. They manage this with some difficulty, encountering unexpected dangers on the way. After beating the Colchians the Greek soldiers feasted on honey from bees that had fed, it is thought, upon the flowers of the *Rhododendron ponticum*, which still grows wild all over the mountains, and 'went off their heads', vomiting and hallucinating for three days. Some died. It is true that Xenophon skirted the southwestern edge of the lands inhabited by the ancient proto-Georgians and their relatives and so can give only a small flavour of their lives, but far from celebrating their culture he damns most of them by comparison. This was, of course, normal for Greeks among the barbarian, concerned always to reinforce their sense of superiority. Many of these Georgian tribes, inhabiting the south-eastern corner of the Black Sea, were, at least nominally, part of the nineteenth Persian satrapy (the Armenians, their neighbours, formed the eighteenth) and had fought with the Persians against the Greeks. Xenophon, attacking one of the strongholds of the Taochi, recounts that when the Greeks had taken it after fierce resistance, the defenders preferred to die rather than be taken captive: 'then came a dreadful spectacle: the women threw their little children down from the rocks and then threw themselves down after them, the men did likewise.' He seems to have had a grudging respect for such courage. Indeed he writes of the Chalybes, that they 'were the most valiant of all the peoples they had passed through'. However, Xenophon particularly marks out the Mossynoeci, some of whom had allied themselves with the Greeks, and tells us that 'Those who were on the expedition used to say that these people were the most barbarous and the farthest removed from Greek ways of all those with whom they came in contact.' He tells us of 'some boys belonging to the wealthy class of people, who had been specially fattened up by being fed on boiled chestnuts. Their flesh was soft and very pale and they were practically as broad as they were tall. Front and back were brightly coloured all over, tattooed with designs of flowers. These people wanted to have sexual intercourse in public with the mistresses whom the Greeks brought with them, this being actually the normal thing in their country.' It did not seem polite to mention this to Gia.

After a long sojourn with his collection of antiquities, Gia took us upstairs to show us his modern art. I began to break out in a rash. Almost all the contemporary art I had seen in Georgia had depressed me, largely because it is so un-Georgian, so lacking in any particularity, so much like everything everywhere. On the other hand, when confronted with a painter who seems to try to work within a different, more defiantly Georgian idiom, such as Lado Gudiashvili, the work seems too garishly oriental, almost kitsch. The addition of painting to the Georgian arts is comparatively recent: there is little apart from icons and church murals, marvellous though these are at times, until the late nineteenth century, something to do, perhaps, with iconoclasts, Monophysites and the influence of Islam. The one splendid and deeply Georgian painter one is always shown, Niko Pirosmanashvili, who painted lovely scenes of Georgian life in the late nineteenth century, is always called a 'primitive', perhaps, some might say unkindly, because he could not actually paint. It is always interesting to speculate on the reasons for cultures producing brilliance in some arts and not others: certainly in the twentieth century one could talk of the brutalisation of the visual under the Soviets, and the crude imagery and vulgar monumentalism that this produced. This was especially vicious in Georgia which has, in contrast to its small store of paintings, a rich and magnificent sculptural tradition, mostly seen in relief on Georgian churches. This tradition has not recently, as far as I am aware, undergone any substantial renaissance, quite the opposite: there is a terrible Mafia of sculptors, favoured during the Soviet years, recipients of considerable funds, who litter the streets of Tbilisi with their efforts.

With surprise and delight, then, I found myself looking at a fine collection of prints, etchings and lithographs, by various young Ratchuelian artists whose names I disgracefully forgot to note down. Here were delicate aquatints of the mountains of Ratcha, subtle interiors in drypoint, painterly lithographs of village life. Gia had the true collector's susceptibility and my enthusiasm kindled and inflamed his most friendly instincts. He rushed us downstairs, shouted at his mother, sat us down at the table and hurried off for glasses and wine. We should have a banquet, a *supra*, immediately!

The *supra* is absolutely central to life in Georgia. It is a word of great antiquity, means literally a table-cloth, and possibly derives from the Aramaic '*soop-rraa*', meaning food placed on a spread cloth. (It is tempting to imagine that our own word 'supper' ultimately derives from this.) It suggests hospitality, toasting, poetry, community, food and drink, the sharing and passing on of tradition, the table as a metaphor for life's purpose and life's pleasure. Perhaps this is even more deeply felt in Ratcha than elsewhere in the country. The effects of Soviet rule and, particularly, of collectivisation in remote rural areas was not as completely devastating in Georgia as in some other states of the Union – it is easy to forget that collectivisation probably killed more people than were lost in sum total by all countries on all fronts during the Second World War. The peculiar organisation of Georgian society, the interconnectedness of communities through ties of family and obligation, meant that the whole idea of sharing or pooling resources and wealth was often familiar and congenial. Households retained much of their traditional structure and most of their ancient values. In fact, the Soviet system, while it certainly brought great hardship, was exploited as far as possible and used to maximise profit and opportunity. Here in Ratcha an extreme form of collectivisation was introduced in a few instances, a sort of ideal 'commune', created to represent a perfected Communist way of life. This experiment was far too successful. Dr Tamara Dragadze, in her study of Ratcha, *Rural Families in Soviet Georgia*, tells a wonderful story of the commune set up at Sori, near Ambrolauri:

> . . . the members of that particular village understood that if they were to share all they had and eat together, this meant they were to feast together and celebrate their love for one another in toasts. They allegedly banqueted every day for a whole month. Supplies ran out and, in the face of disaster, the commune was disbanded forthwith.

Our feast, materialised by some hospitable incantation, was set before us. Equally mysteriously friends appeared, attracted by the psychic pull of our *supra*. Very soon all were merry and Levan, an actor, bearing the most unnerving resemblance to my local builder, Reg, and behaving as actors do, stood to recite a few of his favourite poems. Within the first hour he gave us all of King Henry's speech before Agincourt, the Seven Ages of Man and, naturally, To Be or Not To Be. By the end of the second hour he had delivered most of the works of Mayakovsky, a smatter of Ratchuelian songs and the greater part of Rustaveli's *Knight in the Panther's Skin*. As he declaimed, Gia, overcome by emotion, leapt up and clasped him to his bosom. Thus they stood, swaying above the table, joined by their shared delight. Unfortunately, I was in that peculiar condition only brought about by listening to hours of unintelligible poetry: a kind of deep, vascular agony. Mindi had seen the panic behind my eyes and, looking for a way out, suddenly remembered my interest in Oni's Jewish community. Catching a momentary pause by the throat, he mentioned this to Gia, and in a stumbling twinkle we were walking through the dusk, down the back-lanes of Oni, into the courtyard of a slightly shabby but substantial synagogue. Gia, smiling, his legs working in different directions, called out to an old man in a flat cap and dusty jacket who popped into the gloom and reappeared seconds later with a suitably impressive key.

Gia took me tightly by the arm and we walked, packed close together like the White Queen and Alice, through the high porch of the synagogue, with its chunky barley-twist columns, up the aisle, stopping at every step as he waved his free arm expansively about, inviting me to enjoy the splendours of the interior. These were few. But while the decoration was deeply uninteresting the fact of the synagogue's existence was profoundly so. Gia beckoned to the old man and sat us all down on a pew.

'Never', he said, 'have the Georgians persecuted the Jews. Only in Georgia have they lived without fear through the centuries. They are Georgians, like us.'

He turned to the old man who nodded and smiled his agreement. So Gia sat content, chanting a charming and sozzled lullaby of peace:

> 'You see, you see!
> No hatred,
> No hatred,
> No hatred!'

And this seems, very largely, to be true. Only in the nineteenth century, with the arrival of Russian Orthodox priests and officials and their virulent anti-Semitism, were there outbreaks of violence against the Jewish population of Georgia. These were provoked by vicious blood-libels, and vigorously decried by many leading Georgians who wrote at length condemning such manifestations of religious hatred as contrary to Georgian culture and tradition. Ilya Chavchavadze and Akaki Tsereteli, two of the greatest poets of late nineteenth-century Georgia and perhaps the most influential voices in the cultural and intellectual life of the time, both spoke and wrote against anti-Semitism, both produced poems on Jewish themes and translated others by Byron (*Jewish Melodies, Eulogy of the Jews*) and Lermontov (*The Prophet*) into Georgian. This attitude can be strongly contrasted to their hostile views on the Armenian population of Georgia. There is a fine painting by David Gvelesiani of the Jews of Oni welcoming Akaki Tsereteli to the town.

The old man told us, with much sadness, that since independence most of the Jewish population of Oni, indeed of all Georgia, had emigrated to Israel.

'Most of us have left. My son, my daughters, my grandchildren have all gone. There are only thirty families still here and most of them have applied to leave. But I shall stay, I am too old now and I am Georgian, I do not want to leave. We have been here for so long.'

'How long?' I asked.

'For ever,' he shrugged and spread his hands wide.

There are various stories of the arrival of the first Jews in Georgia. The first, an oral tradition which is also found in Daghestan, says that they came to Kartli in the ninth century BC after the Assyrian King Shalmaneser had driven them into exile – that they formed a part of the so-called Ten Lost Tribes. The second story gives the arrival a slightly later date and is found in the *kartlis tskhovreba*, the *Georgian Chronicles*: they arrived after the destruction of the first Temple and the capture of Jerusalem by Nebuchadnezzar in 586 BC. Of course, even the entry in the *kartlis tskhovreba* was probably based on oral tradition and not written down till around the eleventh century, so should be regarded with a little caution, if one is of a scholarly or cautious disposition, that is. The third date given for their arrival is around AD 70, some time after the sacking of the second Temple by the Romans and the destruction of Jerusalem. Though the earliest archaeological evidence, gravestones from Mtskheta inscribed with Hebrew and Aramaic letters, dates from the fourth century AD, it is fair to conclude that there was a Jewish community in Georgia, as in the rest of the Caucasus, well before the birth of Christ. In fact the Jews of Azerbaijan, the *Bain Israel*, when living under the tsar were said to have escaped the tax levied on Jews elsewhere by persuading the authorities that since they had left the Holy Land before the Crucifixion they could not be blamed for Christ's death and should therefore be granted a special exemption.

The Jewish presence in Georgia is central to the story of Georgia's conversion to Christianity, for it was among the Jews of Mtskheta that St Nino, the great Illuminatrix, began her work of preaching and conversion in AD 332. She was herself from Cappadocia but had learnt Hebrew and was, therefore, able to talk to the Jews, who received her kindly: some of them followed her while she pottered about doing miracles among the Georgians, baptising the Kartlian King Mirian and his Queen Nana (almost all Georgian women are called Nino, Nana or Nunu) along with most of their court and their subjects. There were Christians active in Georgia before this but the official conversion had the most profound effect on Georgian history and would fix Georgia's gaze to the West and Christian Byzantium, rather than to the East and Zoroastrian, later Muslim, Persia.

Throughout the Caucasus there are strange whispers of the Jewish origins of various peoples and tribes. The old Georgian word for Jew, *uria*, is a sound that one hears often repeated in place names, and suggestions of Jewish ancestry are rumoured from Daghestan to the Crimea, giving a certain provenance to the antiquity of many a lineage. The most celebrated of these claims is that of the Royal House of Bagration, the Bagratids, who ruled in Georgia, or in some fractured element of Georgia, from the ninth to the nineteenth century. This vigorous family seems to have emerged in the sixth century as leading lords and princes along the fluctuating march-lands between Georgia and Armenia. They also, of course, became the Bagratuni, kings and princes of Armenia, and just how far they were originally wholly Armenian or wholly Georgian is something that keeps the historians of both countries well exercised, each desperate to prove the purity, originality and individuality of their respective royal houses. Georgian scholars seem to insist that the Bagratids originated in Speri, the oldest township in Georgia (now Ispir in Turkey, a filthy place full of secret policemen), and that a branch of the family later settled in Armenia, while the Armenians insist that . . . Well, they have been at it for years, bashing away at each other in their battle for primacy.

There is a story, shared by both Bagrationis and Bagratunis, that the progenitor of the Bagratids was Jewish, one Sumbat, Smbat, or Sbat. The tenth-century historian Moses Dasxuranci wrote in his *History of the Caucasian Albanians* that the 'King of Armenia, son of Hayak, asked the King of Babylon for a certain Jewish captive, named Sbat, whom he took and settled in Armenia with great honour. From him originated the Bagratuni family.' Versions of this tale were widespread in Georgia. The great Turkish traveller Evliya Chelebi, who spent some time in Georgia and the Caucasus in the seventeenth century, wrote in his *Narrative of Travels* a rather sketchy 'Genealogy of Georgian Kings', at the beginning of which he states with marvellous certainty that 'Their first kings were Jews'. Certainly the historians of the *kartlis tskhovreba* insist, in a very deliberate attempt to add splendour and prestige to the genealogy, that the line of the Bagrationis stretched back to King David. On the royal coat of arms are David's sling and his harp, an inscription from the Psalms, the seamless coat of Christ (bought to Georgia, it is said, by Jews from Mtskheta and buried there under the great cathedral of Svetitskhoveli) and a pair of scales.

To all these tales and to the evidence of ancient Jewish communities in the Caucasus, the Jews of Mtskheta, the Mountain Jews of Daghestan and Azerbaijan, another dimension must be added. In the sixth century AD a strange, nomadic Turkic people, arriving from Central Asia, began to make their presence felt around the

Caucasus. They quickly became a great local power, took more land, subdued more of the local tribes and, by the eighth century AD, ruled over a vast area, an empire, that reached along the top of the Black Sea beyond the Crimea to the west, up as far as Kiev, across the Dnieper, the Don, the Volga to the foothills of the Ural mountains, all along the northern and north-western shores of the Caspian, resting, to the south, along the base-line of the Caucasus. These were the Khazars, relatives of the Bulgars, the Bashkirs and many others who formed part of that great rolling migration westward of Turkic tribes and confederacies that culminated in the Seljuk and Ottoman settlement of Asia Minor and Eastern Europe.

The Khazars became of critical importance in the political and military struggles of the time; their strength and power had huge repercussions in the history of the region and of Europe. They became the valued allies of the Byzantines, first against Persia and then, after the explosion of Arab armies out of the Middle East in the seventh century, against the Arabs. The Arab–Khazar wars raged for more than a century as Muslim armies tried again and again to penetrate the wall of the Caucasus, sometimes breaking through the mountains of Daghestan, sometimes through the Daryal, more often pouring up along the shoreline of the Caspian and through the Iron Gates at Derbent, always being thrown back again and then fighting desperate defensive battles as the Khazar cavalry penetrated deep into Persia and towards Baghdad, sacking towns and gathering booty on the way. A trace of their exploits has lodged in our own language: the words 'hussar' and perhaps also 'cossack' derive from their name. Nor was their hegemony just a transient flash of nomad ferocity: the Khazars settled, founded cities and for at least three hundred years held the key to the lands of the North Caucasian steppe and prevented Arab encroachment in the east with as much significance for Byzantine, Russian and European history as the far more famous victory of Charles 'the Hammer' Martel at Tours in 732 which threw the Arab armies back over the Pyrenees at the other end of Europe.

But perhaps the most extraordinary fact about the Khazars is that they were Jewish. That is to say that they converted to Judaism around AD 740, it is thought, though there are also convincing arguments for later dates. They formed, in the eighth or ninth century, a Jewish state more than a thousand years before the inception of the state of Israel. This was as much of a surprise to their contemporaries as it is to us. One of the historical sources for the Khazar conversion is an exchange of letters, the so-called Khazar Correspondence, between the Khazar Khagan, or King, Joseph, and the Jewish vizier to the Umayyad caliphs of Cordoba, Hasday ibn-Shaprut, around the middle of the tenth century. Hasday was an extraordinary man: foreign minister, court physician, patron of poets in Hebrew and Arabic, he dealt with ambassadors from the Christian kingdoms of northern Spain, from Byzantium, from the German empire, corresponded with the leading rabbis of Baghdad, translated medical treatises into Arabic. Upon hearing of this strange Jewish kingdom to the east from a couple of merchants from Khorasan, this most erudite and well-informed man was, at first, extremely sceptical. However, intrigued, he tried to discover more and eventually some Byzantine ambassadors confirmed what the merchants had told him. So he wrote a letter to the Khagan Joseph, which, after much delay and many adventures, arrived in Khazaria in AD 954. Hasday received his reply, in Hebrew, a year later and Joseph confirmed all that Hasday had heard, informing him not only of the events of the conversion but also of much about the nature and extent of the kingdom.

All the historical sources for the conversion of the Khazars – Jewish, Arab and Byzantine – give slightly different versions, varying in degrees of melodrama, stuffed with argument, duplicity and supernatural visitations. The story I like best is that of the Khagan Bulan who, convinced of the superiority of monotheism over his ancestral, pagan ways, and having in his kingdom many rabbis, priests and imams, ordered a debate between the most revered religious leader of each faith. All three agreed on the truth of the Torah but the veracity of the New Testament and the Koran was supported only by each book's particular proponent. The rabbi, too, had a direct route to God, while both priest and imam had their religion mediated by a third party. The logic was overwhelming and the Khagan was immediately inducted into the Jewish faith.

Leaving aside the theological, philosophical and mystical impulses which may or may not have contributed to the conversion, the question of how and why it took place still remains. Neither can be answered with certainty but it seems that there was a large influx into Khazaria of Jewish refugees during the sixth and seventh centuries, fleeing from fierce persecution both from the West and the torments ordered up by the Byzantine emperors, and from the East and the ministrations of Zoroastrian priests at the Persian court. These refugees included, of course, rabbis and religious leaders who seem to have spread Judaism among the population with considerable success. But the decision to convert to Judaism must also have had a strong political motivation: the Khagan had, to either side, the hugely powerful empires of Christian Byzantium and Muslim Arabia which were in almost perpetual conflict; Judaism, while it suggested all the advantages of coherence and control that seemed to characterise the other monotheistic faiths, was a politically neutral space, did not necessarily propel the Khazars towards one side and alienate them from the other, was a bulwark against that influence and penetration which always went hand in hand with proselytism from Islam or Christianity. Byzantine history, particularly in relation to the empire's northern and eastern neighbours, is a vivid testament to the way in which priests, like that great pair of sainted brothers Cyril and Methodius, were used as the shock troops, the vanguard, of imperial expansion. In fact it is quite probable that it was St Cyril who was the Christian priest in the great Khazar disputation, thus fixing the date of their conversion at AD 861.

It used to be thought that the extent of the conversion was limited to the ruling élite but the latest scholarship shows that Judaism penetrated and spread deep throughout Khazar society. It was a society which was singularly marked by its tolerance, inclusiveness and multi-ethnicity. The Khazars were Turks, it is true, but this appellation describes a linguistic grouping much more than a single race. They were an agglomeration of collected peoples; their physical appearance was described extremely variously: tall, short, white-skinned, dark-skinned, red, fair, smooth, hairy, with shaven heads, with long hair, living in houses and living under the open

The market, Tbilisi.

(*Overleaf*) Oshki, Tao-Klargeti.

Ishan, Tao-Klargeti.

Yayla, Shavshat.

The sheep co-op, Mestia.

Picnic, Svaneti.

Taxi, Mestia.

Children, Svaneti.

Cemetery, Ushguli,

Ushguli, Svaneti.

Girl blowing bubble, Tbilisi.

sky. There was certainly a Mongol or Uighur element. When the Khazars first appeared in Georgia as allies of the Byzantine Emperor Heraclius in AD 627, having just sacked Derbent, they set about besieging Tbilisi, then under Persian control. Unhappy in the summer's heat, sitting about unsuccessfully, the Khazars were jeered at and taunted by the Persian and Georgian defenders who put a large pumpkin on the battlements to represent the head of the Khazar leader, Ziebel, with his Mongolian features, disgracefully beardless. They then did unspeakable things to the pumpkin. This was a terribly bad idea. When Ziebel returned the following spring he ransacked the city, then tortured, mutilated and executed the governor and many inhabitants, finally exposing them on the same battlements. There is the most fantastic description of this in Moses Dasxuranci's *History of the Caucasian Albanians*:

> . . . the tempest from the north suddenly roared a second time and lashed the great eastern sea [the Caspian]. The savage, putrid beast came down with its bloodthirsty whelp Sat' and fixed its eyes upon the kingdom of Georgia and the city of Tiflis; and there were none of the courageous men previously to be found among them, and the Khazars had the occasion to vent the spite that had rankled within them since the recent insult. Surrounding the town, they fought and harassed the inhabitants, who turned and fought back and for two months worked and strove in vain against the sentence of death which faced them. Fear of the shedding of their blood, a danger that was very imminent, spurred them on. Then the terrible beast roared, and hunting down and slaughtering enough for its brood filled its lairs with game and its forces with loot. Raising their swords, as one man they stormed the walls, and piling one on top of the other, their numbers were so great that they topped the wall. A dark shadow fell upon the wretched inhabitants of the city; the joints of their limbs were loosed and their arms grew powerless. They were defeated. They fell back from the ramparts, terrified as sparrows trapped in the engines of bird-catchers. No one had time to warn his family of the dread

disaster, to instruct his beloved wife to care for the fruits of her womb, or to think about their duty as parents. Exhausted with fatigue and terror-stricken, they strove to conceal themselves; some hid in the rooftops and others in the drains, while many made for the sacred refuge of the churches and clung to the horns of the altar. The cries of mothers lamenting for their sons rose up like that of a huge flock of sheep, like that of ewes calling to their lambs. And after them came the merciless reapers, their hands shedding torrents of blood, their feet trampling upon corpses, their eyes beholding the dead fall like a shower of hail. When the wailing and groaning subsided and not a single person was left alive, the Khazars knew that their swords had drunk their fill. They brought the two princes, one the Persian governor and the other a native Georgian, as captives before the king, who commanded that their eyes be put out as retribution for having insultingly represented his image as blind; and with dire tortures he strangled them to death, then flayed the skin from their bodies, stretched it, stood it up, filled it with straw and suspended it from the top of the wall. Then they laid their hands on the chests full of treasure, and the whole army, each man heavily laden, carried it before their ruler and placed it in great heaps and piles.

No one writes history like that any more! The great Edward Gibbon, in his *Decline and Fall of the Roman Empire*, writing eight hundred years after Moses Dasxuranci, also writes of the Khazars wonderfully, and describes the meeting between Ziebel and Heraclius outside Tbilisi:

At his liberal invitation, the horde of Chozars transported their tents from the plains of the Volga to the mountains of Georgia; Heraclius received them in the neighbourhood of Teflis, and the khan with his nobles dismounted from their horses, if we may credit the Greeks, and fell prostrate on the ground to adore the purple of the Caesar. Such voluntary homage and important aid were entitled to the warmest acknowledgments, and the emperor, taking off his own diadem, placed it on the head of the Turkish prince, whom he saluted with a tender embrace and the appellation of son. After a sumptuous banquet he presented Ziebel with the plate and ornaments, the gold, the gems and the silk which had been used at the Imperial table, and, with his own hand, distributed rich jewels and earrings to his new allies. In a secret interview he produced the portrait of his daughter Eudocia, condescended to flatter the barbarian with the promise of a fair and *august* bride, obtained an immediate succour of forty thousand horse, and negotiated a strong diversion of the Turkish arms on the side of the Oxus.

The Khazars' later contemporaries, particularly Muslim travellers and commentators, were amazed at the variety of races and creeds that were tolerated and encouraged under Khazar dominion. The early Khazar capitals in Daghestan were probably rather provincial affairs, but when the capital was moved, finally, to Itil, or Atil, in the throat of the Volga delta, it soon became a teeming, thriving city, controlling trade down the Volga to the Caspian – known to the Arabs still as the Khazar Sea, *Bahr-ul-Khazar* (and to the Turks as *Hazar Denizi*, to the Persians as *Daryaye Khazar*). Along the Don, a second city, Sarkel, set half way between the Don–Volga portage (the Khazarian Way) and the Sea of Azov, led to the Crimea, the Black Sea and the wealth of Constantinople. Trade flourished: from the south came Arab silver and Byzantine gold; from the east, as far away as China, came silk, perfumes, pottery; from the north, Viking and Slav traders brought amber, skins, furs and slaves down the Volga. The great riverways that linked the Baltic with the Black Sea were under Khazar dominion. Under their tolerant rule the empire flourished, held together by a remarkably efficient administration and set of laws. Members of each faith were tried in their own courts: Jews, Muslims and Christians had two judges each, while pagans had one. The rabbinical Judaism that they adopted was, for the Khazars, a matter of conscience and was never imposed upon the varied communities of Khazaria. Despite their new faith, they held to their Turkic ways. They kept for some time to their strange form of dual kingship, the titular head of the kingdom being elected for an allotted period and then ritually strangled, and though they may have held aloft the scrolls of the Torah as they went into battle, battle order, dress and customs remained Turkish at heart.

What happened to the Khazars? The short answer is that the Russians destroyed them. At this period the name Russian, or Rus, was used variously to describe either the eastern Slavs or their Viking overlords or both. Those amazing Vikings, a little before their cousins the Normans were conquering England, were establishing the new state of Russia. They had taken Kiev from the Khazars (and their Magyar relatives) and, piling down the great rivers and across the Black Sea, soon appeared at the gates of Constantinople, the fabled Miklegard of the Northmen, wheeling their boats under sail across the land when they found the entrance to the Golden Horn barred by the great chain, much to the terror and amazement of the Byzantines. Four hundred years later Sultan Mehmet used the same trick to greater effect, but the Byzantines had to pay off the Rus with huge bribes. Even so they came back again five times during the tenth century. Despite the service that the Khazars had done the Byzantines against the Arabs (who also joined the queue to besiege Constantinople), in the face of this tremendous threat the empire turned from them to placate the aggression of the Rus and began to find alternative allies, the Pechenegs, among the Turkish tribes in the wild steppe lands to the north of the Caucasus. The Khazars had been fighting the Rus who had penetrated down the Caspian shore as far as Baku; the Byzantine emperor, displaying that treachery for which his court became a byword, encouraged the Russian Prince Oleg to attack the Khazars on the Straits of Kerch. Russians and Khazars fought fiercely in the Crimea and along the Volga throughout the mid-tenth century, with the Khazars getting much the better of the conflict. However, in 965, the Russians under Svyatoslav, Grand Duke of Kiev, took Sarkel from the Khazars and two years later, sailing down the Volga, having just defeated the Bulgars, they laid siege to Itil and overran the Khazar capital. Some kind of Khazar confederacy held on for at least another fifty years; in 1016 a joint Rus and Byzantine army defeated the Khazars in the Crimea and captured the Khazar khagan. There is evidence to suggest that a vestigial Khazar state hung on until finally dispersed by the Mongols in the thirteenth century, but to all intents and purposes they were finished.

But the Khazars did not simply vanish. Where did they go? Some must have stayed roughly where they were, some were resettled by the Russians, but the majority seems to have migrated westward into Europe. A branch of the Khazars, the Kabirs, had already settled in Hungary with the Magyars in the ninth century and helped to found the Hungarian nation; early Hungarian coins have been found with Magyar inscriptions on one side and Hebrew on the other. Now Khazar émigrés spread into Poland, the Ukraine, Byelorus, Lithuania, even, some small numbers, into Spain and elsewhere. This is the basis of a huge, unresolved and fascinating argument that perturbs Jewish scholars to this day. How far was European Jewry, particularly Eastern European Jewry, descended from the Turkic Khazars and not from the Tribes of Israel? Are many European Jews Turks? A wonderful question which will not detain us beyond the suggestion that, according to some estimations, as many as 60 per cent of Ukrainian Jews may have been descended from the Khazars.

This brings us back to the Caucasus and the same question. How much of the Jewish population there is of Khazar origin and how much do the many legends of Jewish descent owe to the Khazars? Almost everything here is speculation. It used to be thought that the Karaite Jewish community in the Crimea was the one population which could claim certain descent from the Khazars and Arthur Koestler in his book *The Thirteenth Tribe* held to this view; but Khazar scholars like D. M. Dunlop and, more recently, Kevin Alan Brook, dismiss the notion. The Russian historian M. I. Artamonov declared it certain that the Khazars had 'intimate links with the Caucasus', and many other historians write of vestigial Khazar communities in the mountains without being very specific about where these are to be found; definite evidence of an unbroken tradition is hard to locate. In the north-eastern corner of the Caucasus, above Derbent, live the Kumyks (not to be confused with the Kumukhs), pastoralists speaking an archaic Turkish dialect related to Komanic.

Most scholars agree that they are of mixed Khazar descent. The old Khazar capitals of Balanjar and Samandar, though their precise location is uncertain, were most probably within the area inhabited by the Kumyks today. Their near neighbours the Nogays, despite their entirely Mongol appearance, are also thought to have mixed with the Khazars. One tribe of Nogays in particular, the Chi-Jughutlari, is said to claim Jewish Khazar ancestry. It seems reasonable to suppose that the already established Jewish communities in the area, under the centuries of Khazar dominion, would easily have mixed and intermarried to some extent with their powerful co-religionists: the Mountain Jews of southern Daghestan, the Jewish Tats or *Dagh Chufut*, living by the hem of the Khazar Sea, are most likely to have done so.

All along the mountains there was probably some degree of inter-mixing. The Alans around the Daryal Pass raided against the Arabs with the Khazars and some converted to Judaism. To the east of them, in Chechnya and Ingusheti, there are what are thought to be Khazar graves, and to the west, among the Karachays and Balkarians (split apart by Stalin but really the same people, speaking a Turkic language), are more Khazar graves dating from the seventh to the twelfth centuries. A medieval town, near present-day Billim, was called Khazar-Kala and on the right bank of the Kuban River, near Hamara, archaeologists believe they have discovered a large Khazar site. Prince Vakhushti, in his *Geographical Description of Georgia*, called the Balkarians and the Karachay '*Basiani*', and derives the name from a particular Khazar tribe called '*Basa*'.

Long before their conversion, Khazars had rampaged through Georgia, Azerbaijan and Armenia and had entered into dynastic marriages with various ruling families, sometimes rather forcefully. A famous Georgian story praises the courage of a Georgian princess so condemned who, horrified at the thought of her future husband, the Khazar Khagan, poisoned herself while being carried off through the Daryal Gorge on her journey towards him. The Khazar Khagan was so furious that he had the commander in charge of the party tied by the neck to two horses which pulled him asunder. There are similar Armenian and Caucasian Albanian tales. The Khazars did marry into the Abkhazian ruling household and helped them strengthen their grip on western Georgia. The most famous Khazar marriage alliance took place at the other edge of the Black Sea in Constantinople: the Khazar Princess Chichak, later Eirene and a most pious Christian, gave birth to the Byzantine Emperor Leo the Fourth, known as Leo the Khazar.

Unfortunately, there is no evidence directly linking Jewish Khazars with the Jews of Oni. I say unfortunately because, as may be guessed, the Khazars are some of my favourite people. The most that I can suggest is, again, that intermarriage took place across the Caucasus and that such a thing is probable, certainly possible. I came near to concluding an academic deal with Professor Neil Bradman, head of the Department of Genetic Anthropology at University College London, who is also interested in the Khazar Question. I was to wander about the mountains with a box of test-tubes taking swabs for DNA sampling from likely inhabitants. These could then be compared with East European Jewish samples and with Turkish samples to see if any possible Khazar conclusion could be drawn. His research so far shows that there are marked differences in the DNA of Ashkenazy Levite Jews from other Jewish populations and these may be, in some part, the descendants of the Jewish Khazars. Unfortunately our deal was dashed on the rocks of time and money, but only in such a way will we be able to understand, finally, what really happened to the Khazars.

*

Mindi's lovely cousin had left for work and her husband, arriving very late at night, had scurried off at first light to find sustenance. The poor chap needed sleep but insisted on feeding us. We break-fasted off omelette and cool little cucumbers from his garden, helped down with a strange chocolate liqueur from Daghestan, which went rather well with cucumber, I thought. He then took me out to see his melons and his dope plants, growing splendidly against the far fence of his kitchen plot. Around mid-morning Mindi and Bomba were ready to leave and we strode out of Oni towards Glola, some twenty-five kilometres away. Douglas Fresh-field, in *The Exploration of the Caucasus*, called the road to Oni from the south 'the most beautiful road in Europe', and indeed, all around was glorious in morning mistiness, with deep green forests rising in waves over the mountains, though the boys grumbled away about possible lifts in lorries as we walked on past the timber yards and the jolly houses with their ornate pierced-metal gutters and hoppers and their little orchards of apples and pears.

Ratcha is famous for its mineral springs and we stopped frequently to taste the rich waters which poured out everywhere along the route. In the village of Utsora an old man, stretching his back from his hoeing, shouted to us from his garden and brought us water of a particularly delicious and health-giving nature, he assured us, and pears and glasses of *chacha*, as we rested a minute by the roadside under a walnut tree. Brosset, the great French historian of Georgia, had written in his *Rapports sur un Voyage Archéologique*, that in Oni he drank '*eaux acidulés, ferrugineuse ou autres, je ne sais, qui sont une boisson aussi saine qu'agréable.*' (Waters that are acidulous and perhaps chalybeate, I think – a drink as agreeable as it is healthy.) I had not yet made up my mind how '*agréable*' the water was, but it was certainly necessary to compliment the inhabitants upon its qualities, of which they were immensely proud. Brosset had also discovered in Oni, in the middle of the main street (so just outside Mindi's cousin's shop by my calculations), a pit covered in branches from which rose clouds of vapour. He sat by the edge of the pit and breathed in the vapours which '*causent une espèce de vertige momentané. Après quelques minutes consacrées à cet exercice, on se sent la tête plus dégagée, le jeu des poumons plus libre, la circulation du sang plus active; on éprouve un bien-être général. Les femmes surtout se plaisent à ces exhalasions, et les bestiaux, qui en connaissent bien la route, n'y sont pas insensibles.*' (. . . cause a kind of momentary dizziness. After a few minutes dedicated to this exercise one feels one's head more free, the play of one's lungs more easy, the circulation of the blood more active; one has a general sense of well-being. Women, particularly, enjoy these vapours, and animals too, knowing the way well, take pleasure in them.) Brosset found a similar hole in Utsora from which flowed vapours of such strength that '*il suffit de deux ou trois inhalations pour mettre un homme sur le flanc*' (that it only needed two or three inhalations to lay a man flat). I searched earnestly in both places for felled men, gangs of stoned women and giddy beasts but found neither them nor the pits with the magic gas. Brosset's description, though, did sound very much like descriptions of the strange exhalations in the cave at the oracle of Delphi where this procedure of breathing in fumes from the bowels of the earth took on a sacred significance. The gas in both cases was probably ethylene – so rather like sniffing glue.

Heading slightly east to Glola (and so back towards the Mamisson Pass and Ossetia) was a diversion due mainly to Bomba's insistence on visiting his cousins there. When I questioned him more closely they seemed to be almost entirely youthful and female and Mindi grinned sheepishly at my interrogations. My own grand plan was to head west through Ghebi and to see if it was still possible to walk through the mountains from Ratcha into Svaneti, following one of Freshfield's carefully marked tracks. Freshfield's book is of a quality that would bring tears to the eyes of even the most blasé bibliophile. Beautifully printed in 1896 by Edward Arnold, it is full of photographs, all taken with one of the enormous, heavy plate-cameras of the time, and all the appendices and notes one could possibly wish for. But best of all, in a little pocket in the back cover of the second volume, is a map. To pull it gently out, unfold it, and spread it across the floor gives a shiver of delight. Though showing only the central part of the mountain chain, from Kazbek to Elbruz, it is even now by far the best map of the Caucasus I have discovered, certainly the most beautiful. It was made by Stanfords, still the finest map shop in London, all in relief, the mountains in shades of brown, their peaks white with snow, the glaciers shaded a slight tinge of purple. And according to Freshfield there was a track that went across the upper reaches of the Rioni River over a high pass into the land of the Svans. This was what drew me, though the boys were deeply uncertain about the entire project and, with studied innocence, kept trying to persuade me that we should take our ease in Glola for a few days.

And so, of course, we did. Mindi and Bomba were so happy playing with the jolly cousins, who were all extremely pretty, that I did not have the heart to tear them away after just one night. We found the cousins' house down a dusty, piglet-snuffled track, a large ramshackle building set in an overgrown garden. After much rejoicing, we joined an ancient grandfather with a withered leg at an outside table and were served from a great cauldron with *lobio*, the endemic Georgian, spicy, red bean stew (especially good when served with *ajika*, a staggeringly hot and bitter relish from Abkhazia) which fuelled us throughout our stay. From the garden gates I could look up at the ruins of Queen Tamara's castle, with a satellite dish and what I took for a large cross, though later found was an aerial, on top, high on a hill. A huge, contented sow lay by the back door.

That evening for my entertainment, to satisfy my need for local culture and to make up for my utter inability to understand the rules of the 'very simple' card game I was invited to join, an old lady was respectfully ushered into my presence. Lively and passionate, Tamara Azanishvili danced and sang the folk songs of Glola and Ratcha in the dusky half-light of the garden, punctuating her movements and her verses with commentary. She apologised for her absent accompanist: he was extremely old and ill and the only *chianuri* player in town, so in the absence of this lute-like instrument and its master (it may only be played by men) she had come with a cassette player and recordings that she and her friends had previously made here in the village. She produced these with such aplomb and seemed so much at ease with herself and with me, that I asked if she had done this before. She replied proudly that professors from Moscow had been to hear her sing. The words to the songs, some of which she kindly wrote down, were difficult even for clever friends in Tbilisi to translate from the rich dialect of Ratcha, and their significance impossible to grasp entirely without the movements and explanations that accompanied them. There were work songs, harvest songs but, most of all, songs of mourning and funeral laments. I have always had a weakness for funeral laments, particularly the formulaic improvisations of Greece, the *moiroloyia*, and think of the Linos myth from the *Iliad*, which explains the very origins of music as lament: the void Linos left behind at his death being itself so perturbed by the loss of such beauty that its vibrant agitation produced music. Tamara explained that there were three types of lament specific to Ratcha: *korkali*, *zrooni* and *ghughuni*, each of which had a set verse pattern and specific function. The *zrooni* is sung immediately after a death, when the body is still within the house; the *ghughuni* when some time has elapsed after the burial. These are still sung to this day in Glola and the *zrooni* that I heard was particularly beautiful: a polyphony for six unaccompanied female voices (all these songs, in fact, are only sung by women), it was wonderfully soft, quiet and moving. The simplest and most self-explanatory of the songs she wrote down tells of a hunter, high in the mountains, lamenting the death of his brother who, it is understood, has perished on the heights chasing some bear or tûr:

> Someone lit a fire on top of the mountain
> We thought it was a hunter
> We learnt that his heart just ached over his brother
> And tears were running down his face.

The following day, after a start that was, even by Mindi's standards, quite painfully leisurely, I was taken out, like some elderly pet, to walk to Shovi. It was a day of soft breezes and bright sunshine; Ratcha and all its inhabitants looked particularly lovely. The girls chirruped gaily and Bomba and Mindi had a marvellous time carrying them across rivers and handing them up and down slopes that, when unattended, they skipped merrily over on their own, stopping here and there to pick bunches of flowers which grew in fantastic profusion and variety about the fields and mountainsides around. This sylvan, summer scene could be very different at other seasons, the Bokos-tsqali River which runs through Glola, and the smaller Tchantchaki, bursting their banks regularly and carrying away people and houses in their fury. The girls told me, with some pride, that many had been drowned in this way and, indeed, the whole of Glola had been moved higher up the mountain slope during the last century after a particularly appalling flood had carried off most of the old village.

Shovi was not so much a village as a resort: a few fine villas and some unappealing hostel blocks set about a great meadow, all now empty, ransacked and fallen into decay. In the 1890s Freshfield had predicted that this area would become the new Baden-Baden of the Caucasus. I had missed the fulfilment of his prophecy and now attended upon its ruin. What had once been a small but thriving resort was now quite deserted and hung about with all the sadness of a shattered dream. We rummaged through the carcasses of buildings with floorboards, doors and windows broken or ripped out, the girls anxiously watching for snakes, and climbed up to a terrace built half way up a hill to look down upon the view and imagine the crowds taking the waters, bathing, escaping from the summer heat of the cities and the plains. The wreckage of this human effort was all the more poignant because the natural world around remained so luxuriant, so extravagant in its beauty and indifference.

A little way back down the road we clambered through the woods to visit a magical rock called *kokwabi*, a great overhang under which the sick would lie for a day and a night, to awaken the following morning in the certain knowledge of a cure. It was particularly efficacious against cases of dysentery and jaundice. The girls all believed this absolutely and crossed themselves repeatedly in front of the rock. We walked on under the trees to a graveyard, the graves all neatly fenced about with elaborate ironwork, polished slate tombstones with etched photographs of the dead, tables set with glasses, bottles and chairs around, so that those left behind could sit and drink and hold communion with their departed loved ones. A tiny church stood above and the girls went in and lit candles for a much-loved uncle and a grandfather. Icons of Mary, of Christ and the Apostles hung about the walls and great horns of tûr leant up against them. Then we walked on past Tamara's castle with its satellite dish, now defunct, and paused on our way home to take our fill of liquid metal.

The next morning, after fond farewells, we crammed into a battered little bus, already impossibly full with villagers heading to market in Oni, and jumped down after five or six kilometres to head on west to Ghebi, rejoining the Rioni River which we would follow almost to its source. The way was easy and we ambled along by the wide river-bed, hopping over the rushing streams which fed it. In the clear air the gleaming mountains marched along beside us. We stopped to admire them and bathed in the freezing waters of the Rioni, then settled in the long grasses on the river's edge for a picnic by the village of Chiora. Thousands of crickets took off in protest, opening up like butterflies, flashing red and making an unbelievable noise, like the sudden ringing of an alarm clock.

Both Brosset and Freshfield wrote fondly of their stays in Ghebi and Glola, though Brosset lamented the disappearance of a wealth of artefacts and manuscripts that he had heard about and read of in Vakhushti's *Geographical Description of Georgia*. Nevertheless he carefully noted every ruined church and tower and copied down inscriptions so that some record of this past glory would remain. He wrote also that this area had once come under the rule of the Svans who, in the fifteenth century, murdered one of the Japaridzes, princes of Ratcha, and were then blockaded by the Ratchuelians for nearly twenty years, their convoys of trade plundered. At length a huge blood-price was fixed which included vast tracts of land, churches and their precious objects, fortresses, monasteries and villages with their inhabitants, both nobles and peasants, and all the villages around Ghebi with four hundred families. He was a very pricey prince. Ever since, the land has been firmly part of the province of Ratcha.

Ghebi stands over the Rioni, a large village near the head of the valley with the great mountains closing in around. Just to the south is the strange twin peak of Mount Shoda, to the north the Domba ridge and further off Mount Laboda. Great glaciers, flat-topped, snow-covered, shone for us in the sunshine. Freshfield described Ghebi's position nicely:

The inhabitants occupy the first place in one's memory, but the situation of Gebi has great picturesque attractions. The village stands 4,400 feet above the sea, where a green knoll projects and bars the valley, below defaced by torrents, above smiling with corn-fields. It is surrounded by forested slopes, golden and fragrant through the early summer with sheets of azalea blossom, by pastures fringed with delicate birches and low thickets of creamy Caucasian rhododendron. Snow-crests look down from all sides over the shoulders of the lower hills.

The village is busy and populous: sturdy houses with wide wooden verandas, neat haystacks, tidy plots of potatoes and of maize. All the inhabitants seemed to be on the move at great speed. A party of grandmothers carrying huge bundles on their backs strode on past me. I tried to keep up with them but soon gave way. Mindi approached a lone loitering child who led us to the broken old village school by which, he said, we might pitch our tents. Immediately, out of nowhere, the village drunk arrived, delighted to see us, and introduced himself as Suzy. Taking me by the arm, he sat us down in the shade of the school among the rubble and bits of broken machinery, and from a plastic bag produced a full bottle of ur-*chacha*, *zhipitaouri*, and some loaves of bread. Within moments all the bad boys of Ghebi had joined in and lined up alongside us against the wall. A cassette player was turned on and *Disco Dance Six* blasted into the sunny and once-peaceful air. Bomba opened his pack and laid out sausage and cheese; more bread and cheese were brought in, bottles of strawberry liqueur. The sole glass went round and round, toasts were proposed and answered. We were formally welcomed and our plans discussed. The route to Svaneti was variously represented as non-existent, quite impossible, very difficult, possible, no problem and a doddle. Suzy, fair-haired, in his early thirties, quite utterly drunk (real name Kwitcho), had by this time removed his shirt and was dancing ecstatically on the football pitch, keeping up a constant stream of chatter with us, our new friends and any passers-by, most of whom he grabbed and waltzed about the field. He declared himself immediately ready to set off for Svaneti, promised us his horse and, after an hour or two drinking steadily in the heat, marched us off singing to stay at his house. I was mildly alarmed at the prospect of Suzy as guide and chaperon, though charmed by his abundance, his superfluity of character. As we walked through the village he kissed and cuddled anyone he could catch, much to their amusement and to the great delight of various old ladies who shrieked with laughter. All except his mother. On opening the door to us she fetched him a ringing slap across his face and scolded him roundly. She apologised to us but Suzy only laughed the more, so we left our packs and then he took us off to see an old friend of Mindi's.

Mindi had thought that his friend Rezo, who lived near him in Gamarjweba, would still be working in the city but we found him outside his family home, playing with his little daughter. He was a tall, slim, immensely tough man, a fine mountaineer, loving and gentle with his child, and I came to like and respect him greatly. We were immediately invited into a long kitchen which looked out across a veranda to the great mountains beyond, and sat at the table while his mother and father welcomed us, brought more *chacha*, hard lumps of salty pork fat, spring onions and *smetana*. As we watched the day darken and the stars come out, grandpa took Suzy outside and gave him a wash at the tap, rubbing him down with a towel, and made him drink glasses of their water which fizzed like soda and was, he said, a sure antidote to a *chacha* hangover. He then fetched his *pandour* and played while his grand-daughter sang, producing a remarkable sound for one so young and tiny. She had a voice that could level a city. Then he sang, wonderful songs about hunters and mountains and death and bandits. He sang of Jamata, a notorious Svan brigand who had terrorised the villagers for miles around and eventually met his end leaping from a mountain top, or, in this version, killed by the men of Ghebi. These songs of the wild *abreks*, outlaws who sheltered in the mountains, are very like the *klephtic* songs of Greece, terror mixed with admiration for their daring and defiance:

The Song of Jamata

They say
    Jamata the Svan
    Is a great enemy of Ghebi
    He goes around Ushguli and Khalde
    And tells the men to go up the mountain
    To lay an ambush for the people of Ghebi:

'We shall throw away our goat skins
and lay hold of their chokhas.'*
They say
Ninia Gagashvili
He is a good man
He hunts at the far end of the mountains
Guarding the heights.
When he sees Jamata
He strikes his chest with his fist
He goes and tells the people of Ghebi:
'Jamata hangs around here,
Men of Ghebi
This is our day
Let us arm ourselves
And scare the enemy
Let us cut the throats of the rotten Svans.
Do not lose time.'
The people of Ghebi gathered
Played music
Arranged their ceremonial parade
Started off in pursuit of the enemy.
When they reached the end of the moun-
    tains
They consulted.
They sent the young men up to the very
    heights.
The boys from Ghebi caught their enemies
    on the very heights.
Devleta from the Tamazi family
Held the silver rifle:
'If I see Jamata anywhere
I shall make the blood flow from his chest.'
Otuka Patshiashvili
Is a young hero,
Kogoshvili Gogia

---

* Traditional Georgian costume.

Strikes fire from his teeth,
Pashela Kamechishvili
Kills four at once,
Kekhsurashvili Basuka
Ties the hands of the captives.
Jamata loses his spirit from fear.
Shame to his courage
He hides in the bushes.
Devleta shoots him with the silver rifle,
Wounds his side,
The blood flows,
Jamata the Svan dies.

(translated by Marika Didebulidze)

It was all too much for Suzy who leapt to his feet and sang along and then started improvising verses of an explicit and improper nature which made grandma laugh so much that she laid her head on the table and wept uncontrollably.

We left with Rezo promising to meet us with his horse in the morning and help us across the pass into Svaneti. The moon was full and high. The Rioni shone and sparkled in the moonlight, the snows upon the mountains gleamed silver against the night sky. The narrow lanes thronged with people, all of Ghebi was out enjoying the warm summer evening air, talking and walking in clusters through the village. Grandmothers sat by their doors knitting, grandfathers lined in ranks on plank benches by the walls, calling out greetings to all who passed. Little children played complex Ratchuelian games of pat-a-cake and I, being something of an Olympian at that particular sport, joined in, to their great astonishment. Suzy, of course, embraced everyone. Our progress was slow and soon the entire population, it seemed, were coming with us to Svaneti. Bomba, who had briefly disappeared, returned, naturally, with a cousin, Vito, a man of about my age, who also had a horse and would come along too.

Then Suzy, heading towards his house, led us through the village cemetery and, suddenly, did something terrible. He stopped by a grave and let out an awful, tortured, piercing cry. It was so shocking, so violent, so loud, that my heart stopped beating, as though cleaved by an axe. He threw himself upon the grave and wept most horribly. His best friend lay beneath him, killed fighting in the Abkhaz conflict. Everyone clustered around, soothed him, and gradually his cries subsided and he was helped to his feet. Gently, we took him home to bed.

He was fast asleep on the veranda when I woke, but soon jumped up and raced off to fetch his horse. His mother and father sat us down to breakfast: a great bowl of *kasha*, *smetana*, more lumps of pork fat and, of course, *chacha* with the wonderful option, this time, of tea. As mother bustled about, Suzy's pretty young wife came into the room carrying their baby son. She smiled at us but her thoughts were on the child. Kneeling on the floor she gently placed him in his cradle, first swaddling him tightly in two broad bands of cloth till he looked like a little mummy, then laying him softly on his back. She stayed by him gazing at him lovingly, gently rocking the cradle, beautifully made with solid rockers at either end, arched at head and foot, with an upper bar along the top which she held and pushed.

I was the first Englishman that Suzy's father, Irakli, had met since the war. Captured by the Germans in the early days after Hitler's attack on the Soviet Union, he had eventually been freed by the British from a German prisoner-of-war camp in 1945. After the terrible hardship of the camp he had looked forward to returning home but as, under Stalin's tender rule, all Soviets taken by the enemy had obviously surrendered and were thus considered *de facto* as traitors (under article 26B, Betrayal of the Motherland), he had been shipped off to Siberia with thousands like him and spent seven years there in the gulags. And so, of course, began the Stalin Conversation:

'A man like Stalin, that is what we need here now.' Irakli smiled at me over his buckwheat porridge.

'But you can't mean that, not after all you have suffered from him.'

'That is not important. We were at war. Everything was upside down.' He shrugged dismissively.

'But what of the terror, the purges, the famines, the millions who died?'

'I doubt there were millions, this is an exaggeration. And Stalin cannot be held responsible for everything. There were many bad people then as now and many traitors. He was a strong man. He did what needed to be done. He led us through the war, a war that we won. He was strong and clever – did he not get Achara back from the Turks? He had an iron hand.'

At least Irakli did not ask me to drink a toast to Stalin, something that I had experienced occasionally and to my great surprise on my first visits to Georgia. I was always torn between insulting my hosts and insulting myself, not a battle that lasted long. At first I usually managed to pick my nose, or have a fit of coughing, then I became quite open in not raising my glass. I found the whole idea, then as now, extraordinary. This was not the usual moaning about the price of sausages but something much more deeply embedded in the Georgian psyche: the cult of the strong man, the idea that the nation needed a great, determined and ruthless leader, that this ruthlessness was a desirable, indeed essential quality. Enthusiasm for the old monster was, of course, by no means universal. I found it particularly among the older generations and hardly at all among the educated middle classes; all my friends had grown up cursing his name. But the effects of years of lies and propaganda and a terrible, fear-induced stasis, an enforced stability, the stability of the cemetery, have left an understandable imprint upon a people now faced with new waves of crisis and conflict, a changing and alien world. Despite Khrushchev's denunciation in 1956 and the awful personal experience of so many, those in the West who had read Solzhenitsyn and the works of historians like Robert Conquest had, until quite recently, a far better, broader idea of what Stalin had really done than most of his erstwhile subjects. The *Gulag Archipelago* did not appear in Russian till 1989. Of course, Stalin organised his own cult and rewrote history, or had it rewritten, so that he could be seen to be its master. One does not have to go very far in Georgia to see and feel the lingering hold Stalin still exerts. There is a Stalin society in Tbilisi (generally, I think, viewed as rather mad), the Society for the Ideological

Heirs of Stalin, where many of his tumbled statues have been re-erected by his devotees. From bits of mountain around, his painted image still stares down. The little cottage where he was born in Gori is still there, inside its absurd mausoleum, and I would not relish standing outside it on my soapbox denouncing Stalin's crimes. Of course, his lingering popularity as a 'strong man' is by no means confined to Georgia.

The fact that Stalin was Georgian is often used as a stick with which to beat the Georgians. It is suggested that he represented them and that somehow they got off lightly, were favoured. This was not the case, though there are valid arguments about territorial boundaries under his aegis and the way in which minorities like the Abkhazians, Ossetians and Acharans (or Ajarians) were subordinated to the central powers in Tbilisi. Stalin was virulently anti-Georgian to a degree that went quite beyond his usual anti-nationalist stance. He nearly destroyed his career arguing with Lenin over Georgian autonomy, and when he could, with his Georgian sidekicks Ordhzonikidze (whom he did not hesitate to kill) and Beria (who was probably involved in Stalin's own death), he deliberately targeted Georgian nationalism, unlike Lenin who took a much more conciliatory approach. Stalin and Beria decimated the Georgian intelligentsia (though not only them, of course) and wanted to use 'the maximum force – especially in Georgia', as Robert Conquest wrote in *Stalin, Breaker of Nations*. He goes on to write of Stalin's 'hatred of Georgia' and quotes from a hair-raising speech Stalin made to the local Bolshevik leadership:

'You hens! You sons of asses! [a common epithet among Georgians and others]. What is going on here? You must draw a white hot iron over this Georgian land! . . . You will have to break the wings of this Georgia! Let the blood of the *petit bourgeoisie* flow until they give up their resistance! Tear them apart! Impale them! Make them remember the days of Shah Abbas! (the bloodthirsty Persian invader who had ravaged the country in the eighteenth century).'

Why did he feel quite so strongly, so madly? There have been many suggestions: a rumoured illegitimacy, a troubled childhood with a violent father, diminutive stature (five foot four, and when a child, shorter), crippled arm, a face pitted with smallpox, bitter experiences at the seminary in Tbilisi. But more than all this, there seems also to be a realisation that his compatriots did not see him as he wished to be seen. From his earliest days he cast himself as different, special. There are two marvellously juxtaposed school photographs in Professor Alan Bullock's study *Hitler and Stalin*, showing the two dictators at the age of about eight or nine, both stood in exactly the same position at the dead centre of the raised back-row of children, both small in comparison to their school-mates, and both with remarkable expressions of fierce determination on their faces, expressions which they carried throughout their lives and which became so horribly familiar to millions. Stalin, from the beginning, had cast himself as a hero but in his early days as a Bolshevik agitator in Tbilisi, Batumi and Baku no one noticed. He wanted to be noticed and he wanted to be revered but in Georgia no one seemed to care. He was thought of, rather, as a small town wide-boy, a petty crook and looked down upon even by his fellow conspirators for his intellectual shortcomings. Politically, he was unacceptable to most Georgians. They vehemently rejected the Bolshevism Stalin espoused and formed a Menshevik government from 1917 to 1920. It was not until the Red Army invaded the country and the agents of the Cheka, the secret police, went about their murderous business, that Georgia had Bolshevism most forcefully and violently imposed.

Stalin did not want to be merely Josef Dzhugashvili so he recreated himself. Like Hitler he was a bright pupil and fond of reading and he became obsessed by one particular story, Alexander Kazbegi's *The Parricide*. Kazbegi did for the people around Mount Kazbek rather what Vazha Pshavela had done for the Pshavs and the mountain folk of eastern Georgia. Like Pshavela he went to live in the mountains and actually spent seven years as a shepherd. He collected their folk tales and stories, wrote of their customs and culture, sharpened their sense of identity and, in tales like *The Parricide* and *Khevisberi Gocha*, distilled a heroic spirit from their lives and struggles. The hero of *The Parricide* is Koba, a Robin Hood figure who stands up for the peasants, defends their rights and fights against some dreadful Cossacks. From the time that Stalin read the story he insisted on being known as Koba, and this remained his name for twenty years or so until he exchanged it for the Russian 'Stalin' in 1912 or '13. And 'Stalin' means, of course, 'man of steel' or 'the steel one', and this time he really did become his name. Then he seems to have done as much as he could to distance himself from his native land. After he moved to Moscow he hardly returned to Georgia, was never heard to speak Georgian in his home (though he did enjoy talking Georgian to Beria to annoy others who could not understand), never taught his children any Georgian or referred to his Georgian homeland, did not even return to attend his mother's funeral. In fact, the contempt he felt for his oldest son, Yakov, child of his first marriage, is thought to have arisen because the boy reminded him of his own Georgian origins. When the Germans captured Yakov in the early days of the war, Stalin refused to exchange him and dismissed him as a traitor because 'no true Russian would ever surrender'. (His daughter, Svetlana, became famously odd and his other son, Vasily, managed to destroy himself with drink at the age of forty-one.)

To put the Stalin Conversation into its proper context, to understand, finally, a man like Irakli, a kind, sincere man who had himself been through the hell of Stalin's camps under a mad, vicious and paranoid policy that was of Stalin's own making; to understand, too, the attitude of mind of Paata's gentle, noble, father-in-law in Dzhuta, and all the thousands like them, I need to quote from *Stalin, Breaker of Nations* once again:

If there is one point that has been insufficiently stressed in this book, if only because it is almost impossible to stress it sufficiently, it is the psychological horrors of mass falsification, more than the physical horrors of mass terror. What was imposed on the population was a disjunction not merely between truth in general and the official interpretation, but between the experienced reality of their own and their country's life and the fantasy world they had mentally to accept. As Soviet historian Natan Eidelman says, in the Stalin period a significant part of the Soviet population 'was living under a special hypnotic spell'. Exorcism proved immensely difficult and painful.

*

During breakfast Suzy had reappeared and in the yard below was saddling up his horse, a fine white mare with a lovely delicate foal of three or four weeks nuzzling her side. Then Vito and Rezo rode in, Rezo apologising for his lateness and explaining that he had had to fetch his own mount from a high pasture. They tied on our packs and adjusted their saddle-bags, taking care to distribute the weight according to the strength of the horse, and we set off, stopping briefly down the lane at a spring of liquid iron to pep up the horses, who seemed to enjoy it greatly. And then, much to my astonishment, Rezo, Suzy and Vito climbed up on their animals and invited us to join them. I had thought that we would walk beside the horses which seemed quite loaded enough but the Ghebiots insisted and I shuddered for the poor creatures as Bomba climbed up behind his cousin. I really did not want to get on, there was simply no room, but Suzy beckoned importunately. So I got up behind in the position of a hurdler at the top of his flight, bags and packs making it quite impossible for me to put my legs down and then, to my horror, we all set off at a gallop. Suzy's saddle had a metal ring behind and as I was thrown violently up and down my testicles were severely threatened, so instead of holding on to Suzy I was forced to hold on to myself. All my yelling and pleading just fired them up the more and soon Rezo-with-Mindi behind and Suzy-with-me were involved in a desperate race over rocks, round boulders, through thickets, across streams. Suzy increased his usual level of noise by directing loud cries and shouts of '*Ho! Ho! Khevsuro!*' to Mindi (translated roughly as 'Yes! Yes! You old Khevsur! Get a move on!) as he came up behind Rezo's horse and gave it sharp thumps on the rump, which amused him greatly and seemed to encourage the horse. The little foal kept up with our mare all the way, whinnying to her softly, Vito and Bomba followed sedately after. I do not think I have ever had a more delightful and more uncomfortable day. After a couple of hours, thinking by then that it was most unlikely that I would ever be able to bring my legs to the vertical again, I managed to fall off, and walked with some great difficulty to a little church by the Rioni where everyone stopped to picnic, for two hours. We went into the church and sat on the floor and drank lots of *chacha* and ate more pig fat; and this seemed to me to be The Essence of Georgian Travel. The idea is that one should spend as little time as possible actually travelling, so it is entirely necessary to hang about for as long as one can doing nothing and then move off at tremendous speed. I would have quite liked to walk along at a reasonable pace, not so amusing perhaps but still enjoyable, for the way was fantastically beautiful: there were mountains, woods, water, all that sort of thing, in abundance. Then we might have rested for a few minutes, but this was really far too weird a concept and not at all in accordance with protocol.

A little further along we crossed over a narrow, half-broken wooden bridge to the northern bank of the Rioni, Suzy picking up the foal and carrying it in his arms when it refused, terrified by the roaring water and the rickety bridge full of holes. I had wanted to make a little detour to the archaeological site at Brili, just to the north of the river, towards the Zopkhito glacier. As both Gia and Beka's stepfather, Gela, had warned me, there was nothing archaeological to see there now, the digs had long since been closed, but it was an extraordinary place: a lovely upland meadow stretching towards Mount Zopkhito, covered in a forest of hogweed and nettles, towering far taller than a man. As nettles are the pre-eminent weed of disturbed ground they suggest the activity that once must have taken place here. It was such a natural place for, at least, some kind of summer settlement that I found it almost odd not to find houses, nor signs of houses. But it was quite empty, there was no habitation here, nor at all between Ghebi and Svaneti now, though once, with iron and other metals being worked in the mountains all around, it must have teemed with human life. The highlands were once far more densely populated than they are today and the whole Rioni valley was a most important route up from the Black Sea coast.

Aboard again we continued along the Rioni, Rezo and Suzy racing and pushing past each other, yelling with laughter as I bounced, imperilled, on the mare's hard rump, until Suzy put me up in front, shoved his broken sunglasses on my face, and gave me the reins. The horses trotted surely over the rocks and through torrents, the mare and foal tight together, talking to each other. I slowed the pace, enjoying the comfort of the saddle. As night drew down upon us, we climbed a little way above the river to the ruin of a house, the *turbaza* of Bartuzweli, a stone hut built here originally for shepherds and hay-makers who came this way, heading for the rich meadows around the Sasvano tarns which we would pass next morning. Vito, Rezo and Suzy had all done this, carrying their scythes and reaping hooks to mow the rich summer flowers and grasses, prized winter fodder for their animals, returning in the early autumn to carry back the sweet hay on their horses and in carts. The hut had half a roof and a little planking on the floor, a small metal stove, a broken table. The horses were wiped down and tethered in the meadow. Order was made of our establishment, the table set outside, jammed upright and laid with a table-cloth of plastic bags, *chacha*, bread and cheese spread out upon it, logs and stones brought round as seats. From here, at the head of this valley, we were very close to the source of the Rioni; directly ahead great Mount Edena, with its glacier, looked over us and the little Lukhumi torrent flowed down from the ice to join the river. Rezo raced off, down to the river to fish, and Suzy, taking a small hatchet from his bag, set about a wooden structure – the remains of a shed – and demolished it. It made a fine bonfire. Mindi and Bomba whittled slivers of wood to form *shampoor*, skewers, and as the full moon came out from behind the clouds and lit the valley and the waters below, Rezo returned with twelve gleaming trout. He had caught them with his hands, tickled them, and was soaking wet in the now-cold night air. He seemed not to notice and, taking off his shirt to dry by the fire, he cleaned the fish, impaled them and set them to cook. Trout and *chacha* in the moonlight, beneath Edena, above the legendary river, stilled even Suzy for a moment as the magic of the night took hold and the stars sparked into life and decorated the coal-black sky like a wizard's robe.

For the sake of general amusement Suzy had decided that I was to be *tamada*. After a moment of solemnity, laughter echoed off the mountains as I stumbled through the litany of toasts with much encouragement and commentary from the company. The Ghebiots sang songs of Ratcha; Mindi and Bomba, sometimes in duet, recited anthologies of verse: Pushkin, Rustaveli, Poe; I gave them 'Jabberwocky' with much movement. This excited Suzy enormously, particularly my swordplay in which he joined, so I cut off his head to great acclamation. But then the chatter and the jokes left me far behind and I sat looking out into the night, warmed by the fire's glow, bathed in the night air, straining to imprint everything, all sensations, all feelings, all impressions upon my mind, so that I should not forget.

I watched with some interest the next morning, after a night on a plank with some very long nails, as Rezo and Vito wound their feet with strips of cloth. This was the traditional mountain sock. Not so long ago, in Vito's father's time certainly, most would have bound their feet like this and then put on soft leather moccasins stuffed with straw, laced beneath, to enable their feet to grip the grassy slopes down which my rigid boots were constantly slipping. Clive Phillipps-Wolley, a friend of Douglas Freshfield and fellow-member of the Royal Geographical Society, wandered about Ratcha and Svaneti in the 1870s, and was much taken by this footwear but when he swapped it for his hobnail boots found that he lacerated his feet on the sharp ridges of stone that lay beneath the grass. Only the mountain men, light of foot, can wear such things. In his book *Savage Svanetia*, Phillipps-Wolley admires the hardiness and vigour of the local men who helped him but he had not the humanity, nor yet the knowledge and understanding, of Baddeley nor even Freshfield, and his pages are tainted with a supercilious Victorian disdain. He loved the mountains and, to be fair to him, his book does give a vivid picture of his travels but his conde-scension gets in the way and his only real interest lay in bagging as much game as possible. He was one of those mad Englishmen who left home for months on end to pursue all sorts of goats and bears across impossible landscapes, a tedious end for all his efforts. He wrote unforgivable poetry to his wife in order to encourage her fidelity during his long absences:

For soft grows the pillar of stone, dear,
All the mountain with beauty is rife
There is nothing for him to bemoan, dear,
Who can trust in his God and his wife.

We lit the stove and breakfasted on tea and home-made black-currant jam which Vito produced from a great glass jar, ideal for a trip into the mountains. A dense mist delayed our start till after nine, but as the sun came out we set off with Suzy strangely quiet. We had run out of *chacha* and the storm inside him had abated. The way became very steep and we led the horses, thank God, while Rezo encouraged them with strange Ratchuelian cries of 'Achoo!' and 'Brrrr!' which made me think, at first, that he had caught a dreadful cold from his night-time dip. Giant beech trees covered the mountainside and we rested frequently beneath their welcome shade. As we came out above the woods, Mount Edena with its great flat glacier stood in full view just to our north and Mount Phasis, slightly to its west, both rising to nearly 13,000 feet. Beneath the snow and ice that clung to Mount Phasis lay the source of the Rioni, the ancient River Phasis which Jason and his Argonauts had entered from the sea on their quest for the Golden Fleece. The Phasis is also celebrated for having given its name to the pheasant, but I looked in vain for the wild ancestors of the bird. The mountain ridge we followed was clothed in a brilliant turf and covered in wild flowers. I rode much of the way on Rezo's horse, giddy with the height and the great space around, and looked down upon a sea of colour which parted for us briefly, then closed behind and covered up our tracks. We climbed steadily past the Sasvano tarns, brilliant pools of shining turquoise, each little lake set like a jewel in a belly-button, and on up until we saw the pass beneath four great standing stones which pointed like fingers into the sky and marked the way into Svaneti. Below us we could see the River Tskhenis-tsqali, the Horse-water, winding down through the mountains, and here we stopped. This pass, lying between the sources of the Rioni and the Tskhenis-tsqali, is marked on Freshfield's map and others as the Vazizveri or Vatsistveri, but none of my companions knew this name and they called it Sasvano. I am still not absolutely certain that they are one and the same and we may have come out at a point just to the south of Freshfield's pass. We lunched briefly upon bread and cheese and then we strapped on our packs as Rezo, Suzy and Vito mounted up and turned away, waving and calling out encouragements.

Most of the long way down I spent upon my arse. The grasses and flowers grew up above my head and every time I tried to walk I fell and slithered. Huge yellow lilies laughed at my descent and Mindi grew concerned lest I castrate myself upon a jag of rock. I tried to stay upright but simply could not manage it, so slid most of the way with legs stretched out in front to feel the ground and brake my fall. I got up quite a speed and when, at last, the ground permitted and I raced off after Mindi who had at once returned to his old ways and disappeared into the distance, I was delighted to find that it was Bomba, trailing on behind, who called out to him to stop. I had found a slow Khevsur. After all my weeks of walking I was feeling almost spry. Fighting our way with difficulty through dense forests of huge weeds and thickets of birch and alder scrub, we reached the banks of the head-waters of the river, clambering over fallen trunks of trees. Here, I suddenly recalled Freshfield's descriptions of the jungles of the Tskhenis-tsqali and thought of all the wonderful advantages a wide reading brings. A machete would have been good, a flame-thrower even better. Mindi grew excited by many fresh tracks of bears and we moved cautiously through the undergrowth, half in fear, half in hope of spotting one. About an hour downstream a track appeared off to the right and we followed it along, moving Bomba up ahead to bulldoze a path when it became too choked and seemed impassable. It led us back down to the river and up its opposite bank. We had no option but to cross. I was not keen. The river flowed deep and fast and carried the rubble of ten thousand winter storms. Our feet sank between rocks and rose over unseen boulders as we struggled against the torrent, holding our packs above our heads. Propelled by fear, by the frozen waters that pounded at my chest and by a determination that surprised me, I fell against the far bank. We hauled ourselves up to the track and set off again, past a solitary fallen farmhouse, and in a broad meadow, as the rain started to pour down, decided to pitch our tents. I lay exhausted on the grass but the boys wanted supper, so we cooked Minestra Primavera by Knorr, then went to bed.

The next day we fought our way along in a similar manner for five or six hours. We plunged thrice more into the water, found tracks of wild pig and bear, were pursued by horseflies as big as dogs and gathered the wonderful sweet strawberries that grew by the rocks. In every puddle along the track, a thousand frogs sang. It was most enjoyable but Mindi had generously shared out all our supplies (with just perhaps a little calculation towards his load) and Bomba was complaining of a desperate hunger. At last we found ourselves on a spit of land where the Zeshko River flows into the Tskhenis-tsqali. We looked up and we looked down but saw only the broad river, black with mud, prancing and bucking over rocks, just as its name implied. Mindi took off his belt and lashed me to him, Bomba held to his other side. He picked out a long diagonal towards the far bank and with many exhortations not to look down, to look only at his hat, he plunged us into the mad torrent. I went down twice but came up again quickly and somehow, dashed against boulders, hurled along in fury by the flood, we gained the shallows at the water's edge and scrambled up the steep slope to the dirt road above, where a Svan astride a horse sat expressionless but eyed us intently.

CHAPTER 7

SVANETI

'Whistles, yells, signals, portents –
what do they matter?'

Joseph Conrad, *Victory*

How we suffer a setback and
decide what to do next

I wanted to turn right along the road and head up towards the village of Ushguli and so link up with the journey I had made through Svaneti some years before but the boys were determined to turn left and reach the village of Panaga in lower Svaneti, where they had friends. Neither had been in Svaneti before and they were nervous. Though I had experienced no problems on my first visit, the reputation of the Svans suggested that some local help would be only sensible. But I was fond of my plan, reluctant to abandon the neatness of our westward line, and also I had some contacts around Ushguli, friends of friends who were restoring some of the early Svan churches nearby. However, as we stood dripping on the road, the humourless Svan on the horse told us that the pass to Ushguli, about twenty-five kilometres off, was perilous and the way hard. We were all shattered and I had not the heart to insist, so we turned to the left and walked easily down the wide track, until an old lady on a motorbike roared by in a cloud of dust and sent us scrambling for cover.

Cows appeared and on the left bank of the river a ruined tower and then another, and soon after we found ourselves once more walking through a settled landscape. In the village of Melo a shop

248

disclosed itself, selling, as far as I could see, only beer and boiled sweets. So we bought a lot of both and distributed the sweets to the crowd of little children that had followed us along. We sat on a bench in the shop and drank our beers and explained ourselves. A pretty, fair-haired Svan, studying English at university in Tbilisi, chatted amiably, eager for practice. As we strode on by the side of the Tskhenis-tsqali, night fell upon us and so, just beyond the next village, Chikhareshi, on a tufted lawn just off the road, we decided to pitch our tents, much to Bomba's disappointment, as he had set his heart on Panaga, a fine dinner and the World Cup Final which, apparently, was on this very night. As I lay in my tent writing my diary by the fading glow from my Maglite, a couple of Svans from the large house nearby wandered down to greet us and invited us to stay with them. But we were settled now and very tired and knew that if we accepted their invitation we should have to stay up all night drinking *chacha* and talking. We simply did not have the appetite. So we declined as gracefully as possible.

A little later, as I was dozing off, still clutching my fix of text, Conrad's *Victory*, I was dimly conscious of strange noises in the night, a loud and prolonged whistle, soft calling and the sound of feet running over grass. What did these noises mean? And then the shooting started, a sudden crack of rifle-fire above my head. I heard yelling and Mindi calling out and, just as I was scrambling for my boots, a large blade appeared through the skin of my tent and settled rather near my nose. I crawled out and in the shadowy half-light of the clouded moon saw Mindi and Bomba sat upon the grass with half a dozen masked men pointing a variety of rifles, a Kalashnikov and two ridiculously large knives at them. And me. The moonlight lent a ghostly, dream-like quality to the scene and I was still half-asleep and far more bewildered than shocked. The leader of the gang, the only one unmasked, spectral and grim-faced in the dark, first confusingly demanded our papers and I handed him my passport, thinking for a moment as he gave it back that they were, perhaps, policemen. This fuddled nonsense was soon dispelled by a gruff demand for money, and as Mindi and Bomba handed over theirs, I pulled out the contents of my pockets, some lari and some dollars, not much. Meanwhile our tents and packs were being ransacked and I became terrified that they would bundle up the lot and run off with my notes. They had given back my passport, which was strangely reassuring and nothing else really mattered. However, our assailants started to get rather excited and pushed us about a bit and Bomba got a little worried and told me urgently to hand over any other money I had. So I gave them the rest of my money. Then the leader and one with a knife pushed me away from the boys and led me up the hill, a little way off. I did not like this much and we had a silly conversation, punctuated by a rifle fired into the ground by my feet:

'Give me your money!'

'I have given you my money.'

Bang.

'Give me your money!'

'I have no more, that's it, you have the lot.'

Bang.

'Give me your money!'

'I really do not have any more money.'

Bang.

'Take off all your clothes!'

So I stripped off, and as they shone the beam of my own torch over me all I could hope, inanely, was that they were not too appalled by my psoriatic limbs. They got cross as I put my clothes back on without being told to and prodded me a little and shouted a bit and waved a knife about. I heard Bomba in the background begging them not to take all his cigarettes. Mr Big, working himself up to a new point of frenzy, then pushed his face into mine and yelled, 'Fuck you! Fuck you! Fuck you!' in English, and this infuriated me far more than anything else he had done, quite beyond the point of reason. It seemed so unnecessarily rude, they had insulted us quite enough already. I remember thinking that this was the global effect of too many American videos and said, quite calmly and rather stupidly, 'Fuck you, too!' At this point we heard voices in the distance, slowly moving towards us, very slowly in the circumstances, though perhaps this was wise. The leader gave a theatrical 'Shush!' listened a moment and then shouted to everyone to run. So the whole gang suddenly fled, springing over the soft turf towards the woods, whooping occasionally in their delight and letting off their guns. The entire procedure had lasted about fifteen minutes.

Three men ambled over, shone a torch about and observed us with mild interest. The oldest, one of the men who had come from the nearby house earlier, made some superfluous remarks about accepting invitations when they were offered and wandered off. The other two treated the event with great good-humour, non-chalantly helped us gather our belongings as though assisting some poor fellows who had tripped and dropped their shopping, and invited us to spend the rest of the night at their home. This time we accepted gratefully and packed up as best we could, rummaging in the dark to find our scattered bits. I saw my notebooks all intact, discarded on the grass. A gang of critics. Our rescuers, Dato, in his thirties, bright and talkative, and Merab, middle-aged, wearing a Svan felt cap, led us back down the road through Chikhareshi to a house at the far end of the village. The village was perfectly quiet, a few lights shone gaily from windows, some pigs runtled about in the dark edges of the road, all at peace. The Svans breezily dismissed our robbers as boys having a little fun, hardly worth bothering about, after all we were unharmed. Mindi looked murderous but I agreed, worse things happened in Piccadilly, and I had left the bulk of my exchequer in Tbilisi with friends. I can not even remember how much I had lost, perhaps 150 dollars, enough to pay for food and expenses in Svaneti. Clever Mindi had managed to shove twenty dollars underneath his tent and so we were not absolutely broke. I was always amazed that nothing remotely like this had happened to me in all my wanderings. Travelling about with a large sign hanging from me marked 'Swag', I had met with only kindness. Young Svans, destitute, without work, living in their remote province and feeling the hardship of the times even more sharply than those in other parts of Georgia, had reverted to the traditional occupation of their ancestors, brigandage.

Of course, this had never completely disappeared, hence the reputation the Svans carried, but what was so idiotic was the effect created by this renewed reinforcement of their old stereotype. Hardly anyone wanted to go to Svaneti any more, to bring in a little money, to encourage others to go and see for themselves the sublime beauty of the high villages or climb its great mountains. Later I learnt of recent attacks on two Austrian geologists, a couple of Americans and a young Scottish mountaineer on the Latpari Pass, besides the many raids on their own people. A bus full of farmers and their wives going to market had recently been held up at gun-point, everything stolen. There was, most definitely, something rotten in Svaneti. Perhaps the Svans were as stupid as all the Georgian jokes about them suggested. This is my rather feeble revenge upon the Svans:

A Svan is chatting to his friend. 'What a wonderful thing these new mobile phones are,' he says. 'Now whenever I ring up my wife she is always at home.'

A Svan was going to meet a woman. His friend advised him not to forget to put on a condom or he might make her pregnant. After several months the Svan complained to his friend: 'How much longer must I wear this thing?'

Some Kakhetians were upset that all the jokes in Georgia seemed to be about Svans. So they decided to do something really stupid. They built a bridge over a dry valley with absolutely no trace of water anywhere and invited lots of people to the unveiling. They made speeches and broke a bottle of champagne and then removed the cloth covering the bridge. On the bridge they saw a Svan. He was holding a rod and fishing.

While Bomba chatted to our two new friends, Mindi and I shared our unease. The whole operation had been too pat, we both had a strong sense that we had assisted in some kind of play: the initial contact and inspection, the attack, the ample time allowed despite the shouting and the gunfire, the neat arrival of the rescue party, their tremendous calm, their utter lack of surprise. This is perhaps to do a terrible injustice, especially in view of the hospitality we received, but something had given both of us the same impression. It is probably nonsense, gunfire in Svaneti, and throughout the mountains, often goes quite unnoticed and is taken as a sign of high spirits or even celebration. Nevertheless we had both felt something strange. Thank goodness Mindi had no gun. Had he been carrying the pistol he used for target practice in Khevsureti, I am certain he would have come out of his tent shooting. He said as much. In fact both he and Bomba behaved with exemplary coolness, though I had been worried at the time. Their pride had suffered a terrible blow and as we walked through the night Mindi was already planning his revenge, swearing to return with Khevsur friends, to find my money, to punish our oppressors. He declared that with what he had earned from me he would purchase a Kalashnikov and I suddenly saw a terrible Khevsur–Svan war, a ghastly vendetta that would last a hundred years. I told him to forget about it, to do nothing so rash nor so wasteful, but it took many conversations over some weeks before he calmed down. Even now I am not too sure.

Merab bade us all goodnight and Dato lead us through a garden gate, up some steps to his front door. His kindly mother, disarmingly solicitous, bustled off to fetch food and make beds. Their front room was full of books and in the far corner a television flickered. We were just in time to see the French football team being presented with the World Cup. A cousin, a man we had seen before in the sweet shop in Melo, sat watching in an armchair. We told our story again, mother letting out cries of '*Vai me! Vai me!*' 'Woe is me!', a frequent exclamation of Georgian women which sounds so much like the Yiddish '*Oi vey!*' that it seemed congratulatory, but the cousin was no more surprised or disturbed than Dato had been. We sat down to lumps of pork fat (I had now started to wonder what on earth they did with the rest of the pig) and jugs of *chacha*, so here we were doing exactly what we had sought to avoid. We counted through our losses: our watches (mine broken), my torch, my daughter's ancient little camera (I bought her a new one), the boys' small sum of money, mine. That was all. However, since the moment the cash was taken I had been trying to work out what to do next. Obviously this would affect our plans and unless I could somehow raise some money locally, we would have to return to Tbilisi to get more. I let the problem stew away in the back of my mind.

Dato's younger brother joined us and we went through the whole rigmarole again. Once more, hardly a flicker of interest. He was, it is true, completely stoned and carried an enormous joint at which he puffed away while cuddling his mother. From our emergence out of the depths of the Tskhenis-tsqali we had walked through two villages, observed by all. It seemed more than likely that our assailants must have come from either one. They would hardly have had time to have heard the news and come from very far, nor was there any sound of cars starting up after they fled. They might have had horses, I suppose, but even so, to have learnt of us, hatched their plot and found us would have taken time. They must have come from nearby. Everyone in these villages knows everyone else; Dato, his brother or his cousin must have had a very good idea of the culprits' identities. I asked them, but they smiled and shuffled and spread their hands, changed the subject and poured more *chacha*. We got to bed at four. I still needed a little text before sleep and so I opened *Victory*, at page 290 in the Penguin Popular Classics, and the first thing I read, and it was so strange that it made me feel quite odd, was this:

> Out in the black night, not very far from the bungalow, resounded a loud and prolonged whistle. Lena's hands grasped the sides of the chair, but she made no movement. Heyst started, and turned his face away from the door.
>
> The startling sound had died away.
>
> 'Whistles, yells, signals, portents – what do they matter?' he said.

At seven that morning we were on the village bus to Panaga, only a few miles down the road but the boys did not fancy the walk. We were tired, heavy-headed and somewhat deflated. A fierce argument was raging in the bus but everyone was shouting Svan, so Mindi was as much at a loss as I was. Despite the turmoil and the crush the Svans all competed to give me their seats. As we drew into the village Mindi spotted his friend walking with some lads along the road, so he called to the driver to stop the bus and we got down. We sat by the roadside, told our tale and were taken home where we did it all again. And again, sitting in the yard, with chickens and charming hairy piglets running round, and again when grandfather appeared, wearing yellow trousers and a woolly hat, peaked at both corners, and many times again at each new entrance and arrival. I was by now thoroughly fed up with the whole thing and being force-fed *chacha* by grandfather who saw it as his hospitable duty to make quite sure that I was never in danger of a momentary dryness. Sometime that day my eyes closed and I was led off to bed, waking much later in the dark to find a large crowd helping me to my feet. They had killed a calf and the *supra* was about to start.

A dozen of us men sat down to dine, girls scurrying forth with vast bowls of boiled calf, a whole ribcage, head and legs poking through a grey soup. A smiling, plump young Svan sporting a T-shirt with the legend 'Substrate of Terror' tore me off a few ribs. All encouraged me with cries of '*tchame! tchame!*' 'Eat! Eat!' but I could hardly manage. It took a long time to eat the calf, to toast the toasts, to tell the story. A demijohn of wonderful wine kept us going, golden, light and dry, we drank it by the tumbler, at each toast draining the glass entirely.

Mindi had decided to stay another day in Panaga to further his investigations, so after a late start, we wandered the leafy lanes and woods around the village, rootling about for information, rather like the tribes of hairy pigs that lay or trotted everywhere. Much of the time was spent up in the pine forests where a couple of the men were working felling trees and dragging them down the mountain with an ancient tractor. These were for export to Turkey and once a month a Turkish lorry arrived somehow up the unmade road to collect the timber. This was the only work around and of all the young men, nine or ten, who lay about with us on the huge trunks of the felled pines, smoking cigarettes and chatting in the sunshine, none had any job. It was lovely here but desperate and most of them seem to have become involved, to some degree, with the Mafia gangs in the cities. Even so they were all broke.

I had come to the conclusion that we would have to return to Tbilisi, there was no other way. I had crossed from Ratcha to Svaneti as I had wanted but failed to reach Ushguli. I could, perhaps, try again but this seemed far too pedantic and there was a further problem. I was committed in a few days to another trip, with Beka to hunt bear in Chechnya, an idea so odd I could not pass it by, and I would simply have no time to come back to Svaneti now. In the morning, with Mindi's twenty dollars, we would take the bus to Tbilisi. It was frustrating but after all I had been to Ushguli before.

CHAPTER 8

THE CHURCHES OF TAO

The Protocols of Sarpi and the *Gurgi-Bughaz*

How we spent our days in Trabzon, came
across the mountains of Turkey and
eventually reached Tbilisi

It was the summer of 1991 and I had conceived a fine idea. I would
go through Turkey into Georgia and Svaneti, returning to travel
through the medieval Georgian kingdom of Tao-Klarjeti, now
north-eastern Turkey. I was with Chris Willoughby, on our first trip
together to the Caucasus, and we had been stuck in Trabzon for
a week, looking for a boat. This was not the original plan. We had
tried to cross into Georgia through the little border post at Sarpi
but been turned back over some disorder with our visas. The stamp
I had been given at the Russian embassy in London, which I had
carelessly forgotten to check, was marked 'Tbilisi', and so, obviously, Tbilisi had to be our point of entry. The border guards were
adamant. Cows wandered back and forth quite happily, queues of
old ladies ambled through, I argued fiercely in no-man's-land, Chris
behind the fence, waving in Turkey, but it was hopeless. The guards,
all fourteen-year-old Russians, had eventually called over a senior
officer, a Georgian, a charming, apologetic man who resisted all
my cajolery and my clumsy attempts at bribery.

'Let me pay a special visa tax,' I pleaded.

'I regret, but that is quite impossible.'

'For goodness' sake, you are supposed to be independent now,
why should these Russians have any say in the matter. They

buggered up my visa, have probably never even heard of Sarpi.'

'It is most unfortunate. When we have our own embassy in London, I am sure you will have no problems of this kind.'

'So I must wait till then?'

'No, you must fly to Moscow and then to Tbilisi.'

'But that's absurd. Thousands of wasted miles.'

'I feel for you. Of course, you could take the boat.'

'The boat? There's a boat? No one told me about a boat.'

'Certainly there is a boat. From Trabzon to Batumi. Yes, certainly, you should take the boat.'

'When does it go?'

'Oh, very often, three or four times a week.'

'Well, that's fantastic. But why do I need a special stamp to cross at Sarpi and not to get the boat to Batumi?'

'It is difficult for foreigners to come through Sarpi. We are not ready for them yet.'

'I see,' I said, bewildered.

'Yes, indeed. Unfortunately the boat is, at present, broken.'

'Broken? Will it be mended?'

'Naturally, it will be mended.'

'Will this be soon?'

'Oh, very, very soon.'

And so we had been waiting for the boat, the mythical, possible, maybe, never boat. It was due today, tomorrow, in two or three days' time, next week. We never saw it. So in Trabzon we badgered many Russians at their consulate, but the answer was always '*Zakryt!*' or else '*Nyet!*' Many kindly Turks came to our aid. Indeed, the whole town was on our side and we were treated to endless glasses of apple tea in the jolly central square of Trabzon. In the Post and Telegraph Office concerned citizens would furrow their brows as I tried again and again to phone friends in Georgia, smiling broadly when I finally got through and they heard me talking, murmuring in frustration when my line was broken. As we walked to and fro, between the Russian consulate, the Turkish ministry, the post office, and sat poring over maps in the square, it became quite obvious that we were involved in some stupendous deal. Nejip from the ministry took us under his wing and introduced us around, lest we should feel lonely. Abdul, a nice Jordanian, was also having problems, though going the other way. He was the manager of the Russian State Circus and he borrowed our maps, worried for his vast caravan of trucks and his lions, his seals, his acrobats and knife-throwers, discussing routes with Nejip and his Turkish guide, attempting to avoid the Kurdish areas held by the PKK as he plotted his way to bookings in Syria, Jordan and the Yemen.

Finally, Nejip had the most definite news from a friend in the dockyard at Samsun: our boat was almost ready and would be in Trabzon in six days. We decided to set off on our journey through Tao-Klarjeti and went to the Hertz office to rent a car. Next morning we would leave, an impossible thought. I had grown fond of Trabzon and was used to its ways. The more I stayed, the more I felt like a character in Rose Macaulay's *Towers of Trebizond*, Father Chantry-Pigg or Aunt Dot, or even Laurie, perhaps. Indeed there was so very much in common between our predicament, experiences, intentions and that fabulous story that I started to confuse what I had read with what I had done. It certainly made me write, and even think, in incredibly long, whimsical sentences with clauses hanging thick upon each other, and ending in a dying fall, so that I wondered, for example, if perhaps the boat did not come, whether we might lash together a raft of those huge water-melons which filled all the greengrocers of Trabzon, and sail along the Black Sea coast to Batumi, and write a book about it called *By Sea and Watermelon along the Black Sea Coast*, but I realised that it had probably been done by all those people wandering around writing their Turkey books, and that anyway it echoed too closely Laurie's projected *Rambling around Anatolia with Rod, Line and Camel*, so it was not to be considered.

The people of Trabzon, courteous and kind, have not changed so much in the fifty years since Rose Macaulay wrote. The Byzantine walls still stand and now enclose smart new restaurants, the little lanes up from the sea, the 'real Trebizond', are still there, the shop-fronts now hung with signs in Russian, Georgian and Armenian. But her 'pretty road to Rize', sadly bereft of camels, is a rash of property development, thrown up by returning Turkish *Gastarbeiter*, great blocks of flats standing empty and incomplete in a littered sprawl, facing out to sea forlornly, in the hope of some future boom in tourism or the price of tea; and the Boz Tepe, the ancient Mithraic site that overlooks the city, is a tea-garden, tasselled with Pepsi-Cola bottle-tops set in concrete. The famous church of Hagia Sophia with its lovely Byzantine frescos, no longer 'derelict and deserted', now pulls in the crowds, all clutching Professor Talbot-Rice's excellent book, and the Sumela monastery, in its mountain fastness behind, lies full of rubbish, its crumbling walls covered in the graffiti of a hundred tongues.

Beyond all the usual progress, though, the change that would have most surprised Rose Macaulay has taken place down by the seashore. All along the front struggles the 'Russian Market'. Crowds of Georgians, Armenians, Russians, a few Uzbeks, some Kurds, desperate for Turkish lira or, better still, dollars, sell off bits and pieces of the old empire: old tractor parts, Zenith cameras, spoons, dolls, toy cars, fishing rods, radios, samovars, tea sets, lipstick, old clothes. Chris and I wandered between them, looking and chatting as they haggled furiously with Turks who seemed hugely amused by the whole fandango. Chris became involved with a gold-toothed Uzbek in a patterned Uzbek skull-cap: a complex and deeply satisfying discussion in no mutually intelligible tongue on how to sex the rabbits he dangled before the crowds. But these new marketeers were not a happy lot. Some sat by their cars, fanning off the flies in the heat, others slumped by the sea wall holding up two packets of Marlboro cigarettes. All were exhausted. Though in some ways depressing and considered almost shameful by other Georgians, I thought the market was a good sign in those early post-Soviet days, especially for the Georgians who, unlike the Armenians, had no real tradition of trade and were not known for their entrepreneurial skills. They were learning how to survive in their new world. However, they all had a terrible fierceness about them, a not-to-be-trifled-with air, which spoke of their desperation. It was a market dominated by women, big blonde ones, small dark ones (hair lacquered back with that harsh, distinctive, unmistakable Soviet hair dye that is somehow far too blonde or far too black), most rather stout, and when they had made some profit they would stream up into the lanes of Trabzon and buy as fiercely as they sold: T-shirts, jeans, jackets, shoes, they packed them all into enormous bundles or crammed them into bags and sacks. The Turkish shopkeepers loved it and so they hung out their polyglot signs and joked and laughed; but the exhausted women bargained with a new fury, determined to make the most of all their efforts. They haggled over coffees, they haggled over rooms, they even haggled with exasperated bus drivers on the road back to Sarpi, and I thought I should try this on the number 16 bus from Victoria when I returned to England. From villages and towns in Georgia and beyond, they had streamed to Batumi, then waited for hours and hours, days sometimes, in cars and buses and on foot, till at last, laden like camels, they fought their way through the sentinels of Sarpi. I have now been through Sarpi many times and its proto-cols are familiar to me, but stuck on a Georgian bus for hours in the damp heat, harried by guards from both sides, going to see the hobo-doctor in his vest round the back by the toilets so that he can certify you free of Aids (which he does by looking at you), cemented between enormous women and larger mounds of baggage, requires a yogic exercise in patience and detachment.

Since the gates of Sarpi were opened (to some) in 1988, this Russian Market has extended all along the Black Sea coast, spreading up into the mountains, along the river valleys to towns like Artvin and Ardahan, through Samsun and Giresun all the way to Istanbul, where it bursts into a riot of commerce, both human and material, just as the old trade routes led there through the many centuries before. Now, instead of the Circassian and Georgian slaves so prized by the Sultans, the Natashas sell themselves in the burgeoning Russian Quarter, to the great delight of Turkish men who earnestly discuss, like anthropologists from leading univer-sities, the relative merits of Russian and Bulgarian girls, explaining that the superior vigour and lovemaking expertise of the Turk has attracted these poor women to their great city.

Chris and I collected our Hertz car early and set off along the narrow strip of coast. All along, the mountains of the Pontic Alps fall sharply into the sea, their heights turbanned in mist and moisture. In this steamy air the odd banana plant springs up surprisingly, but this is the land of tea. Tea bushes undulate invitingly like soft green pillows in neat rows up all the slopes around, hanging perpendicular as far as the eye can see, and on over the border, spreading out into Georgia and across the wide, sultry Mingrelian plain. This was, a hundred years ago, a desperately poor land and, during the interminable fighting between tsarist Russia and the dying Ottoman empire during the last half of the nineteenth century, often came close to famine. Tea, introduced in the 1920s, saved it, and all the endless tea drunk in Turkey is grown here. Down the green aisles of tea the women work and at once something different becomes apparent. Women. Nowhere else in Turkey do women work and walk so openly, for only women pick the leaves of tea, their fingers shuttling furiously through spring and summer. They also seem to grow most of the produce of the fields which they sell in all the village markets around. The men sit about the tea-houses playing backgammon, wearing their shabby jackets (I feel entirely at home) and their flat Kangol caps (made in England, the factory now defunct with who-knows-what consequences for Turkish fashion), as everywhere in Turkey. But the women are all different: the Turkish villagers in their striped shawls, deep red or orange, white and black, the *keshan*, and wearing checked and striped dresses; the women from the high damp hills behind, the Hemshinlis, in dark woollen skirts, multicoloured stockings and bright orange scarves, arrayed around their heads like the headdresses of troubadour maidens; and the Laz in their gaily patterned skirts, bright tops and plain white headscarves.

Such diversity suggests the great mix of peoples that cohabit in this far corner of the Black Sea. In the villages just east of Trabzon many still speak Greek as their first language, though most would no longer describe themselves as Pontic Greeks and are, in some villages, famously devout Muslims. How far they are descended from the Greeks who lived here before the Turkish invasions and how far from later migrations, is not clear but their presence cannot fail to re-ignite a splendid vision of the fabulously wealthy and corrupt empire of Trebizond that outlasted Constantinople, though it too eventually fell to Mehmet the Conqueror. What lineages may go beyond this to the ancient Greeks that settled the Black Sea coast? The Greek they speak, Pontic Greek, is strange and wonderful to the ear of any speaker of modern demotic, though intelligible. Some modern words are not understood and given in Turkish. But the speaking of the language is done discreetly with many glances around and about if other Turks seem imminent. This is also true of the Georgians who come from the high villages around Borchka and Shavshat by the border. Some seem to think of themselves as Georgian-speaking Turks. Others are more conscious of their ancient roots and have fought more openly for their language rights, achieving some recognition from the Turkish government during the 1990s. Though delighted to speak Georgian, most appear nervous when doing so with strangers. How far was such an attitude simply my impression, or peculiar to just a few, or based on any reality? Many Turks, in their usual way (and the Turks are most extraordinary about their own history) give out with utter certainty the myth that all the Greeks and Georgians, not to mention Laz and Hemshinlis (and absolutely not to mention the Armenians) are late arrivals, emigrants from Russia when, in fact, all the migration of Greeks and Georgians were quite in opposite directions and all of them have been here a lot longer than the Turks. The Turks have an absurd paranoia, a holy fear of being reminded of their own later invasions lest their polity be threatened and separatist bogies escape and rush across the land. They desperately expunge alternative histories from the collective memory, a process that continues today with disastrous results, particularly for Armenians and Kurds. Apart from being appallingly oppressive and an abominable contempt of history, this is particularly silly when it is considered that contemporary Turks are themselves the mixed amalgam of descendants of Turkic tribes, of Paphlagonians and Phrygians, of Lydians and Lycians, of Hittites and Hurrians and of all the past peoples of Anatolia and Cappadocia, as well as Greeks and Kurds, Armenians and Georgians, their slaves and subjects and visitors and aunts and uncles. The extraordinary service done to modern Turkey by its hero and founder Kemal Atatürk was to give all of Turkey a singular coherence and I have listened to Georgian Turks, and all manner of others, while they stood proudly to attention and recited by heart portions of Atatürk's declarations. But this coherence has come at a price. The exterminations of Greeks and Armenians are well known (of Assyrians less so): the massacres, the forced marches into the deserts, the dreadful butchery of Armenians at Shadaddie and Greeks and Armenians at Smyrna. The Turks, of course, deny all this and say that such rumours spring from Greek and Armenian propaganda, even CIA plots. They point out, too, with some justi-fication, that in the general chaos after the First World War, Armenians and Greeks were perpetrating their own massacres and were trying to reclaim or to carve out bits of old Ottoman Turkey for themselves. They were at war. The Greek invasion of Turkey, the famous 'Great Idea' which sought to re-unite the Greek areas of Asia Minor with mainland Greece, saw massive numbers of foreign Greek troops in the country. The British, particularly, had encouraged this 'Idea', and the British Prime Minister, Lloyd George, for his part in the whole débâcle, should have been taken out and publicly flogged up and down Pall Mall. At one point, just after the armistice, the Pontic Greeks tried to resurrect some echo of the old empire of Trebizond as a new independent state of Pontus, and gangs of Pontic guerrillas, under the command of one of their fiery bishops, roamed the countryside around Trabzon terrorising the local Turks. Until 1921 Trabzon was still very much a Greek city. The terms of the eventual treaty at Lausanne involved a massive and compulsory exchange of populations between Greece and Turkey so that it comes almost as a surprise, now, after so much enmity, to find Greek spoken here at all.

The Hemshinlis, the people from the Kachkar Mountains behind Rize, Ardeshen and Hopa (though the name is often used to describe all highlanders), are another of the pre-Turkish if not autochthonous inhabitants here, with their own dress, customs and, in a few villages around Hopa, their own language, an ancient dialect of Armenian. Whether this reflects settlement from else-where or a later cultural influence is unclear. Their mountain villages, remote and difficult of access, were never really controlled or much bothered by either their Byzantine or Ottoman overlords. But the Laz who live along the coast and dominate the towns between Trabzon and Sarpi have a very different history. They are a Georgian people speaking a language, Laz or Lazuri, which is very close to the Mingrelian that is spoken over the border. Indeed, the two are close enough to be mutually intelligible. Lazuri's relationship to the Kartvelian family of languages is easily heard. For instance, the word for 'three' in Georgian is *sami*, in Svan *semi*, in Mingrelian *sumi*, and in Lazuri *sum*. Mingrelian and Laz are sometimes thought of as dialects of a single language, Zan, which diverged from Georgian nearly three thousand years ago.

The ancient kingdom or principality of Lazica was the direct descendant of the fabled land of Colchis, Kingdom of Aeetes, destination of the Argonauts, and covered large areas of what is now western Georgia, Mingrelia and Abkhazia, and north-eastern Turkey. Colchis was the great western hub of that Graeco-Georgian society that helped to mould and form the Georgian nation. One must not forget the Persians, of course. They also claimed Colchis as part of their world and, indeed, laid some of the blame for Graeco-Persian enmity on the abduction of Medea (from whose son, Medeus, the Medes are said to have taken their name) by Jason after he had taken the Golden Fleece. When Xenophon arrived at Trapezus (Trebizond, Trabzon) in the fifth century BC he described it as a Greek town in the country of the Colchians. Colchians and Trapezuntines were again closely connected during the time of Mithridates Eupator, King of Pontus, scion of a Hellenised Persian family. That great monarch's vigorous expansionism brought him into direct conflict with Rome and, after many years of fierce fighting, Mithridates finally saw his kingdom shattered and had his personal slave stab him to death, after he had repeatedly tried to poison himself unsuccessfully. He had at one time controlled all of the Black Sea littoral and had even planned to invade Italy. Pompey's armies took over and the Colchians found themselves under Roman control. This kingdom of Lazica, as the Romans came to call it after the most dominant of the Colchian tribes, became crucial to Roman, then Byzantine, success on the east coast of the Black Sea. During the fourth and fifth centuries the Laz, who had subjugated the Abkhaz to the north and the Svans in the high mountains to the north-east, had a military alliance with Rome, their main purpose being to guard the passes over the Caucasus. They also traded with Rome, probably largely in slaves. In the sixth century the Byzantine historian Agathias described them as:

> a strong and courageous people who dominate other strong peoples. They are very proud of being called Colchians, doubtless with reason. I know of no people, vassals of a foreign power, who are so renowned for the abundance of their wealth, the number of their subjects, the extent and fertility of their land, the beauty and spirited character of the inhabitants. [They] practise the art of navigation and carry on lucrative trade. Thanks to their relations with Rome they have built their country into a solid structure under the rule of law.

At this time Lazica became an important pawn in the game being played out between Persians and Byzantines who both eyed the country covetously, seeing it as the key to their ambitions against each other. The Laz tried to play their own game but, having kicked out the Byzantines with Persian help, found the Persians just as ghastly and, getting wind of a Persian plot to deport the entire population to the interior and replace it with loyal Persians, so that the kingdom might be used as a launching pad for attacks along the Black Sea coast against Constantinople, returned with some reluctance to their Byzantine alliance. Eventually the Persians ceded control of Lazica to the Byzantines under the terms of the appallingly ineptly named 'Treaty of Eternal Peace', eternity lasting, on this occasion, for eight years.

In 1204, with Seljuk Turks swarming all around and Crusaders chewing up Constantinople in their greed, Queen Tamar, at the height of Georgian power, sent the Georgian army into the Laz lands and occupied Trebizond, Samsun and Sinope, setting up a kind of protectorate and so bringing, for the first time, all the Kartvelian people (along with a lot of Greeks) under the power of one kingdom. This 'protectorate' was the so-called Empire of Trebizond, a silly title which Georgian historians mock, for this glorious empire was really a client state, its emperors related to the Georgian Royal House by marriage, promoted and maintained by their relatives in Tbilisi. Queen Tamar had sheltered the grandchildren of Andronikos Comnenos, Alexi and David, after they had been exiled from Byzantium and set them up in Trebizond; their descendants became a great feudal family in Kakheti and still live in Georgia today under the name of Andronikashvili.

The Laz have a remarkable history. They used to know this: in the sixth century, during their negotiations with the Persians, they constantly referred to the ancient associations that had existed between the Colchians and Achaemenid Persia a thousand years before. Now a vigorous part of the Turkish republic, they are beginning to rediscover themselves. The Turks, again, do not like this much. Neal Ascherson, who must have wandered about in this area at roughly the same time I did, wrote movingly in his *Black Sea* about the problems of the survival of Laz culture and, particularly, of the Laz language. He tells the story of Wolfgang Feuerstein, the German scholar who has been working on the Laz language, Lazuri, for many years, has given them an orthography for the first time, an adapted alphabet, both in Turkish Latin script and in Georgian, and was thrown out of Turkey for his scholarly pains, after a thorough beating by the Turkish police. Even such tremulous activity as this towards any declaration of an identity not wholly Turkish sends the authorities mad with anxiety. I have found various estimates of the Laz population in Turkey, ranging from three million to 90,000 but probably only 30,000 to 40,000 speak Lazuri as a mother tongue. The figure usually given by linguists for a healthy language is 100,000 speakers, upon which basis over half the world's 3,000 languages face the threat of extinction. There seems, therefore, especially to foreign linguists and academics, a very real danger, with greater penetration of Turkish through all the media (there is only one little Laz newspaper, *Ogni*, set up in Istanbul), that Lazuri could wither away. This is not, on the whole, a worry that is shared by the Laz, it seems. Some, undoubtedly, may be nervous of trouble and fear upsetting the authorities but most remain quite happy to speak Lazuri at home, to learn Turkish at school and to use it as the language of wider intercourse, acknowledging the opportunities this brings.

*

But we were after Georgian churches and so Chris and I in our Hertz rent-a-car left the Laz villages and the Black Sea, calm and rather green, at Hopa. We turned into the mountains and drove up, through plantations of tea and tobacco and maize, through the mists, past little wooden huts built on stilts, on the lovely road to Artvin. We picked up a Georgian farmer from Borchka who sat forward on the back seat and clapped me on the shoulders as I wobbled above the Choruh River, past fierce torrents and wonderful, terrifying bridges of Seljuk or Ottoman design. Chris tried to distract our friend with a story involving an Armenian he knew from Milton Keynes but this led to smiles and nods of incomprehension and further embraces as he called me his '*dzma*', his brother, and inquired after our children, the cost of the car, the cost of our air tickets, the price of hotel rooms. When I asked if he was Georgian or Turkish he had little hesitation in declaring for Turkey though, again, with some unease, as if I was impugning his character or his loyalty.

There are possibly over three hundred Georgian churches and monasteries in various states of collapse in Tao-Klarjeti and hardly any contemporary Georgians had until very recently seen any of them. It is rather as though no Frenchman had been permitted to see Chartres, nor any Italian Assisi and they were forced to content themselves with old photographs and bits and pieces of ancient scholarship. My own friends from the Georgian Institute of Art, a small flock of specialist art historians, had spent their working lives dreaming of one day being able to visit these great cathedrals and managed finally, in the summer of 1996, to borrow a minibus and mount a little expedition. They were on their way to see the church of Doliskana when they were stopped and arrested by the Turkish police and held in custody for days in Artvin and fiercely interrogated. Ordered out of the country, forbidden to continue their travels through Tao-Klarjeti, they eventually won through by arguing and telephoning furiously in Trabzon for a week and enlisting the help of various Georgian ministers. They received a grudging permission to visit some of the churches. However, they were escorted and forbidden to take any photographs, make any sketches, write down any notes and observations, which destroyed the whole point of the mission and the very reason they had been given a grant by the Soros Foundation in the first place. Outside Ishan they were actually confronted by a hostile group of soldiers whose officer informed them that he knew their goal: to restore the Georgian kingdom in Turkey. The Turks could cope with the odd Briton but Georgian scholars looking at Georgian churches were most suspicious and obviously a danger to the entire state. (It has to be said that these scholars also had problems in Jerusalem with the Greek patriarchate and Russian clergy; they had to hide in a bush and look at the Holy Cross monastery through binoculars, having been refused permission to study there, members of the synod being just as paranoid about old Georgian remnants as Turkish policemen.) After the Turks conquered Tao-Klarjeti in the sixteenth century and the process of Islamicisation began, some churches were deliberately destroyed, while most simply fell into ruin, their great stones pillaged now and then, so that one can still see, poking out of some low barn, the most exquisite tenth-century carving. Ironically, the best-preserved are those that were converted into mosques and it always surprised me to find, as some imam tugged at my sleeve or shuffled along behind, crosses, stars of David and frescos of saints, some wonderfully clear, almost pristine and untouched.

At the time of my first visit I had to piece together a route through these ancient Georgian lands. Since then Wachtang Djobadze's magisterial *Early Medieval Georgian Monasteries in Historic Tao, Klarjeti and Shavsheti* has added immeasurably to the store of current knowledge easily accessible beyond the academic circles of Tbilisi. I planned a journey along the Choruh River, the Georgian *tchorokhi*, with looping diversions which would take us to some of the greatest of these monasteries. They represent a staggering cultural achievement, little known in Western Europe and, like the rest of Georgian architecture, hardly ever referred to in any discussion of Christian art. It is a terrible omission. These wonderful buildings are, after all, not lost in some impenetrable jungle of the Far East, but have stood proud against the mountains for a thousand years. They make magnificent ruins, set in one of the most beautiful landscapes in the world.

*

We dropped our farmer friend in the centre of Artvin and settled with glasses of *raki* in a tavern overlooking the chasms of the town. Cheerful and engaging Turks clustered round, offering cigarettes and plates of chips and much of the usual historical advice upon the Russian origins of the Laz, the Georgians, the Greeks, the Armenians, anyone, in fact, who was not entirely Turkish. They could not have been nicer. Outside, a small band of Georgians had set up another 'Russian Market' and, as we entered the little rickety lift to take us to our room, our host entertained us with a story of five large Georgian ladies who had crammed into the lift the week before and caused it to plummet down three floors. At some point in the conversation he branched eagerly off into a strange dialect which caused Chris a terrible fit of hysterics:

'*Shavshat rumet randop clering vestman snars.* You understand?' he said.

'Er, a bit,' I answered, propping Chris against the door.

It took a little while but eventually we realised that he was speaking English and informing us of the next day's festival just off the road to Shavshat. During the summer months everyone heads for the *yayla*, the high mountain pastures where for millennia the people of the Black Sea have driven their cattle and sheep and escaped the heat of the lowlands. It is a great excuse for a continuous party and the festivals that punctuate the *yayla* calendar have a Bacchic air. Indeed, the characteristic *horon*, the great circular dance which starts sedately and climaxes in a spinning frenzy as the bagpipes play faster and faster, derives from the ancient Greek *choron*, danced to honour the god of wine.

Imagine Tao-Klarjeti at the height of Georgian power in the Middle Ages, a lozenge of land (the 'Georgian Throat' in Turkish, *Gurgi-Bughaz*, which says it so much better) that stretched nearly from the present border right down to Erzurum. Imagine the churches and monasteries full of treasures, the monks and scholars who worshipped in them busy translating and scribing and singing their wonderful polyphonic chants (so much more moving and interesting than the dreadful dirge of the English hymn and the awful wheezing of that dire instrument, the church organ); the craftsmen and artisans producing icons of dazzling *cloisonné* enamel; architects, masons and stone-carvers moving across the mountains building, restoring, refining; merchants with their caravans and gossip making their way from Tbilisi and Ani and Kars along the valley of the Choruh river to Trebizond: a landscape boiling with activity and creativity. Even what is left now, in the clear air and quiet villages among the mountains, has a fantastic vitality and force. Immediately, the sheer size of some of the churches seems extraordinary; there is no vernacular architecture anywhere around that is remotely comparable, rather like finding a skyscraper among the huts of a bushman village. Then the style of these buildings is so very distinctive. The obvious point of comparison is with Armenian architecture and quite clearly both come from the same stable, though Georgian and Armenian historians fight, as always, about who was first, best, built what, when. They use the same kinds of masonry, have the same distinctive shape of polygonal cupola or dome, often sprout a complexity of roofs in odd places. There are, however, differences: Armenian churches seem far more massive, darker, more compact and fortress-like, their domes often appear disproportionately large, the decoration and carving quite different. Some eloquent essayist might trace these similarities and differences in practice and aesthetic to the similarities and differences in the historical experiences of the two peoples, their national characters, even to the different landscapes of the two countries. Clearly, though, while local historians insist upon the native genius that produced them, both styles were influenced from the East, from Syria, from Sasanian Iran and beyond, as well as from the Byzantine West. Both countries are fiercely proud of their architects and masons who early gained an international reputation. In 989, when the dome of Hagia Sophia in Constantinople collapsed, the Byzantines sent for an Armenian architect, Trdat, to repair it. Hagia Sophia was the largest domed building in the world for a thousand years, till St Peter's was built in Rome, but on the whole the Byzantines didn't really excel at domes and did not understand them. Nor are there, I think, with the obvious exception again of Hagia Sophia and one or two others, Byzantine churches as large as the cathedrals of Ishan or Oshki in Tao-Klarjeti. Here there were two major styles of basic architectural design: the cruciform church with its exotic cupola, and the more austere, plainer, three-naved basilica with no dome. How far these designs or any other practices of Armenian and Georgian architecture influenced the buildings of Byzantium and of the European Renaissance remains, at present, a relatively unexplored subject. However, the received wisdom of a one-way traffic of ideas from West to East is certainly not the whole story.

I could have stayed for ever in Artvin, wandering its chasms, but at five in the morning, woken by the muezzin's loudspeaker, just beyond the wall behind my pillow, we set off to Sumbat's church of Doliskana in the little village of Hamamli, high above the Artvin to Shavshat road: a breathtaking, dizzying drive to a snug and bosky village. Muslims do not seem to have this same obsession with building their places of worship on top of mountains, overhanging precipices, in inaccessible chasms. They prefer to have their mosques within their cities where people can get to them. But Christians send their masons climbing towards heaven, as though the higher a church is built, the closer it gets to God. The remoteness, the height must have added to the security, the seclusion, a freedom from too much distraction, but there must also have been a spiritual aesthetic at work, a response to the sheer beauty and drama of the place. All through Tao-Klarjeti, Chris and I would wonder why? why here? why there? The answer always came in our exclamations of admiration and delight.

Sumbat's church is now used as a mosque, a loudspeaker on top of the dome, the imam's house tucked into its side. It has been rebuilt in parts, its roof restored by the imam, ethnically a Georgian. There is wonderful relief carving, something that is always so striking about Georgian churches where statuary, sculpture in the round, is unknown. I have never seen inscriptions carved directly into the walls of a church in the same way as was frequently done in Georgia, the beautiful lettering of the ancient Georgian *mrgvlovani* script becoming an important decorative feature, always in harmony with the whole. Here the inscriptions offer prayers for King Sumbat (died 958) and King Bagrat:

Jesus Christ help our kings
builders of this
holy church during the Last Judgement. Jesus help!

and there is a little carved portrait of King Sumbat, levitating slightly, rather damaged, holding in both hands a model of the church which he is, presumably, offering up to Christ. There are a couple of rather chunky angels, Gabriel and Michael, and next to Gabriel a sunburst with a portrait of the mason inside. All the faces have been chipped away more or less but the weave pattern above the doors and windows remains bright and clear. The setting of the church is magical, high in the mountains of Tao-Klarjeti, their rugged shapes set like a defensive wall all around, the high summer pastures of the *yayla* stretching out between.

To understand something of the importance of Tao-Klarjeti it is helpful to understand a little of Georgia's always complicated history. At the turn of the ninth century Ashot Bagrationi moved his capital here, to Artanuji, just a couple of miles east of Doliskana, and well away from the interference of the Arab emirs who dominated the Georgian heartlands. In the tenth century the province became the springboard for the unification of Georgia, a process that culminated in the crowning of King Bagrat (who is known, helpfully, as Bagrat the Third) as the first king of a united Georgia in 1008. Actually it did not really culminate so much as begin, for the political situation at the time was extremely complex and many problems remained for Bagrat and his heirs. However Tao had a remarkable ruler, David Kuropalates. He held his title as the gift of the Emperor of Byzantium and, after sending 12,000 cavalry to enable the Emperor Basil to put down the rebellion of Bardas Scleros, he was granted extensive lands and became the most powerful ruler in Caucasia. Geographically and politically Tao was the most important of all the Georgian kingdoms at this time: Byzantine lands directly bordered Tao to the south-west, Armenian lands, ruled over by Arab emirs, bordered to the south-east. Tbilisi was also in the hands of the Arabs. The rest of Georgia was fractured into four main parts: the Kingdom of Abkhazia, the Eristavate of Kartli, the Kingdom of Hereti and the Chorepiscopate of Kakheti. All of these fought with each other and a variety of enemies and allies. David of Tao, ably supported by a group of nobles and statesmen, was determined to bring order to a chaotic internal situation by welding the country together and, as he himself was childless, he fixed his succession upon the young Bagrat Bagrationi whose grandfather had been King of Kartli and whose mother was a princess of Abkhazia. But the unification of Georgia did not unfold smoothly from Bagrat's various coronations. He and his successors had to struggle against many internal and external threats. Arabs loyal either to the independent emirate of Tbilisi or to the caliphate in Baghdad – mutually antagonistic, fighting sometimes with Georgians of one principality, sometimes with others – tried to exert control. Byzantines, jealous of any threat to their domination, suborned ambitious nobles and discontented younger sons and, through the eleventh century, fought openly against the Georgian crown with a terrible ferocity. Byzantium incorporated southern Tao into the empire for some years. But the great achievement of David Kuropalates of Tao was to firmly and ineradicably implant the idea of a united kingdom of all the Georgians, to set it up as a desirable and attainable goal. It is from this time that the word Sakartvelo, the Country of the Kartvelians, the Georgian name for Georgia, came into use and it is from this time that it becomes possible, despite its endless vicissitudes, to speak of Georgia as a single, national entity. David was also responsible for building many of the greatest churches of Tao-Klarjeti and these foundations were, of course, political watchtowers which helped to establish and protect a firmly Georgian national, cultural and religious consciousness.

*

The *yayla* folk were setting up their summer fair in the Sahara Dagi mountains beyond Shavshat and we found them just off the unbelievably beautiful road towards Ardahan which winds through the pine trees along the upland valleys, past spreading meadows full of flowers and hay-makers. I became more and more convinced

that the Georgian princes and kings of Tao who built their monasteries here had done so out of love. They had fallen in love with
the land. The crowds were gathering in a great meadow, ringed by
trees and sloping down to the south with a miraculous view of the
mountains around. The real party would not start till late in the
evening and we had decided that we had not the time, if we were
to see our churches and catch our mythic boat, to wait till then. I
regret this deeply: it was an act of cowardice and self-preservation.
We knew that if we stayed it would take days to recover. But tents
were popping up under the trees and villagers and townspeople,
gypsies and nomads, all the *yayla* folk, were gathering to trade, to
dance, to wrestle, to fight their bulls, to drink and to fall in love.
Already makeshift stalls were doing a roaring trade in *rakı* and beer.
Musicians dressed in sheepskins, with their bagpipes, drums and
fiddles, led dancers in circles and snaking lines across the grass.
Chris with his camera was pursued by a merry shepherd who,
unused to society and already very drunk, had mistaken him for a
houri. Knots of small boys raced everywhere and clustered on boulders, posing for photographs.

North of Shavshat, up a little track and a stone's throw from the
Georgian border, is the church of Tbeti. It stood intact for a thousand years until, in 1961, it was blown up by a band of Poshas,
Armenian gypsies, looking for treasure, an ever-present local obsession which is almost universally used to explain the presence of
any new face in the area. Chris and I would protest our purely
academic interest in old churches but were always answered by a
knowing smile. The church now makes a splendid ruin, even what
little there is left is extraordinary. It stands in a magnificent grove
of mulberry trees in a village of balconied wooden houses, looking
down along a lovely valley. Though the centre of the church was
blown sky-high, the massive vaulting of the side apse still stands
and, somehow, bits of the dome remain. There are wonderful
remnants, too, of tenth-century frescos here: in the dome the figure
of Christ in triumph with His angels and prophets, in the apse the
Apostles. The pure, dry mountain air has kept them fresh and alive
through eleven centuries. It is, or was, a huge building, and gives
some idea of the wealth and power of the Georgian kings. Founded

at the beginning of the tenth century, it soon became an outstanding centre of culture and learning. Some suggest that Shota Rustaveli studied here though, more usually, he is thought of at the Ikalto Academy in Kakheti. It would have been, one might have thought, quite enough cathedral for an entire province, but it was just one of many such foundations in Tao-Klarjeti.

Having looped back to Artvin for the night we arrived next morning in another fine village, Yeni Rabat, looking for the monastery church of Shatberdi. The technique recommended is to approach any inhabitant and ask for the '*Kilise*', though quite which church and at what distance it might be located can never be determined. Earlier, near the village of Ortakoy, a small child was detailed by the village elders to lead us to our destination: after a two-hour climb we were rewarded by a ruin that I have never managed to identify. Not that this mattered at the time. The old church was perched high on a ledge overlooking a tranquil valley full of flowers. Next to it was a waterfall and as Chris and I stripped off and stood under it, much to the amazement of the boy, epigone of a once proud race, mouth open, a thick rope of snot dangling from one nostril, it seemed quite obvious that our church had been built for the sublime view. Here in Yeni Rabat, the infant teacher, a young man of intelligence and culture, led us to the ruined church, perched looking out across the slopes, a couple of miles along a path which wound through bean fields and around the hillside. Many of the loveliest Georgian illuminated gospels came from Shatberdi. But this overgrown and crumbling ruin may or may not have been Shatberdi. Even Djobadze is uncertain as to the monastery's precise identification and location, though it is frequently referred to in Georgian texts as one of the great scriptoria of the region. My confusion total, my research slipshod, my notes inadequate, I left the church to itself. On the way back, we stopped for a moment with a family sitting at their lunch in the cool shade of a spreading cherry tree, on a steep slope they had just scythed. At first the women shyly drew their scarves across their faces but after polite introductions smiled and relaxed. Boys rushed up the tree and brought down great branches of cherries for us, no question of picking just a few bunches.

We moved off along the Artvin to Erzurum road, a long run to find the church of Khakhuli. As we followed the River Tortum, the scene became harsher, craggy, parched and bare. The huge, bald canyon gradually widened towards Lake Tortum. There was little traffic. A few figures materialised spontaneously about the roadside, coming and going nowhere. The land seemed desolate, unpeopled. However, as soon as we turned up through the hills, the little valleys became green once more, shaded by trees, fertile and full. The villages here are deeply conservative and the women instinctively turned away from us, pulled their long, wide veils tight about their faces, and hid themselves. Khakhuli church in the village of Dikmen is magnificent: huge, massively intact and used as a mosque, set along the left bank of the little Khakhuli River. It is one of the great cruciform, domed churches built by David Kuropalates. Many of its details are still visible: carved weave patterns of an almost Celtic look, faded frescos, sun wheels and stars of David. However, all the human figures have been defaced or removed. The imam leant against the front, smoking, and seemed dispirited by our interest in the building. When I remarked upon the church's beauty he just shook his head gloomily and ground his cigarette stub under his heel. All the dwellings, the scriptorium, the refectories have disappeared but there are ruined little chapels scattered nearby and throughout the hills around, giving some idea of how populous and busy this monastic community must once have been. It was a great creative centre: the Khakhuli Triptych, now in Tbilisi, originally whisked away from the monastery in the early twelfth century to save it from the Turks, is one of the loveliest and most famous pieces of Georgian art, the central icon of the Virgin, though incomplete, wonderfully vivid, like a Fayum portrait.

This little valley lies just off the Erzurum road, once the main highway from the east to the Black Sea, and travellers and caravans must frequently have passed through. The church is not as richly ornamented as others but what detailing there is appears strikingly beautiful and sometimes peculiar. On the south façade, particularly, are carved the oddest assembly of figures: above the twin windows a rather ugly eagle carries off a deer; above the doorway four angels hold the Cross; to either side, rather worn and partially obscured, are figures with a strangely Mesopotamian air, doing incomprehensible things. There is a man in a chariot; some griffins; someone holding two fish is being swallowed by a monster, and a creature that is probably a lion seems to be enjoying a bull. All this Djobadze explains: the man in the chariot is Alexander the Great on his celestial journey. Quite what it is doing here he does not say, though the accumulated mythology around Alexander which prefigures him as an archetype of Christ was widespread throughout the Christian East. The man with the two fish is, apparently, Jonah, though the whale has confusingly become 'Ketos', a mythological sea-monster with legs and a lion's head. A lion, a cockerel and a griffin are all derived from the Near East where they were frequently employed as guardians at gateways.

Khakhuli and Oshki, another of David's churches, just to the north down a little tributary of the River Tortum, are two of the most outstanding Georgian tenth-century buildings. Most Georgians have never seen them. Anywhere in western Europe they would be enshrined as great architectural treasures and set about with tea-shops. They laid down the architectural pattern for much of what was to follow and they are so huge, so impressive, that coming upon them up a mountain track, through a little Turkish village, is startling. It is difficult not to burst out clapping at such a sudden, incongruous and magical manifestation. Oshki is larger still than Khakhuli and although all the aisle roof has fallen in, the dome is still standing, neatly supported by four freestanding piers. The church has a fantastic number of inscriptions and much lovely detailing and carving. Little boys led us around, pointing with real pleasure at the faded frescos, the little figures of David and Bagrat, carved angels and animals, the scallop-shaped niches and the lovely raspberry fruits carved around the bases of the pillars. These massive ruins are now cared for by the villagers, they say, though they were neglected and plundered for centuries.

Djobadze's study of Oshki revels in its bold articulations, its blind arcades, its triangular niches and the twenty-four-sided drum of its dome, and stresses the many architectural innovations and the fearless originality of Oshki's masons. From the hillside to the northwest, there is a fine view of the cathedral towering above the little houses of the village and one can start to understand its grand symmetry. Its desolation, though, produced a feeling of sadness, almost of despair; perhaps because it is so nearly perfect its ruin was all the harder to contemplate. As we left the church we found our tea-shop, a lean-to nestling up against the church wall. We were beckoned inside, seated and given tea, all payment vehemently refused, and we left with many courteous valedictions. The little boys instantly reappeared and escorted us with smiles to our car.

From Oshki we drove north across the wild mountains through a haze of blue and purple flowers, descending by crazy hairpins in the growing dark to Yusufeli. On a balcony over the fast flowing Barhal River we ate trout, drank *raki* and made friends with a driller from Detroit and his Turkish colleagues. They were looking for gold in the mountains. The driller, a tall spare man in his fifties with a Zappa mustache, had never been further than Texas before and could not wait to get home. The Turks, too, were bored by their months in the wilds and looked forward, their eyes wide and shining, to some leave in Erzurum and a visit to its whorehouse, most highly recommended. Might we care to join them? One girl there, a lame girl – of course, we knew what that implied – could perform the most extraordinary acts of love.

Later that evening, as I leant back in my chair, I started to feel rather odd, the back of my head had merged with the pillar behind and the rest of my body was following. Consciousness sucked at the edges of my mind like a withdrawing tide. In the night I had the most vivid and appalling dreams. I woke in the dark with no knowledge of where or who I was. Such temporary dislocations are not unusual but this time I feared the condition might be permanent. The effects of the hallucinogenic *raki* of Yusufeli lasted for some days and my nights became a surrealist playground. It was almost pleasant. The liquor, I assume, had been steeped with wormwood, or its local equivalent; I came to understand the madness of Lautrec and the old absinthe addicts of France and Spain.

By no means deterred and clinging to my mission, I sat, next morning, in fractured sunlight as Chris, who had drunk only beer, hurled our now battered rent-a-car along the Barhal valley through twenty miles of twisting, broken dirt and rubble track to Altiparmak, to find the monastery of Parkhali. Whenever I leant from the window to ask a rare inhabitant if we were heading in the right direction (once from the middle of a delightful plot of onions into which we had somehow strayed) the answer, inevitably, was '*Yok!*' and so '*Altiparmak yok!*' became our bourden. Once found by this process of negation, bounced like a pinball between the mountains, the village still refused to reveal the church till we discovered it nestled on a shelf in the hillside, along a narrow track, cloaked by trees. The church is not as lovely as Oshki or Ishan but has a grand solemnity that slowly takes hold. It is also well-preserved, in use as a mosque. A grumpy man made us pay to see it: all the other monastery buildings have disappeared but the great three-naved basilica stands in monumental grandeur, its tenth-century sandstone exterior clean and pure with a few wonderful carvings in relief: crosses of interlaced ribbon in different patterns, left unharmed, the brows above the windows of intricate geometric and vegetal design. On the north façade, carved into the keystones of the window arches, a lion prances and two peacocks strut with jewels suspended from their beaks, indicative, Djobadze says, of the adaptation of ancient oriental, Sasanian themes, found typically on churches throughout Tao-Klarjeti. There is also a rather endearing carving of a little man with a beard, thought to represent the master mason in charge of the church's construction, another characteristic of the churches of Tao and one which would win the approval of builders everywhere. The interior of the church with its soaring barrel vault has been whitewashed over and the inscriptions and paintings which once decorated the walls are either chipped away or covered. Somehow the very bareness of the space adds to its majesty. The grumpy man, though, hovered over us and his bad temper forced us out before we quite realised that we had left. He shut the door firmly behind us.

From surviving manuscripts it is clear that there was much exchange between the churches of Tao, with monks and calligraphers lending each other materials to copy out, translating religious and liturgical works and helping each other in their tasks. There were certainly close connections between Parkhali and Ishan, the next church we visited, perhaps the most magnificent of all, though now in ruins. We drove through an extraordinary landscape: an arid, desert, denuded canyon with mountains of sand and shale until, in a burst of green and shade, surrounded by orchards of apple and chestnut and cool gardens, softened by clouds of butterflies, we found Ishan, miraculously towering above its vast levelled court, now the village football pitch. The air was so clear that the view seemed almost unreal. Standing just behind goal, the great dome or cupola of the church, with its many-sided drum and pointed roof, rose above walls that appeared at first quite intact. However, as with Oshki, the roof of the church has gone, which makes the dome all the more surprising and wonderful, balancing as it does on supporting arches that burst from the four massive pillars which rise from the floor beneath. The revealed skeleton of the church demonstrates exactly how the whole structure was joined.

Ishan was the most important of all the five bishoprics of Tao-Klarjeti and is at once one of the earliest and one of the last of the great churches, the culmination and distillation of an architectural practice that evolved over many centuries. The oldest part of the church dates from the middle of the seventh century, a marvellous colonnaded apse, a columnarium, stout little pillars which curve about its eastern end. It is thought to have been built by Nerses, the Catholicos of Armenia, who escaped to find sanctuary in Tao after he had expressed support for the Chalcedonian orthodoxy, espoused by Georgia and most of the churches but rejected to this day by the Armenians. It was the cause of the split between the Georgian and Armenian churches, one of those wonderful and only marginally comprehensible arguments that rived the Orthodox world so often, causing all manner of rioting, anathema, dissension, death and damnation among the faithful. It has been said that no one could cross a road or buy a carrot in Constantinople without having to argue about the triune nature of God, or exactly to what extent Christ was human or divine, or whether iconoclasm was a good thing. The taxi drivers of the time must have been a nightmare. Not all of this reached into Georgia. Iconoclasm, for example, never really took hold and the Georgians remained firm iconodules, lovers of images, displaying that wonderful disobedience of the Second Commandment for which we are all so much the richer. The Council of Chalcedon had been called to settle the knotty matter of the nature of Christ. The Monophysites believed that the Incarnate Christ was wholly divine. This was in contradistinction to the Nestorian heresy which had caused such trouble a few years before and which stated that there were two distinct persons in Christ, the human and the divine. (There was another famous heresy, the Arian heresy, which stated that Christ was wholly, though perfectly, human and not divine at all.) The Monophysite position caused absolute turmoil so the emperor convened a council of 600 bishops who met in the Church of St Euphemia at Chalcedon in 451 and managed to produce a piece of wonderful fudge, the Chalcedon Definition, which stated that Christ was one person with two natures, united indivisibly, both perfectly divine and perfectly human at the same time. Most, extraordinarily enough, went home happy but the eastern churches, the Armenian, Syrian, Abyssinian and the Copts of Egypt all rejected it. The Georgian church went with the Definition though it too had flirted with the Monophysites for a time, influenced as it was by the teachings of the Syrian church in particular. Syrian holy men, the thirteen Syrian fathers of Georgian legend, had helped to establish Christianity in Georgia and, indeed, the Georgian church had, at first, been subordinate to the Patriarchs of Antioch. However, after Chalcedon, the Georgian church allied itself firmly to the Greek, leaving a schism between itself and the Armenians which caused all kinds of bitter feuds and argument for centuries thereafter. Nerses, despite being the Armenian Catholicos, was also of the Chalcedonian persuasion and had to flee Armenia for Ishan where he set about building his church. Unfortunately, a couple of centuries later, Arabs dispatched by the Caliph of Baghdad on a punitive raid destroyed it almost entirely, though they left the lovely columnarium. It was rebuilt at least once again early in the ninth century, the site revealed by God in a vision to its restorers, Saba and Grigol, who were having difficulties finding Ishan as it was 'inaccessible to man', proving that Chris and I were not alone in having problems locating some of these great churches of Tao. (The Bagrationis were especially devoted to Grigol, who founded a dozen monasteries. His biography, the *Life of Grigol Khandzteli* is one of the great works of medieval Georgian literature.) However, Ishan did not reach its final state till 1032, about fifty years after Oshki with which it can be compared, the earlier foundation almost certainly influencing the form of the later.

The exterior of Ishan in its form and detail displays much that seems to typify Georgian architecture at its best and most distinctive: the cruciform church with its characteristic dome or cupola, facings of smooth, beautifully dressed stone, exterior walls decorated by blind arches, strange triangular niches on the east and west façades, the frames and brows of the windows and doors richly carved and patterned, carved lettering on the tympanum. The interlaced crosses carved on the walls are unharmed and lovely leaf patterns spring from their bases. It is an incredibly elegant and sophisticated architecture yet without any showy exhibitionism, dignified, restrained, almost reserved. The churches of Tao do not seem to display those strange carvings that one finds sometimes on churches within Georgia jutting haphazard from the walls and suggesting some old looted, pagan temple, but all over Tao are fine zoomorphic reliefs as exotic and compelling as the wonderful creatures at Nicortsminda in Ratcha or the great bulls' heads that peer out from Svetitskhoveli in Mtskheta. By the time of the last period of building in Ishan these animal forms have become smaller and were soon to disappear as the Georgian church fell more in line with the Greek church and had less to do with the churches of the East. Beneath one window is a lovely small carving of a lion eating a dragon which, according to Djobadze, alludes to an ancient belief that eclipses were caused by a giant serpent which swallowed the sun, extinguishing light and life. The lion represents the sun itself and the carving is placed at the source of light for the church, the window. On the little chapel or oratory which stands just to the south-west of the church, there are more animal carvings over the windows and doors, tiny figures of lions, elephants, peacocks, griffins and winged horses set within an intricate weave. Most of these motifs derive ultimately from Iran and Mesopotamia and, carved around the openings (doors and windows) to the sacred space, have a symbolic, protective force.

Inside the roofless church a few patches of brilliant blue and some red fragments still visible along the aisle suggest the blazing colours which once decorated its walls, but the frescos inside the drum of the dome remain and angels' faces still look down from above its tall windows. The angels carry the Cross, beneath them race the chariots of the Apocalypse, on the other side a strange female figure rides upon a bull, said to represent the sun. Though the exterior of the dome is sixteen-sided, inside it is perfectly round and, where the four central pillars meet the supporting arches beneath it, lovely scallops have been carved.

One question puzzled me. Why did all this building activity, this fantastic flurry, comparable in intensity to the building boom of post-Norman England, seem to stop suddenly towards the middle of the eleventh century? Perhaps there were by then simply enough churches and monasteries in Tao. The answer is probably, however, more political and in two related parts. First, the unification of Georgia after the death of David Kuropalates (who was himself responsible for the building of Parkhali, Otkha Eklesia, Oshki and Khakhuli) meant that the focus of attention shifted away from this south-western edge towards the centre. And then there suddenly appeared upon the scene a whole new entity which changed for ever the face of Transcaucasia and hugely reinforced the drive for a strong centralising power in Georgia. The Seljuk Turks arrived. They had overrun Persia, Mesopotamia and parts of Syria and now poured into lands the Byzantines considered theirs and so, in 1071, a large Byzantine army, led by the Emperor, Romanus Diogenes, confronted a far smaller Seljuk force under the able command of Alp Arslan, the Seljuk Sultan, and was completely thrashed at the battle of Manzikert, just a few miles north of Lake Van. The battle has often been characterised as one of the great turning points of world history. The Emperor himself was captured. One of the reasons given for his defeat, apart from the brilliance of his enemy, was the ragbag nature of his army, too hastily assembled, dispirited, starved of funds after years of sharp decline in the fortunes of an empire led by a dreadful succession of incompetents. Diogenes' force consisted of many untrustworthy mercenaries and unwilling allies who hated him, including some of his own commanders, Turkomans that went over to the enemy, Georgians that the Byzantines had been bullying for years, but more especially Armenians who were being horribly persecuted by Byzantium for their adherence to their Monophysite beliefs. The irony of this defeat, which was absolutely critical and destroyed at a stroke Byzantine power in Armenia, most of Anatolia and the Transcaucasus for ever, creating in its place the great Sultanate of Rum, was that there was really no necessity for the Byzantines to have given battle in the first place, certainly not in such a hurried and disorganised manner. Scholars believe that Alp Arslan (whose mustaches were so long that they had to be tied behind his back when he fought) initially had no intention of settling in the area, certainly no idea at all of destroying the Byzantine empire in Asia Minor which was an entity as fixed and immutable in contemporary minds as the mountains themselves. Looting and pillaging, certainly, some wilful destruction of course, but not permanent conquest. The Seljuks, recent converts to Sunni Islam, were merely on an outing to go and pulverise their arch-enemies, the Egyptian Fatimids, Shi'ites who had set up a rival caliphate in Cairo and whose empire reached up through the Holy Land to Aleppo, which Alp Arslan was besieging at the time of Romanus' mobilisation against him. There was actually supposed to be a truce between the Byzantines and Turks. It is true that the Turks under Alp Arslan's uncle, Tugrul Bey, and as freebooting bands of Turkoman raiders, had been causing havoc in Armenia and making periodic incursions into Georgia for some years, just about reaching Trebizond around the middle of the century, which must have given everyone in the area, including the church builders of Tao, a dreadful shock. Alp Arslan himself had ravaged parts of Georgia in the 1060s, in 1064 penetrated Tao-Klarjeti, and two years later exterminated most of the population of Kartli. But after Manzikert everything changed, not because of the battle itself but through the utter idiocy of Romanus' successor and the implacable rivalries of the Byzantine court. Romanus had been released by Alp Arslan after concluding a treaty that really did the empire little harm and would have maintained a balance of power in Armenia. Unfortunately, when he got home, Romanus was defeated, deposed, blinded, mounted on a mule for a 500-mile journey into exile and degradation and soon died, the factions at the court of Constantinople conspiring against him and replacing him with the weak and malleable Michael. The new Emperor refused to accept the terms and obligations of the treaty between Romanus and Alp Arslan and so gave the Seljuks and the Turkoman tribes every excuse they needed. Tens of thousands of them poured into Anatolia and within a couple of years had removed from the empire the source of much of its grain and half its manpower.

The effects of all this upon Georgia were at once disastrous and dazzling. The Seljuk invasions led to one of Georgia's darkest periods – known still as the *didi turkoba*, the Great Turkish Troubles – and also, eventually, to its finest flowering. As the Turks went on their usual rounds of devastation, enslavement and destruction, turning cultivated fields into nomad pasture, killing, burning and looting, a contemporary chronicler wrote that 'the country became empty and turned into forest. And in the place of people, wild animals roamed.' The Georgian people, in their usual fashion, sought refuge in their mountains and the Georgian king had to make the journey to Isfahan to submit to the Seljuk sultan and agree to pay him tribute. The devastation and misery in Armenia were, if anything, even worse. Both peoples felt that they were facing complete extermination.

Then, in 1089 a sixteen-year-old king was crowned in Georgia. He was King David, known to the Georgians as *aghmashenebeli*, the Builder or the Restorer. If ever anyone lent credence to the Great Man theory of history it was he. Careful, brilliant, utterly focused and determined, as well as being a great scholar, linguist and poet, he totally transformed the fortunes of his country and the whole of the Transcaucasus in the thirty-six years of his reign. He saw precisely what he needed to do and exactly how to do it. First he

gathered loyal supporters about his throne and placed them in all
high positions of church and state, firmly repressing the rivalry
and greed of the Georgian nobles and ecclesiasts. Then he made
the necessary alliances, marrying one daughter to the son of the
Emperor of Byzantium, another to the Shirvansha. He himself
married a princess from another Turkish tribe, the Kipchaks, who
lived in the steppes to the north of the Caucasus, and he built a
fort in the Daryal to ensure safe passage to his allies. He needed,
above all, a professional standing army and he recruited busily
among his own people, among the Ossetines around the Daryal
and among the Kipchaks themselves, bringing 40,000 horsemen
and their families into Georgia and settling them. He recruited
mercenaries from Daghestan and from the Kurds. Slowly, surely,
he began to push the Seljuks out. They would come every autumn
into Kartli and up the valley of the Mtkvari River with their herds
and flocks and bowmen, making settled life impossible, so David
harried them and ambushed them and drove against them till they
fell back. The population gradually returned to their homes. In
1110 he pushed them from Somkheti and defeated in the field a
great force sent against him by the Seljuk rulers of Persia. He
cleared them from Tao and Klarjeti in 1116, and in 1121 at the
battle of Didgori crushed and destroyed a huge Seljuk army of
300,000. In 1122 he took Tbilisi, releasing it from Muslim control
for the first time in 400 years and making it his capital. By the
following year Georgia was whole and cleared of Seljuks. David
then went on the offensive again and drove deep into Shirvan
which passed into his control in 1124. He fought his way into
Armenia, castle by castle, town by town. The citizens of Ani, the
ancient capital, ruled by an Arab emir, invited him in and
Armenians fought side by side with Georgians in a war of libera-
tion. In the same year David's forces took Ispir on the Tchorokhi.
He planned not only to make all Georgia's frontiers secure but
also to gain control of the important trade routes of the Caucasian
Middle East and by the time he died in 1125 Georgian hegemony
stretched from the Black Sea to the Caspian. He was a ruler of
tremendous vision, tolerant and wise and much loved by his
subjects. Muslim historians writing shortly after his death praised

him unreservedly: 'He rejoiced the hearts of the inhabitants . . . visited the principal mosque each day, listened to the prayer and the lesson from the Koran; gave money to the Khatib for the soothsayers, Sufis and poets, and allowed them pensions.'* Sixty years later, when Queen Tamar came to the throne, something very much like a single Caucasian state existed thanks to David, ruled over by Georgia, with considerable local autonomy for Muslims, Armenians, mountain tribes, Kipchaks and all its disparate elements but nevertheless reasonably coherent and relatively peaceful, in the Caucasian sense, and prosperous. And then, of course, after the great days of Tamar, the Mongols arrived and shattered Georgia once more and the whole awful process of history started all over again.

I may have strayed a little from the churches of Tao but not really that far. There are connections everywhere. Shota Rustaveli studied at Tbeti, wrote his poetry at the court of Queen Tamar, died in Jerusalem. His great poem was set in India and Arabia and adapted Persian themes. Georgia looked out upon the wider world and the world looked at Georgia. In the same year as Manzikert, the Seljuks took Jerusalem and then the Pope started the Crusades. At the battle of Didgori, David the Builder had a force of two hundred crusaders fighting alongside the Georgians against the Turks. At roughly the same time Alexius Comnenus, the new, able young Emperor of the Byzantines, was tidying up his empire and turning its shattered bulk into a great power once more, despite its loss, dealing effectively with terrifying Normans, greedy Crusaders and yet more Turks, this time the fearful Pechenegs who besieged Constantinople in 1090 and whom he destroyed with the help of still other Turks, the Cumans. There really were the most absurd number of these Turkic tribes wandering about and one can only thank goodness that they all now have somewhere pleasant to stay. All these worlds were by no means separate and the actions of one impinged upon the other. The arrival of the Seljuks may have ultimately stopped the further building of churches in Tao and caused chaos, death and destruction in Georgia but they also

* El-Aini; See W. E. D. Allen, *A History of the Georgian People*, p. 97.

removed the Byzantines and took control from the Arabs and Persians, simplifying the local situation considerably. Their arrival also provoked the Crusades which diverted at least some of their attention and gave David his opportunity. In this new world, Georgia, far from being the remote and obscure country it later became, was a great light to all in the west, Byzantines and Crusaders alike, and its power and prestige were upheld by its armies, its court, its diplomats and its churchmen. There were no rigid boundaries here: soldier-priests, noble-monks, ambassador-bishops filled the ranks. Almost all the great churches of Tao lay within a monastic foundation, they were like universities, and the priests who peopled them travelled to sister foundations within Georgia and over the Christian world. Georgia had for many centuries great monasteries in Syria, in Palestine (about twenty), in Sinai, in Bulgaria, in Constantinople and above all on Mount Athos. Here the great Iviron monastery was founded and staffed by Georgian monks, as might be deduced from its name: Iviron deriving from Iberia, the ancient Roman name for Georgia. It was second in importance only to the Great Lavra (whose founder, St Athanasios, came from Trebizond and had a Georgian mother) and became one of the most important centres of the whole orthodox world, possessing vast wealth and huge tracts of land.

*

So much heat, history and architecture were taking their toll. Chris was looking a little madder and I only had to mutter 'architrave', as we passed a likely looking track, for him to push his foot firmly to the floor and send the rent-a-car flying down the main road to Ispir. Besides, we had a boat to catch. All along the Choruh River ruined fortresses clung to cliffs, guarding the way into Tao. This was death-valley canyon, the dirt road wild and difficult, a landscape of jumbled rock and broken mountainside, huge moonscapes of sand and baked mud stained with mineral ooze. We found our gold drillers in their little camp – a couple of caravans and a tent with a deep freeze – working at their rig, just off the road, parched in the torrid heat, covered in sweat, sand and flies. As we shared some iced water they spoke of Erzurum again, and I could understand the force of their longing, even for that unappetising dump. After Ispir the road climbed up and up, became wilder and even more arid until, high in the mountains, nomadic bee-keepers lined the way with their tents and hives, and deep, green, mossy grass, wild thyme and wild flowers spread all around. Then, at the very top of the Ovitdagi Pass, the scene changed again, and shepherds with their flocks and herds of cattle wandered through thick fog. Little rough, low huts, *kosh*, roofed in turves and plastic, serve as their summer homes and give refuge to travellers caught on the mountain. Up above the snow line, cloud covered everything and we inched the car down over the pass, quite blind in the whiteness. Suddenly we could see again and this was a good thing as the road was deeply cratered where boulders had crashed down upon it. Houses soon sprang up: built of wood, with a rubble infill and plastered with clay, they had a strangely Tudor air. Now, on these north-facing slopes, dense pine woods closed about us and then the broad-leaved trees, green and luxuriant, and then the dark green bushes of tea, as the valley broadened out towards the sea.

But where was our boat? We found Nejip in the square in Trabzon and he informed us sadly and with many apologies that it was still broken. And so we started our peregrinations again, crossing and re-crossing Trabzon like mysterious extras in a Tati film. Over more endless glasses of apple tea we had many conversations with men from various ministries whom Nejip produced like rabbits from a hat. All were sympathetic and soothing, till in the midst of one conversation I suddenly woke up.

'Why do you not go to Kars and take the train?'

'There's a train? No one told me about a train.'

'Certainly there's a train. You must go through Armenia, of course, but you will have no problem.'

'Well, that's fantastic. But why don't we need a visa to go by train?'

'There is no requirement. That is all.'

'I see. Do the trains go often?'

'Certainly they go often. There is one tomorrow.'

And so Nejip phoned a friend at Kars station and booked us two seats and we rushed off to buy bus tickets to Kars and phone my friends in Tbilisi to tell them that finally we were coming via Armenia and they laughed. I found out later that when asked why we had not yet arrived they would answer truthfully that we were in Trabzon, and that this is a frightfully funny joke in Georgia, Trabzon representing the far-off and faintly implausible, rather like Timbuktu in English. So if in Tbilisi you hear the one about the two Englishmen stuck in Trabzon you will know its provenance.

I love Turkish buses. We took our seats and were instantly sprayed with perfume. The bus conductor inquired after our health, our families, and moved people around so that we should have congenial souls to talk to. We drove back along the lovely road to Artvin again, then through the multicoloured hills and moonscapes around Ardanuj, and then into nothingness. A huge endless plain at the end of the world. And suddenly I could see the Mongolian Hordes and the Seljuk Turks pouring out of Asia and through Armenia, wheeling their cavalry around to point at Georgia, trotting freely with the wind behind them and nothing at all in their way. Nearer Kars a few nomad tents appeared, a few sheep and more low, mean and decrepit-looking crofts. In this huge landscape a few piles of turf, the odd cart, some simple strip-farming, gave intermittent signs of a hard and poor life. Kars was no better. It felt like the last outpost on earth, which it was for many of the Russian and Turkish soldiers stationed there, counting the days, as it changed hands back and forth between the two powers. Why either of them should have thought it worth fighting for is not immediately apparent. Beyond the occasional startling reminder of the town's ancient Armenian past and the solid Russian buildings of its more recent tsarist one, it is full of dust and rubble and poverty. However, as it was Gurdjieff's birthplace, I was determined to find it interesting, so Chris and I went in search of some salon where we might find poetry and music and other graceful arts. We heard only the low moan of the wind and saw only tumbleweed, blowing down the streets. This was a tremendous disappointment as I had been informed, most unreliably, that in Kars one might still hear the *ashok* sing. Gurdjieff's father was an *ashok* (or an *ashug* in Georgian). They were the tellers of tales, the poets, the singers, the bards who would improvise verses and fight each other in deadly battles of poetry, like the *chattismata* in Cyprus or the *ragga* battles of Jamaica. Once common all over the Caucasus, Central Asia, Asia Minor and Turkestan, some were supposed still to sing in a particular tavern in Kars. However, Chris and I found nothing along the dark, deserted streets and I had to content myself with thoughts of Gurdjieff lying on a pile of wood-shavings in his father's workshop, somewhere in Kars, listening to him sing the story of Gilgamesh to his friends.

Strangely enough, that night, lying in bed, listening to the thunder, the room illumined by lightning, I heard what seemed to be one of those poetry battles raging in the room above. It sounded thrillingly archaic. I sat up in some excitement and strained to listen. Fascinating. The language was strange, not Turkish, perhaps a local dialect. Or Finnish. Or Hungarian. Or Norwegian. I asked Chris. 'English,' he said, and went back to sleep. Sure enough a few recognisable words began to fall from the ceiling. Here on the dark corner of a street in Kars, two Geordies were having a fight:

'You never think of anyone but yourself. It's me, me, me all the time.'

'You think I'm selfish, you should hold up a mirror sometimes.'

'You know I like Nescafé for breakfast and you took it all.'

'And what about me? I like Nescafé for breakfast and all.'

I thought they were doing quite well. It almost rhymed and nearly scanned and the rhythm was potent with anger.

At eight in the morning we were at the station. At ten the little train arrived. By midday we were squashed inside with a couple of Jordanians, three Syrians, forty Armenians and their vast mounds of luggage, great bundles of goods bought in Turkey to sell in the new commercial shops in Yerevan. Their whole operation was masterminded by a young man in a checked coat with huge lapels and a mouthful of gold and far more teeth than were strictly necessary, who disposed the sacks and suitcases carefully throughout the train. Slowly we moved off over the broad plain, stopping occasionally in the emptiness where one or two locals got on or off.

We passed a few low huts with grassy roofs, turves stacked outside, a few horses, some sheep, strips of wheat, beet, potatoes until, at last, we reached the border control. We all got out, had our passports stamped. The Armenians dragged their heaps of baggage through the station house and on to the other platform. We waited. Three hours later the old Soviet train appeared. We pushed our way on and after an age the train began to move. Very slowly. All around watchtowers and fences and armed guards marked our progress. And then the train stopped in no-man's-land. Everyone looked about nervously. Nothing but the clearing of throats and the clutching of passports. Four armed guards appeared. Silently, inspecting us carefully, they removed our passports. This was it. We waited. The Armenians waited. The Syrians and Jordanians waited. We all waited. A friendly Jordanian chatted away, fidgeting furiously, loosening his tie. He was trying to get to Kharkhov to see his Russian wife. He wondered whether there was something wrong with his visa. Or his friends' visas. Chris and I thought that we might be the problem. The Armenians slumped in resignation. Three more hours passed in the sticky heat of the carriage. There was no word from outside. Then, at seven in the evening (by which time we had foolishly imagined we might be in Tbilisi) a ripple of rumour spread along the train. A guard appeared and silently, looking at us intently, handed back our passports. Normal procedure. By eight we were in Leninakan station (or Gyumri station as it now is), having taken twelve hours to travel sixty kilometres.

Fighting our way through laden Armenians, we found ourselves in the customs shed. We were questioned and searched perfunctorily and then a very nice security officer took us away and locked us into a small room. He was quite firm about it in wonderfully exact French and resisted all my blandishments when I tried to persuade him that we needed coffee, or water, or food. '*Je regrette, Monsieur,*' he said, repeatedly, and he did look deeply sorry. So Chris and I sat and then stood and then sat again for four more hours until we heard the train pull in and then the officer re-appeared and led us through the station and on to the train and stood there watching us steadfastly till we departed.

The train was utter chaos. We all waved our tickets about and made the resident Armenians laugh. Each seat had been over-booked a dozen times and the crowds sat and stood, glued together in the sticky night, packed tight along the corridors, in the compartments, in the toilets and on the grinding metal plates between the carriages. Small scuffles broke forth. The Syrians, particularly, pushed their way through in an admirably tight scrum towards a carriage already so full that there were families camping in the luggage racks, but which they felt should certainly be theirs. This was the holiday express to Sochi on the Black Sea coast and it was full of excited boys off to the seaside. Chris and I were grabbed by two lads and pushed into their compartment, heaving our way over bodies and bags through the swelter, and hassled all along by Armenians eager to buy everything we had. Our trousers? Shoes? Watches? Socks? Toothpaste? Anything? We must, surely, have something we could sell them? Something, no matter what, from the West! The lads and their mates kindly gave us the top bunks and then we all stood smoking and chatting next to the stinking bog. We swap addresses, I am invited to be a godfather, we are asked to assess any women who squeeze by. Eventually, as the train rolled gently on, I got to doze fitfully, waking often to look over at Chris who, head and knees drawn up, appeared to be stuck between the ceiling and his bunk in some agonising asana. He was, however, happily asleep and I could hardly wake him when, much to my amazement, at eight the next morning, our train pulled slowly into Tbilisi station.

CHAPTER 9

SVANETI

Dining at the Savoy

How we came through Svaneti, from Mestia to
Ushguli, and tried to leave Georgia (with some
remarks upon the character of the Svans)

The city was nervous. Newly independent, half way through
Gamsakhurdia's regime, no one had the faintest idea what was
going to happen next. There were crises of all kinds, refugees
from South Ossetia were wandering forlornly through the streets,
rumours of imminent Russian occupation ran like a blazing fuse
about the land and there had just been a terrible earthquake.
Matters, of course, were to get much worse, the deposition of
Gamsakhurdia, the civil war and the Abkhaz war were still a few
months off, but friends were bewildered and anxious. It was difficult to move about, petrol in very short supply, few cars around
to flag down for lifts. Prices had been 'liberalised', the price of
bread rising daily and causing havoc. The wheat supply had been
cornered by the Mafia. The old state shops were virtually empty,
and though there was plenty of food in the market, it was expensive. Indeed, money had gone mad. The various parallel universes
through which money circulated were impenetrable to the non-
Soviet mind even in the old days: things could appear both ridiculously expensive and absurdly cheap at the same time, depending
on the position of the observer, rather like some strange experiment in particle physics. The average wage was about two
hundred, two hundred and fifty roubles a month. A hundred

roubles, two weeks' wages, would buy three chickens, one blank video, four kilos of beef or an air ticket to Batumi. It was all quite insane and impossible to make out how people survived. Everyone was selling off the family silver. Anyone with a few dollars was, of course, quite fabulously wealthy. Strange men with suitcases stuffed with cash sidled up to us at every corner. The official rate of exchange was 47 roubles to the pound, black market rates many times this. At the official rate our putative chicken, therefore, cost about 75 pence, or about a fifth of the monthly wage. A fifth of an English monthly wage (£800) would have been £160. So the chicken cost either 75 pence or 160 pounds. It was all quite simple.

By my calculation we must therefore have eaten a few thousand quids' worth of chicken the night we sat down to supper at Tsira Gugushvili's. She and her sister Marina had been cooking since Chris and I were sent back from Sarpi, and though their friends had tried their best to clear each day's *supra* as it had been produced, we were expected to make up for all those lost dinners. Since we had arrived most of Tbilisi had been feeding us regularly and we were stuffed like bears before winter. However, Tsira's chicken *satsivi* was a work of art and if I ever suffer from an impaired digestion I shall, like one of P. G. Wodehouse's characters, have the recipe read out to me at night by my butler. I tried making it at home but it turned out quite wrong. It goes something like this:

> Boil a number of chickens
> When cooked remove chickens and spread salt over them
> Stew finely shredded onions in the fat from the broth
> Crush large quantities of walnuts
> Pound garlic, coriander, saffron, cinnamon
> Soften them with vinegar
> Leave two-thirds of the broth in the pan
> Put everything except chicken in and cook for ten minutes
> Cut chicken into pieces and add to pot
> Stew a little more

Tsira's flat, one of those lovely old Tbilisi apartments with a wide wooden balcony running along each floor and overlooking a central courtyard, was a cool oasis away from the horrid heat and uncertainty of the streets. It was full of friends, most of whom had stayed with me in England: Gocha and Katy from the Rustaveli Theatre, Ghizo the director, his son Ghoki, Katy's new husband, Irakli, her mother, Nana, Zura with whom Chris and I were staying. The evening filled with chat as we tried our best to make headway against the ever increasing tide of dishes – piles of *chadi*, Georgian maize-bread, stacks of *khachapuri* – Tsira and Marina leaping into the kitchen as soon as any slight progress was made and covering the table with more, bottles marching like breakwaters into the flood. Eventually, despite much encouragement, I was reduced to toying with a few pomegranate seeds, and a little cabbagey thing with spicy, walnutty stuff, and the conversation, inevitably, turned to the only real subject, the situation, the *situatsia*. It was definitely bad, everyone agreed upon that, but the young, who in England are probably the most cynical and disenchanted group in society, here were much more optimistic, more forgiving than the older generation. Little did they know. Gocha, who had been heroic during the Russian crackdown in April 1989 – rescuing fallen friends, barring the way to the Rustaveli Theatre against Russian troops and receiving a terrible beating for his efforts – argued passionately that Gamsakhurdia must be allowed to go through these various stages towards democracy, that he was doing what was necessary as part of a process of profound change. Marina argued just as passionately that Gamsakhurdia was a dreadful person, she knew him of old, they had been at school together. He was, and always had been, ruthlessly ambitious, corrupt, authoritarian, a Fascist who was systematically perverting the course of democracy.

The next day Chris and I gave a little interview to one of the pro-Gamsakhurdia newspapers that had sprung up in Tbilisi. It seemed odd that they should want to haul in a couple of wandering Englishmen but so eager were they to see what the world might think of them in those times that they would probably have interviewed my dog, if he had been available. We gave them our impressions, talked of John Baddeley, discussed our planned trip to Svaneti and they published it all at length. The staff were all very young, excited, jolly and full of hope and desperately wanted our approval. Within a couple of months this paper had become little more than a propaganda rag and, as the opposition to Gamsakhurdia gathered force, started to belabour the population in exactly the way that Marina had predicted. In the autumn, a couple of months after we left, Marika Didebulidze wrote me a distraught letter:

This has been a dreadful autumn. The situation is very tense and our government acts disgracefully, it has become dangerous to live here. Everyone who opposes the government is treated very badly – some put in prison (a handful as yet but the state wants to punish everybody). The situation reminds me of the French Revolution, with mobs of people screaming in the streets and demanding execution. It is very sad. Do you remember the young ladies from the newspaper who interviewed you? They are in the forefront of persecuting the opposition. We spent the whole of September and October on the streets. Even Mako [our close friend of absolutely no political bent and retiring disposition] left her flat and attended the demonstrations. During these foolish confrontations a dozen young boys have already been killed, for nothing. I have no hope that anything will change – we shall become a kind of Albania in a very short time. They already speak of closing the borders – it is almost impossible to get permission from the Ministry of Foreign Affairs to go abroad, especially so for those who are not devoted to the President. But the worst thing for me is the dreadful mental condition of our people. This man, our President, has succeeded in spreading his notions of hatred, deception and enmity all over the country. It is really terrible. The only thing I can do now is not to let this hatred into my heart and mind. He really has something of Satan in him. You feel it in the air. It has become difficult to live with and associate with people. The worst of the situation has been in the district where I live, around the university and the television station. Lots of guns and heavy weapons and shooting in the night. Imagine me running around the university gardens in my nightgown screaming with fright. Many foolish things have been said and done by both sides, but our government champions fraud, dishonesty and cruelty. If it were not for the reality – the screaming crowds of Gamsakhurdia supporters, the deaths, the fear – this might all be quite amusing, a kind of Theatre of the Absurd. Can you imagine the president of a country yelling on TV, 'Help! Come and defend me all you true patriots! Destroy the false democrats! Ruin them! Kill them!' – all this because twenty boys tried to start a hunger strike in front of the Parliament. He does not want any real independence for the Georgian people, he wants to rule here.

With all this looming it was, of course, completely frivolous to go wandering about in pursuit of pleasure, even of knowledge. The only case I can put in mitigation is that everywhere people wanted to talk, to see other creatures from another world, to feel that they were not utterly cut off and drowning unnoticed in their own particular mire. However, the *situatsia* did throw all my elaborate plans for Svaneti into confusion. I had been trying to organise my journey through an affable fellow who ran something called The Peace Temple Project Union. What this was exactly I never quite understood, though I had reams of paper attempting to explain it. There were a plethora of such potty-sounding would-be organisations at the time, all called The International Fund for Peace, or the Georgian All-Party Peace Initiative and suchlike. They were, I think, scams for extracting money from abroad. Our man Michael, as charming as he was, as much as he had promised and assured us, turned out to have done nothing. All his brandied talk of guides and horses, mountain passes, churches and towers, was so much thin air, air into which he had, in fact, vanished. Marika had been pursuing him for weeks to no avail. So Chris and I decided to set off on our own. And so Marika and Mako decided they would come too.

It is absolutely recommended that any adventurous traveller, when striking off into wild and unknown parts, should enlist the help and protection of at least one, preferably two, lady art-historians of elegance and distinction. They have a calming effect upon the natives, whose base intentions are at once confounded by their presence, and the profound understanding they acquire through years of study brings an unparalleled degree of refinement to any society into which one might fall.

So Chris and I bade farewell to our hosts, Zura and his kind parents – who had all expressed nothing but horror and alarm at our departure for Svaneti – and found ourselves, with our two bodyguards, chugging through the night on the slow train from Tbilisi to Zugdidi. We were not at all certain that we would reach Svaneti: there had been terrible landslides across the road up into the mountains and the Svans were revolting. Upset at the appointment of a new prefect, a woman of all things (though she had a reputation as a fine shot and a devastating pugilist), they had decided to add to nature's work by blockading the road and patrolling day and night with armed guards. Fortunately, on the morning we arrived in Zugdidi, they suddenly realised that not only were they preventing strangers from entering Svaneti but that they themselves could not get in or out and were running desperately short of vodka. So they cleared the blockade, dug away the landslides, and the taxi that Marika had somehow cajoled with her art-historical charms in Zugdidi was able to take us all the way up to Mestia.

The road north is breathtakingly beautiful and very unsafe in places, twisting up beside the fierce Inguri River, so the journey was full of excitements. (The Svans are rather proud of their road and its dangers. Here is a bad Svan joke: A man from the lowlands asks a Svan if the road to Mestia is good. The Svan replies that there are two roads, good and bad. The one from which your car plunges into the Inguri never to be found is the bad one; the one from which your car plunges into the Inguri but your body is recovered is the good one.) Best of all, after the road and the river turn off to the east, are the high glens of Upper Svaneti, the great upland basin of the Inguri River. Endless hyperboles extolling nature become incredibly tedious to read, as to write: beautiful, lovely, wonderful, amazing – but there is something very special about this little corner of the wide world. Douglas Freshfield thought so and returned here seven times on three different expeditions to explore its mountains, writing that it far exceeded in drama and beauty even the Alps, which he spent a lifetime climbing. The mountains are higher, the permanent snows and glaciers more numerous (679 listed in the Central Caucasus) and greater in extent, the flora more abundant and extraordinary. As you approach Mestia all the great peaks line up above and stretch away towards the horizon: Elbruz, 18,470 feet, beyond the borders of Svaneti just to the west; then Ushba, 16,405; Tetnuld, 15,918; Shkara 17,038. Freshfield contrasted this sunny southern flank of the Caucasus with the darker northern slopes:

In scenery this highland basin is in every respect a contrast to the northern valleys on the other side of the chain . . . 'Smiling, sylvan, idyllic,' such are the epithets that rise on a traveller's lips as he suddenly emerges from the dark treeless glens and chilly recesses of the Northern Caucasus on to a region of gentle slopes and wide distances, of forests and flowery meadows, of fields golden with barley. Compared to the warrens, or stone-heaps, that serve the people of the northern valleys for dwellings, the towered villages and castellated farms of Suanetia assume at a distance a false air of mediaeval romance. North of the chain the traveller feels himself at the bottom of a well. He knows hours of climbing are required in order to enlarge or vary the outlook. Here the landscapes are wide and constantly changing: the visible sky is not a narrow strip but a broad arch. The pines no longer predominate or press on one another until they become mere ragged staffs. They present themselves as dark, shadowy cones amidst the fresh green of the deciduous forest, of beeches and alders, of ash and walnut, of copses that in June and July are bright with purple rhododendron and fragrant with golden azalea blossom. The glades are gay with lupines and lilies and the spires of a ten-thousand-blossomed heracleum . . . When the azaleas and rhododendrons thicken, and the tall flowers cluster among them round the mown, open spaces, the epithet 'park-like' is inevitable! . . . Space, variety sunniness – these are the constant and characteristic qualities of

Suanetian scenery. The great mountain basin is broken by no heights that approach the snow-line. The glens are divided only by long grassy or forested ridges. Their gentle, undulating crests furnish the most effective contrast to the icy clefts and rigid cliffs of Shkara and Ushba. From the beauty of flowers and forests close at hand, the eye is carried through soft gradations of distance to the pure glaciers which hang down like silver stairs from the snowy chain . . . To the natural beauties man has added something. It is a land where every man's house is his castle. The meadows and the cultivated valleys are strewn with high white towers. In one spot a single tower stands isolated, in another they cluster in groups of fifty to eighty. Every hamlet has as many towers as the cities of Tuscany in the middle ages. Nothing so fantastic as these family fortresses can be seen outside San Gimignano or the frame of an Old Master.

Mestia had been a lively centre for mountaineers from all over the Soviet Union and abroad – there were a couple of small hotels. These we christened the Ritz and the Savoy. There was little to choose between them. Both were half-wrecked in that all-too-familiar post-Soviet fashion. When we walked into the Ritz a small hairy pig rushed out of the door past us, squealing. The whole town was overrun by tribes of these friendly and attractive little porkers that had a grand time of it fighting with the local dogs. Having inspected the rooms, Mako decided against the general squalor and we marched off to the Savoy down the road. It was, if anything, worse but the rooms looked out upon the snow-tipped pyramid of Mount Tetnuld. Marika, Chris and I went back out into the rain-swept, piglet-infested central piazza (a great, open, indeterminate space inhabited by an old lady leaning on a broom and smoking a cigarette) to inspect the tall, white towers of Mestia while Mako stayed behind with a determined look on her face, and closed purposefully with the bed-linen.

There are many towers still in Mestia, most about ninety feet high (a height equal to the perimeter at the base) and they differ somewhat from the towers of Khevsureti and Tusheti. They are formidable buildings and have stood through centuries of storm, avalanche and warfare, plastered and whitewashed on the outside to withstand the penetrative effects of frost and rain. Though new windows have been punched through the walls of some, many seem to have almost no openings at all beyond the door, perhaps one or two gun-slots, and they must have been incredibly dark, lit only by torches made of birch bark. The roofs, as I wrote in Chapter 2, are very distinctive, mostly wooden, shallow-peaked, with over-hanging, crenellated machicolations, which give the towers a strangely playful air, like so many kings and castles waiting to be moved in some giant game of chess. Many of them are still inhab-ited (the latest built towards the end of the nineteenth century) with a solid, square house butting up to the base of the tower and, very often, a high, impenetrable, padlocked iron gate set within a surrounding wall. The impression is of a guarded people, extremely careful of their privacy and safety. There are none of the 'Galgais' towers of Khevsureti and Tusheti, nor are the towers placed upon some dreadful crag, as in Mutso or Kvavlo, but rather cluster in the centre of the valley as if to say that they themselves, the high peaks around and the snows which cover the land for eight months of the year afford protection enough. Walking through the village, we managed to find one tower deserted and climbed up by way of a veranda and some rungless ladders, through its dark floors, to find three maidens from Tbilisi sheltering from the rain under its wooden roof. Their expressions of abject terror turned quickly to smiles of relief when they realised that they were not about to be gobbled up by the foul fiend. On the ground floor, the main living area, were carved stalls for cattle, benches and chairs, all decorated with sun symbols. In the old days, not so long ago, humans and cattle, as in Khevsureti, would have huddled here together through the many months of winter.

Svaneti is divided north and south by a ridge of mountains: Upper (*zemo*) Svaneti, along the basin of the Inguri River, and Lower (*kvemo*) Svaneti, along the basin of the Tskhenistsqali. This division becomes a little confusing: while Lower Svaneti is often referred to as Dadiani's Svaneti, because it was held by the ruling family of Mingrelia, the Dadianis, the western part of Upper Svaneti

is known as Dadeshkiliani's Svaneti, after the princes of that name
who ruled there, while the eastern part is known as Free Svaneti
because it was never subjugated by any feudal lord and was
governed by a rather attractive-sounding council of communities
where no one family, in theory at least, was permitted more power
than any other. Unfortunately, this had its drawbacks: as there was
no real authority to exercise control over any decision that might
be taken, indeed as the taking of decisions was in itself a fraught
process, the families that made up these communities constantly
resorted to arms and so lived in a state of perpetual warfare with
each other. The towers, therefore, as with many of these tower
communities elsewhere, were as much a protection from each other
as from incursions into Svaneti from outside. But who would have
come from the outside and how? To the north, between Mount
Elbruz and Mount Phasis, there are, I think, four or five main
passes (though a larger number of trickier, more seldom used
routes) leading into Svaneti: the Donguzoron, the Betsho, the
Mestia, the Zanner and Sharivesk passes – though names vary on
different maps. (Here I follow Freshfield.) These passes are of
varying degrees of difficulty, and open only for a few months in
the year. Through these, over the centuries, local tribes from the
north like the Kabardians, Karachays and Balkarians came stealthily
to raid cattle. During the Persian–Byzantine struggle over Lazica,
probably long before the towers were built (though some Georgian
historians date the earliest from the first millennium BC), Svaneti
became important as a potential route of invasion from the North
Caucasian steppe – the Huns, at least once, poured through on
their way to the Byzantine territories in the south, following the
course of the Inguri River, and there were possibly further incursions by them and the Scythians, Sarmatians and others. Certainly
the Romans, then the Byzantines, had many fierce arguments with
the Persians over Svaneti, poised as it was above the sensitive marchland of Colchis, later Lazica. Svaneti was, nominally, a vassal state
of Lazica and its kings were appointed with Laz approval and with
the ultimate authority of Byzantines or Persians, depending on who
was in control at the time. Certainly Byzantines and Persians were
both supposed to have been present in Svaneti, the Byzantines

invading the province and kicking out the Persians finally in 575, though how far this implied the permanent presence of either power through anything but their local representatives is difficult to tell. There is little sign of Persian, or even Byzantine, refinement in the customs or manners of the Svans. However, the routes to the south down the Inguri, across the Laila Pass or through to Dadiani's Svaneti via Kal and Lentekhi, and the route to the east through to Ratcha, were important links with the outside world along which the Svans raided and traded, bartering honey, beeswax, skins, gold and silver for the grain they desperately needed to sustain themselves throughout the year.

Though Svaneti is often represented as an almost totally closed world, it can never have been quite this. At certain times over the centuries Svaneti drew near to the world beneath the mountains and at other times withdrew from it but, whether for plunder or peaceful profit, or as allies or mercenaries in Georgia's endless wars, Svans needed and maintained contact beyond their mountain homes. With these reservations it is true, however, that they inhabited a natural fortress, a safe refuge readily defensible. The last major incursion till the Russians arrived in the nineteenth century was in 1397, when Tamerlane's Tatar–Mongol hordes devastated the country on their rampage. In the chaos and desolation that followed Tamerlane's invasions of Georgia the Svans saw their opportunity and, scenting plunder, raced down south into the plains and ransacked Kutaisi. After this, darkness descends again upon the affairs of the Svans, though in Georgia's troubled history, and in the oral traditions of the Svans themselves, Svaneti was always considered a place of safety in dangerous times, where kings and princes, treasure and holy objects were brought to hide away until the storm should pass.

For this reason the Svans look upon themselves (however the rest of the world might see them) as the guardians of Kartvelian culture, keepers of secrets, nurturers of the true tradition and are fiercely proud of their race and its customs. More than this they feel that they represent the true, pure Kart blood, untainted by the miscegenating plains. This is, of course, nonsense, and a look at the variety of colouring and facial types among the Svans shows that quite possibly the reverse was true; there must have been a real need for a purposeful exogamy among such close and closed communities and wife-lifting was as much a part of their raiding as cattle rustling. The rest of the world, it is probably fair to say, considered the Svans (when they were not finding refuge among them) a dreadful nuisance. From the earliest references to them among the classical authors, they were written off as 'thieves and plunderers, who committed appalling, impious acts', as Menander has Chosroes, the Persian Emperor, describe them. Over the centuries such views did not alter greatly.

We, however, found them wholly pacific, helpful and charming, particularly the much-hated Prefect, Tsiala Geledani, to whom we presented ourselves the next morning. This was thought politic and sensible. She gracefully allowed Chris to take her photograph as she sat behind her desk in the little town hall, a large portrait of Gamsakhurdia looking down from the wall behind. A cheerful, impressive Svan, an ex-policewoman, she wrote us out a note of permission for the Svan churches Marika wanted to show us, then volunteered her car and driver for our explorations, said they would be ready outside in an hour and they were. First, though, we walked across the centre of town to see her great enemy, another Tsiala, Tsiala Chartolani, the director of Mestia's little museum, who equalled her in affability and was the passionate curator of Mestia's cultural treasures: ancient fragments of cloth, embroidered purses which held offerings of precious stones and had been found inside the walls of Svan churches during restoration, gospels, crucifixes and icons, painted on cloth or worked in metal (a particular specialty of Svan artists), some of them very old and very lovely. Upstairs was a little collection of ancient weapons. A part of the museum was dedicated to Svan alpinists, particularly to the exploits of Michael Khergiani, a local hero known as the 'Lion of the Rock', killed climbing in the Dolomites in 1969. His father, Beknu, had won fame during the Second World War when he climbed to the top of Mount Elbruz and took down the Nazi flag, planted there by the Edelweiss Corps as the Germans advanced upon the Caucasus.

We set off in the Prefect's jeep to the south-west, down the road which runs beside the Mulkhura River, to the community of Latal above the junction of the Mulkhura and the Inguri. The tract of land between the two rivers, running from Latal to the base of Mount Tetnuld, some ten miles to the east, forms a natural terrace of wide lawns, thick with flowers and set about with azalea and rhododendron, perhaps the loveliest part of Upper Svaneti. Here in Latal, as elsewhere in Svaneti, clusters of villages, closely related by ancient family ties, are grouped together under a single title, so there is actually no village of Latal but a number of hamlets: Sidianari, Matskvarishi, Ipkhi, Lakhushti, Ienashi. We turned north up a little track to Sidianari, a simple, remote place just under the Bal ridge, where children and pigs ran happily about the mud and rubble path, and the elders came out to greet us. Polite, reserved, with many a handshake and '*gamarjobat*', they inspected our note thoroughly and sent a child off to find the man with the key. Freshfield tried many times to get inside the little churches of Latal but was never allowed: they are, like all the churches in Svaneti, jealously guarded, kept always locked, the sacred property of their community.

The churches of Svaneti could not offer a greater contrast to the great cathedrals of Tao. They are tiny, single-naved, simple structures, rather like the little Byzantine churches familiar in the Greek countryside and throughout the Balkans, probably owing more to the early missionary activities of Byzantium than to the influence of the eastern Christian churches that marked the grander buildings elsewhere in Georgia. What so distinguishes Svan churches is not their architecture but their decoration. Most of them are covered with frescos, sometimes even on the exterior walls of the churches where their preservation seems almost miraculous. Our bodyguards devoted themselves to our education.

I shall resist a blow-by-blow account of all the frescos of Svaneti and the various techniques employed by their painters, largely because I cannot fully understand my notes but also out of a dainty regard for my readers. These murals should properly not be called frescos at all, an invention of the Italian Renaissance, but should anyone wish to pursue the problems of painting on dry plaster or the development of the wet-plaster technique, the mixing of animal glue with paint, the use of earth pigments and an orange pigment made from squashed cattle ticks, there is a short article available in English on the Internet, *Materials and Methods of Execution of early Mediaeval Murals in Upper Svaneti,* by Irakli Iakobashvili. (A fuller, more general, account of Georgian frescos can be found in *The Treasures of Georgia,* edited by Vakhtang Beridze and others.) The murals vary a great deal in quality, some rather crude, others very lovely. The saints, angels and Apostles who provide much of the subject matter are often drawn with a realism and expressiveness quite unlike the more familiar, rather deadpan work of their Byzantine contemporaries. Most of the best work dates from the tenth, eleventh and twelfth centuries and a couple of the painters are known by name, though their biographical details are rather sketchy. With two of the elders of Sidianari, we first went to the church of Matsqvari, The Saviour, in the hamlet of Matsqvarishi. The frescos here, from 1142, were painted by Michael Maglakeli, some shining out with fantastic clarity, some rather battered: an Entry into Jerusalem, St Demetrius looking very worried, a Deesis with the Apostles below and on either side the six-winged seraphim (much loved by Georgian painters), those strange creatures that guarded the Throne of God, one of which appears to be riding upon a scooter. This is probably why he needs his feet, which are supposed to be hidden by the lower set of wings but here dangle down sweetly. In fact these wheels come from Ezekiel's visions of God (Chapter 1: 15–21 and Chapter 10: 2,6 and 12–19) and are most obscure but thought of as representing the Thrones, the first rank in the celestial hierarchy. Anyway the six-winged seraphim with their four faces raced about on them. There is a rather touching inscription in Old Georgian by the entrance, next to the figure of a clergyman: 'Who ever will be the abbot [or perhaps "guardian", the word used is, interestingly, *mamasakhlisi*] of this church, please spare the paintings from smoke, so as not to damage the colours.' Marika said that this was clear evidence of fresco conservation in the twelfth century, giving her profession a tremendous pedigree. Whoever wrote the inscription, probably the painter himself, had understood a real problem – unfortunately many of the frescos in Upper Svaneti have been blackened by candle smoke over the centuries.

Heading back towards Mestia we stopped in the community of Lenjeri at the tiny church of Taringzel, The Archangels, in the hamlet of Laschtkveri. This church is so lovely that the Svans have built a little lean-to drinking shed outside, where they can sit and celebrate their pleasure properly. Or they can move to the grave-yard and celebrate with the dead: tables, chairs, glasses and ashtrays help to make their stay more comfortable. Some early travellers, seeing few cemeteries in Svaneti, thought that the Svans were curi-ously careless of their dead; there was no necropolis like Anatori of the Khevsurs. They would sometimes bury their dead under tracks, by the side of roads, anywhere. However, in truth, the dead here were and are mourned perhaps even more seriously than in other parts of Georgia: men do not shave for a year, the Svan funeral ceremony, the *zari*, is, as in Ratcha, full of laments and poetry, and mourning seems to go on for years. The *zari* itself is a special ritual cycle of songs and lamentation in three parts, performed by two separate choirs of men and women. The literal meaning of the word is simply a 'bell', but it is often used to indi-cate a terrible tragedy or great misfortune. However the Svans have now borrowed or resurrected ancient traditions that were never theirs in the free market for the superstitious that has accompa-nied the post-Soviet religious revival. As in pagan times people have taken to placing goods and belongings in the grave alongside the departed. In Georgia, as throughout the rest of the old USSR, other symptoms of the age include outbreaks of aliens, faith-healing, cults of all sorts: all the disorders of the half-baked.

On the northern facade of Taringzel are brightly painted scenes from the great national epic-romantic poem *Amirandarejaniani*, one of the poems that inspired Shota Rustaveli, a retelling of the Amirani story as a tale of knightly superheroes. There is a great picture of Amirani killing a Devi, demon of Iranian and Caucasian folklore, his huge curved sword slicing through its horned head and sticking out the other side, blood flowing down. I was very keen on this and paintings of non-religious themes are rare but the fifteenth-century work was a little late for the taste of Marika and Mako. Inside the church, painted from top to bottom, are scenes from the Transfiguration, the Entry into Jerusalem, depictions of holy hermits and the Archangel Michael, splendidly winged, Lazarus, the Resurrection. Here also is St George slaying not the dragon but the Emporer Diocletian, persecutor of Christians. The Svans love the more martial of the saints, St Theodore, St Dimitri and particularly St George, *dzgrag* in Svan, whose image appears in many if not most of their churches and on some of their most beautiful icons, and whom they revere, like the Khevsurs, above all others. In the Svan pantheon many of the saints have simply taken on the attributes of their pre-Christian counterparts: St George is the god of the moon; St Quiricus is the god of hunting; St Barbara the goddess of the sun; the archangels are the spirits of the mountains.

In the same community is another little church, also called Matsqvari, in Nesgun where some of the oldest frescos in Svaneti, from the ninth to tenth century, rather damaged in places, show Christ in Glory, the Madonna and Child, saints and prophets. These were all done by a certain Giorgi, a 'provincial painter' according to Vakhtang Beridze, which probably means he was not very good, though apparently they show a clear similarity with Georgian relief sculpture of the same period. They are certainly rather archaic and angular, the colours limited, though perhaps all the more interesting for that. How and where the Svan painters learnt their trade is not clear. Echoes and influences from other parts of Georgia and from Byzantium are certainly there but no record of any specific link. The most famous of all the Svan painters, Tevdor or Theodore, working at the end of the eleventh century and beginning of the twelfth, was certainly a Svan by birth and called himself 'the King's painter', though there is no evidence of him working in any of the churches commissioned by the kings of Georgia. However, Marika was intrigued by the many similarities in style and manner between the murals known to be by Theodore in Svaneti and some of the murals in Tao-Klarjeti, particularly those in the cathedral of Oshki, especially the Crucifixion in the south transept.

Why there was so much activity in Svaneti is, I think, a more interesting question than how and where the Svan painters developed. This must connect with the explosion of church-building in Tao-Klarjeti at the same time and have at its root some of the same historical causes. The tradition took hold and grew in the years before the unification of Georgia, when Svaneti, like the mountains of Tao, was a place of refuge, a crucible for national and religious feelings and aspirations. One of Michael Maglakeli's murals shows a group of noblemen, among them the Lord of Svaneti, dressing King Demetrius the First with his ceremonial sword at his coronation. Later, during the *didi turkoba*, the Turkish Troubles, and then the Mongol invasions, Svaneti became again the nation's eyrie.

We walked back to Mestia in the afternoon sunshine, stopping to drink at a sulphur spring, looking in Mestia's three shops, all empty, and, as we came to the Savoy, fell in with a handsome, tough, middle-aged Svan, Nopé, who eyed Chris and me rather doubtfully (understandable, of course) but with a glimmer of hope in his eyes.

'Are you climbers?' he asked.

'No, I am afraid not,' I replied.

'Oh dear,' he said and gazed at us mournfully.

'But we would very much like to walk up as high as we can before the going gets too difficult,' I volunteered, hoping to cheer him up.

'No one comes any longer. We used to have many climbers. Now it is all finished. *Kaput*! *Perestroika* has killed us!'

Nopé was heart-broken. A great alpinist, he co-ordinated expeditions to Svaneti's high peaks, had climbed them all himself. He waved a despairing hand at the dilapidation around us, everything was run-down, nothing worked, no one came. He took us to his little office, photographs of Tensing and Hilary pinned on the wall, and, promising to find us a guide, talked mountains. He was, as Mako remarked rather wistfully – and I thought I detected a slight weakening of the knees – 'a very manly man'.

Describing Mount Ushba, he became so excited that he herded us outside and into his jeep, collecting a stray Austrian geologist on the way, and drove off through the forested slopes above Mestia, up to a ridge opposite the mountain so that we could see it in all its glory. Its great twin peaks rose above us, its glacier curled around to the south-west, its southern face a great wall of ice known as 'The Mirror', or '*Dalis Panjara*', The Window of Dali, the goddess of hunting and animals, a beautiful and highly erotic being who liked to lure hunters into perilous amorous adventures. Nopé called Ushba the 'fiercest mountain in the world' and said that it had claimed sixty-seven lives. He had climbed it twice. No one had climbed its southern peak by the time Freshfield published his *Exploration of the Caucasus* in 1896. J. G. Cockin, who contributed a chapter to Freshfield's book and managed to climb the north peak in 1889, called Ushba 'the most imposing mountain I have seen' and noted dryly that it was 'often very dangerous'.

Nopé was a great admirer of Freshfield and knew all about his climbs in the Caucasus. His eyes lit up when I mentioned the Englishman and we went through the list of his achievements: in 1868 the first ascent of Kazbek and the first ascent of the east peak of Elbruz; in 1887 the first ascents of Tetnuld, Gulba and Shoda and the exploration of Shkara; and then, in 1889, when he set out to find the body of his old friend Donkin who had never returned from an attempt on Koshtantau, just to the north-east of Shkara, the first ascent of Laila. During all these expeditions he traversed many passes, having one named after him, and explored the whole of the central range. It was an extraordinary record of achievement for a man of that time who climbed without pitons, swivels or crampons, wearing the grey cutaway tailcoat and trousers that he wore habitually in England. His exploits in the Alps were similar – he climbed Mont Blanc at the age of eighteen. While Freshfield was searching for Donkin (and his companion, Fox, who also died) he had the strange experience of seeing his dead friend and talking to him, and wrote a poem about this 'vision', not Shakespeare, certainly, but an attempt, perhaps, to crystallise his feelings for the mountains:

> I lay, alone with the sunset, hard by the Caucasian snow,
> And gazed, from my eagle's eyrie, over infinite space below,
> And infinite space above me, the lifeless wastes of the sky,
> And the fields where men, as of old, are born, grow weary and die!

All radiant, self-illumined, the wonderful landscape
  shone,
While the face of the earth still glowed with the rays that
  from heaven had gone;
And the mountains stood transfigured, each hill and
  hollow and stream
Distinct as a mapman's model, yet fair as a poet's dream
  . . .

. . . Then again earth's memories found me, my
  schoolfellow stood at my head,
And those we sought came round me, the living talked
  with the dead.

Nopé's Austrian geologist, an engaging professor from Vienna,
was collecting data on the moraines and glaciers of the Central
Caucasus, and beamed at the mountains with all the pride of a
father at his child. The two men looked ready to join hands and
skip about the slopes singing. The professor had just come from
inspecting the Tien Shan with a Georgian colleague and had been
walking about the great glaciers of Ushba and Zanner, studying
the movement of the ice. He explained that the lovely sweep of
land along the Mulkhura River, leading to Tetnuld and known as
the Mujal, was a deep moraine left by the ice sheets as they retreated
ten thousand years ago, scouring the ground beneath and carving
out a chasm. He grabbed the air with his hands and drew them
towards his chest, becoming himself a great ice monster, illustrating
the tremendous power of the withdrawing glacier. In geological
time the whole process was over in a flash, the valley formed in a
mere one thousand years.

That evening, the Ritz having denied categorically the existence
of food, we attempted to dine at the Savoy. There, in the greasy
half-light of the shabby restaurant, in which Chris and I felt quite
at home (though Mako had to be induced inside with the promise
of fine wines), we found a very hungry French musicologist (half
the professors of Europe seemed to be in Mestia) who had been
in residence for over a week. The poor man had been sent to

Svaneti to record Svan funeral laments for the Musée de l'Homme, but the eagerly anticipated death had not happened. In fact, the elderly Svan in question seemed to be making a remarkable recovery and the torments of Svan cuisine, or the lack of it, were speedily doing for the Frenchman. His mind was slipping from Svan culture towards pâtés and terrines and he was plagued by olfactory delusions, smells of freshly baked baguettes drifting to him through the mountain air. I became very fond of the dining room at the Savoy, largely because of its cook whose manner and demeanour were firmly based upon the cook in *Alice's Adventures in Wonderland*; all that was missing from her kitchen was a large cat and a duchess nursing a baby. Her temper was entirely in character. Terrible crashings and bangings and muttered curses echoed from the kitchen so we sent in Chris to order some food. I am not sure what he did in there but he emerged looking a little dazed, followed soon after by the cook who had rearranged her grumpy features into something resembling a grin. She thumped down some bowls of dark soup. In its murk lay lumps of fat and pieces of rhinoceros pizzle. I had developed a theory that every *provodnitsa* and *dezhurnaya* in the Soviet Union (those frightening and implacable women who made sure that nothing was available or worked or was in any way pleasant and sat about all day in trains and hotel corridors) had been specially schooled to the task in some remote gulag in Siberia. Obviously there was also a great Institute of Cookery hiding somewhere near Irkutsk. It may have recruited particularly in Svaneti: there was a famously irascible Svan cook at the ski resort in Gudauri where Mako taught English to the staff in summer. He once attacked a Mkhedrioni thug with a butcher's knife after a complaint about the food and started a gun-battle in the hotel restaurant.

The rhinoceros soup was a subtle counterpoint to the sublime view of the mountains. Having begged the cook for the recipe we turned towards them and, while drinking aviation fuel from a large jug, talked of gold and legend. The Svans believe with certainty that their mountains conceal huge veins of precious metals and, indeed, they do, or did, pan for gold in the rivers. From this has developed the great story of Ancient Svans laying fleeces in mountain streams to catch the particles of gold and so, it is said, giving birth to the legend of the Golden Fleece that Jason stole from Colchis. It is a marvellous explanation, taken up by several authors including Tim Severin in his *Jason Voyage,* a most enjoyable book. He quotes from Janet Brown's *The Voyage of the Argonauts,* which argues that Jason's journey was 'a real quest for real gold'. Severin's discussion of the Jason story and his account of building a replica *Argo,* rowing from Greece through the Bosphorus up the Black Sea coast of Turkey to Georgia and on up the River Phasis, the modern Rioni, are vivid and exciting. His argument that Svaneti was the ultimate source of the Fleece, that it was given as tribute by the Svans to the Colchian kings, had me reaching for Homer and my old school *The Voyage of Argo,* Apollonius of Rhodes' retelling of the legend. Severin was given a demonstration of the Svan gold-panning technique and describes it thus:

. . . Svanetia was the prime source of Colchian gold. Next morning we were to witness how the gold was obtained, and that has a crucial bearing on the legend of the Golden Fleece. Four Svan gold miners were awaiting us. They were standing in the shallows of the Enguri river which runs through Mestia, and they were there to show me how the Svans mine their gold. Three of them had once made their living as professional gold gatherers; the fourth, as a young lad, had helped his father in the same trade until the end of the Second World War, when the last government agent to whom these men brought their gold for sale was withdrawn.

Nugzar had arranged the demonstration. The Svan's chief tool was sheepskin. Every spring, when the snows and glaciers in the high valleys began to melt, the Svan miners would climb to the upper valleys, to the feeder streams of the Enguri. Each man went to his favorite place, where he knew by experience that the meltwater was carrying small quantities of gold washed from veins in the rock. Into these streams the Svans placed sheepskins with the fleece side uppermost. The skins were nailed out flat on wooden pallets which were sunk on the stream beds and weighed down so that the stream flowed across them, often in a series of steps from one pallet to the next. As the water ran across the fleeces, the flecks of gold, being heavier than the sand and silt, were trapped in the wool. Each Svan gold gatherer knew when to inspect his gold trap, depending on the richness of the stream and the amount of the water flow according to the season. When the time was ripe, the gold gatherer would remove the sheepskins from the stream, wash out the accumulated silt from the wool, and search through it for gold particles. Exceptionally, in the very richest area, the first fleece, the highest one in the stream bed, would be so impregnated with gold dust that it was virtually a golden fleece.

Strabo, the Greek geographer, had suspected the truth as early as the third century BC. 'It is said that in their country [Colchis] gold is carried down by the mountain torrents, and that the barbarians obtain it by means of perforated troughs and fleecy skins, and that this is the origin of the myth of the golden fleece.' Two thousand years later it was astonishing to find men who still knew the ancient technique and had practiced it in their own lifetimes. Standing ankle-deep in the icy cold waters of the Enguri, they showed me the tools of their craft: sheepskins pinned to a board, a mattock to spread out the silt on the wool, a scraper to clean the fleece, and a simple wooden trough to pan out the silt in a final search for gold.

Sadly, the truth of the matter may not be quite so simple. Firstly, the story is not of a Golden Fleece that originated in Colchis or Svaneti but of one that belonged to a magical ram that, sent by Zeus to rescue Phrixus and Helle from their horrid stepmother, flew to Colchis from Thessaly, unfortunately dropping Helle into the sea on the way – hence the Hellespont. The ram was then sacrificed to Ares, and King Aeetes of Colchis, Medea's father, got to keep the marvellous fleece. Professor David Braund, in his *Georgia in Antiquity*, explains the symbolic significance of the Golden Fleece as evoking 'supernatural power, kingship, and prosperity, and thus suggesting a golden age'. He also shows how the legend parallels others: golden lambs, golden apples, myths of foundation with animal-guides as agents of supernatural powers, by no means confined to the Caucasus. Furthermore, Strabo – who was writing at around the time of the birth of Christ and not, as Severin says, in the third century BC – was trying very hard, just like us, to find a rational explanation for the legend. In fact, this attempt to rationalise the myth started very early on among the Greeks, so the ram is a boat, Helle gets seasick, the ram is Phrixus' schoolmaster, the fleece his flayed skin, torn from him by hostile Colchians.

At the heart of Severin's explanation is his witnessing of Svans panning for gold using sheepskins. Though it may be that this technique really did give rise to the legend, it is just as probable that the legend gave birth to the technique. The story of the Golden Fleece is central to Georgian culture, all children grow up with it. Colchis, from the fifth century BC, was strongly affected by Greek language (it became the language of the court) and by Greek thought. The rational explanation that Strabo offers was probably well-known then. Certainly, it is widely believed now. Also, the myth itself is much older than the Colchian gold that has been found, and the gold artefacts that Severin and others use to support their claims of this gold technology come from the fifth century BC and later, not from the Bronze Age of the thirteenth century BC. The academic accounts of Svans panning for gold with fleeces in modern times are based on the work of a Georgian anthropologist (Botchorishvili, 1946) who did not actually see this herself and merely relates that she was told of it by three old Svans who failed to agree among themselves on the precise method used. There seems to be no other independent evidence and so questions arise as to just how commonplace this practice was. What struck me as odd was that though I had seen plenty of pigs and cattle when I was in Svaneti, I cannot remember seeing many sheep. Perhaps they were all hiding in some distant valley. None of this, of course, gainsays Severin's own eye-witness account nor his wonderful journey. It merely adds a note of caution and suggests that myth may work its way back into a culture in the most remarkable fashion. Every myth or legend, every fragment or fraction of history in Georgia (and throughout the Caucasus) is clung on to passionately, used to shore up or add weight to the national story, to throw hooks into the past so that they might anchor the people more securely, more tightly to the loose sands of antiquity. The Svans and the Golden Fleece have a major place in this process. Any hint or tentative suggestion that Severin's gold-panners and their demonstration might not have quite represented the continuous tradition to which they laid claim is met with displeasure, especially from some Georgian archaeologists, as Professor Braund discovered when he first, politely, questioned it.

When Severin landed in Poti harbour he was given a fantastic Georgian reception: crowds cheered, speeches were made, dances danced. There was singing and drinking and feasting – a tremendous celebration. He was welcomed by Miss Tbilisi, dressed as Medea, with whom I later danced in the Nightbar of the Iveria Hotel and who has had to put up with a lifetime of bad jokes about her magical and disastrous effect on men and children. Behind the scenes there had been a certain amount of chaos that has passed into local legend: it was feared, for example, that the water level in the Rioni in summer would be insufficiently high for Severin's *Argo*, so sluice gates were opened causing such a flow of water that progress became impossible and the Argonauts arrived in Vani, the great Colchian site excavated by Otar Lordkipanidze (hurriedly cleared of pigs and chickens), by bus. This, anyway, is the story I have heard, though Severin writes only of rain and mudbanks halting him.

The Georgians had in fact tried to recreate the last part of Jason's voyage themselves some years before. A group of Georgian professors had commandeered a boat to row up the Rioni. They had dressed as ancient Greeks with a few carefully pinned old sheets but, unfortunately, got stuck on a mud-bank as they tried to head up stream and jumped ashore to find help. By unhappy coincidence, at the same time a call had gone out to the police that a number of lunatics had broken out of the local asylum. The policemen, scouring the countryside for these dangerous escapees, spied the professors running across a field, their sheets flapping out behind, and grabbed them. The professors, handcuffed and thrown into the back of a police van, tried to explain that they were not lunatics but ancient Greeks. The policemen said of course they were and locked them in jail. After many hours and the inter- cession of various colleagues, they were eventually released. No one found the lunatics. Before Tim Severin arrived many irreverent jokes circulated about the fate that awaited him.

Next morning we went to see the lady Prefect once more to borrow her jeep for our trip to Ushguli, but she was gone. She had been removed in the night and sent back to Tbilisi. In her stead was a small, hopeless, plump young man, the Sub-Prefect, who knew nothing, thought nothing and did nothing. So Chris and I sat in the piazza watching the pigs while Marika and Mako went to hunt for a friend. They returned with a young Svan, Dato, a junior colleague of Mako's much-loved brother, who scurried off to find a jeep, though he was worried by the shortage of petrol, particu- larly as the petrol depot in Zugdidi had just blown up in a terrible conflagration, probably started deliberately. Svans and Mingrelians fomenting rebellions. However, he arrived shortly with another friend and we all motored off down the bumpy track alongside the furious Inguri River, past forests and chasms and villages of towers, past the sacred drinking site where Marika had nearly met her end a few years previously at the hands of some very drunk natives, and eventually came to the stretch of valley where the community of Ushguli lies. Utterly beautiful, the four villages – Murkhmeli, Chvibiani, Chajushi and Djibiani – cluster on gently rising folds, with the great mountain Shkara, the highest in Svaneti, just behind. Shkara's glacier and the Inguri glacier to its east, where the Inguri River rises, pointed down towards us. The towers here are bunched tight together and seem more solid, broader than the others, offering a more formidable prospect to intruders. Some of these, it is thought, date from the sixth century. Ahead of us, alone on a ridge, was the tiny church of Lamaria; we stopped outside it, and waited for the man with the key. He soon came trotting up, a neat and tidy Svan, full of history, in whose presence Mako and Marika remained respectfully quiet, though I was dying to hear what they had to say about the church, as they knew a great deal more than he. The church was from the ninth century, with traces of frescos of warrior saints, St Theodore and St George, the Deesis on the vault of the apse and the six-winged seraphim, this time with eyes in the wings, from Ezekiel's vision. There is also a portrait of Queen Tamara, *tamar mepe*, though Marika muttered that every church liked to claim one and only three or four are definitely attributable. However, Tamara did come often to Svaneti. Outside on the façade were more scenes from the *Amirandarejaniani*. Inside were piles of tûr horns dedicated as offerings to the church.

The churches here are not frequently used, opened perhaps twice a year for celebrations or feast days but they remain a tremendous and potent force within the local culture. There are few priests in Free Svaneti; they were dispensed with years ago along with lords and nobles, so the churches belong to and are looked after by the community. It is still reckoned a great honour and spiritual benefit to take care of your church. Nopé had told us a story about a young man who had plunged off a bridge into the Inguri while driving a tractor. He showed us the spot. It was fearful, the river ran a hundred feet beneath the track. The boy climbed out unharmed. This was due, Nopé assured us with absolute sincerity, only to the fact that he and his family had been protected by the saint of their local church to which they were particularly devoted.

A museum had just been opened in Ushguli. It was certainly the highest museum in Europe, probably in the world unless there is one in Tibet, and very likely the most remote, inside a converted tower, extremely well done and full of curiosities. It was opened for us with much ceremony and we were guided around the three floors by the curator, a man who fixed Marika with his beady eye and talked like a badly tuned radio. He was quite bonkers and expounded at length his theories linking the Svans with ancient Sumerians who, as far as I could gather, had made their way up into the high mountains to preserve their culture, threatened by an early and virulent outbreak of feminism. Apparently the desire to preserve their patriarchal customs had driven them to Svaneti. Well, they had certainly managed this, though men from slightly lower altitudes do not seem to have suffered much in this regard. It seemed rather an extreme reaction.

The first and second floors of the museum had lovely carved

chests, a great embossed cross, wonderful icons, early and beautiful. This was all serious stuff. But the top floor was rather like my cabinet at home, at once familiar, and I would not have been at all surprised to find my wife's rabbit-dropping necklace or her copulating frogs in plastic among the odds of jewellery, fossilised sea urchins and the great fur ball taken from the stomach of a goat. I definitely wanted the last and wondered if I could swap it for our spare mammoth tooth.

We walked through Djibiani, the highest village, past the towers with their abutting houses and carved wooden balconies, through the usual swarms of pigs and children, and on up the slope overlooking the village with Shkara opposite, lit by the setting sun. Dato announced that we would have a picnic and set us to gather brushwood, birch scrub, while he took from his pack many bottles of wine and put them to chill in a stream. Little figures on the far slopes whistled down their cattle, a group pulling a long sledge brought down a great pile of hay, horses trotted towards home. We made a fire and the two Svans prepared shashlik from a small pig they had concealed about their persons. Night came on and the stars shone out and the valley and mountains around were bathed in moonshine. Dato had forgotten glasses so ran off to the village and returned with a whole fresh cheese, a gift. Then the pig was roasted and we made a feast in the great stillness of the night, under the mountain, warmed by our fire, at the far end of Free Svaneti.

Douglas Freshfield's account of his first visit to Ushguli in 1868, the first time he had entered Svaneti, is worth retelling, if only for the complete contrast it offers to our own:

As the green featureless glen we were descending opened out towards a larger valley, a great company of towers met our astonished eyes. We could count at least fifty, clustered in three separate knots, and most of them covered with a rude white plaster. Square in form, they were redeemed from a resemblance to factory chimneys by their roofs and battlements, pierced for musketry. Round their base clustered barn-like dwellings built of dark slate. The scene was weird and strange.

My mind wandered far for a comparison: first to some woodcut familiar in childhood, an illustration to Lane's *Arabian Nights*, then to Tuscan San Gimignano.

We hurried on towards these habitations with all the eagerness of men who have been rained on for several days, and have had little to eat or drink beyond high sheeps-brains, wild raspberries, and water flavoured with the dregs of tea-leaves. In 1868 our tent was not waterproof, and our commissariat was simple in the extreme. We found quarters in a barn slightly above the village, a gloomy building without windows. Many of the houses at Ushkul have no windows, and depend for light on what can pass through the chinks between the unmortared stones of the walls. In this gloomy lodging we spent two nights and a day, surrounded by the most savage and dangerous-looking set of people I have ever come across, outside Arabia. The men went about armed with flint-lock guns and pistols; even the small boys carried daggers. Their arms seemed their only possessions; their clothes were sheep-skins, or rags and tatters, their coats as often as not sleeveless, their headgear dirty *bashliks* tied up into turbans, or small shapeless pieces of cloth, from the size of a crown piece upwards, fastened on the top of wild, unkempt locks. The women were as a rule hideous, and their dress was shapeless, the children wore a single piece of sacking or nothing at all. We could not sit outside our barn without being mobbed: if we retreated for peace into the black interior, we were pursued by individuals who planted themselves a yard off, took a steady stare which lasted any time from five to fifteen minutes, and then began to overhaul our persons, with as little scruple as if we had been figures in a waxwork show. Here a line had to be drawn and the sightseers requested 'not to touch any of the objects exhibited'. But still, on one pretext or another, visitors crowded in, and as the day wore on, grew more and more aggravating. Towards evening a short revolver practice, and a bold statement by our Mingrelian interpreter, an old servant and travelling companion of Gifford Palgrave, that our weapons were self-loading, produced a certain pause in the persecution. But we barricaded ourselves in for the second night, not without some apprehension as to how it would pass, or how we should get away from the place next morning.

Our final departure was a singularly dramatic scene, and gave promise at one time of a tragic ending. After an attempt on the part of the people to separate us, by shutting our interpreter and our Chamoniard, Francois Devouassoud, up in the barn, had failed, we succeeded in hoisting our slender baggage, partly on the one horse we had secured, partly on our own shoulders. Then forming in close order, and holding our revolvers in our hands, we made ready for a sudden start. Meantime some of the inhabitants, yelling and jabbering, barred the way, others brandished swords, daggers, and pistols on either wall of the sunk lane which led through the village: a few ran off making signs they would fetch their guns. The women, screaming and apparently endeavouring to restrain the passions of their relations, added to the picturesque confusion.

Things seemed getting worse and worse, and the issue more and more doubtful, when a demand of some sort, shouted out by a man on the right-hand wall, suggested a simple stratagem. I flung a handful of kopeks into the crowd, and at the same moment we all made a sudden push down the lane. The crowd scrambled and fought for the coppers, the men in the roadway yielded as the cold muzzle of the revolver touched their faces, and in less time than it has taken to describe the incident, we were outside the hamlet and among open fields. With our fifteen barrels we now felt comparatively safe. When roused to passion the Suanetian will occasionally use his dagger in open fight – I have more than once seen daggers drawn – but he much prefers the safety of a neighbouring thicket, whence he can take a deliberate aim with the help of his forked gun-rest, and shoot his enemy unobserved. The owner of our horse, a native of another village, who had disappeared during the disturbance, now came up to tender his services and offer his congratulations, while our Mingrelian interpreter explained to us the voices on the wall: 'Let us tie them up, let us rob, let us kill.'

In Baddeley's copy of Freshfield's first book, *Travels in the Central Caucasus and Bashan*, are scrawled impatient exclamations suggesting that the hostility Freshfield encountered was his own fault for having 'the help of a Cossack in all dealings with the villagers'. This was, Baddeley scribbled, with many exclamation marks, his 'fatal error', for the Russians were the new conqueror, the oppressor, and Russians considered, not long since, legitimate targets. Baddeley's own delight in the native people and his willingness to communicate with them was unusual. However, Freshfield, who had also his Mingrelian guide, was by no means alone in his experiences. Other travellers like Dr Radde and Phillipps-Wolley wrote accounts of similar tribulations. And it is clear that Baddeley had never actually been to Svaneti. There are references to Svan customs and folklore in his *Rugged Flanks of the Caucasus* but no first-person account. Though I found some wonderful photographs of Mestia, Tetnuld, Laila and Ushba in the material he left to the London Library, he wrote that he had 'only seen in photographs' the towers of Svaneti, so must not have taken these himself. He was used to travelling the northern slopes with his friend and companion, Ourousbi, a local Ossetian, well-known and respected in many of the villages he visited and so unlikely to cause the sort of mayhem experienced by Freshfield. When Freshfield returned to Ushguli nineteen years later, he was amazed by the change: he was left in peace, seldom mobbed on his walks and provided with food with no difficulty. The people, he wrote, had lost their 'strange, hunted look'. This he put down entirely to the effects of Russian rule: curtailing of vendetta and brigandage, some education, greater communion with the world. He noted that 'the Svanetians are beginning to find life endurable without the daily excitement of killing or being killed' and that 'In repressing disorder, improving communications and welding different races into a polit-ical unit, Russia is at once carrying on the work of civilisation and strengthening her own position in Western Asia.' Freshfield was firmly a child of empire himself and was quick to mark its beneficent effects. Baddeley too, though he was far more critical of Russian policy, not that Freshfield was unaware of the problems this might cause. In a passage that says as much about the attitudes of an intelligent Englishman of the times as it does about his perspicacity, he wrote: 'The chief native races, the Armenians and Georgians, are intelligent and progressive . . . they are also the inheritors of national languages and traditions with regard to which they are justly sensitive. Whether these peoples are to prove to be the Scotch or the Irish of Russia will depend mainly on the wisdom of the Imperial Government during the next half century.' All these travellers carried, inevitably, certain amounts of Victorian baggage with them. (None of us escapes himself.) They all thought the Svans needed a firm and civilising hand. Phillipps-Wolley, certainly, was unequivocal: the title of his book, *Savage Svanetia*, though it referred also to the terrain, left his readers in no doubt as to the character of its people and he continuously refers to the 'uncivilised Svans', 'these filthy householders', and writes that he has never seen 'a place in which there was an utter absence of all authority and discipline as in these Svanetian villages'. Only a decade before, Francis Galton had published his *Advice on Travel* in which, in his passage on how to deal with savages, he wrote 'if a savage does mischief, look upon him as a mule or wild animal'. Freshfield rose well above this level, was far too interested in everything around him to settle for such stuff.

Chris and I stood next morning at six thirty outside the Ritz waiting for the young Svan, another Dato, a protégé of Nopé's, who was to take us on our walk. Tall, fair-haired and strong, he arrived, eventually, with an even more frighteningly vigorous-looking friend, who went off, he said, to collect some more friends. Meanwhile another friend turned up and we waited half an hour and Dato said, 'Where are they?' and another half an hour and he said, 'I am getting angry!' and another half an hour and he said, 'Now, I am really angry!' at which point a very pretty young girl appeared round the corner of the hotel and his anger quite evaporated. 'Ah, now they are coming,' said Dato, and Chris and I looked at each other quizzically, and they came. Six of them, young maidens from Tbilisi in dainty footwear, three of whom we had already met under the roof of the tower. Our virile strut through the peaks had been subverted and quite transformed. Chris and I, imagining ourselves at the centre of some wild and manly expedition, became at once supernumerary ancients at a jolly picnic. The girls, however, could not have been more charming and we all set off, past Dato's family tower, collecting a few more friends, up and up, past slopes of scything men, through hazel scrub and pine, and out above the trees. The day was wonderfully clear, the sun blazed as we made our way towards Mount Ushba, its twin, snow-covered peaks dead ahead. The meadows were thick with flowers and horseflies like Heinkels pursued us. Horses, scattered over the slopes, grazed on the sweet summer grasses and herds of great bulls crowded to drink the brilliant water from tiny tarns and dotted the sky line. Plod-plodding past herdsmen and their grannies, Chris and I thrust out our chests and strode forth, for England! for Freshfield! for St George! Red in face and drenched in sweat, we reached the snows, and there, high upon a final ridge before the glacier, lay down. A very old man and two little boys bounded past us, grinning. Chris thought we might find a Walls Ice Cream van somewhere around. Two eagles wheeled above us and a falcon shot by disdainfully. All about grew carpets of gentians. Dato ambled up to join us, he had just been to check his bulls, and pointed to them away in the distance. They were used to pull sledges (wheels were useless on the steep slopes and in the winter snows) and slaughtered at weddings and at feasts. They were a measure of wealth and of social standing and carried, still, a sacred significance: I thought of the bull totems found at Colchian sites like Namcheduri and the bulls' heads jutting from the great cathedral of Svetitskhoveli, of the sacred bulls Jason had to tame, of the bull cults of ancient Greeks and Romans, of Mithras and Zoroaster, which all made their way into Georgia. The Svan bulls, Dato said, were a cross between domestic cattle and wild aurochs, still to be found in the high pastures across the mountains, and they did look stately, fierce and untamed.

After a fine picnic among the flowers, taking the quick way down, always a mistake, Chris and I suffered with our knees, but the Svan boys leaped over precipices like goats, dancing, racing each other down sheer slopes of rock and rubble in a game they must have played since childhood. Back in the square in Mestia, after our ten-hour hike, we said good-bye to the girls and guides and hobbled towards the Savoy where Mako and Marika were waiting for us in the dining room. This was our last night and, in celebration, Kalbatoni (Madam) Darghiza, the fabulous cook, made us chips to go with our rhinoceros soup.

We left Svaneti in the standard bus. Old ladies fainted in the crush and, during the five hours of mad descent to Zugdidi, numbers of them were thrown out, vomiting by the roadside. Standing in the back, wedged between a fearsome woman with a bosom of jutting rock and another who barked at her friend continuously, so that I thought she might have swallowed a small dog, Chris slept upright for most of the way while they passed dainty snacks to one another across his chest. We fled Zugdidi and spent the night in Kutaisi, the old capital of the Kingdom of Abkhazia and of western Georgia, wandering again the partly restored ruins of Bagrat's lovely church and the great monastery at Gelati, one of David the Builder's foundations and the site of a famous neoplatonist academy. In the town, as in Tbilisi, new commercial shops with strange English names, like *Risk* and *Capital* and *Big Ben*, were taking root. But we could not, and sped on to Tbilisi, for we were booked on a plane to Batumi – a slightly mad and needless journey as we were nearly there already. However, it was time to leave Georgia and we had to plan our escape through Sarpi and to gather our belongings.

At the airport, piled with presents – a conveniently large painting, a samovar, books, quantities of daggers, drinking horns and Svan felt hats (of which I now possess the largest collection in Western Europe) – we pushed our way up the backside of a small jet, settled on the broken, beltless seats, only to be told that we must all get off again as someone had forgotten to refuel the plane. Standing under its wing in a haze of aviation fuel, the young pilot, about fourteen years old, smoked and joked with the passengers, as Chris, Tsira, Guliko and I edged back off the tarmac. There were no more concessions to faint hearts on the flight: not a word, not a stewardess, not a friendly note as the plane hurried to Batumi. Just up, briefly along, then down. The joys of Aeroflot are well documented – there already exists a substantial literature on the subject, a sub-genre of its own, to which I cannot add greatly. However, I frequently observed that the citizens of the old Soviet Union seemed to fly under the mistaken apprehension that they were, in fact, travelling on a bus. On coming in to land, everyone leapt to their feet, put on their coats, grabbed their huge belongings and piled towards the front of the aircraft so that they might be the first to get off. This flight was no exception. The pilots, too, are charmingly idiosyncratic. Once on a flight from Tbilisi to Moscow the plane I was on made an unscheduled stop at Krasnodar so that the captain might feed his dog. We landed, very puzzled, at the end of a remote runway, the stewardess opened the door, and there, on the horizon, steps were being wheeled towards us, on top of which sat a large black dog. A plate of food (none had been offered to the passengers) was put out, the dog ate, was wheeled away and we took off again. Our young pilot on this flight to Batumi had merely forgotten to close the door, so one of the passengers had to leap up and shut it as we lifted off.

Having established the principle, it was now clear that Chris and I would travel nowhere in Georgia without at least two distinguished ladies to look after us. So Tsira Gugushvili and her best friend Guliko decided to escort us out of the country. Tsira, all kindness, uttering many cries of '*Vai me!*' and stricken by the awful prospect of our having to fend for ourselves without friends or compan-ionship in Batumi (a major seaside town, capital city of the province of Achara, with many hotels, and stocked with most necessities), had taken the matter in hand and arranged that we should all stay together at her cousin's house. I was just beginning to have slight doubts about the impression Chris and I gave out.

Tsira's cousins lived in the faded comfort of a large, ramshackle house, fronted by a dusty garden long since gone to seed. Guram, epigonous adopted son of the Zhordania family, welcomed us, waving his arms about and crying, '*Restavratzia! Restavratzia!*' as he introduced us to his property, smiling and shrugging his shoulders. I knew the feeling exactly and warmed to him at once. Tsira looked at him fondly and said, 'He is a good, kind man and I love him but he is so lazy, so very lazy.' He was small and plump, vested in the sticky heat and he lay on his bed in the garden all day chain-smoking Gonio cigarettes and playing backgammon, *nardi*. Peach trees, loquats and kumquats grew all about and vines, left to go their own way, tangled through their branches. Chickens scratched in the dust and a large sow lay in one corner by an equally inert dog, who, occasionally mad, rushed once or twice to the front gate, barking, only to return exhausted. Guram's wife, Maria, with fine, intelligent Mingrelian features, did all the work and served us with cold drinks and food. As we sat in the cooling evening air the next-door neighbour, another Maria, joined us. Enormously fat, she launched at once into a tale of present misery and, with no indication of any irony, told us of her poverty and her imminent death by starvation. She recalled the good old days of Stalin when there was plenty and Guram, lying on his bed, smoking, joined in to bemoan the lack of discipline in contemporary society. It was not worth it but I just could not help mentioning the millions who were killed. 'Only a few, very few,' came the gentle reply. Such stuff no longer shocked me but I was a little surprised because this family's most famous son, proudly remembered, was Noe Zhordania, the Menshevik President of Georgia from 1918 to 1921, who had turned Georgian social democracy away from Bolshevism in the early years of the twentieth century, negotiated his country's brief independence and remained a bitter opponent of the Bolsheviks all his life. Considering what was to happen a few months later, and for the next seventy years, the post-revolutionary government's recognition of Zhordania's independent Georgia in May 1920 must rank high among the great betrayals of history. The Soviet government declared that 'Russia recognizes without reservation the independence and sovereignty of the Georgian State, and voluntarily renounces all sovereign rights which belonged to Russia with regard to the Georgian people and territory.' When the Red Army invaded Georgia in February 1921, Zhordania took his last stand in Batumi and three weeks later sailed with his government into exile in Paris, from where he fulminated against the Soviet occupation of his country. 'I cannot consent to government by assassination,' he wrote, 'and will not return until my country is freed from Bolshevism.' And so he never did come home.

Next morning, we all jammed into a friend's car and drove to the shipping office to buy our tickets for the Kometa, the hydrofoil to Trabzon. This was our mythic vessel and, apparently, it really did exist and had lately been seen, though it would, in fact, deliver us to Giresun. As we turned to go the manager mentioned ominously that if there was bad weather we would have to take the bus. But, he assured us, there would be absolutely no problem. We could go. Clutching our tickets, we left to do a little shopping. It is astonishing that anyone should deliberately go to Batumi in the height of summer: the climate is vile, appallingly hot and humid. But now the once-thronged beaches held only a few brave bathers and the streets and cafés were almost empty. The petrol crisis, tales of poisonous pollution in the sea and the economic collapse had kept the crowds at home. We wandered slowly through the heat, drinking juices and eating ice-creams, getting stickier by the second and advanced upon the market, where Guliko terrorised the stall-holders, sniffing chickens and shrieking in disgust, throwing tomatoes and aubergines aside, collecting the ingredients for our supper. The market was full of food, no shortage here, and great torn bits of meat, like flesh shredded in a bomb attack, hung like flypapers about the hall.

Half way through our supper under the trailing vines, Tsira got up to phone the manager of the shipping office and came rushing out of the house crying, Cassandra-like, 'Bad news! Bad news!' He had received instructions not to let us leave for Turkey, neither by boat nor by bus through Sarpi, so we picked ourselves up out of our wine-dark haze and charged into the night. We pushed at every open door, invading offices and ministries, where Tsira denounced all loudly. The sight of her attacking various puzzled KGB officers was profoundly moving and impressive. She raced up and down the dark streets of the town, trailing Chris and me behind. Getting nowhere, we laid siege once more to the shipping office. Chris and I could only watch in admiration as our champion exhorted, cajoled, explained, begged and persuaded. The manager was only mortal man and staggered beneath the weight of her argument. He smiled and held up his hands. He would see what he could do. We should come back in one hour. We took Tsira, now prostrate with nervous exhaustion, for a coffee and when we returned the manager greeted us like family, beaming. 'Ho! Ho! Ho!' he cried. 'Yes! Yes! Yes!' that wonderful Georgian affirmative that turns all agreement into laughter and Christmas, with just a little undercurrent of policeman. We all cheer and clap and embrace. But we must go by bus. Chris and I look anxious but, the manager assures us, the border patrol at Sarpi has promised to let us through, two Englishmen only, no Syrians, no Bulgarians, nobody else, just us for this one time.

And they did.

CHAPTER 10

HUNTING BEAR IN CHECHNYA

The Axioms of Bakar

How we sat about in Shatili, crossed into
Chechnya and pursued our quarry

I was back in Shatili once more, in the summer of 1998, just after
my rout in Svaneti, sitting on the veranda of Dato's hut, looking
out over the Argoun River. I had spent a few days in Tbilisi with
Mako and Marika, and loading Beka's Niva with supplies: sacks of
flour, tinned fish, coffee and ammunition. Then Beka, Levan, Mindi
and his brother Malkhaz, Tom Clark (who had flown out specially
for this trip) and I had all jammed ourselves among the baggage
and set out along the mountain road for Khevsureti.

Tom and I were watching the soldiers in their little compound
on the far bank of the Argoun and looking deep into ourselves.
We thought that we did not really want to shoot any bears, in fact
that we really did not want to shoot any bears, nor did Tom have
any overwhelming desire to go into Chechnya, but here we were,
somehow. Most of the soldiers were marching up and down in
ragged lines, others were carrying stones across the bridge to Dato's
hut for some planned extension. Tom perspicaciously remarked
that a wheelbarrow might have saved both time and effort. The
soldiers, marchers and carriers, were starting to grumble. Suddenly
one of them had had enough and swung a punch at his
commanding officer and a tremendous brawl broke out. Rocks
were hurled, bodies flew about, everyone yelled at once and the
entire village, Mindi and Malkhaz in the lead, streamed over the

bridge and into the mêlée to interpose themselves and calm the army down. Peace restored, Mindi and Malkhaz returned, grinning. The soldiers were bored and fractious, insults had been hurled, blows traded. Honour had been satisfied, all would now be well with the Georgian army.

Beka had disappeared with Dato and Bakar to fetch horses. We had been promised a mount each and I was looking forward to a comfortable ride over the mountains. But there were problems. All the horses in Khevsureti seemed to have gone missing. First we would have seven, then four were thought available, then two. Now we would have one, it seemed, but it was up in some high pasture and had to be caught. Beka returned disconsolate. Dato had produced rifles for Tom and me, two Lee Enfield 303s. Our pockets stuffed with bullets, we pottered up the river with the others for some target practice. Bakar and Dato carried their Kalashnikovs, Beka and Levan had their hunting rifles. Everyone opened fire at once, a terrible din, and I successfully hit a large mountain. This was the only violence I was to do with my rifle the entire trip, apart from repeatedly striking myself on the head with it as I fell wildly down various rocks. However, to have refused the weapon would have been impossible: I may as well have declared myself a homosexual or a vegetarian.

That evening, pondering the mysterious ways of huntsmen, trying to glean some idea of what, if anything, was going on, I looked up from my seat on the veranda to see a tall, fair, bearded young man, dressed in corduroys and a smart V-necked sweater, striding towards us. He introduced himself as Daniel, a Dutchman, educated in England, finished with his studies in Moscow, up from Tbilisi to see Khevsureti. He declared himself instantly ready to hunt bear and joined our party. Absurdly, we had all manner of strange connections and mutual friends. It soon became apparent that he knew almost everything, from the price of helicopters to the best way to shoot a bear and the Khevsurs approved of him immediately. He had no jacket, no tent, just a small quantity of plastic sheeting in which he rolled himself at night, looking for all the world like a large fish, freshly purchased.

Next day, after hours of inconsequent debate, we started walking, very slowly, waiting for our horse, first along the track to Mutso that Chris, the Mindis and I had travelled a few weeks before, then branching off up a lovely valley to Khonischala: a tiny settlement of stone huts with woven hurdle fences around, a few cattle, a donkey, a couple of ruined towers and lots of young men, all very stoned. Tom and I were strolling by the river, bemused, muttering to each other, when they issued forth, one waving an enormous, smouldering joint a foot long, and demanded to know what we were doing. This rather tense encounter was at once defused with smiles and handshakes when we told them we were with Bakar, off to hunt bear in Chechnya. They inspected our rifles earnestly. Tom, who had mumbled something about 'the village from hell' as we nervously answered their challenge, wondered if we were wise to hand over our weapons.

Mindi had decided to stay in Shatili but soon Malkhaz, Beka, Daniel and Levan arrived and we walked on. Only Bakar was missing, still pursuing his horse. We made camp by the river and waited. We built a fire and Levan went on upstream to fish for trout. First he scrabbled about under the rocks on the riverbank and collected a number of tiny creatures, black and brown, that looked exactly like miniature scorpions. He produced a short length of line and a hook, skewered a couple of scorpions and dangled them in the quiet pools that formed along the torrent's edge. After some hours he returned with a few magnificent fish, three or four inches long, which we cooked with great ceremony. In the middle of the night Bakar arrived with his horse and a complicated tale of capture and subsequent escape – the animal had made a dash for Azerbaijan and was only persuaded to return with the greatest difficulty. It had obviously heard something that Tom and I had not.

Next morning we found another horse at a little summer camp (a hut, a makeshift tent, two drovers and some cattle) and so, free of our packs, we climbed on towards the heights. It was just begin-ning to dawn upon me that some of the surrounding scenery was becoming vaguely, troublingly familiar. I suppressed a moment's panic and asked Bakar how, exactly, he intended to enter Chechnya, over which pass? I had asked this question of various others before and had somehow convinced myself, among all the contradictions and confusion, that we should enter Chechnya by the shortest route. But no! The answer fell lightly off Bakar's tongue and struck me like a stone between the eyes: 'The Atsunta Pass!' I nearly sat down and cried. I railed and groaned and everyone laughed. There was nothing else for it. I was stuck in the middle of this potty expedition going precisely where I had sworn I should never go again. I would have to continue. And so next morning there we all were shuffling up to the top of the pass. But it was not so bad. The great collar of snow and ice that had blocked us before and forced us down the mountain had melted away and we were able to approach from the west at a more civilised angle. Even so it was an effort, the ground at the top was all sliding slate and mud and the horses were having considerable difficulty. As we broached the crest of the pass one stumbled back and one of our packs went cartwheeling over the edge into the depths below, down and down like Kipling's Daniel Dravitt into the chasms of Kafiristan. Tom, in no way yet acclimatised, feeling odd and dizzy, exhausted by the pace of our ascent, riding whenever the ground allowed, was seized by a momentary terror as he saw the body fall. Dato raced down after it and was back in a few minutes. It was the only time I ever saw him even slightly out of breath.

We came down from the Atsunta and made our way towards Mount Tebulos. The way was scarred by steep ravines, great fun to slither down but tiresome crawling up. My rifle was a bloody nuisance. We crossed a wide grassy plateau, full of flowers and nettles, then climbed to the base of a distinctively shaped hill, just like Glastonbury Tor: a long ridge of mountain ending in a sudden cone with a cairn on top. Just beneath this, in a shallow bowl, we stopped to camp. It was raining hard and freezing cold so we huddled in our tents a while then emerged in a dazzle of sunshine to look about. Our little plateau, Kvalkhidi, stood over the confluence of several streams that merged in the valley bellow, a wide and open space, the mountains set about, as lovely a spot as I had seen in all the Caucasus. When the wind stilled, a soft quiet blanketed the air, no people, no cattle, that extraordinary hush and peacefulness that lies within the mountains' heart. Ahead, massive

and barren, stood Mount Tebulos. Tom, large, ramshackle, hetero-
clite, emerged half-dressed from the tent in search of tea, favouring,
this afternoon, a purple underwear which hugely alarmed the
Khevsurs. Bakar appeared on a grassy knoll above our tent and
asked us if we had seen the bear. Resisting an impulse to jump
into each other's arms we took his proffered binoculars and looked
in the direction he indicated. There, in the distance, on an almost
perpendicular cliff-face, a large black bear was digging for roots.
We lay in the long grass and watched it slowly moving across the
cliff. It went about its business with a calm and easy grace, at one
with itself and the world around, and I became suddenly fearful
that Bakar might kill it.

'No, of course not,' Bakar replied. 'It is far too simple hunting
bears, they are easy to kill.'

'But I thought we had come to hunt bear.'

'Whatever gave you that idea? No, we shall hunt tûr. Tûr are
difficult. We must climb very high and make no noise at all. This
is real hunting. For this you must be strong!'

So we were not, after all, going to hunt bear! Bakar then pointed
high to another peak, jagged in the distance, and told us that up
there were tûr. I could make out little, just flecks that glinted gold
in the sunshine. Apparently, there were fourteen of them.

Next morning, at first light, after a night of bitter cold, Tom
strode about the plateau making loud noises and calling out for
tea. The large roll of plastic that was Daniel wriggled slightly. Levan
appeared in full camouflage, boots shining, trousers creased, and
marched off with his rifle. Malkhaz had a headache, Beka tended
his blisters, even Bakar had a bad back. Dato made a fire. As the
sun came over the eastern rim of mountains, the horses stamped
and whinnied at their tethers, the terrors of the night now over,
arching their backs and tossing their manes in pleasure at the sun's
warm glow.

Tom, still unbreakfasted, was finding it difficult to attract attention, not one of his usual problems. 'If I were covered in fur, it
might be different,' he said. He had woken me with the oddest
remark anyone has ever made before breakfast:

'I have just had an idea for a revolution in retail shopping. Shops ought to change more often. You should go to a shop one day and buy chocolate and then you go there the next day and the shop-keeper would say, "Sorry, mate, no chocolate today but I've got a nice piece of haddock." Much more surprise would open the pockets of the punters. There's a bit more work to be done on this, probably.'

'Really?'

He was finding the plateau inspiring. But 'challenging, very chal-lenging'. Shattered after the exertions of the previous day, breathing still difficult, he thought that he might stay and read his Gurdjieff, gazing out over the mysteries of the Caucasus and preparing for a spiritual awakening. I was horrified at the thought of leaving him all alone in this great and empty space but the Khevsurs said that he was right: the way on was hard, impossible to ride over, he would not keep up. Daniel thought he might leave us before crossing into Chechnya and return to stay with Tom at camp that evening. So we gathered the barest minimum of supplies, left Tom with the tents, food, a horse, a rifle (for the bears and the Chechens) and set off, travelling light, waving to Tom who stood, growing ever smaller, watching us, as we climbed past the tor towards the great peak of Mount Tebulos. It was hard work over loose stones and shattered mountain rubble, the rocks stained with minerals and ores. Down below a few square holes pierced the mountainside, ancient workings for gold, Bakar said. Eagles wheeled overhead. We crawled up through the rocks by the side of a great waterfall and I, foolishly, went off to drink from its clear stream. This was far more difficult than it looked and I found myself clinging to the rock-face in panic, shouting, 'Fuck! Fuck! Fuck!' paralysed for a moment by vertigo, unable to move up or down.

We traversed great snow-covered slopes, the mountain peak rising just above us to 4,500 metres, and walked around it towards the pass, a small lip of rock that Bakar pointed out which looked to me no more passable than the rest. We sat awhile to gather our strength then started up. Dato sprang straight for the pass. I followed Bakar and the horse, keeping to my golden rule, zigzag-ging over sliding rock and mud, the horse clambering almost upright. The rocks were covered in a green lichen and shone strangely in the glare, folded and crushed, slates loosely sticking together in sheaves, like playing cards in a shuffle, crumbling away as we pulled ourselves upwards. Everything fell away beneath us, wafers of mountain slid down as we climbed along the spine of those broken rocks, unable to hold fast or gain purchase. Then, suddenly, we were at the top. I stepped forward, one foot still in Georgia, the other in Chechnya. And there, stretched out before me, was absolutely nothing. We were enveloped in thick cloud and could hardly see each other, let alone the view beyond. At this point Daniel decided to head back, much to my relief, assuaging some of the guilt I felt at leaving my old friend stuck alone in the middle of nowhere.

We were on the Brolisghele Pass, the Pass of the Crystal Stream, and though I saw no stream there were hundreds of crystals scattered all around. Dato and Bakar had bent to the ground and picked up handfuls and spotted many fresh prints of tûr. They hushed us all to quiet. I immediately sneezed violently. We picked our way carefully across shale and snow and a wasteland of rubble. Momentarily, the freezing cloud started to clear and I could see Chechnya unfolding before us, beautiful, green, these northern slopes covered in many more trees than those we had just ascended. Everyone stopped, crouched, rifles ready: ahead were tûr, far off, almost impossible to spot against the mountain, golden shapes moving cautiously over a shingle bank. But too far off! Thunder cracked and the rain started to fall, thick and cold and heavy. The cloud closed all about us once again.

It was getting dark. We walked on down. In the strange half-light of dusk and cloud, all sound distant and muffled, picking my way over a snow bridge, I woke out of my reverie to find myself alone. I could see no one. I whistled softly and heard a soft reply and followed after it. Climbing on to a steep ridge I saw Bakar, Dato, Malkhaz and the horse, way ahead, Mindi's close relations. Behind came Beka and Levan. I waved them on and followed in the track of trodden grass. Soon I was near the tree line. Huge hog-weed, nettles and thistles towered above my head. I slithered down and, there below, our horse stood grazing in the rain by a ruined hovel, our shelter for the night. Three walls of rough-laid stones crumbled among the weeds. Across their top Malkhaz was laying Daniel's plastic sheet, which we had somehow stolen. In one corner Dato was trying to coax a fire out of sodden wood. We stripped off our wet clothes and delved around for dry ones. We were exhausted and freezing and whoever should have been in charge of catering wasn't. We seemed only to possess three tins of condensed milk and a couple of chocolate bars between us.

That night it was impossible to sleep. The rain poured into our tiny shelter, sharp rocks pierced our bodies, jammed together on the broken ground. I sat huddled by a wall, racked and pinioned through the night, taking, in my delirium, a perverse kind of pleasure in my sleeplessness in this ruin in Chechnya, amid this strange tangle of humanity and its self-imposed discomforts. Lines from 'The Hunting of the Snark' kept filling my head and I wondered if we would all just softly and silently vanish away. Cigarettes and occasional conversations marked the passing hours. Bakar talked of Russians and of the Chechen War again and of his particular love of this area about Mount Tebulos. He had been given the freedom of the mountains by the local Chechens and acted as an unofficial warden, keeping an eye on people and animals, watching over the land around. Beka and Levan pondered gently, from time to time, the fact that we had spent five days on this expedition and so far not managed to kill a thing. Bakar, Aristotle of the hunt, replied epigrammatically as usual:

'Hunting is only possible if man is strong.'

I asked Malkhaz, who was keeping very quiet, what he thought of the trip so far.

'I want to go home,' he said.

And suddenly there was a flurry of talk about walking to the nearest Chechen village and getting a lift to the end of the new Shatili road. Bakar snorted, all subsided and tried to get some sleep.

As dawn broke I waited for everyone to seize their weapons and rush off up the nearest precipice. But no, the grass, apparently, was too wet. So we lolled about as the sun came up, bright and clear. Birds chirruped, the horse whinnied and finally we were ready. We plunged downwards through the still-dripping over-growth, hacking our way through towards the river and the valley bottom. Stands of birch, dainty and elegant, lined the river's banks and the valley opened out towards the shining mountains ahead. About the ground shattered bits of Russian helicopters lay grim and rusting. An old camp fire blackened the grass, charred bones of tûr poked out among the weeds. Behind, two gaunt peaks revealed a further valley, empty, wide and still. We paused to gaze about and understood at once Bakar's great love for this place.

Nearby, a low saddle of rock indicated a further pass, the secret road through Chechnya, the 'Black Way', where smugglers carried weapons and narcotics into and out of Georgia. We climbed towards it. The route from the pass through to Shatili took only one and a half days, Bakar said, and was far easier than the one we had come by.

'Why did we not come this way, then?' I asked.

'When hunting tûr, you must not take the easiest path,' he replied.

'We must come back this way next time,' said Beka, growing more enthusiastic. 'Each with a horse. We have food, we have water and we sit here and hunt tûr all the time.'

'Brilliant!' I said, 'but I thought that was supposed to be the plan this time.'

'Me too!' replied Beka, 'but you know how it is. Many times I asked Dato to hire horses, to make sure they were ready and he always said, "No problem, no problem! Of course I will get you horses, no question of payment." And, of course, when we arrived there were no horses. What could I do?'

We sat by the river in the heat of the day and waited. Levan sunbathed, Beka fell asleep, the others stripped and cleaned their weapons. The poor horse stamped and shimmied as clouds of horseflies like bright green zeppelins settled over its head and body. Bakar scanned the peaks with his binoculars. He had found some tûr: bright gold maggots moving across the face of the mountain, crossing a patch of black shale, dizzyingly high and gleaming in the sun. They were heading slowly down towards us, about eight of them. Dato immediately picked up his Kalashnikov and raced off. He would have to scale the peaks behind them, then flush them down towards us. The climb looked utterly impossible, sheer towering walls of rock.

Now Bakar led us off at a fantastic pace. Then we hid in a birch wood, whispering. On the opposite slope we could see a mother and its two young, nervously listening, sniffing the air. Between us and the tûr lay a long ridge. There we would wait for them. We set off up at a run, hiding among the trees, then hanging desperately on to a tangle of azalea as we started the steep climb, trying to keep quiet. Malkhaz decked me out with an entire Burnham Wood of azalea blossom in an effort to disguise me as a flowering shrub. We hung on to the bushes and saw the tûr clearly now, wonderful, vivid yellow gold, bounding down the cliffs, racing along the mountain folds and across the fissures of rock, disappearing from time to time among the trees, stopping to look about, coming closer, almost at our level. The mothers came out first into the open, made sure all was safe, then beckoned to their young which darted out from behind the trees and scampered along. They were utterly beautiful, much larger than I had imagined, with bright golden coats and the soft warm faces of deer. None of the adult males, with their great curved horns, were yet among them. They would follow on behind, going more slowly. I hung on to my shrub, entranced. But the tûr had sensed something. Perhaps Dato behind somewhere, or us in front, and they started to gaze about nervously and to retreat back up the mountainside. So Bakar told us to make a break for the ridge and we left our cover at a crouching run. Trying to keep quiet, scrabbling up excited, hearts pounding, we reached the ridge and lay along its grassy edge, rifles ready. Opposite, the great mountain glistened in the sun, its peak towering over us, its base just below, a great ledge of rock running around like a pedestal.

Suddenly, shockingly, we heard Dato's shots. I never had such a fright in my life. Down the mountain poured a river of tûr, fleeing in panic. There seemed hundreds of them, a great herd, perhaps sixty or seventy animals, bouncing and prancing and leaping down the rocks. It was, I think, the most beautiful and exciting sight I have ever seen. Great males and tiny young, tûr of every age and size, raced across and down the cliffs, gleaming gold, jumping chasms, moving with a wonderful grace and at incredible speed. I lay upon the ridge, mouth open, my rifle quite forgotten and then World War Three broke out. Bakar with his Kalashnikov, Levan, Beka and Malkhaz with their rifles, all opened fire at once. I put my fingers in my ears. I saw the bullets strike the rocks behind the tûr showering them in bits of stone and ricochets. They were close, terribly close to the animals but, fantastically, not one was struck in all that eternity of firing, which lasted, at most, two minutes. Such a relief! Everyone jumped up, roaring with laughter and yelling with excitement, our expedition vindicated in the mad rush of those few seconds.

But where was Dato? We lay along the ridge and chattered and peered about for him and eventually Bakar, Malkhaz and Levan went off to look while Beka and I made our way back to the grassy knoll where we had tethered the horse and left our packs. As we walked we heard another burst of gunfire and saw Bakar high up, a half-inch speck against the sky, calling to Malkhaz. We sat upon our knoll as lovely bands of cloud trickled down towards us and wrapped themselves around the slopes. Ahead, the mountains and their foothills receded along a distant valley, its river flowing down to the Chechen lowlands and Itoum Kale beyond. Levan returned saying that he thought Dato had killed a tûr. The sun began to set, it was getting late and Chechnya was turning pink. It would soon be dark. How on earth would they get back down the mountain with their tûr? We set about the azalea bushes, pulling up dried roots and dead branches and, as night enveloped us, lit a huge bonfire, in part to help them on their way, in part hoping for some late-night barbecue. We finished the last half-tin of condensed milk. Beka fired off a shot and way in the distance another answered. We sat and gazed upon the night.

Just before midnight Bakar, Malkhaz and Dato arrived carrying an enormous sack and the head of a large, adult, male tûr. Dato, concealed behind a rock high up the mountain, had shot it as it wandered past him, not ten metres away. It was a clean kill, a single bullet just behind the shoulder. He had then butchered the animal on the spot and brought it down the mountain in the dark in pieces. All gathered round to admire the head which Dato presented to Beka: the huge curved horns ringed like a tree, this tûr, *jikhvi* in Georgian, ten years old. Quickly the Khevsurs prepared shashlik, cutting tender pieces of meat and delicate bits of organs and using the cleaning rods of their rifles as skewers, *shampoor*. Hungry for the past two days, we ate and ate till bursting, Dato and Bakar solicitously pressing further peculiar cuts of innard upon me. I drew solace from the fact that it had taken seven men nearly seven days to kill this one beast. I did not mention that these tûr, *Capra cylindricornis* (closely related to *Capra caucasia*, found a little further west), were variously listed as a vulnerable or endangered species, though I was impressed by Dato's attitude: he had waited for an old male and only killed one animal when he could certainly have taken more.

I awoke the next morning in agony, not from stomach ache as I had expected, but to find that I had slept all night upon a box of ammunition. Bakar still snored beside me under our makeshift cover, clutching his Kalashnikov. The others lay in heaps about the knoll between bloody bits of carcass and the great severed head of the tûr. Vultures already circled overhead, waiting their turn. We ate more, packed up and Dato machine-gunned the skull to free the great horns. The horse was loaded with the bulging sack of meat: it left a trail of blood as we wound our way up to the pass. We asked Bakar how long we would take to reach it. 'Two hours! *ori saati*,' he replied, which is what he always said, so we laughed. It never was. I followed the horse up a winding track and across the snow and four hours later we were staring down into Georgia once more. And then, later still, exhausted by the steep descent and various gullies I had fallen into, the Khevsurs way ahead, lost in the distance, I looked down upon our camp by the Tor, Kvalkhidi. I could just make out the horse and a bright purple blob that must have been Tom, skittering hither and thither so still alive, and a browner blob that was Daniel.

As I got lower I tried to call out to them but I was so tired nothing came out. As I stumbled on to the plateau Dato was already cooking but Tom and Daniel had left a note pinned to the tent which read 'Gone Fishing!' I lay down on the grass and fell instantly asleep. Later, in our tent – after we had all huddled round the fire, talked of our adventures and eaten bowls of Dato's gizzard soup, particularly invigorating, he said – I asked Tom how his two days had been. 'Strange and most enjoyable.' He had communed with nature and then with Daniel, watched the horse and the eagles, listened to the silence and the wind, gazed at the mountains, read Gurdjieff. He felt he had probably had a 'primal experience' but was too full of gizzard soup to remember what this was. He expressed some concern and foreboding about the journey back.

I could hardly face it myself. We left our camp next morning and, after cutting down through a series of deep ravines and crossing a natural stone bridge high above a torrent, had to call the Khevsurs back as they rushed off over the horizon. We persuaded Malkhaz to walk with Tom while he rode on the horse. This was an extremely good thing as he managed to catch Tom a number of times as he fell off. We climbed back up over the bald skull that led to the Atsunta Pass and I thought that I was probably walking in my own footsteps. As I neared the top Dato raced down past me, after another fallen pack, and clambered back up with it shortly after, passing Beka and Levan, hardly breaking stride. At the top we froze again and the cloud hung thick about us, then we swung over the shoulder of the pass, heading west. The weather greeted us with peals of thunder, great forks of lightning and hailstones of enormous size as we slid down through the mud. We came to the extreme left-hand edge of the valley under the mountain, not the central route I had taken with Chris and the Mindis, and headed off up a little track that ran towards a high ridge. The storm continued in its fury and Tom upon his horse was soaked to the skin, and I the same but, running to keep up with Bakar, much warmer. This long, high ridge, a flat, wrinkled table of grass, *Khidotani*, Bridgebody, crowned with a cairn, pointed towards Ardotti and ended in a steep bank, a great natural platform which looked out across the land. It was beautiful there, lashed by the storm, with the lightning flashing and the thunder booming around the peaks and the mountains green all around. Ahead two valleys branched out and, though wetter than a fish, I stopped a moment to gaze about and then we tracked along over the ridge and passed above Ardotti, way below. Sliding and skiing down the mud for hours, we came through the scrub and the birch trees and then on to level ground once more, back through Khonischala, past Mutso and so to Shatili once again.

And that was the end of my walk through the mountains of Georgia. Tom and I swore solemnly that we would, in future, walk no further than our local post office. That evening, back in the little room where the Mindis, Chris and I had eaten our first meal in Shatili, we had a grand *supra* of tûr. We feasted on a great Khevsur speciality, *khinkali*, large raviolis stuffed with tûr meat, drank volumes of *chacha*, toasted each other, friendship, families, hunting, the mountains, Georgia, and by the end of our celebration were feeling so remarkably well that we stood and raised our glasses to the next trip, the next expedition, a greater, more glorious hunt. It all seemed quite definitely, probably, possible.

*

Conclusion of the tale, the tale,
Maize-bread with ashes hast thou ate,
Hast drunk poor wine of evil taste,
Hast likewise eaten rotten nuts.

*(traditional stock deprecatory ending
of Mingrelian story-tellers)*

Abercrombie, J. *A Trip Through The Eastern Caucasus* (Edward Stanford, 1889).

Allen, W. E. D. *A History of the Georgian People* (Barnes & Noble, New York, 1932, 1971).

Allen, W. E. D. (ed.). *Russian Embassies to the Georgian Kings* (Hakluyt Society, Cambridge University Press, 1970).

Altstadt, Audrey L. *The Azerbaijani Turks* (Hoover Institution Press, 1992).

Amiranashvili, Shalva. *Georgian Metalwork* (Hamlyn, 1971).

Anderson, A. R. *Alexander's Gate, Gog and Magog* (Mediaeval Academy of America, Cambridge, Massachusetts, 1932).

Apollonius of Rhodes. *The Voyage of Argo* (Penguin Classics, 1959).

Arbel, Rachel, and Margal, Lily. *In the Land of the Golden Fleece: The Jews of Georgia – History and Culture* (Tel Aviv, 1992).

Aronson, Howard. *Georgian – A Reading Grammar* (Slavica, Ohio, 1990).

Artamonov, M. I. *Khazar History* (Leningrad, 1962).

Ascherson, Neal. *Black Sea* (Jonathan Cape, 1995).

Avalishvili, Zourab. *The Independence of Georgia in International Politics 1918–1921* (Headley Bros, London).

Baddeley, John F. *The Rugged Flanks of the Caucasus* (Oxford University Press, 1940).

Baddeley, John F. *The Russian Conquest of the Caucasus* (Longmans, Green & Co., London, 1908).

Baddeley, John F. *Russia in the Eighties* (Longmans, Green & Co., London, 1921).

Baddeley, John F. *Russia, Mongolia and China* (Macmillan & Co., London, 1919).

Bennigsen-Broxup, Marie, and Gammer, Moshe. *The Chechen Struggle for Independence* (C. Hurst & Co, 1996).

Beridze, Vakhtang. *The Treasures of Georgia* (Century Publishing, 1984).

Bey, Essad. *Blood and Oil in the Orient* (Grayson & Grayson, 1925).

Bey, Essad. *Twelve Secrets of the Caucasus* (Nash & Grayson, 1931).

Bitov, Andrei. *A Captive of the Caucasus* (Weidenfeld & Nicolson, London, 1992).

Blanch, Lesley. *The Sabres of Paradise* (John Murray, London and New York, 1960).

Braund, D. *Georgia in Antiquity* (Oxford University Press, 1994).

Brook, Kevin Alan. *The Jews of Khazaria* (Jason Aronson Inc., New York, 1999).

Brosset, M. F. *Histoire de la Géorgie* (St Petersburg, 1849, 1851, 1858).

Brosset, M. F. *Rapports sur un Voyage Archéologique dans la Géorgie et dans l'Arménie* (St Petersburg, 1849).

Brosset, M. F. (ed.). *Description Geographique de la Georgie, par le Tsarevitch Wakhoucht* (St Petersburg, 1842).

Bullock, Alan. *Hitler and Stalin: Parallel Lives* (HarperCollins, 1991).

Burney, Charles, and Lang, David Marshall. *The Peoples of the Hills: Ancient Ararat and Caucasus* (Praeger, New York, 1972).

Chantre, E. *Recherches anthropologiques dans le Caucase du Sud* (Paris, 1855).

Chanturia, A. *Matiane Kartlisa* (Academy of Sciences, Georgia, Tbilisi, 1996).

Chardin, John. *Travels of Sir John Chardin into Persia and the East Indies, Through the Black Sea and the Country of Colchis* (London, 1691).

Chelebi, Evliya. *Narrative of Travels in Europe, Asia and Africa* (London, Oriental Translation Fund, 1834–50).

Chervonanaya, Svetlana. *Conflict in the Caucasus* (Gothic Image, 1994).

Conquest, Robert. *Stalin, Breaker of Nations* (Weidenfeld & Nicolson, 1991).

Conquest, Robert. *The Great Terror* (Pimlico, 1992).

Conquest, Robert. *The Harvest of Sorrow* (Pimlico, 2002).

Devdariani, Jaba, and Hancilova, Blanka. *Georgia's Pankisi Gorge: Russian, US and European Connections* (CEPS Policy Brief No. 23).

Djobadze, W. *Early Medieval Georgian Monasteries in Historic Tao, Klarjeti, and Shavsheti* (Franz Steiner Verlag, Stuttgart, 1992).

Dowsett C. J. F. (ed.). *The History of the Caucasian Albanians by Moses Dasxuranci* (Oxford University Press, 1961).

Dragadze, Tamara. *Rural Families in Soviet Georgia* (Routledge, 1988).

Dumas, Alexandre. *Adventures in the Caucasus* (Chilton Books, 1962).

Dumbadze, Vasili. *The Caucasian Republics* (New York, 1925).

Dumézil, Georges. *Légendes sur les Nartes* (Honore Champion, Paris, 1930).

Dunlop, D. M. *The History of the Jewish Khazars* (Princeton, 1954).

Farson, Negley. *Caucasian Journey* (Evans Brothers Ltd., London, 1951).

Fraser, George MacDonald. *Flashman and the Tiger* (HarperCollins, 2000).

Freshfield, Douglas W. *The Exploration of the Caucasus* (Edward Arnold, 1896).

Freshfield, Douglas W. *Travels in the Central Caucasus and Bashan* (Longman, London, 1869).

Goldenberg, Suzanne. *The Caucasus and Post-Soviet Disorder* (Zed Books, 1994).

Goltz, Thomas. *Azerbaijan Diary* (M. E. Sharpe, 1998).

Grove, F. C. *The Frosty Caucasus* (Longmans, London, 1875).

Gugushvili, A. *The Georgian Alphabet* (Georgica, Stephen Austin & Sons Ltd, 1936).

Gurdjieff, G. I. *Meetings with Remarkable Men* (Routledge & Kegan Paul, 1945).

Herodotus. *The Histories* (Penguin Classics, 1954).

Hewitt, B. G. (ed.). *The Abkhazians* (Curzon, 1999).

Hewitt, B. G. *Yet a third consideration of Völker, Sprachen und Kulturen des südlichen Kaukasus* (Central Asian Survey, 1995).

Hewitt, B.G. *Book Reviews* (Central Asian Survey, 1995, 14, and 1999, 18).

Hewitt, George. *Georgian – A Learner's Grammer* (Routledge, 1996).

Hewsen, Robert H. *Armenia: A Historical Atlas* (University of Chicago Press, 2001).

Hillery; P. J. *Georgian, The Kartvelian Literary Language* (The Languages Information Centre, 1994).

Hunter, Shireen. *The Transcaucasus in Transition* (Center for Strategic and International Studies, 1994).

Iakobashvili, Irakli. *Materials and Methods of Execution of Early Mediaeval Murals in Upper Svaneti* (www.opentext.org.ge/art/ swaneti.htm)

Kazemzadeh, F. *The Struggle for Transcaucasia* (George Ronald, 1951).

Kelly, Laurence. *Lermontov. Tragedy in the Caucasus* (Constable & Co., 1977).

Keun, Odette. *Au Pays de la Toison d'Or* (Flammarion, Paris, 1922).

Kinross, Lord. *Atatürk, The Rebirth of a Nation* (Weidenfeld and Nicholson, 1964).

Klaproth, H. J. von. *Reise in den Kaukasus und nach Georgien, 1807–8* (2 vols, Halle, 1812–14).

Koestler, Arthur. *The Thirteenth Tribe* (Hutchinson, 1970s).

Korkut, D. *The Book of Dede Korkut* (Penguin Classics, 1974).

Lang, David Marshall. *The Georgians* (Thames and Hudson, 1966).

Lang, David Marshall. *The Last Years of the Georgian Monarchy* (Columbia University Press, 1957).

Le Carré, John. *Our Game* (Hodder & Stoughton, 1995).

Lordkipanidze, M. *Georgia in The XI–XII Centuries* (Ganatleba, Tbilisi, 1987).

Lermontov, Mikhail. *A Hero of Our Time* (Penguin Classics, 1966).

Macaulay, Rose. *The Towers of Trebizond* (Flamingo, 1995).

Maclean, Fitzroy. *To Caucasus, the End of all the Earth* (Jonathan Cape, 1976).

Marsden, Phillip. *The Crossing Place* (Flamingo, 1994).

Merzbacher, Gottfried. *Aus den Hochregionen des Kaukasus* (Verlag von Duncker & Humblot, Leipzig, 1901).

Morrison, Sir T., and Hutchinson, G. *The Life of Sir Edward FitzGerald Law* (William Blackwood & Sons, 1911).

Minorsky, Vladimir F. *A History of Sharvan and Darband* (W. Heffer & Sons Ltd., Cambridge, 1958).

Nasmyth, Peter. *A Rebel in the Caucasus* (Cassell, 1992).

Nisanyan, S. *Black Sea* (Boyut, Istanbul, 1990).

Norwich, John Julius. *Byzantium* (Viking, 1991).

Obolensky, D. *The Byzantine Commonwealth* (Weidenfield & Nicholson, 1971).

Peradze, Archimandrite Gregory. *Georgian Influences on the Culture of the Balkan Peoples* (Georgica).

Rawlinson, A. *Adventures in the Near East 1918–1922* (Andrew Melrose, 1923).

Rayfield, Donald. *The Literature of Georgia* (Clarendon Press, 1994).

Reiss, Tom. 'The Man from the East' (*New Yorker*, October 1999).

Rosen, Roger. *The Georgian Republic* (Odyssey, Hong Kong, 1991).

Rustaveli, Shota. *The Knight in the Panther's Skin* (Sabchota Sakartvelo, 1986).

Said, Kurban. *Ali and Nino* (Simon & Schuster, New York, 1972).

Salia, Kalistrat. *History of the Georgian Nation* (Orientaliste, Leuven, 1980).

Severin, Tim. *The Jason Voyage* (Hutchinson, 1985).

Smith, Anthony. *National Identity* (Penguin, 1991).

Sproat, Robert. *Chinese Whispers* (Faber & Faber, 1988).

Steinbeck, John. *A Russian Journal* (Minerva, 1994).

Suny, R. G. *The Making of the Georgian Nation* (I. B. Tauris, 1989).

Suny, R. G. (ed.). *Transcaucasia, Nationalism, and Social Change* (University of Michigan Press, 1996).

Temple, Robert. *The Crystal Sun* (Arrow, 2000).

Tolstoy, Leo. *Hadji Murat* (Penguin Classics, 1960).

Tolstoy, Leo. *The Cossacks* (Penguin Classics, 1960).

Toumanoff, Cyril. *Armenia and Georgia. Cambridge Medieval History* (Cambridge University Press, 1966).

Tsagareishvili, Tamila. *traditsiuli kultura da ecosistemebi* (Tbilisi, 2000).

Vinogradova, Galina. *Saint or Satan? The Life and Times of Vladimir Kashpirovsky* (Gothic Image, 1996).

Wardrop, O. *The Kingdom of Georgia* (Sampson Low and Co., London, 1888).

Wright, John. (ed.). *Transcaucasian Boundaries* (UCL Press, 1996).

Xenophon. *The Persian Expedition* (Penguin, 1949).

INDEX

Abana, 176
Abbas, Shah, 45, 238
Abercromby, J., 138, 139
Abkhazia, Abkhazians, 20, 109, 176, 225, 265, 273, 274, 295, 327; separatist war, 191–204; origins and history of, 193, 97–199; language and alphabet, 81, 82, 83, 192, 198; relationship to Georgians, 198–199; causes of conflict, 192, 194, 195; diaspora, 197; and Chechens 109–110, 203
Abkhazian Popular Forum, *Aidgylara*, 195
Abreks, 233
Achara, 176, 328
Adyghe, 83
Aeetes, King of Colchis, 265, 316
Aeroflot, 328
Aeschylus, 169
Ajaria, see Achara
ajika, 228
Akhieli, 92, 107, 129, 140, 141
Agathias, 266
Agdam, 23
Agdash, 25
Ahura-Mazda, 143
Alp Arslan, 284–286
Alans, 65, 158–160 , 224; *see also* Ossetia, Ossetians
Alaunts, 159
Alaverdi, 43–45
Alazani River, 44
Anabasis, see Xenophon
Ani, 287
Albania, 14
Albanians, Caucasian, *see* Caucasian Albanians
Aleppo, 285
Alexander Gardens, 80
Alexander of Kakheti 5, 6
Alexander the Great, 151, 278
Alexander's Gates, 161; *see also* Daryal Gates
Aliev, Haydar, 23
Allen, W. E. D., 53, 54, 59, 65, 86, 107, 141n, 143, 151, 159n, 160n, 175, 288n
Alp Arslan, 285, 286
Altiparmak, 280
Al-Qaeda, 111
Alvani, 43, 45
Ambrolauri, 211
Amharic, 14
amirandarejaniani, 168, 309, 320
Amirani, 168–171, 309
Amazons, 151

Anatolia, 263, 285, 286
Anatori, tombs of, 100, 101, 309
Andaki River, 89, 92, 94
Andronikashvili, 267
aoul, 5
Apollonious of Rhodes, 207, 315
Arabs, 107, 111, 162, 216, 218, 222, 273, 282, 288
Aragvi River, 134
Aramaic, 83, 143, 214
Archi, 81
architecture, 43, 44; Georgian compared to Armenian, 271; in Tao-Klarjeti, 269–289; in Svaneti, 301–311; *see also* churches, towers
Ardahan, 274
Ardeshen, 264
Ardon river, 175
Ardotti, 82, 88, 89, 92, 93, 344, 345
Argoun River, 100, 102, 332,
Arkhoti, 137–146
Arkhotis Pass, *see* passes
Arian heresy, 282
Arrian, 169, 207
Argonauts, *see* Jason, Golden Fleece
Armenia, Armenians, 21, 24, 25, 30, 31, 268, 273, 287, 288, 289, 293, 325; architecture, 271, 272; alphabet and language, 31, 81, 82; and Byzantium, 285; christianity of, 100, 281, 282, 285; in Cilicia, 14; history shared with Georgians, 209, 215, 286, 287; relations with Georgia, 24, 25, 213; relations with Azerbaijan, 24, 36; invaded by Seljuks, 285, 286; in Tbilisi, 24; in Baku, 36, 37; Turkish massacres of, 263, 264; *see also* Bagratuni, Karabakh, Mesrop Mashots
Armazi, Armazian, 143
Armaziskhevi, 143
Armazistsikhe, 143
Arrian, 169
Artamov, M., 223
Artanuji, 273
Artvin, 268, 270, 277
As, 159
Ascherson, Neal, 200, 267
Ashkenazy Levite Jews, 226
ashog, 292
Asia, 181–184
Assa River, 93
Astrakhan, 175
Assyrians, 207, 213, 264
Atatürk, Kemal, 263, 264
Athos, 289

INDEX

Caspian Sea, 173, 181, 182, 221, 287

Castelli, 96

Caucasia, Caucasus, 65, 266, 317, 334; common culture, 54, 55; political geography, 177; and British interests, 28, 29; and Russian conquest, 17–19; attitude of Russians to, 17–19, 115–124; languages, 55, 80–85; Europe or Asia? 181–184; metallurgy, 171, 207, 208; myths of, 164–171, 315–319; see also passes, mountains, glaciers, Georgia, Chechnya, Svaneti, Transcaucasia

Caucasian Albanians, 14, 30–31, 82

Caucasian Journey, see Farson, Negley

Caucasian Middle East, 287

Caucasian Prisoner, see Pushkin, Alexander

Caucasian race, 15

Caucasian Wall, 53–55, 160

chadi, 138, 297

Chajushi, 319

Chalcedon, Council of, 281, 282

Chalybes, 207

Chanchakitsqali River, 92

Castelli, 96

Chavchavadze, Ilia, 46, 123, 124, 165, 213

Chechnya, Chechens, 17–19, 20, 54, 55, 59, 177, 332, 334, 337, 338, 339, 342; and Abkhazia, 109, 110, 197, 203; and Georgia, 108–112; and Russia 17–19, 59, 104–120; and terrorism, 106, 109–115 ; the Genocide, 110; see also Kists

Cheka, 239

Chelebi, Evliya, 81, 215

Chernomirdin, Victor, 114

Chervonnaya, Professor Svetlana, 191–192, 195, 200, 201

Cheso, 134

chianuri, 228

Chichak, Princess, 223

Chi-Jughutlari, 224

Chiglaourta, 49

Chikhareshi, 249–254,

Children's Aid Direct (CAD), 20, 27, 34

Chiora, 231

choron, 270

Choruh River, *tchorokhi,* 268, 269, 287, 289

Chosroes, 306

Christianity, established in Georgia, 100, 214; and paganism in Caucasus, 27, 58

Church, churches, Georgian, 269–289, 307–311, 319, 320; and Byzantine, 282, 310; separation from Armenian, 282; wealth of, 289; foundations abroad, 289

Chvibiani, 319

Cimmerians, 158

Circassians, 29, 198, 261

CIS, see Commonwealth of Independent States

Civil War, 295, *see* Georgia

Cockin, C. J., 312

Colchis, 14, 265, 304 , 315, 318, 326; Abkhaz and Georgian tribes of, 198, 199; see also Aeetes, Abkhazia, Medea, Jason, Lazica, Georgia, Golden Fleece

Cold War, 203

Commonwealth of Independent States (CIS), 197, 201

Communist, Communism, 45, 211; see also Bolshevik, Cheka, Menshevik, Soviet Union, Stalin

Comnenos, connections with Georgians, 267; Alexius, 288; Andronikos, 267

Conquest, Robert, 237, 238, 240

Conversations with Eternity, see Temple, Robert

Constantinople (Istanbul), 29, 262, 271, 286, 288, 289

Cossacks, 115, 175

Cossacks, The, see Tolstoy, Count Leo

Crooked Gates, 160

Crusades, 42, 89, 289

cult of dead, 95

Cumans, 288

Chvibiani, 319

Crystal Sun, The, see Temple, Robert

Cyril, Saint, *see* St Cyril

Dadeshkiliani, princes of lower Svaneti, 304

Dadiani, rulers of Mingrelia, 303

Daghestan, 4; languages and peoples, 5, 55, 56, 80, 81, 83; Jews of, 214; and Georgia, 287

Dagh Chufut, 224

Dali, 168, 312

Daniel, Sultan, 6,

Dartlo, 41, 57, 59

Daryal, 53, 158–162, 224, 287; description of in classical times, 160; importance of route through, 158; Alans of, 158; difficulty of 161, 174

Dasxuranci, Moses, 215, 219–220

Datvis-Dzhvaris Pass, 133

David the Builder, *davit agmashenebeli,* 85, 286–289, 327

David Kuropalates, 273, 274, 284

deda, 151

Dede Korkut, 31

Derbent, 53, 83, 160, 173, 216

Devi, 168, 309

diasakhlisi, 149, 150

Dickens, Charles, 60, 91

didi turkoba (The Great Turkish Troubles), 286–289

Didgori, battle of, 287, 288

Dido, 55

Diklo, 41, 52,

diklos mta, 45

Dikmen, 277

Diogenes, Romanus, 284, 285

Djarego, 100

Djibiani, 319, 321

INDEX

Glola, 176, 225, 227

Gog and Magog, 158, 187–188

Gog, Theatre Company, 187–191

gold, in Svaneti, 315–319

Golden Fleece, 14, 85, 168, 265, 315–319

Golden Horde, 175

Goltz, Thomas, 176

Gorbachev, Mikhail, 23, 178

Gori, 238

Gounib, 7

Grachev, Pavel, 114

Great Game, 28

Great Lavra, 289

Greeks, 209, 263–265, influence of in Colchis and Georgia, 15, 265, 318; myths in Caucasus, 168–171, 315–319, 337; and iron, 207; *see also* Byzantines, Pontic Greeks

Grigol Khandzteli, 282, 283

Grozny, 107, 110, 115, 119, 179

gudani, 97

Gudanistsqali River, 134

Gudauri, 314

Gudauta, 197,

Gudiashvili, Lado, 210

Gugareti, 15

gughuni, 229

Gulba, *see* mountains

Gurdjan, 15

Gurdjieff, G. I., 80, 291, 292, 337

Gurgi-Bughaz, 257, 270

Gvelesiani, David, 213

Hadji Murat, 118–120

Hagia Sophia, 271

Halizones, 207

Hamamli, 272

Hamara, 224

Hamlet, 187

hammam, 7, 8, 9

Hemshinlis, 262, 263

Heniochi, 207

Heraclius, Emperor, 220, 221

Hereti, 274

Herodotus, 207

Hermit, The, see Chavchavadze, Ilia

Hewitt, George, 82, 192–194, 198, 200, 203

History of the Georgian People, see Allen, W. E. D.

History of Sharvan and Darband, see Minorsky, V.

History of the Jewish Khazars, see Dunlop, D. M.

History of the Caucasian Albanians, see Dasxuranci, Moses

Hitler, Adolf, 33, 239

Hitler and Stalin, see Bullock, Alan

Hittites, 207, 263

Homer, 207

Hopa, 264, 268

horon, 270

horses 333, 334, 337; racing, 95; burials, 95

Hungarians, 87

Huns, 31, 54, 159, 304

Hunzib, 55

Hyenas, 154–157

Iakobashvili, Irakli, 308

Iberia, 14, 84, 289

ibn Shaprut, Hasday, 217

Ienashi, 307

Ilisu, 1–12; history of 5, 6

Inguri River, 300, 303, 307, 319

Ingush, Ingusheti, 18, 92–93, 112, 177; *see also* Galgais

Ioseliani, 179

Ipkhi, 307

Irakli, King of Kakheti and Kartli, success against the Turks, 121, 161, 162

Iran, *see* Persia, Sasanians

iron, Caucasus as source of, 171, 207, 208, 242

Iron Gates, 216; *see also* Derbent

Ishan, 271, 281, 283, 284

Iskander, Fasil, 150, 189

Islam, 27, 59, 100, 210, 214, 218, 262, 269, 272, 285, 287, 288

Ismayilli, 35

Ispir, 287, 289

Istanbul, 267; *see also* Constantinople

Itil, 221

Itoum-Kale, 105, 342

Iveria Hotel, 186, 188, 318

Iviron Monastery, 289

Jamata, Svan brigand, 233–235.

Japaridze, 231

Jason and Argonauts, 14, 168, 315–319

Jason Voyage, The, 315–319

Javakhishvili, Alexander, 15

Jerusalem, 269, 308, 310

Jonah, 278

Jordania, Noe, *see* Zhordania

Judaism, 110; history of in Georgia and Caucasus, 212–214, 216–218, 221–225

Joseph, Khagan, 217

Kabarda, 177, 304

Kabirs, 223

Kabul, 28

Kachkar Mountains, 264

Kakheti, 5, 6, 42, 65, 121, 174, 274

Kal, 305

Kandahar, 28

Kangal, 56

kaphioba, 97,

Karabakh, 4, 20

Karadzic, Radovan, 86

Karaite, 223

Karata, 55

Kars, 291

Kasara, 175

BREAD AND ASHES

INDEX

Magyars, 223
Mahachkala, 5, 53
Maiden Tower, 30
mamasakhlisi, 149, 151, 152, 308
Mamisson Pass, 176, 227
Mani, 50
Manitch, 181, 182
Manzikert, 284, 285
Marienfeld, 142
Marr, Nikolai, 86
Martel, Charles 'the Hammer', 216
Matsqvari, 308, 310
Matsqvarishi, 307, 308
Mazdaism, 100
McDonald's, 20
Medea, 168, 265, 316, 318
Mehmet, Sultan, 262
Melo, 248
Mensheviks, 329
Meshech, 207, 208
Meskhetians, 193
Mesrop Mashots, 31, 82,
Mestia, 301, 302–304, 306–309, 311, 313, 324, 327
Minaret Group, 26–27
Mingrelia, Mingrelians, 193–198, 200, 202, 265, 345
Military Highway, Georgian, 157, 158, 162 , 173
Mineralnye Vody, 178
Mingechevir, 21–25
Mingrelia, Mingrelians, 84, 192–198, 200, 202, 203, 265, 319, 329, 345; *see also* Egrisi, Colchis, Lazica
Minorsky, V., 160n
Mirian, King, 121
Mitchell, George, 27
Mithras, 260, 326
Mithridates Eupator of Pontus, 265
mkadre, 97
Mkhedrioni, 202, 314
mkinvartsveri, see Mount Kazbek
moiroloyia, 228
Molerats, 172
Mnasi, *see* glaciers
Mongols, 14, 50, 219, 223, 288, 289, 311; invasions of Georgia, 61, 62; census of, 61, 62
Monophysites, 210, 282, 285,
mountains: Blanc, 312; Diklos, 45; Edena, 243; Elbruz, 76, 169, 301, 304; Gulba, 312; Kazbek, *mkinvartsveri*, 64, 153, 158, 163–173; Koshtantau, 312; Laila, 312, 324; Phasis, 245, 304; Shkara, 301, 312, 319, 321; Shoda, 312; Tebulos, 69, 74, 88, 94, 336, 337, 339; Tetnuld, 301, 307, 312, 324; Ushba, 301, 311, 312, 324, 326; Zopkhito, 242
Mountain Jews, 215; *see also* Tat *and* Judaism
Mountain Peoples of the Caucasus, Federation (Union) of, 25, 110
Mossynoeci, 209
mrgvlovani, 272

Mtiuleti, 154
Mtskheta, 121, 143, 214, 215
Mtkvari River, Kura, 287
Mujal, 313
murals, *see* frescos
Muridism, 29
Muslims, *see* Islam
Mulkhura River, 306, 307, 313
Murkhmeli, 319
Mutso, 88, 94–97, 106, 334, 345
My English Grandfather, 143
mze (sun), gender of, worship of, 151

nabacchusevi, 127
nabadi, 55
nakalakari, 63
Namcheduri, 326
nardi, 329
nasakhlari, 63
nasophlari, 63
naptha, 63
Nakh, 55
Nana, Queen of Georgia, 214
Narts, 164–168
Narzan Springs, 9
National Guard, Georgian, 197
Nebuchadnezzar, 213
Neo-Platonism, 70
Nerses, Catholicos of Armenia, 281
Nesgun, 310
Nestorian heresy, 282
Nicholas, Tsar, 118–119
Nicortsminda, 283
Nino, St, converts Georgians to Christianity, 100; and Jews of Mtskheta, 214
Nokhchi, *see* Chechens
Nogays, 11
Notes of a Journey from Vladikavkaz to Tiflis, see Chavchavadze, Ilia
Nussimbaum, Lev, *see* Bey, Essad

Obolensky, D., 174
Oghuz Turks, 31
Ogni, 267
oil, in Baku, 32, 33
Oleg, Prince, 222
Omalo, 49, 57, 106
Oni, 206–213, 225, 226
Ordhzonikidze, 238
Ortakoy, 276
Ortsveri, *see* glaciers
Oshki, 271, 278, 279, 281, 284
Ossetia, Ossetians, 158–160; language, 84; conflict with Georgia, 176–180; as descendants of the Alans, 158; as descendants of Narts, 165; *see also* Alans
Otkha Eklesia, 284
Ovitdagi Pass, *see* passes
Oxfam, 26

INDEX

Sasvano, 243, 245
satsivi, 296
Savage Svanetia, 244
savages, how to deal with, 325
Sbat, 215
Scythians, 95, 304
Shah Abbas, 45
Shalmaneser, 213
Shaprut, Hasday ibn, 217
Secret History of the Mongols, 14
Seim of Transcaucasian States, 25
September 11th, 111
Severin, Tim, 315–319
Shadaddie, 264
Shamyl, Imam 6, 7, 18, 29, 41, 116, 118
Shatberdi, 276
Shatili, 41, 100–32, 332, 333, 339, 345
Shavshat, 263, 270, 274, 275
Shavsheti, 270
Sheki, 35
Shenako, 57
Shevardnadze, Eduard, 49, 108–109, 112, 179, 203; in Abkhazia, 192, 197; in Ossetia, 179; joins CIS, 201; attitude of Georgians to, 109, 203, 204; interview with, 201
Shevkal of Ghimri, 5
Shevkal of Tarku, 5, 173
Seljuk Turks, *see* Turks, Seljuks
Shida Kartli, 177
shrines, 67, 91, 92, 99
Silk Route, 174
Silzibul, Khan, 174
Shirvan, 287
Shirvansha, 287
Shkara, Mount, *see* mountains
Shoda, Mount, *see* mountains
Shovi, 229
Shuvaloff, Count, 16
Sidianari, 307, 308
Sigua, Tengis, 179
Sinai, 289
Sioni Cathedral, 188
siskhli, 107
snakes, 74
Socar, 27
Sochi, 294
Solzhenitsyn, Alexander, 237
Somkheti, 287
Sori, 211
Soros Foundation, 269
Soslan, Prince David, 70, 160
Sounzha River, 173
Soviet Union, 19, 36, 144, 176, 177; *see also* Communism, Russia, Stalin, USSR
Spenser, Edmund, 72, 73
Speri, 215
Spiritual Mission of Georgia, The, 85, 86
Stalin, 33, 115, 152, 176, 192, 194, 236–241
Stalin, Breaker of Nations, see Conquest, Robert

Steinbeck, John, 120
steppes, 287
Strabo, 54, 207, 315, 316, 317
suleti, 47
Sultanate of Rum, 285
Surakhani, 28, 31
Sumbat, 272, 273
Sumela, 260
Sumerians, 52, 320
Sumgait, 37
supra, 210, 211, 255, 345
Suny, R. G., 161n
Sounzha River, 173
Sukhumi, 196, 197
Svaneti, Svans, 248–256, 265, 295-327; cult of St George, 310, 320; feminism, 320; funeral laments, 309, 314; Free Svaneti, 304, 321; and gold, 315; and Golden Fleece, 315–319; Huns in, 54, 305 ; language, 265; lawlessness, 249, 251–253, 321–324; passes into, 304; Tamerlane in, 54, 305; Dadiani's Svaneti, 304; Dadeshkiliani's Svaneti, 304
Svetitskhoveli, 215, 283, 326
Svyatoslav, Grand Duke of Kiev, 222
Svytich, Vladislav Illich, 84
Syria, Syrians, 271, 282, 289, 293

Tabasars, Tabasaran, 80
tamada, 150
Taliban, 111
Tamar (Tamara, *tamar mepe*), 49, 50, 126, 228, 267, 288; extent of kingdom, 50; adulation of, 49, 70, 71; visits Svaneti, 320; marries David Soslan, 160
Tamerlane (Timur), 18, 305; campaigns in Georgia, 62–63
Tao, Tao-Klarjeti, 257–289, 307; conquest of, 269; importance of, 270, 273, 274; David of, 273, 274
Taochi, 207, 208
Tarku, Shevkal of, 5, 173
Taringzel, 309
Tashkent agreement, 108
Tat, 83, 224
Tbeti, 275, 276
Tbilisi, 19–21, 121, 158, 185–191, 257, 267, 287, 287–299, 327; pogrom in, 166, 188, 297; under Muslim rule, 287; siege by Khazars, 219, 220; theatre in, 187–191
Tbilisi Revolution, 179
Tchantchaki River, 229
Tchanti-Argoun River, 100
Tchorokhi River, *see* Choruh
Tskhenistsqali River, 246, 247, 249, 303
tea, 11, 262
Tebulos, Mount (*tebulos mta*), 69, 74, 88, 94, 336
Telavi, 39–41
temi, 140, 141, 151
Temple, Robert, 170, 171

INDEX